OPTIONS AND OPTIONS TRADING

A Simplified Course that Takes You from Coin Tosses to Black-Scholes

ROBERT W. WARD

Boston, Massachusetts   Burr Ridge, Illinois
Dubuque, Iowa   Madison, Wisconsin   New York, New York
San Francisco, California   St. Louis, Missouri

The *McGraw·Hill* Companies

Library of Congress Cataloging-in-Publication Data

Ward, Robert W.
  Options and options trading : a course that takes you from coin tosses
to Black-Scholes / by Robert W. Ward.
        p. cm.
  ISBN 0-07-143209-4 (hardcover : alk. paper)
  1. Options (Finance)   2. Derivative securities.   I. Title.
HG6024.A3 W36 2004
332.64'53--dc22

                                        2003016489

  3 4 5 6 7 8 9   BKM BKM   0 9 8 7 6

ISBN 0-07-143209-4

This publication is designed to provide accurate and authoritative information in regard
to the subject matter covered. It is sold with the understanding that neither the author
nor the publisher is engaged in rendering legal, accounting, or other professional service.
If legal advice or other expert assistance is required, the services of a competent
professional person should be sought.

> *—From a declaration of principles jointly adopted by a committee of the*
> *American Bar Association and a committee of publishers.*

McGraw-Hill books are available at special quantity discounts to use as premiums and
sales promotions, or for use in corporate training programs. For more information, please
write to the Director of Special Sales, Professional Publishing, McGraw-Hill, Two Penn
Plaza, New York, NY 10121-2298. Or contact your local bookstore.

CONTENTS

Wall Street—oh, the stories I could tell and the tales of intrigue I could write—and don't think I haven't been asked or been tempted. Maybe it comes back to that old market adage regarding time and price—I haven't the time and no one has yet offered my price! But no matter, my memoirs will have to wait for another time as this is Bob's option book. Some day when life slows down a bit maybe I can make the time to dictate those stories. Bob took some time off and did just that, but he focused on sharing his hard-earned knowledge and experience with those who want to know how it really works.

Wall Street is a world of finance, a world of ever-changing prices and ideas—here today, gone tomorrow. Change is in the air. Only on Wall Street could the Nasdaq be priced at more than 5000 before crashing to almost 1000 in two years. Meanwhile, Bob and I have been toiling away in that Rip Van Winkle of a market, gold, which after slumbering for 20 years has just begun to awaken, and in two years has bounced back from $250 to $425. It has been a long, long wait for those of us not asleep the past 20 years. This is the market Bob and I have been shackled to, seemingly forever.

It takes real hardscrabble instincts to survive in such a barren environment and to help us thrive and prosper at Prudential Securities we fall back on old Ben Franklin's adage: early to bed and early to rise. Things start early in our office. At the southernmost tip of Manhattan our day starts at 6:45 a.m. and we are, paraphrasing Michael Lewis in his book about Salomon Bros., "ready and eager to bite the backside off a bear each morning."

But you need more than enthusiasm to prosper on Wall Street. Our survival over the past 25 years has been based primarily on the philosophy we embrace and to which Bob devotes a whole chapter: "The customer is king." We ply our daily efforts solely in the direction of helping our customers survive and thrive in the gold and foreign exchange markets. For the past 20 years we've operated an around-the-clock desk—an increasingly rare phenomenon these last few years. As Bob likes to remind me, "in good times it seems everybody's a genius, but only the shrewdest manage to survive in style when a decade of dry years hits." And gold has been in a coma for at least that long.

Our business is primarily based on derivatives, the very ones described in Bob's book: futures, forwards, and options. They are our stock in trade, comprising roughly three-quarters of our deals. To many on the outside of Wall Street they seem to be unfathomable and, by implication, unmanageable. But this is not the case at all. Despite the fact that my education prepared me far more for literature and philosophy, learning the ins and outs of derivatives was more a matter of time and application than of mathematical wizardry. Mathematical theory has its place, but it often seems wide of the mark and leaves many of us shaking our heads with a "so what" attitude. The market is not a respecter of simple formulas, or things would be more orderly than they are. Most of us require an intuitive feel for the derivatives we trade, rather than depend upon mathematical abstractions. Bob shows you how and why forwards, futures, and options work from the inside out. Take it from one who knows—his descriptions are as real world as they come and properly describe the way the markets work.

His chapter on how traders make money (and the importance of customers) is clearer and truer than any I've ever seen. It not only has the ring of truth, but the real-time experience to back it up. Bob was a head trader for many years and learned these things first hand. I can verify the realities he lays out—it's as true a description of the trading dilemma as you will ever see. You can fool around with taking positions all you want, but the customer is king and the moment you forget that is the moment your department starts downhill. You will never survive the dry years.

Bob has taken his deep understanding of the markets, options in particular, and turned them into a step-by-step textbook to help aspiring students. You won't find complex ideas broken down more simply, or explanations made as real-life and visual in any other books. And nobody worries like Bob does about the reader getting lost. While academic books might show more rigor, they also miss the point: What matters to a trader on a desk is the nitty-gritty intuitions of how and why something works and how to fix it when things go awry. Bob can troubleshoot problems instantly and figure out simple solutions faster than anybody I know. I've seen him do it. If you pay attention to the details in this book you will learn the most important lesson in troubleshooting—good solutions always depend on a clear understanding of the basics. The more basic a thing is, the easier it is to see the problems and find the right answers. In several in-famous disasters of recent years, such as Enron, derivative posi-tions were not simplified and clarified but were used as vehicles of obfuscation. That alone tells you about the intentions of man-agements who failed.

Bob is able to take esoteric concepts and translate them into simple, everyday examples. He then helps anchor the ideas in your mind with memorable visual images—making recall so much easier than the classically dry textbook formulas. I know this for sure—I have never run into a better blend of risk manager-teacher-trader than Bob. His knowledge of markets in general and precious metals in particular is encyclopedic. His desire to share knowledge and help others learn comes through clearly from page one.

If you are hoping to find the one and only answer to beat Wall Street, you will be looking for a long, long time. Everybody wants a quick fix and an easy answer, but in the high-stakes game of finance with so many brilliant players there are no easy answers—only complex ones. And the answers can change from minute to minute. You don't go to the World Series of Poker if you don't know whether a flush beats a straight—because the players who show up are not merely knowledgeable about poker, they are obsessed. Only the best of the best need apply. So it is, also, on Wall Street. Your training in derivatives begins with the basics in Bob's book and then it's up to you to develop experience and practice. If this is too much trouble, then maybe you don't really want to work on Wall Street.

If you will read only one book on derivatives, this is it. If you find a book that makes complex market concepts simpler than this, buy the book and keep it forever. You'll have the first edition of a classic. What Graham and Dodd did for simplifying and ex-plaining security analysis, Bob's book does for derivatives. Wall Streeters do not have the mind or temperament to explain basic details to beginners. That's what makes Bob's book so different—there aren't any other books like this out there.

Years ago, when I was a neophyte trying to understand the vagaries of the markets and the esoterics of the forwards and fu-tures, I would have given a month's salary to have the simplistic clarity that Bob brings to this topic in a single chapter. In another chapter he shocks you by taking simple things you already knew (but didn't realize) and showing you how they come together to make a simple option formula. It's like looking at the answers to a *New York Times* crossword the next day—it makes complete sense and you can't believe you didn't see it all along.

Bob has flattered me by saying that I'm the best salesman he's ever met. Well, I could hardly live up to that standard if I couldn't convince you to buy this book. So here is a hard fact of life learned after 25 years in the business: No one gives away a dime on Wall Street. The closest thing to a freebie on Wall Street that you will ever find is the knowledge and experience shared with you in this book. The education you will receive in this book is a gift—take it and run.

JOHN W. FALLON
Head of Forex and Precious Metals
Prudential Securities
New York, February 2004

P.S.   If you run across a clearer, better book than Bob's let me know—I'll free some time to write that foreword, too. As long as I'm writing forewords I want to make darned sure I do it only for the best!

On Taking Risk and Blowing Up

No one could believe the news. Impossible. A billion dollars had disappeared overnight. The bank's star trader, a newly minted whiz kid, had lost more than a billion dollars almost overnight in the Tokyo stock and bond markets. The money was just gone— lost forever to other, better players. It was as if someone had thrown open a door latch and a billion borrowed pigeons had flown the coop seeking to return home. There is a saying in markets: *Money always returns to its true owners.*

This was not a government agency playing with imaginary resources and 5-year plans or even a Hollywood blockbuster about Wall Street trading gone bad. This was *real* money earned penny by penny for over a century. Unfortunately for the depositors and shareholders, the bank was broke. This international bank had weathered depressions, famines, and world wars, but was now insolvent, its life force completely drained. And the blame fell to a single trader.

It would be hard even for the great Houdini to make money disappear that fast. There was no smoke, no mirrors, and no secret offshore compartments. Most fascinating of all is the fact that no arcane knowledge was needed, just super-aggressiveness and an extremely poor understanding of the leverage inherent in derivatives.

It sounds incredible that a firm could lose everything in virtually no time at all through poor trading strategies. But this is not just a fanciful hypothetical or an abstract theoretical discussion. It is the reality of our times, and has happened over and over again.

In the past 10 years there have been more than half a dozen spectacular blowups. And it will happen again and again. We've had billion dollar debacles at Barings Bank, Metalgesellschaft, Orange County, Sumitomo Trading, and Long Term Capital Management (LTCM); the latter required intervention by the Fed with an orchestrated multibillion dollar bailout. And then in 2002 there was Enron Trading, the biggest energy trader in the world. Enron's billions and billions in market capitalization have disappeared in the blink of an eye. The stock, once at $80, is worthless today. All of Enron's banks and counterparties are still in shock. Many employees were wiped out, their pensions and incomes forever lost. What occurred is still being argued in the courts, and no clear explanation has been forthcoming. You can be sure that, just like the other debacles, at the core is an exceedingly large market exposure, bad trading practice, and a complete lack of appreciation for the proper use of derivatives. It's a blueprint followed over and over.

This is not just about luck. Luck has to do with runs of winners and losers. It has nothing to do with blowing up and ruination. Everyone is subject to bad luck, but *good traders never lose everything*. You can take that to the bank. If you take too much exposure in the option market and an earthquake sends the Nikkei down 10 percent, you will get wiped out. This is not merely bad luck, it is irresponsible trading. You can never bet the ranch! That is rule no. 1 in Trading Strategy 101. Sooner or later there is *always* a bad swing of luck, and you can't afford to allow that swing to ruin you or your company.

Simply put, the billion dollar losers had taken on much too much risk. Either the traders and management agreed on a spectacularly bad strategy, or the traders told management that they had it under control—and management didn't understand the size of the risks. Any way you look at it, they lose.

Cautious, knowledgeable traders do not make a single wrong turn and end up in the war zone. It takes continuous disregard for crucial market tenets and huge overinvolvement to lose billions. They failed to learn the hardest truth of trading: *You can never be bigger than the market*. For when you finally think you've got control, *its got you instead!* If you are big enough to be important in a market, you can't get out without paying a price. The market is a very hard and uncompromising tutor. The tuition is very steep indeed.

The problem is not in the derivatives, but in the lack of understanding risks and leverage. Derivatives are complicated. The study and experience necessary are time-consuming. But it's even more daunting than that for some. Many market professionals try hard to get up to speed and then run into a brick wall. They get books on options, but find the books speak in foreign languages: mathematics and Greek, as a matter of fact.

To get your hands around the main concepts of derivatives requires a nodding acquaintance with the mathematics of statistics and probability. Most managers have too many things on their plate to spend weeks trying to understand the math necessary to grasp the basics of options and derivatives. But without this they can only partially understand what their traders and operations people are telling them. And less than half the traders really understand the math, preferring not to overintellectualize what they have previously succeeded at with intuition and gut feel. They bluff the rest.

So management hires math geeks and "quants" to oversee the traders. Management then learns a new lesson: traders are game players, first and foremost. This means that the traders start spending time figuring out the new quants who are supposed to be watching *them*. Traders are always searching for new angles and ways to push the envelope. How far can they go when bending the rules? How can they most selectively represent their risk to management? How far can they blow through their limits when they have a really good thing? And, scariest of all, how can they rationalize their losses and hide them until things get better? The rocket scientists hired by management usually have limited experience with traders and trading. They are typically a few steps behind. The two cultures rarely mix well.

So where is one to turn? Risk management is too important for a trader or manager to be entirely out of the loop and clueless. The only proper answer is to get a book that translates the foreign languages into English and to get down to studying. There are a half dozen very good books on options, but they use at least mid-level math formulas and explanations. That is just too difficult a leap to make for the nonmathematician without spending a thousand hours of intense research and review. This book tries to fill that gap.

Our goal is to get the reader up to a level where he or she can look at the intermediate books and actually grasp what is being discussed. The ideas and the math won't look like gibberish any longer if you put in some time studying this primer. Our goal is introduction and translation, not advanced trading strategies; our goal is to give the reader the confidence to look at the intermediate books for answers.

Derivatives seem like magic potions to a lot of people. And maybe they are in a way. But more than a few spectacular bankruptcies might have been prevented had the warning labels on the magic bottles been translated into plain English.

As you proceed, some of the work might seem a bit thick. Just remember the inscription from a 1910 math book we adore: "What one fool can do, another can." The great majority of options people are not even close to being math wizards; they just work at the basic stuff day after day until it starts to make sense. It will make sense to you also after a bit.

Another important issue: Reading a book, no matter how terrific, will not give you enough of an edge to make money in the markets. Contained herein are the rules of the game and an introduction into how options and derivatives markets work. You can succeed just as you would in the games of chess and bridge: You learn the rules, start with beginner's strategies, and then you gradually learn how to out-finesse your opponents. Failing that, they will beat you time after time. The opposition already knew the rules of option trading and had their moves down long before you picked up this book. With a bit of work you can get there too.

Good luck!

ACKNOWLEDGMENTS

I would like to take a moment to thank all those who contributed to this book in various ways. While inspiration and a rush of enthusiasm may play a major role when producing the mythical Great American Novel, producing a technical book seems to require endless patience, scrutiny, and painful attention to detail. I doubt I would have finished were it not for the support and encouragement of a wide range of friends and family.

From my family: Claire and Walter, Jaclyn and Michelle, Tom and Joette, Veronica, Erin, and Colin, Chloe and Dobie, John and Sue, Steve and Jackie.

Good friends who have read and made detailed observations on the original manuscript and urged me to continue when the task seemed endless are: Charlie, Mark, E.B., Jane, Alan, Randy, Steve, Ray, and John.

Special thanks to Robert Rotella, who recommended the book to McGraw-Hill, my editor Steven Isaacs for publishing it, and Pattie Amoroso for running a crackerjack editorial staff.

And, of course, there would be no book except for the peer-less typing, organizing, and dedication to detail of Charlotte Fisher. In the bustle of deadlines I've no doubt forgotten someone important to me, only to remember when it's too late. If so, I'll try to make amends in the next edition. Thank you one and all for your help and support. I am truly blessed; thank you for being my friends.

PART ONE

The Basics

CHAPTER 1

What a Derivative Is and What It Isn't

INTRODUCTION

In the past 5 years the price movements in the markets have been positively spectacular. In fact, it might be more accurate to say that the markets seem to have gone volcanic, erupting and spewing fire in all directions before lapsing back into a period of relative quiescence. For a long, long time certain high-tech industries and individual stocks seemed as invulnerable and mighty as Superman: faster than a speeding bullet, more powerful than a locomotive, and able to leap above their 52-week highs with a single bound. To even seasoned traders the events of this period were startling, the price movements mind-numbing.

Since the invention of money, there has never been a period of boom and bust to rival the trillions of dollars made and lost in the stock and bond markets over the last several years. As such there has never been a more exciting time to be involved in the markets. We are living through an historical period. And it is not over yet.

As a result of this there has never been a more appropriate time or more of a need to be studying finance and investments than right now. This is true despite the fact that the markets are in the process of losing some of their allure as they give back a large portion of their gains. While many might believe that the party is over and it's time to wander off home, they are not seeing the bigger picture. Now, more than ever, there are growing opportunities for those who understand markets and the myriad financial instruments available to be traded. It's when the easy money's gone that knowledge and experience pay off the most. It is sad to say, but only a handful of people involved in the markets over the last 10 years really understood what they were doing. One of the oldest adages in the markets is: Never confuse brains with a bull market. Once again the wisdom of old proverbs is being proved true.

In the market reversals of the last few years so many investors have gone from being "geniuses" to "idiots" that the nation's intelligence seems to have dropped 20 IQ points. Many day-trading stock speculators, who were never burdened with the knowledge of how markets work, have gone overnight from millionaires to bankrupts as their technical trading methods plunged them into a death spiral of losses. This is a classic beginner's mistake that can be easily avoided with a little discipline and risk management. But this type of overreaching speculation has little to do with the search for knowledge about finance and investments. And it has little to do with rational, level-headed people. Only suckers are gullible enough to think that becoming rich overnight is easy. They have now learned the painful way that what looks easy *isn't*, that what you see is *not* what you get, and that taking high risks brings insolvency far more often than riches. Most of the short-term technical traders, who were spectacularly successful for a while, have now "crashed and burned," in the colorful vernacular of traders. It's tough out there. Much tougher than many thought when the money was coming in fast and furious. The ones who succeed from here on in will have to work harder and learn their craft more properly than they did before. They might even have to go back to the basics to learn what makes the markets and financial assets tick. If they're smart, they'll start with a book like this.

There are two primary reasons that studying finance and investments right now is a very good idea even though the markets are no longer in runaway "bull" mode:

1. The stock market boom attracted many millions of new, inexperienced investors over the past 10 years. Although they think their baptism of fire over the last few years

has turned them into seasoned veterans, they are still novices who don't know what they're doing. The market has a lot more moves yet to show them.

2. The enormous growth in the numbers of different types of financial assets over the past 20 years is staggering. Very few people, even in the industry, can get a handle on all the changes. This creates opportunities for those who can understand what's going on and why.

Such a huge number of newcomers were lured to invest their nest eggs over the past 10 years that there are now millions of novice investors, more than ever before in the history of the markets, following dubious advice and strategies. And these investors are beginning to realize they are very, very lost and in need of help. The demand is bigger than it's ever been, and it is growing. Many of the newcomers would like to stay invested, but want to learn how to hedge their exposure and lower risk. This opens opportunities for those who know what they are doing when it comes to measuring risk and hedging it, and there are far fewer professionals qualified to do this than you might think.

Furthermore, this new group of inexperienced investors is likely to create good trading opportunities in the future as they chase the hot money trends, which has been their habit. The better you understand the markets, the more likely you are to recognize when the newcomers have occasion to start a stampede of over-buying or overselling which will make some investments more attractive than they ought to be. It is from such ideas that successful trading strategies are woven.

Alongside this is the enormous growth over the past 20 years in the number of different types of financial assets. Very few people can keep up with all the various financial products available. There have been more financial innovations in the last 2 decades than in the 4000 years preceding them. The markets have never been more alive or faster-growing. With change and innovation comes added complexity. *Never have so many financial assets been so complicated and understood by so few!* The financial innovations that helped spark this revolution are known as *derivatives,* and we will be getting very familiar with them since they are central to our studies.

The term *derivative* describes a new type of asset whose value is derived from the more familiar markets. That is to say that the centuries-old markets of stocks, bonds, and commodities have given birth to a whole new asset class that is derived from them. Derivatives always depend on their underlying parent markets to support them. Sort of like that black sheep brother-in-law who's been staying at your parents' house. Derivatives are similarly dependent on their underlying parent markets, but they never mooch beer money or run up the phone bill.

The most basic derivatives are *options, forwards,* and *futures.* It is our task here to come to grips with what they are and what they can do for us. Our primary focus is options, but as you will see, we need a nodding acquaintance with forwards and futures to get the whole picture. And that is a good thing, for it makes the financial world a whole lot clearer after a bit. Options, forwards, and futures are the building blocks and backbone of most of the derivatives out there. When you understand these three basic building blocks, you will understand the concept behind almost all derivatives.

This book is about learning options the easy way. That does not mean it will be a breeze, for anything worth knowing cannot properly be learned via speed-reading. It just means that there is a difficult, complex way to learn options (one that requires a Ph.D. in math) and an easier, more basic way for those of us who don't consider ourselves math geniuses. We are going to present the more basic course, and we think we can teach it better than anyone else has been able to. We also believe that a lot more people would learn options if they had the opportunity to learn about them in this simplified fashion.

WHERE WE ARE HEADED

So, let's spend a moment talking about the path we will follow. Using very simple analyses we will investigate and discuss options in ways similar to those uncovered by the economists who pioneered the earliest option theories. For them, at that time, many of the most appropriate answers were not as clear-cut or straightforward as they will be for us. We have the benefit of their errors and pains to guide us properly. Options have been part of the markets for centuries, but the theories of fair value are, relatively speaking, still in their infancy. Before the 1970s successful option traders had to develop a superior "gut feel" to enable them to price options, for there was little theory to back them up. Slowly, over many years, option theorists started to spring up in academia. They began puzzling over the fair valuation of options much like their academic predecessors mused over counting "how many angels could dance on the head of a pin." Applying knowledge learned from *games of chance,* the option theorists began to understand options well enough to translate their findings into the one true universal language: mathematics.

We will, in essence, become apprentices to these theorists and learn the ropes in a fashion that someone working directly with them might have. Working with the simplest of examples, like coin tosses, we will work our way to the point of understanding the underpinnings of the basic option formulas. We believe that you cannot understand options successfully without fully grasping the implications inherent in the option formulas. This does not mean that you must be fluent in advanced math or that you must memorize the formulas. It merely means that since the formulas are the heart of the market's method for valuing options, you cannot possibly understand option markets unless you have a working familiarity with the formulas. When you are making money or losing money in options, the answer as to why lies within the inner workings of the formulas: what risks you have hedged away and what risks you maintain. This cannot be understood from a distance; you must get up close and personal with it. These formulas, that the academic theorists only uncovered in the 1970s, are largely responsible for fueling the greatest growth and innovation in the history of finance. Without exaggeration, options are the backbone of today's enormous financial derivatives markets.

But finance is a very broad and diverse area of study. And options are certainly not the only financial derivatives. In our studies we will run into other financial derivatives that are not only important to specialized traders but to us as well. The world of derivatives is one of complex interrelationships. To understand options we must have at least a smattering of knowledge and awareness of several other derivatives. Life is never simple.

Options can become very complicated. To help us simplify our studies we will avoid many of the small, intricate questions that those who wish to become experts must answer but are only of minor interest to the rest of us. While these small pieces are necessary to pull together a complete option theory, in 95 percent of all situations you'll never incur them. In many options books this attention to small detail can overwhelm most readers. We've opted to cover more ground by taking a less detailed, more general approach. If you would like to scrutinize such details at some other time, there are a half dozen books readily available.

In this chapter we cover a lot of territory and describe a host of market terms, but don't let it overwhelm you. Our plan is to briefly describe in broad strokes the many various markets and financial assets that can become intertwined with and impinge on options. This is an introductory walk-through of the markets that hold interest for us, in very general terms. We could have made this chapter into half a dozen very small chapters, but then you would be itching to get onto the good stuff. This way we present lots of background information in this chapter and jump directly into our option basics in Chap. 2. We might discuss markets or terms that are new to some of you, but to the degree that they have importance to us we will provide more detail later on in this chapter. And, failing that, throughout the remainder of the book we've sprinkled reminders of what many of these terms mean. We've erred on the side of redundancy to encourage you to keep moving forward and not get too hung up on details the first time they are presented. You'll do best to just let it wash over you to get a sense of where everything fits and not worry too much about the small specifics. You can always come back and review the material later if you need to.

Since options belong to the category of financial assets known as derivatives, it makes sense to review more specifically what we mean by derivatives. As it turns out, it is not always clear as to what should be considered a derivative and what should not. We try to show that it is more by convention, that is, general agreement, than by strict rule that certain assets are called derivatives. Many assets that should technically be called derivatives are not. It's important to discuss what does and does not make the cut as a derivative if we want to understand the big picture about markets more clearly. We start off gently by describing a derivative relationship that isn't financial at all, but you will find it very familiar.

GETTING COMFORTABLE WITH DERIVATIVES

Every day we see and easily understand real-life derivative relationships all around us, yet many of us are confused by the derivative relationships in financial markets. Once you get the hang of it you will see that most financial derivatives are not so difficult to grasp. While the mathematics might be daunting at first, merely getting an intuitive feel for the purpose and function of an individual derivative isn't tough at all.

Let's talk about the derivative relationship between parents and their children for a bit. We often see a child that looks like a dead ringer for one of its parents. We might be slightly taken aback at the amazing likeness, but this is, nonetheless, a familiar situation for us. Sometimes members of a large family look like differently scaled versions of each other. And we have all witnessed the schoolmaster who projects past experiences onto the new arrival: "Young Smith, I pray you don't give me as much grief as your brother did!" Likewise, we are familiar with the fundamental adage that children are derivatives of their parents: "The apple doesn't fall far from the tree."

Derivatives in financial markets also follow paths and values similar to those taken by their parents. Financial derivatives have been blamed for the sudden, inexplicable blowups of a dozen trading companies, but this is a bum rap, an oversimplistic explanation of a complex issue. Derivatives have gotten bad press simply because they are believed to be unpredictable and uncontrollable. But this is just plain wrong. Their ways and actions can be understood, predicted, and controlled. Many firms do it very nicely every day.

Financial derivatives such as options, futures, forwards, and swaps inherit their value directly from their parents. In fact, a financial derivative would not have a price at all if the parent ceased to exist (stopped trading). The parents are the three basic financial groups that we are already quite familiar with: stocks, bonds, and commodities. (For our purposes, we consider currencies to be commodities.)

Every day more and more derivative products are being churned out by inventive marketing departments. These "innovations," however, are merely variations on the theme of the most

important fundamental derivatives: options, forwards, and futures. *These three derivatives are the three basic building blocks of all
complex derivatives, such as swaps.* (We discuss swaps later.)

Three Basic Spot Markets (*not* Derivatives)
1. Stocks
2. Bonds
3. Commodities

Three Basic *Derivative* Markets
1. Forwards
2. Futures
3. Options

The goal of this book is to give you a deep enough understanding of these three building blocks so that you will be able to
evaluate any derivative product. We will spend our time focusing
on and explaining options, forwards, and futures: how they derive
their values from their parent financial assets, how the financial
community analyzes their risk, and how this risk can be hedged.

In a sense we will become financial investigators, delving into
the whys and wherefores of the basic three derivatives. As such
there is a lot of math involved, but it need not be painful. We will
assume the reader has little background in math. We will follow
the most intuitive paths possible and avoid as much complexity
as we can. Options are far more complex then forwards and futures, both in the math needed to analyze them and in their implications. As such we will spend almost all our time discussing
and analyzing options. On the journey we will build a base of
knowledge on the Black-Scholes option formula, the master tool
of the options world.

Two of the basic three derivatives, forwards and futures, are
almost interchangeable in many ways. Many professionals trade
them as if they were equivalent to each other. After our discussion
of them later in this chapter, we require only a single chapter to
further analyze the math behind them.

We mentioned swaps earlier. Swaps and swaptions are considered the most complex derivative products and are well beyond the scope of an introductory text. We won't spend much
time with them except to explain what they are at the end of this

chapter. You will see that swaps are merely a complex agglomeration of the three more basic derivatives: options, forwards, and futures. As you get a deeper understanding of the basic three, you will see they are the key to learning swaps as well.

A FUZZY AREA: WHAT IS AND ISN'T A DERIVATIVE?

What is and isn't a derivative is more a matter of convention and definition than you might at first imagine. Some things that are considered basic, primary assets are actually less basic and primary than common knowledge would lead you to believe.

Corporate America is ruled by two predominant financial market sectors: stocks and bonds. Stocks are often referred to as the *equities market* and Bonds are referred to as the *debt market* (corporate debt, that is). Governments also borrow through the government sector of the debt market. By law, the government is not allowed to sell an equity interest in its ownership or control (some cynics might argue this issue).

Many people feel they have a good handle on how stocks and bonds work, how they are used, and their purpose. They know stocks and bonds are the two most basic building blocks of finance. It turns out, however, that stocks and bonds themselves are actually *derivative products*. The world is rarely as simple as we'd like to believe.

Let's say that a corporation needs cash to expand. It sells ownership rights and/or borrows money tied to its inventory and properties. The pieces of paper conferring rights of ownership are called shares of stock. The pieces of paper enumerating the contractual liens and performance clauses backing the borrowings are called notes or bonds. When you buy stocks or bonds, you are really buying pieces of paper that confer rights. The value of the stocks and bonds, are derived from the earnings, assets, and progress of the corporation. They are derivative to the company's well-being and its ability to remain a profitable, ongoing concern. Without a healthy company those rights are pretty much worthless.

Some theorists go even further and suggest that stocks are an option on the bondholders' claims. Stockholders' rights are contingent on the successful repayment of the corporation's bonds and notes. If the bondholders are paid interest and principal as due, there should be something left over, perhaps, for the stockholders to share. But if the bondholders are not paid, then a default takes place and the stocks, which are subordinate to the bonds, might receive nothing and thereby be deemed worthless. Over the last few years there has been far too much of this going on. So much in fact that they've coined a new phrase for it: distressed securities.

While this discussion might bend your mind a bit, it is really just to show you that it is never completely clear, except by creating our own definitions, as to what a derivative is and what it is not. Also it shows that you were already comfortable and familiar with a number of derivatives even though they aren't conventionally considered to be derivatives. *From this point forward we will consider stocks, bonds, and commodities to be the three basic, primary trading assets.* We define them to be basic trading assets and *not* derivatives. These three assets underlie all derivatives and are thus called the *underlying assets.*

What we are investigating in this book, and what most people are uncomfortable with, are the slightly more arcane derivatives called options, forwards, and futures. These derivatives use stocks, bonds, and commodities as their underlying parent assets. For example, traders would categorize an IBM $95 call option as a derivative. The shares of IBM stock, however, would be considered the underlying parent asset. A single stock, like IBM, can easily give birth to a whole litter of IBM options: $85, $90, $95, $100, $105 strikes; January or April expiry; puts or calls, and so forth.

OTHER NONDERIVATIVES: PORTFOLIOS, MUTUAL FUNDS, AND THE DOW JONES AVERAGES

The "basket of stocks" concept is related to three investment concepts that might also be termed derivatives: portfolios, mutual funds, and averages. No one calls them derivatives, but you can plainly see that the classic definition of a derivative applies: an asset whose value is derived from the other assets that underlie it.

For example, if you went out and bought seven stocks and three bonds, your portfolio's value would be a derivative of the value of those 10 assets. It would have a perfect correspondence to, and move dollar for dollar with, the value of the underlying 10 assets. If we registered it, broke it into a thousand pieces, and sold it to the public, it would be a mutual fund. The name has changed, but the game remains the same.

If you created your portfolio from the 30 industrial stocks in the Dow Jones Industrial Average (and weighted it appropriately), then the change each day in the Dow Industrial Average would fairly reflect the value in your portfolio. Clearly the market averages derive their value from the underlying stocks, as does a portfolio and a mutual fund. We won't call them derivatives, however, as that is not the standard convention. But you should know that some options, forwards, and futures base their values on averages and other basketlike assets that might be called derivatives *but are not*. It can get very confusing. To help avoid some later confusion we're going to make an adjustment right now.

There is a generic phrase commonly used in the industry for market averages and baskets of stocks: stock indexes. To avoid later confusion we're going to include stock indexes along with stocks, bonds, and commodities and call them the fourth basic market of underlying assets. This is technically not correct, but it makes things easier for nonexperts. And it helps show you how wacky the question, "Is it or isn't it a derivative?", has become. The following table lists the most typical derivatives available to the public. Using the three basic derivatives and the four basic markets (with stock indexes) there are 12 combinations of simple derivatives.

The Simplest Derivatives

Forwards on	Futures on	Options on
Stocks	Stocks	Stocks
Bonds	Bonds	Bonds
Commodities	Commodities	Commodities
Stock indexes	Stock indexes	Stock indexes

Use the table as a reference; don't try to memorize it. It's here to help you get a feel for the many, many possibilities that exist. Just keep in mind there can be derivatives (forwards, futures, and options) on each of the underlying parent markets (stocks, bonds, commodities, and we've added stock indexes).

THE ORIGIN OF FUTURES AND FORWARDS

For hundreds of years the marketplace did just fine with the three basic financial assets: stocks, bonds, and commodities. People placed their orders to buy or sell and in a few days cash and assets were swapped. These are called the cash or spot markets, in reference to the delivery date. The term *cash* comes from the phrase "cash on the barrelhead," meaning immediate payment. And *spot* comes from "on the spot" deliveries and payments. Over the years the terms *cash* and *spot* became almost equal in meaning, and traders began to allow a few days of delay for purposes of convenience and safety (known carriers of cash are at risk). Instead of traders worrying about dragging away their purchases and validating authenticity, they could hand it to their traffic departments to arrange preparations for taking physical delivery. Today, typical cash or spot deliveries take place 2 to 3 days *after* the trade date. Some professionals have recently begun to use more technical phrases such as "T + 2" and "T + 3" which refer to "trade date + 2," and so on.

A few commodities markets began to offer alternative delivery dates more than a century ago to meet the farmers' needs. The Chicago grain market was one of the first. Farmers with crops in the field wanted to be able to plan their budgets for the year. Without a hint of the price they would receive at next month's delivery they couldn't estimate income at all. They couldn't borrow money at the bank. And in order to decide on which new crops to plant at season's end it was critical to get a handle on what the market would pay for next year's crops of wheat, corn, and soybeans.

The only prices available, however, were for same-day delivery of wheat and corn. Unless you had already shipped and placed your crop into a warehouse you wouldn't have the warehouse receipts needed for same-day delivery. This process of harvesting and delivering into a registered grain elevator could take a month or two. A farmer with wheat still in the field or one trying to decide on what to plant next season was left without a clue as to the anticipated future price.

Slowly there developed groups of traders and dealers who would quote delivery prices for forward or future dates. Thus began the first derivatives market in the United States. Over time it became centralized in Chicago on the floor of the Board of Trade (CBT) as a futures market. In the 1980s, with the explosive growth of bond futures, the CBT became the largest derivatives exchange in the world. In the 1990s the rival Chicago Mercantile Exchange (CME), which is home to currency futures, Eurodollar futures, and the S&P500 Stock Index futures, overtook the CBT as the largest derivatives exchange.

DERIVATIVES TODAY

There are about two dozen world commodities. These days almost every actively traded commodity has a futures market, a forward market, and an options market associated with it. This is true of currencies and government bonds, too.

Stocks, however, have more controls placed on them by the U.S. Securities and Exchange Commission (SEC). Individual stocks like IBM have an options market, but their futures and forward markets are very restricted. There are about 2500 securities in North America that have options trading. For the most part they are all individual stocks, like Intel, Cisco, or AT&T, although more than a few stock indexes and the like have options also.

Up until now the SEC has limited futures trading to baskets of stocks (stock indexes) like the S&P500. This market is huge and growing. In November 2002, after 20 years of turf battles and infighting, individual stocks began trading futures also. They are called single stock futures (we say a few words about them at the end of this chapter). Of course, it's just a matter of time until someone will shoot for having options on these futures. The variety of derivatives might seem overwhelming at first, but all you need remember is that there are four basic underlying assets (stocks, bonds, commodities plus stock indexes) and they are the parents of the three basic derivatives (options, forwards, futures). *Remember:* There are four basic underlying assets (with stock indexes) that can support three basic derivatives each.

All successful derivative products must fulfill some want or need of the marketplace. Unless the products are useful they slowly wither away and disappear. Here is a short list of attributes shared by many successful derivative products:

1. Easy credit
2. Delayed delivery
3. Narrow price quotes
4. Improved liquidity

The three most successful derivatives are also the most basic: options, forwards, and futures. These three all allow for huge leverage (easy credit), offer great liquidity, and have the cachet of get-rich-quick appeal. But, of course, some things that look appealing from a distance might give you indigestion when you get too close. Delayed delivery plays to our eternal tendency to procrastinate and our hope that things will be better tomorrow. During the summer of 2003 the economists are hinging all their recovery hopes on the robustness of the consumer, a "healthy" consumer who continually borrows and buys. It seems like our economy has been based on the increasing use of credit cards for the last 40 years. There is no clearer example of our tendency to procrastinate. "Buy now, pay later" is no longer just a catchy advertising phrase; it's an American shopper's mantra.

Another reason that certain derivatives are so successful relates to our need for fantasy and our hopes in discovering buried treasure, like those who buy lottery tickets every week. Many options *are* lottery tickets: low risk, high reward, and no chance. Our wildest dreams and our worst nightmares may never happen, but options exist for those who feel the need to hedge for and against those possibilities.

Let's end this introductory chapter with a brief section on each of the derivatives we have been discussing.

OPTIONS

Options, despite their complexity, are easily defined by a single word: *choice*. All financial contracts are based upon locked-in commitments for both buyer and seller—except options. Buying an option allows you to have choices. You can see how the world turns out a bit down the road and then decide if you wish to make or take delivery at the original price. You have the choice. This lowers your risk. You can allow unfavorable deals to expire and walk away. This is a very nice convenience, but it isn't free. The price you must pay to buy an option—its cost to you—is called its *premium.*

When you buy an option, you are buying a price insurance policy. Your risk is limited to your premiums. Depending on how events unfold you can be protected against certain price moves and may receive monetary compensation.

On the other hand, if you *sell* options, you are granting insurance to someone else. If certain unfavorable events unfold, you must compensate the other party and it might be highly expensive. You could be in deep jeopardy. The companies who lose megamillions in the options markets are invariably option *sellers.* They pretend they are insurance companies, but haven't the knowledge or capital required. When four standard deviation moves occur, it is the option sellers who get hammered. It turns out they've written hurricane insurance, but they've only been paid "fair weather" premiums. Let's look at two simple examples of IBM options:

> *Example 1:* IBM stock is $100 a share now. If you want protection against the price going down over the next 6 months, you would buy a 6-month IBM $100 *put* (cost: say $7.50 per share). If you haven't got an IBM position, we would say you are speculating. If you have already bought IBM and are seeking protection, then we would say you are buying insurance. Same action, different viewpoint.
>
> To continue, if the price of IBM falls to $80 during the next 6 months, you are protected at $100 since you are allowed to put the IBM stock to the option grantor and receive $100 a share. It did cost $7.50 per share for the insurance, though, so you have lost that, but you protected yourself against a $20 drop.
>
> *Example 2:* IBM stock is $100 a share now. If you want protection against the price going up over the next 6 months, you would buy a 6-month IBM $100 *call* (cost: say $9.20 per share). [*Note for advanced readers:* The put cost is $7.50, but the call cost is $9.20. This is typical of spot options because the forward price is considered the fair price of IBM stock. If spot IBM stock is trading at $100, the 6-month forward is worth $101.70 at 3.4 percent rates. If so, the right

to call it at $100 is worth about $1.70 per share more than the right
to put it at $100.] You might want to own IBM stock, but you
haven't yet done so and you are afraid the market may get away
from you. This call gives you the choice during the next 6 months
of buying IBM stock from the option grantor for $100 a share no
matter what price it is trading for at that time.

So that's it in a nutshell. There are only two basic types of
options. They have been given the names *puts* and *calls*, which,
respectively, give you the choice of selling or buying, *if you choose
to do so*. You need not sell or buy if it is not beneficial to you. Thus,
you do not have an obligation, but a choice. *Only options allow this
choice*. As a comparison, forwards and futures are locked-in obligations in which you must deliver on the agreed date whether
you like it or not.

Puts and calls are mirror images of each other. The first protects the downside; the second protects the upside. It can get very
confusing when both are discussed at the same time. For purposes
of keeping things simple *we will limit our discussions to only* calls.
Once you grasp all the rationales related to calls you will easily
understand puts.

Under certain conditions there are ways to synthetically turn
a call into a put and vice versa. Based on this there are simple
formulas to equate the price of a call to the price of a put. That
concept is a bit advanced for now, so beginning with calls is the
best way to go.

Let's conclude with one other option concept: *moneyness*.
Traders are forever discussing at-the-money, in-the-money, and
out-of-the-money options. The following table shows strike prices
versus moneyness if IBM is trading at $100 per share.

Moneyness of IBM Calls (If IBM Is Trading at $100 per Share)

Strike Price	Moneyness
$120	Out-of-the-money
$110	Out-of-the-money
$100	At-the-money
$90	In-the-money
$80	In-the-money

IBM stock is trading at $100 per share, so the $100 call is the *at-the-money* option. The $120 call is far from being worth exercising, so it's called the *out-of-the-money* option. The $80 call can be exercised immediately to put $20 in your pocket, so we say it is the *in-the-money* option. It's easiest to remember it as a "pocket" thing. Does it put money in your pocket or take money out of your pocket if you immediately exercise your option?

THREE MARKET TIME FRAMES: CASH, FORWARD, AND FUTURES

Let's suppose for a moment that you are a wealthy financier, like Warren Buffet. You decide that silver bullion is the next hot investment, and you call your broker to buy. Your broker asks, "In which market: cash, futures, or forward?" Being well known to investment bankers allows you to choose your market. You can buy silver in the cash market (same as spot), you can buy futures on an exchange, and you can call a dealer and buy forwards. The silver you will buy in these three markets is essentially identical. The prices are comparable with only minor adjustments. The cash, forward, and futures markets trade very closely in line with each other. Because you are Warren Buffet there are no restrictions as to which market you have access to. Everybody wants your business. This is certainly *not true* for most investors.

The overwhelming majority of people never use the forward or futures markets. Their buying and selling is transacted in the cash or spot markets. Less than 10 percent of all investors ever get involved in the futures markets or even vaguely understand them. And only a tiny 1 percent of all investors, the most elite traders, are invited to participate in the forward markets. Figure 1–1 shows a rough diagram of the relative number of players in each market.

It's all a matter of financial wherewithal. If you are a little guy, you need cash on the barrelhead to trade. No one trusts you. But everyone with cash is welcome to trade in the cash or spot markets. If you have good credit, you can open a futures brokerage account that specializes in futures exchange traded assets and you'll need a lot less cash up front. The forward markets, however, trade by invitation only. You must have a relationship with a

F I G U R E   1–1

Relative Number of Players in Each Market

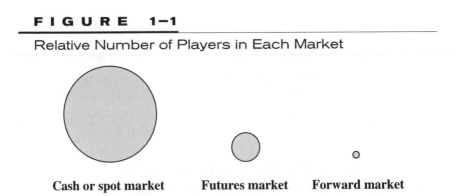

Cash or spot market   **Futures market**   **Forward market**

dealer specializing in forwards. Different markets attract a different breed of participants and have different credit requirements.

All three markets might trade during the same hours. The products traded and the prices charged in all three markets closely parallel one another. Cash, forwards, and futures are always in line after adjusting for deferred delivery costs. They can only trade far apart when there is a hiccup in the circumstances surrounding delivery. Otherwise, dealers would quickly arbitrage them.

Forwards and futures are competitors to the cash market and to each other. Clients who prefer delayed delivery and credit concessions lean toward using the futures and forward markets rather than the cash market.

COMPARING FUTURES AND FORWARDS

The futures market is the average person's marketplace for deferred delivery. These markets trade standardized contracts (e.g., every gold contract traded on the New York Commodity Exchange [Comex] is identically the same), and they transact "downstairs" in a "pit" on Commodity Futures Trading Commission (CFTC) regulated exchanges. They typically call themselves *futures exchanges*. If you can't find what you want on the futures exchange and you have a relationship with a forward market dealer, you can trade there. They will create specially tailored contracts for *anything* you want—for a price.

That's one primary difference between the two markets: Futures have only one standard item that you can trade. Take it or leave it. One size fits all. On the other hand, the forward market dealer will make any changes you want (if you are a client), but charges extra.

Let's use the gold futures contract as an example. On the New York Comex you can trade gold futures with a contract size of 100 ounces. The bars can have only a small weight tolerance, say, plus or minus 2 percent. You cannot deliver 142 ounces, for example. There are six main delivery dates each year: the first business day of February, April, June, August, October, and December. The bars can't be forged at just any refinery, there are lists of acceptable assayers and refiners. And you can't deliver gold in London or Tokyo, it must be a registered receipt for a New York warehouse.

Those are the main requirements, but the list of specifics goes on and on. The exchange publishes rule books with dozens of pages per commodity to legally specify all the standards for deliveries. And they discuss myriad market scenarios, like defaults.

There is an important benefit that derives from standardizing. Standardization allows fungibility and liquidity. *Fungibility* means that, in the eyes of the market, each item is identical and interchangeable. Each unit is considered exactly equal to another. This is true of our currency: each $1 bill is identical and exchangeable with every other $1 bill. Otherwise chaos ensues. Fungibility encourages liquidity. *Liquidity* is the ability to quickly and easily exchange an asset (buy, sell, or transfer).

Futures markets create enormous liquidity by funneling all the buyers and sellers into a single fungible asset. If everyone is interested in trading December 1 gold then there will be many potential buyers and sellers. But if an offbeat request comes in to buy, say, July 19 gold, then very few people will be willing to participate in offering it. The customer must deal with those few specialists who trade offbeat dates. The price quote will be far less competitive.

Futures pits are amazing places. You have hordes of crazy traders yelling and screaming at each other and changing direction as quickly as a flock of birds in midflight. They are executing trades for themselves and for "upstairs" customers. All the business of the world is channeled into one tiny arena as thousands of traders around the globe place orders via direct phone lines. Hundreds of brokers try to rip each other's throats out while screaming for bids and offers. How could a market be any more liquid than this?

On balance the futures exchanges offer the best prices and the best liquidity, but you are stuck trading the same old standard contract. It's like going to McDonalds to eat. The prices are cheap and the service is quick, but the menu is scanty. You can't expect elegant service or high-quality food. But the price is right if you want a quick hamburger. On the other hand, in the forward market you might feel like you are being served the down-home cooking at Alice's Restaurant. And as Arlo Guthrie told us, "You can get anything you want at Alice's Restaurant." But it might cost more. Oh, yes indeed, lots more.

Futures (On a Regulated Exchange)	Forwards (Upstairs, Off-Exchange)
Standardized date, quantity, delivery point	Customized to fit your needs
Market makers in the pit "downstairs"	Dealers "upstairs"
Extremely liquid	Occasionally liquid
Average person's market (anonymous)	Elite one-to-one relationships

There are other differences such as regulatory oversight, margin requirements, marking-to-market, and right of offset. Many of the remaining differences are highly technical in nature and only useful to experts. For our purposes here we wanted to show that forwards and futures are viable alternatives to the cash and spot markets. That for the most part forwards and futures prices closely parallel one another and are closely linked by a network of dealers looking to take advantage of any price discrepancies. Later, when we describe the formula to price forwards and futures, you won't be stunned to find out we use the very same formula for both of them. One formula fits all.

Many floor exchanges are moving toward electronic Internet trading. Any such electronic Internet trading, even though it is no longer occurring from the floor, still falls under the heading of futures. The CFTC remains the regulator presiding over any futures products that originated from an exchange floor.

OTHER MORE ADVANCED DERIVATIVES

In order to round out your knowledge we're including a very short table of the more complex, specialized derivatives, some of which are considered to be rather exotic. From this list we'll only discuss swaps, and those only briefly, since a proper treatment of this list belongs in books far more advanced than ours.

More Advanced/Exotic Derivatives

Swaps

Swaptions

Asian options

Digital options

Rainbow options

Knockout options

Compound options

Swaps

These are the most complex derivatives because they are often combinations of all the other derivatives and assets we have mentioned. On top of that, they have two sides to them. Something is given, something is taken.

In market lingo *spreads, switches, rollovers, repos,* and *swaps* all mean two-sided trades. An exchange of one asset for another. You give something and you get something else in return. You might buy gold for delivery in New York tomorrow and simultaneously sell gold for London delivery next week. Or buy a T-bill for delivery tomorrow and sell a 2-year T-note for delivery tomorrow also. The assets can vary, the dates can vary, and so on. But something is bought and a different thing is sold.

Over time the term *swap* grew up to mean a special kind of complex, long-term deal. And it is usually not a one-shot deal, but an ongoing deal. For example, it won't fully settle tomorrow, but it might continue in force as an exchange of two assets for the next 6 months or 2 years, or more. Maybe the swap settles only at the expiration of the deal, or perhaps a piece of the deal settles every month. These are all struck over the counter between upstairs dealers, and the rules vary deal by deal.

Some enterprising trader came up with the idea of swapping risks or swapping cash flows. Remember the song "You've Got Your Troubles, I've Got Mine . . ."? This is the major thesis behind the swaps market. You can give your troubles and take someone else's. Apparently so many people feel that this is a good deal that the market is thriving.

The swaps market has found its largest acceptance in the interest rate markets. An example might be swapping fixed interest rate risk for floating interest rate risk. For example, the prime rate is a floating (variable) rate. It changes whenever it suits the banks. When you book loans based on the prime rate, you can never be sure what the rate will be tomorrow, since it "floats" up and down. But suppose you are willing to borrow money at a fixed rate, say 8 percent. You might be able to give away your floating prime rate obligation and take a new fixed rate (8 percent)—for a price, of course.

That is the main principle behind swaps and is only one example out of thousands. Dealers call it "give floating, take fixed." Swap one for the other. Remember when we said futures markets were enormously liquid? Well the Eurodollar interest rate futures (the interest rate of dollars in Europe, not the new currency) became the biggest futures contract in the world only after swaps became active. It turns out that Libor (London interbank offered rate) is really the dollar interest rate in Europe (called Eurodollar rates). Libor is one of the most swapped interest rates, and so traders started hedging themselves with the Eurodollar futures contract. The volume is now $400 billion each day. The dealers hedge one type of derivative (a swap) with another type of derivative (a futures contract).

We could go on and on describing swaps, but it is far too complicated to tackle in an introductory text. Swaps will make a lot more sense to you when you fully understand options, forwards, and futures. You will see then that swaps are more intricate, complex versions of the three basic derivatives. (*Note:* If options are added to a swap, it is sometimes called a *swaption*.)

We end the chapter with a brief discussion about the newest kid on the block: single stock futures.

SINGLE STOCK FUTURES

In December 2000, after 20 years or more of internecine warfare, the federal government finally passed legislation to allow for the trading of futures on individual stocks like IBM and ATT. It took another 2 years of red tape and regulatory posturing until the exchanges began trading in November 2002. What could have been a slam-bang start in 1999 was a bit anticlimactic in November 2002 since it represented the third down year in a row for the stock market. In fact, this has been the worst 3-year run since the great depression. Nonetheless, single stock futures are finally with us.

These single stock futures offer many possibilities for shrewd traders, but have not, as of this moment, reached the critical mass of volume and liquidity needed to break through to the next level of acceptance and popularity. Success begets success, to more than a small degree. We believe that single stock futures will someday be one of the hottest derivatives on Wall Street. Only time and a bull market will tell.

Single stock futures, like all other futures products, are margined securities. This means that if you qualify to trade them you will get easy credit and need not put down $100 to buy a $100 stock. Making such easy credit available for stock futures traders was a very hotly argued topic by the SEC, the CFTC, and the Federal Reserve, among others. At the moment (and margins can always change) the margin is set at 20 percent, meaning you have to post $20 a share for buying (or selling) a $100 stock. The Federal Reserve regulation for buying stock in the normal cash markets of the New York Stock Exchange (NYSE) or the National Association of Securities Dealers Automated Quotations (NASDAQ) is 50 percent. So, as is usual for futures, the credit is much easier than for the cash market.

As befits a futures market the deliveries are deferred in time relative to the cash markets. Whereas you must always take delivery on the NYSE and NASDAQ 3 business days after your trade is made [known as "T + 3" (trade date plus 3)], for single stock futures there is only a once-a-month delivery, based on third Fridays.

If you buy June futures, for example, you should expect delivery the day after the third Friday in June. You can buy and sell June futures to your heart's content until the last trading day, which is the third Friday of June. But if you fail to zero out your position by that date, you must make or take delivery. Most traders do trade out of their June positions shortly before the third Friday and then switch to trading the September contract, with the same idea in mind. Never take delivery, but never stop trading either. In many businesses delivery time is when everyone settles up, but in futures trading most traders are long gone by then. Therefore, the industry standard is to continuously charge profit or loss hits to the account each and every night. That way all monies owed are paid by the next morning and the chances for default are greatly decreased.

One question on everyone's mind is, are the futures stock prices comparable to the cash stock prices? No need to worry—the futures price of IBM will match the NYSE cash price for IBM, almost penny for penny. *Arbitrageurs* are the traders who make this occur as they try to earn a free penny per share. There will be a spread between the futures and cash prices based on a well-known fair value (let's pick $0.25 a share for our example here). If IBM is trading on the NYSE at $100.00 a share, then the futures will be trading very close to $100.25 (based on our fair value of 25 cents). If the futures trade at $100.30 instead, an arbitrageur has either locked in about 5 cents profit (before costs) or a whole lot of screaming is going on in his or her trading room. It's probably the boss screaming that free money was given away to the competition. But it might also be the trader screaming at his or her clerk or broker for failing to get a "fill" on a standing order. Or everyone might be screaming at once. In trading rooms it's sometimes hard to know who's screaming and why. We'll go into concepts like arbitrage much later in the book when we discuss how traders make money.

So, for an average investor, the price advantage or disadvantage of buying on the NYSE or in the futures market is often a moot point. The prices are, given proper volume and liquidity, substantially identical. Given active markets, which we expect will occur one day, the ability to execute smoothly and quickly will be equivalent in either market for the average investor. There are additional advantages that accrue only to those who trade single stock futures, however:

1. Investors get easy credit, only 20 percent down.
2. There are no broker loans requiring interest on the other 80 percent.
3. Less trading capital is tied up in each position.
4. Delivery can be postponed indefinitely.

5. Investors can "short" as many shares as they want without extra fees, margins, or the need to borrow stock (*shorting* is the selling of shares you don't yet own).

6. There may be advantageous tax treatment since different capital gains rules apply.

That concludes our opening chapter. There were a great many topics we needed to make you aware of, so don't expect to remember them all. Anything of particular importance to our studies on options will be reviewed again later, so don't panic if it seems like a lot. There's plenty of time to panic later if you really feel compelled to do so. We're going to wrap up all our chapters with a review, some things to think about, and the often feared questions and answers (so you can prove to yourself that you know what's happening so far). The Answer Key in the back of the book is quite extensive with long, detailed discussions and might well suit many readers as an extended means of review.

KEY CONCEPTS REVIEW

- ♦ Options, forwards, and futures are the three basic derivatives from which all others spring.
- ♦ Derivatives depend on underlying assets to give them their value.
- ♦ Stocks, bonds, and commodities are the three financial assets that underlie these derivatives.
- ♦ Stock indexes, like the Dow and S&P500, have come to be considered a fourth underlying asset class.
- ♦ While this suggests 12 possible combinations (three derivatives for each of four underlying assets), there exist many other exotic (complex) variations. For our studies we will avoid the exotic variations and focus on the three most basic derivatives: options, forwards, and futures.
- ♦ Options are far more complex than either forwards or futures and are thus far more difficult to understand. Once you clear the hurdle presented by options the door to understanding derivatives is thrown wide open. We show how to unravel the option mystery over the next several chapters.

- Forwards and futures are very closely related in many ways. They ought to be since they are based on variations of the very same financial concept: delayed delivery. Many professional traders consider them almost identical for trading purposes, and our method of valuing them does also.
- Swaps and other exotic derivatives are merely more complex versions of our three most basic building blocks: options, forwards, and futures. Traders take a piece from here and a part from there to create more complex trading vehicles such as swaps, but in the end they all depend upon the simple and basic three.

THINGS TO THINK ABOUT

Deliveries   The world's largest markets are known as *cash* and *spot* markets (2- to 3-day delivery). Actual physical deliveries are the rule almost 100 percent of the time. Forward deliveries are an extension of this that allow for delayed or deferred delivery, but come the forward date delivery is due. In practice such deliveries take place more than 50 percent of the time; the balance is allowed to be offset or extended again. The futures and options markets are, however, quite different. Futures and options traders almost *never* want to take delivery. Only 2 percent of all contracts are delivered while the other 98 percent are offset or extended. Can you see why cash, spot, and forward markets are considered to be physicals or actuals markets while futures and options are often called "paper" markets? Can you see how paper markets open the doors for a far wider array of investors, hedgers, and speculators and how less money is needed to trade paper markets because the full price is not needed until the delivery date?

You Can Get It Wholesale   Suppose today is April 1 and you'd like to buy deferred delivery gold for December 1 of this year. Forwards and futures are the markets that allow this. The quality of gold offered in each market is the same as are many of the contractual arrangements. For insiders the price quoted for December 1 gold is essentially identical in either market. To which market should you go?

Here are a few extra facts to help you decide:

* Small retail clients have no access to the investment banks that run the forward markets, whereas almost anyone with $10,000 can open a futures market account at a brokerage firm.
* In futures markets both insiders and outsiders get the same price, but only insiders get an equivalent price in forward markets.
* The traders who make markets in the forward markets always look first to the futures markets to hedge themselves after a deal.

QUESTIONS

1. What are the three basic derivatives?
2. What are the three primary markets or assets that underlie all financial derivatives?
3. What are *delayed* or *deferred deliveries?*
4. Why are cash, spot, and forward markets often called *physicals* or *actuals* markets?
5. Why are futures and options markets considered paper markets?
6. Where are forwards traded? Where are futures traded?
7. Why are futures like eating at McDonalds and forwards like eating at "Alice's Restaurant"?
8. Which prices are more competitive, futures or forwards?
9. What is *fungibility?* Why is it important to markets?
10. What is *liquidity?* Why is it important?
11. How do futures exchanges magnify liquidity?
12. How are options a separate class from any other financial contract?
13. How are insurance and options linked?
14. Suppose you decide shares of Amazon.com are going to run up in price shortly. Which market can help you more clearly define and limit your risk: spot, cash, forward, futures, or options?
15. What is a *swap?*

WHY COIN TOSSES?

Unless we understand the mechanics that underlie our world we are at a loss to explain what is happening on a moment-to-moment basis. We must remain dependent on the knowledge of others and default to their judgment if we do not have sufficient expertise in the fundamental forces that drive the events around us. In the world of finance ignorance is rarely bliss.

Take cars for instance: everybody drives one, but few people know the basic mechanics of what goes on under the hood. A driver's nightmare is to break down in the dead of night on a deserted highway. Occurrences like this can be minimized by making sure your car is well-maintained and running smoothly. That's pretty obvious. What's not so obvious is that only someone with a fundamental knowledge of the mechanics of cars can properly judge if it has been well-maintained or if it is running smoothly. Knowing what should be happening under the hood helps one develop the right feel for what is in tune and what is out of tune. Few of us ever spend the time and energy to learn the mechanical side of cars. Suddenly the car stops working, and it seems like a random curse from the gods. An expert would have seen it coming, more often than not. This is why we should know all about our cars—but we don't.

Options are a lot like this. In the world of finance almost everybody is involved with options directly or indirectly, but hardly anybody understands what is going on under the hood. And when you don't understand the basic driving forces, you must depend on your traders and operations people to explain the often quirky financial outcomes—far too late to allow you to intervene. Only someone grounded in the fundamentals can participate in the day-to-day decision making. There is no alternative.

Our tack in this book is to rip the hood off options and show you what is going on, step by step and inch by inch, with simple examples in clear, understandable math. This is no easy task; a proper introduction to options math requires at least a nodding acquaintance with probability and statistics, as well as several other mathematical functions. Luckily for us we can build the basics of our option education on a wonderfully simple game we all know well—the coin toss.

There are a half dozen math concepts, ranging from very simple to very complex, that are critical to valuing options. They must be learned if we are to grasp the inner workings of options formulas. We can do it the hard way by delving into textbook after textbook on statistics, distributions, random walks, and so on. Or we can do it the easy way. Every math concept we need to understand has a simple analog that can be learned step by step as we work through the math of coin tosses. This allows us to use the clearest explanations possible for a complex subject.

Most options books demand a high level of math proficiency and seem to be written for engineers and mathematicians. Starting on a high plane they expect the reader to get each mathematical point immediately, and little time is spent fleshing out the whys and wherefores. We take the opposite policy here, slowly developing each concept from the ground up.

By using coin tosses we can gradually build up a base of knowledge that explains frequency of occurrence, probabilities, statistics, and distributions. We discuss the concept of *fair games* wherein each participant is expected to break even. We show how to easily assign a probability of occurrence to each coin toss outcome. Once the probability of occurrence is known, the payoff is simple to deduce because the sum of all payoffs must be zero in a fair game (all players must break even). It turns out that these two, the probabilities and payoffs, are the most critical pieces of information needed every time you want to compute any option's price. Whether we are describing options for coin tosses or options for the stock market, the math concepts remain the same.

This is by far the smoothest, fastest road to take us where we want to go. Fewer bumps, fewer potholes, fewer twists and turns. If you persevere for just a few chapters, you will begin to see the big picture on options come quickly into focus, sharper and clearer than ever before.

PROBABILITY AND GAMBLERS

If you were a gambler shooting dice just a few hundred years ago, you were treading in unknown territory. And it was hard to find a game; there were no Vegas or Atlantic City casinos to provide action. Maybe that was because probability theory hadn't yet been invented and games of chance such as dice and coin tossing were still unsolved puzzles. Intuition and experience were the only available guidelines, and no one knew how to calculate the precise odds or payoffs.

But gamblers are nothing if not crafty. They petitioned renowned men of learning to provide the answers to their ignorance. The first documented inquiries were about important, weighty topics such as, Which comes first when tossing three dice: a pair of sixes or any three-of-a-kind? Over time, several mathematicians took up these types of questions as a challenge among themselves. They used dice and coins to develop simple, but intriguing, mathematical propositions. These studies later formed the basis for the mathematics we now call probability and statistics.

Just as mathematicians learned a great deal from coin tosses, so can we. Coin tossing, it turns out, is the perfect example of a random result which has only two possibilities. It, therefore, can be thought of as the physical representation of what mathematicians call a binomial.

The word *binomial* means "two names" or "two terms." We often view the world through a binomial choice system: yes or no, black or white, on or off. Computers were created using such a choice system—the binary math of 0s and 1s. Although binomials can be very simple, the complexity can be increased to any level you desire.

In math, the typical usage of binomial is that of *two terms that cannot be combined* and are connected with a plus or a minus sign, for example, H + T (heads and tails). The two terms are often unknowns, such as $A + B$ or $X - Y$. Since $A + A$ can be combined into $2A$, it is not a binomial. Other typical binomials might be $3A + 4B$, $6X - 9Y$, or $2H + 3T$. The numbers in front can vary and are called *coefficients*. For example, $A + B$ implies coefficients of 1 and 1, whereas $4X - Y$ implies coefficients of 4 and -1.

Binomials have been found to play a critically important role in stock option modeling. The stock market has been likened to a random generator that spews out only two choices moment after moment: price upticks or price downticks. Clearly, a coin toss generates heads and tails randomly. We can use it then as a random generator of price upticks and downticks by merely substituting the H and T of the coin for the up (U) and down (D) of a price move.

Virtually all studies by mathematicians and economists for the past 100 years agree on one main point: to a very good approximation, price changes in markets act like randomly distributed variables. To learn about markets, then, it is necessary for us to become acquainted with probabilities, statistics, and distributions. There is no simpler or more clear-cut demonstration of the actions of a random variable than the common coin toss. It is by far our easiest introduction to the math of probabilities, statistics, and distributions.

Here is a hurdle we must overcome: there are no known models that perfectly match price movements. The best match found is that of the log-normal distribution which, through a simple transformation, can be turned into the normal distribution. One reason we study coin tosses is to become acquainted with the binomial distribution which looks, acts, and smells like the normal distribution if we toss enough coins. We then have a simple introduction to an otherwise complex concept, the normal distribution, which is essential to modeling stock prices and evaluating options. We won't be discussing any of these complex ideas for a while yet, so relax.

We will spend a good portion of our time trying to come to grips with what binomials and coin tosses can help us learn about the options market. When it all comes together, it will be quite impressive, for they can help us learn a lot.

ANALYSIS OF COIN TOSSES

Of course, every specialized area of study requires an understanding of key expressions to facilitate communication. You need to be familiar with some basic phrases by the time we finish, so let's begin their introduction now. We've linked phrases that are related with a slash (/).

Paths/outcomes

Relative frequency/probability

Histograms/frequency distributions

Relative frequency distributions/probability distributions

Payoffs/odds/returns

Mathematical expectation

Many of these phrases may look familiar because they have many common uses in our everyday world. But having come into common usage they have also developed different meanings over time, some of which are just plain wrong from our perspective. We need a vocabulary that helps us to analyze and discuss coin tosses, and then allows us to segue into the world of prices and markets.

Our purpose in listing these phrases now is so that you might see that they are important to our studies and thus perk up your attention whenever you run across them. Rote memorization is definitely not required. Rather than give you textbook meanings, which might be quite unmemorable, we'll repeat our meanings again and again.

Let's use a simple coin toss example to see if we can help you clearly visualize the first two concepts, paths and outcomes. The other phrases will be explained in detail as the next few chapters unfold.

Tossing a Coin Four Times

Our prime example, which we use over and over again, will be to toss a single coin four times in a row. Such results are *mathematically indistinguishable from tossing four coins at once*, so if we say "a coin tossed four times" or "the tossing of four coins," it means precisely the same thing. We are not trying to point out something special if the phrasing changes from time to time.

Since you are no doubt very familiar with the possible results of tossing a coin four times, it makes for a nice simple example that can be used to wondrous effect. It will facilitate our easy entrée into the somewhat arcane world of probability and statistics. Using simple examples will allow us to make the often hazy concepts seem perfectly transparent.

There are 16 different possible *paths* that result when we toss a coin four times, but only five different possible final *outcomes* in terms of head count. Figure 2–1 shows a diagram of the *paths* followed to get to these *outcomes*. All *paths* will be different and occur only once, as befits their probable likelihood. The diagram has come to be called a *binomial tree* by options analysts.

Notice that a coin tossed four times leads to *only* five possible different head count outcomes but to 16 different paths. Paths 2 and 3, for example, are certainly different ways to arrive at the final result, but both *outcomes* yield 3H (3 heads) and *so are equal*.

We are concerned with coin toss games because they mimic trading games with their random moves and because they have winning and losing payoff procedures. How much you can win or lose is crucial to option valuations. So, in terms of *outcomes* or *results* we only care about *"payable events,"* and this is evaluated by the *number of heads* (0H, 1H, 2H, 3H, 4H). For coin games, the payoff amounts are usually linked to the *excess* of heads over tails.

A toss of HHTT and a toss of THTH would each produce two heads and so are equal *outcomes* by our definition, despite having followed a different *path* to get there. They would both be "paid out" equally since the head counts are equal (2H). In this case the payout would be zero since 2H out of four tosses implies that we broke even between heads and tails; no excess heads at all. [*Note:* For a simple game of tossing one coin four times we have five distinct payable events: 0H, 1H, 2H, 3H, 4H. If we win

F I G U R E   2–1

Binomial Tree Diagram for Four Coin Tosses

Path Number	Path	Head-Count Outcome	Path Number	Path	Head-Count Outcome
1	H H H H	4H	9	T H H H	3H
2	H H H T	3H	10	T H H T	2H
3	H H T H	3H	11	T H T H	2H
4	H H T T	2H	12	T H T T	1H
5	H T H H	3H	13	T T H H	2H
6	H T H T	2H	14	T T H T	1H
7	H T T H	2H	15	T T T H	1H
8	H T T T	1H	16	T T T T	0H

$1 for each head and lose $1 for each tail, then zero heads (0H) means we are $+0 -4 = -\$4$; 1H means $+1 - 3 = -\$2$; 2H means $+2 - 2 = -\$0$; 3H means $+3 - 1 = + \$2$; 4H means $+4 -0 = +\$4$.] Of course, we could just as well have described HHTT and THTH as *two-tail results,* but for simplicity we will describe results by *head count* only, since the resulting tails are easily deduced. *Results* and *outcomes* are interchangeable phrases and refer, in our usage, to the final *head count.* We will use the term *outcome* more often, and we usually mean payable outcome. Any final head count of two heads (HHTT, HTHT, HTTH, etc.) is equal to any other for our present analysis.

Four Coin Toss Payoff (Betting $1 per Head)		
Payable Outcome	Net Heads over Tails	Profit or Loss
0H	−4	−$4
1H	−2	−$2
2H	0	0
3H	+2	+$2
4H	+4	+$4

We could use a little help from algebra here. Algebra was cleverly defined in a *New York Times* crossword puzzle as "the search for the unknown." That aptly gets to the core of what algebra really does. The number of coin tosses we wish to make will vary. It is unknown right now. If we call this unknown *number* of coin tosses N (for *number*), we find that the following simple rules consistently hold for *any* number of coin tosses:

$$\text{Number of coin tosses} = N$$

$$\text{Maximum number of heads} = N$$

$$\text{Possible different payable outcomes} = N + 1$$

$$\text{Possible paths to these outcomes} = 2^N$$

[*Note:* In math, 2^N is read as "two to the Nth power." N is the power or exponent. It is math shorthand for repeated multiplication, N times. That is, $2^2=2\times2$, $2^3=2\times2\times2$, $2^4=2\times2\times2\times2$, $2^N=2\times2\times2\times2\times2\times2\cdots\times2$ (with N 2s in a row). By the rules of exponents, $2^1=2$, $3^1=3$, $5^1=5$, etc. Strangely, any number to the zero power is 1: $2^0=1$, $3^0=1$, $4^0=1$, etc.]

In our example of tossing a coin four times, N would equal 4. Therefore, by these rules the maximum number of heads (N) is also 4, the possible different outcomes ($N + 1$) is 5, and the number of possible paths is 2^N which is $2^4 = 16$. So 16 paths will be distributed over only five possible outcomes. This means some outcomes will have many more than one possible path to them. Let's recap.

Tossing a Coin Four Times

Number of coin tosses (*N*)	= 4	
Maximum number of heads (*N*)	= 4	
Different payable outcomes (*N* + 1)	= 5	(0H, 1H, 2H, 3H, 4H)
Number of paths (2^N)	= 16	(HHHH, HHHT, . . . , TTTT)

We will now look at the binomial tree in Fig. 2–1. Refer to it as we describe it. You can see that the diagram could get very complicated and messy indeed if we were to toss the coin more than four times. This is one reason we didn't do a higher number of tosses. This binomial tree shows each path has four *decision points* called *nodes* which are the points at which the coin is tossed and a new decision reached. A tossed coin will follow one of the forks randomly. Within this tree we show all the possibilities. The route taken to reach an endpoint is called a *path*. We sort the end-point results into categories of head-count *outcomes*.

In our four-toss example there are five different head-count outcomes: 0H, 1H, 2H, 3H, 4H. Looking at the table in Fig. 2–1, you can see how many paths result in 4H, how many result in 3H, and so forth. Each of the 16 paths falls into one of the five categories 0H, 1H, 2H, 3H, 4H. The number of *occurrences* for each category is critically important in our study. We'll see this later on. It turns out that there is an interesting pattern in the *frequency of occurrence:* 1, 4, 6, 4, 1 for the 0H, 1H, 2H, 3H, 4H outcomes, in that exact order. This has a mirror-image symmetry that will help us later on.

A similar type of symmetry exists also for 5 tosses, 6 tosses, 10 tosses, and so forth, and allows us to fashion rules around it. So the 16 different paths can be broken down into a symmetrical distribution of outcomes using the 1, 4, 6, 4, 1 pattern. But the path followed by a coin toss or an investment is not usually important for payoff purposes, unless we specifically make it so (such as exotic path-dependent options). Usually, only the final outcome matters. For example, we normally don't care *how* IBM stock got to $119 a share today, only that it *is* $119 at today's option expiration.

Similarly, our payoff for the coin toss game is based on *final outcomes,* not on which path was followed. So when 3H is the final outcome, we will be paid $2.00 (3H and 1T equals a winning margin of 2H) regardless of which of the four possible paths may have been followed (HHHT, HHTH, HTHH, THHH). The only payable event is the *final outcome* in this game.

Now pay attention here: It does not matter which path was followed, but it is immensely important that there were four paths, since it is the way to *measure the probability of winning.* The *number of paths* to any final outcome is critical to our later analysis. And the symmetrical pattern of 1-4-6-4-1 will help pin it down easily. We'll show examples as we go along.

What Happens When We Toss Many Coins?

Let's create a general table of coin toss results. When you see N, just remember it means the number of tosses. It can vary and be any number of tosses that you would like. At the bottom of this table pretend N is 100, for example.

Coin Tosses	Maximum Head Count	Different Payable Outcomes	Possible Paths
1	1H	2	2
2	2H	3	4
3	3H	4	8
4	4H	5	16
5	5H	6	32
10	10H	11	1024
⋮	⋮	⋮	⋮
N	NH	$N + 1$	2^N

Let's discuss the table line by line until we clearly see the pattern.

One Coin Toss (N = 1)

If you toss one coin, you can have only two outcomes: 0H or 1H. There is a single path to each outcome and thus two paths total. The frequency of occurrence of 0H and 1H is 1, 1.

Two Coin Tosses (N = 2)

When we toss a coin twice, we have three outcomes: 0H, 1H, 2H. But there are four possible paths because the 1H outcome can arrive in two ways: HT and TH. That is, 1H has twice the frequency of either 0H or 2H, which occur only once each. The frequency of occurrence is, therefore, 1, 2, 1.

Three Coin Tosses (N = 3)

Tossing the coin three times gives four possible outcomes: 0H, 1H, 2H, 3H. There are eight possible paths. The frequency of occurrence of outcomes is 1, 3, 3, 1.

A pattern begins to emerge. Let's create a new table to visualize it.

Possible Head-Count Outcomes

Tosses	Zero Heads	One Head	Two Heads	Three Heads	Four Heads	Five Heads
$N = 1$	1	1				
$N = 2$	1	2	1			
$N = 3$	1	3	3	1		
$N = 4$	1	4	6	4	1	
$N = 5$	1	5	10	10	5	1

The frequency of occurrence for each possible outcome is shown in the preceding table. (If an outcome is not listed, then it is not possible.) If you were to sum across each line, you could tell the total number of possible paths. This table is a mini-version of Pascal's triangle, which is an integral part of the binomial expansion theory. We discuss this in Chap. 3.

Here are the possible paths for tossing a coin four times ($N = 4$), if you'd like a further example. We expect $2^4 = 16$ possible paths.

HHHH	THHH	THHT	THTT	zero heads = 1
HHHT	HHTT	THTH	TTHT	one head = 4
HHTH	HTHT	TTHH	TTTH	two heads = 6
HTHH	HTTH	HTTT	TTTT	three heads = 4
				four heads = 1

There are five outcomes: 0H, 1H, 2H, 3H, 4H with a frequency of occurrence pattern of 1, 4, 6, 4, 1. This covers all 16 paths.

These patterns hold up for all N no matter how large N gets, and it would be pointless and very, very tedious to write them all down. Suffice it to say that if you toss a coin N times, you will expect to get $N + 1$ different outcomes and there will be a total of 2^N different paths to these outcomes. That implies that some final outcomes will have multiple paths to them. We call the number of paths to each outcome the *frequency* or the *frequency of occurrence* of this outcome. Pascal's triangle describes these frequencies perfectly and is an important tool to help us with the binomial theorem, both of which we investigate next.

KEY CONCEPTS REVIEW

- Tossing a coin is the perfect example of a random result with only two possible outcomes.
- Binomial means "two names" or "two terms" as in the heads and tails of a coin toss.
- Coin toss math (binomial math) grants us a simple, but helpful, entrée into statistics.
- Binomials play a critically important role in stock option modeling.
- Coin tosses can help us learn the binomial distribution, which is a sister to the all-important normal distribution. Option models require knowledge of these two distributions.
- Coin tosses easily allow us to learn about head-count outcomes and frequency of occurrence.
- Knowing the frequency of occurrence of all possible outcomes gives you their probabilities.

 • There are two keys to option evaluation: probabilities and payoffs.

THINGS TO THINK ABOUT

Law of Large Numbers   When you toss a coin a large number of times, you will get almost 50 percent heads and 50 percent tails. This is known in statistics as the *law of large numbers*. It's frequently called the "law of averages" by nonstatisticians and used improperly. Many people believe it can help predict a trend that's ready to reverse, as when a coin comes up heads, say, 8 times in a row. They believe a great many tails are due in the near future to balance things out. At roulette they might keep betting black after a wheel has spun red seven times in a row, also believing black is now due.

The reason this does not work is that the events themselves, a coin toss or a roulette spin, are totally independent of all previous tosses or spins. The law of large numbers says simply that after a huge number of coin tosses, say a million, the percentage of heads will tend closer and closer to 50 percent. But if it turns out to be 49.9 percent that, too, would be okay. The law does not predict exactly 50 percent but suggests a range near to 50 percent. A range of 0.1 percent either way would not be out of the question. But 0.1 percent of a million tosses would suggest 1000 heads more or less than most people would expect. If any given series of tosses gets 5 or 10 or even 20 heads out of kilter, then many people would bet the ranch. But the odds do not favor them even a tiny bit more than before the run started.

Mathematical Expectations   The mathematically expected outcome of a series of coin tosses is 50 percent heads as previously described. But expecting some percent outcome based on the mathematics of a situation is a far cry from attaining that percentage over any short run of events. The mathematical expectation is merely an average, a long-run average. It is nothing at all to see such long-run expectations blown out the window in the short run. The casino that has an edge in all its games can still have losing days. Likewise, traders, even those with an expected advantage, can still lose in the short run and must protect themselves against negative excursions or runs of adverse luck. Protecting one's capital is a critical component of trading skill.

QUESTIONS

1. What is a *binomial?*
2. How can coin tosses be linked to binomials?
3. If we toss a coin one time, how many different headcount outcomes are possible? What are they?
4. Answer the same question for tossing a coin two, three, and four times.
5. What is a *binomial tree?*
6. Figure 2–1 depicts a binomial tree diagram for a coin tossed four times. Use this diagram and the table that accompanies it to answer the following questions: How many 3H outcomes were there? How many 2H outcomes?
7. How do we mathematically express the number of possible paths and number of possible outcomes for a coin tossed N times? If we let N equal 3, what are the number of paths and outcomes?
8. Is there a difference if we say "a coin tossed three times" or "three coins tossed once"?
9. Compute $N + 1$ and 2^N when we let $N = 1, 2, 3, 4,$ and 5.
10. Are the number of possible paths typically more or less than the number of possible outcomes? Why?
11. What is meant by *possible outcomes* and *possible paths?*
12. If it doesn't matter which path was followed to get to the head-count outcome, why are we so interested in tracking and counting the number of paths?
13. Tossing a coin three times yields how many different possible paths? List each path.
14. If tossing a coin 9 times yields 512 different possible paths, how many different possible paths are expected when we toss a coin 10 times?

15. For tossing N coins the number of different payable head-count outcomes is $N + 1$ and the number of different possible paths is 2^{N}. If we toss five coins, calculate these two values. Do the same for 10 coins.

16. When we toss a coin four times, how many different paths lead to an outcome of exactly 3H? List all the paths. Is this more or less likely than an outcome of exactly 1H? (*Hint:* Use the binomial tree diagram in Fig. 2–1 to compare 1H paths versus 3H paths.)

CHAPTER 3

Pascal's Triangle and the Binomial Theorem

CHAPTER OVERVIEW

Chapter 2 opened our discussion of binomials and coin tosses. In this chapter we learn to use one of the most powerful tools of the trade, the binomial theorem. The binomial theorem shows us how to easily *expand* (or *multiply*) the same binomial two times or many times. Later, when the need arises to multiply a binomial 10 or even 100 times, you will be very pleased that the theorem allows easy multiplication (called binomial expansion).

But why would we want to multiply binomials at all? It turns out that all the outcomes of tossing a coin *N* times magically reveal themselves when you multiply the binomial H + T times itself *N* times. We can use the resulting expansion to deduce the patterns for one coin toss, or two, *or 2 million.*

We could quickly find, for example, that if we tossed a coin four times there are five possible outcomes (0H, 1H, 2H, 3H, 4H) and 16 possible paths followed to get to those outcomes ($2 \times 2 \times 2 \times 2 = 16$). Also, the occurrence frequency follows the 1, 4, 6, 4, 1 pattern. We can show how to link the paths, outcomes, and frequencies of occurrence to odds, payoffs, and probabilities. Options are derived from these basic concepts.

Pascal's triangle cuts out a lot of the hard work. For example, if we wanted to toss the coin 10 times, it would result in 11 outcomes with exactly 1024 paths. The pattern of occurrences of number of heads (0 to 11) would be 1, 10, 45, 120, 210, 252, 210, 120, 45, 10, 1. Notice the left-hand and right-hand symmetry? That is the eleventh tier (line) of Pascal's triangle. Pascal's triangle was developed specifically to show the recurring pattern of binomial symmetry. It gives the answer for *any* number of coin tosses and helps us juggle huge numbers. Let's review it in detail.

PASCAL'S TRIANGLE AND ITS USES

The brilliant French mathematician Blaise Pascal (1623–1662) was a guiding light in early probability work. He showed how a simple triangle of numbers could form a pattern that would predict accurately the *number of paths* to each outcome. (His method is critically intertwined with the binomial theorem as we'll soon see.) Here is a 10-tier Pascal triangle, but it could go on for *N* tiers as *N* grows to 100, or 1000, or more.

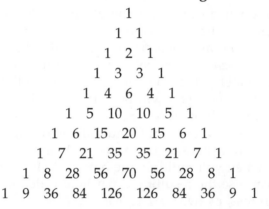

The 10-Tier Pascal Triangle

```
                    1
                  1   1
                1   2   1
              1   3   3   1
            1   4   6   4   1
          1   5  10  10   5   1
        1   6  15  20  15   6   1
      1   7  21  35  35  21   7   1
    1   8  28  56  70  56  28   8   1
  1   9  36  84 126 126  84  36   9   1
```

If you play with the triangle a bit, you will quickly notice its simplicity and symmetry. It took only 2 minutes to create from memory because we knew its "code." Like the DNA of a living organism, this triangle has a genetic code that easily allows creation of its next tier. Without a computer we could easily create a 20-tier or more triangle. It's all simple addition. Let's review the first six tiers. You might recognize that they are identical to the table in Chap. 2 titled Possible Head-Count Outcomes.

To create the first two tiers you merely place a 1 on top and then two 1s on the second line. (All leftmost and rightmost members of the table are 1s.) So far it looks like this:

$$1$$
$$1 \quad 1$$

A simple start. For the next tier we must insert a value below (but between) each pair on line 2. The value is always the *sum* of the two above. Let's see how this looks:

$$1$$
$$1 \quad 1$$
$$2$$

Since there is no other pair remaining on line 2, we now finalize the third line by inserting 1s (since they are always the leftmost and rightmost members).

$$1$$
$$1 \quad 1$$
$$1 \quad 2 \quad 1$$

The fourth tier is merely 1, 1 + 2, 2 + 1, 1 which is obviously 1 3 3 1:

$$1$$
$$1 \quad 1$$
$$1 \quad 2 \quad 1$$
$$1 \quad 3 \quad 3 \quad 1$$

The fifth tier is 1, 1 + 3, 3 + 3, 3 + 1, 1 = 1 4 6 4 1. (Remember this from the four coin toss?)

The sixth tier is 1, 1 + 4, 4 + 6, 6 + 4, 4 + 1, 1 = 1 5 10 10 5 1. Let's look at this final six-tier Pascal's triangle:

$$1$$
$$1 \quad 1$$
$$1 \quad 2 \quad 1$$
$$1 \quad 3 \quad 3 \quad 1$$
$$1 \quad 4 \quad 6 \quad 4 \quad 1$$
$$1 \quad 5 \quad 10 \quad 10 \quad 5 \quad 1$$

This is precisely the same as the Possible Head-Count Outcomes table in Chap. 2. The sixth tier could be found by methodically listing each of the 32 possible paths—HHHHH, HHHHT, HHHTH, and so forth—and sorting out all 32 paths into the six outcomes giving us a frequency count for each. The sorting gets horrendous as we toss more and more coins. *Pascal has given us a quick way to sort this out with no difficulty at all.*

Notice the sum of the numbers on each tier. The total across for each tier of the six-tier triangle as we move downward would be, respectively, 1, 2, 4, 8, 16, 32. The total paths are merely 2^N with N being the number of coin tosses: $1 = 2^0$, $2 = 2^1$, $4 = 2^2$, $8 = 2^3$, $16 = 2^4$, $32 = 2^5$. So it turns out that Pascal's triangle can give us a quick and accurate representation of the results for N coin tosses, no matter how big N gets.

We will move on to the binomial theorem now and show how it simplifies our life by automatically sorting out the different outcomes (head counts)—and it uses Pascal's triangle to tell us how often each different outcome occurs. That is, Pascal's triangle can give us everything we need for probability analysis: the total number of paths and how they are distributed across each of the possible outcomes.

The binomial theorem helps group all the outcomes making it much simpler for us to handle. The five coin toss example has 32 paths, but only six different outcomes. The binomial theorem will show us all the six outcomes and incorporate Pascal's triangle to show us that the six outcomes have occurrences of 1, 5, 10, 10, 5, 1. It does this precisely and with no fuss; no messy list of 32 which we must sort out ourselves.

Consider that a 10 coin toss has 1024 possible paths, but only 11 different outcomes. The binomial theorem will show each of the 11 outcomes in order and let us know that their Pascal pattern of occurrence is 1, 10, 45, 120, 210, 252, 210, 120, 45, 10, 1. Can you imagine the mess of having to disentangle 1024 different paths?

HOW TO USE THE BINOMIAL THEOREM

We will start by using the standard algebraic binomial $A + B$. You probably remember from high school algebra that we can use the small, raised (superscripted) numbers called *powers* or *exponents* to signify multiplication. Or as they used to say, "times-ing something by itself." For example, $A^2 = A \times A$ as well as $A^3 = A \times A \times A$ and also $(A + B)^2 = (A + B) \times (A + B)$, and so on. When the raised symbol is a 1 as in $(A + B)^1$, it implies you shouldn't really multiply at all, so $(A + B)^1 = A + B$. The use of zero as an exponent, as in $(A + B)^0$, is very strange. Any value to the zero power is defined as being worth 1, no matter how large or small it was before being raised to the zero power. That is, $(A + B)^0 = 1$, $A^0 = 1$, $B^0 = 1$, $(9C + 88Q - 124Z)^0 = 1$.

Let's see how to actually multiply $(A + B) \times (A + B)$. We can put it into our old high school algebra format for multiplying polynomials longhand.

$$
\begin{array}{r}
A + B \\
\times\ A + B \\
\hline
AB + B^2
\end{array}
$$
Result of B times top line

$$
\underline{A^2 +\ \ AB\ \ \ \ \ }
$$
Result of A times top line

Summed result: $A^2 + 2AB + B^2$ Notice the 1, 2, 1 pattern of coefficients. (1 is implied if there is no number.)

Multiplying by a third $(A + B)$ results in

$$
\begin{array}{r}
A^2 +\ 2AB + B^2 \\
\times\ \ \ \ \ \ \ \ \ A + B \\
\hline
A^2B + 2AB^2 + B^3
\end{array}
$$
Result of B times top line

$$
\underline{A^3 + 2A^2B +\ \ AB^2\ \ \ \ \ \ }
$$
Result of A times top line

Summed result: $A^3 + 3A^2B + 3AB^2 + B^3$ Notice   the   1,   3,   3,   1 pattern.

Similarly, multiplying by a fourth $(A + B)$ we would arrive at $A^4 + 4A^3B + 6A^2B^2 + 4AB^3 + B^4$. (Notice the 1, 4, 6, 4, 1 pattern.)

This gets increasingly long, messy, and tedious. Also, lots of mistakes are possible in toting up longer and longer numbers. Luckily we can discern a pattern here that harkens back to Pascal's triangle and also note a further increasing/decreasing pattern in the powers or exponents of the A's and B's. These are the pattern rules of the binomial theorem! The values that have been multiplied out are called *expanded* and thus it is called the *binomial expansion*. [$A^2 + 2AB + B^2$ is the expanded version of $(A + B)^2$.]

Let's look at these for a moment. Expanding (multiplying out) these binomials as required by raising $(A + B)$ to the exponent N gives us $(A + B)^N$. This gives us

$(A + B)^0 = 1$

$(A + B)^1 = A + B$

$(A + B)^2 = (A + B) \times (A + B) = A^2 + 2AB + B^2$

$(A + B)^3 = (A + B) \times (A + B) \times (A + B)$

$\qquad = A^3 + 3A^2B + 3AB^2 + B^3$

and so on.

Now let's do something that will cross back over to our study on coins. Exchange (H + T) for (A + B).

	Coefficient Pattern
$(H + T)^1 = H + T$	$1 + 1$
$(H + T)^2 = H^2 + 2HT + T^2$	$1 + 2 + 1$
$(H + T)^3 = H^3 + 3H^2T + 3HT^2 + T^3$	$1 + 3 + 3 + 1$
$(H + T)^4 = H^4 + 4H^3T + 6H^2T^2$ $+ 4HT^3 + T^4$	$1 + 4 + 6 + 4 + 1$
$(H + T)^5 = H^5 + 5H^4T + 10H^3T^2$ $+ 10H^2T^3 + 5HT^4 + T^5$	$1 + 5 + 10 + 10 + 5 + 1$

Although the exponents add a strange look to our coin toss analyses, they can easily be converted as follows: H^3 = HHH (means three heads), H^2 = HH (means two heads), and so forth. This method nicely keeps all similar outcomes together. For example, we know that both HHT and HTH are 2H outcomes. They are both automatically channeled into the H^2T category. And the frequency of each outcome is merely the coefficient in front (H^3 has no coefficient and implies a frequency of 1, whereas $6H^2T^2$ implies a frequency of 6).

There are several interesting things about this expansion process:

1. Note that the coefficient values in front of the H's and T's are from the tiers of Pascal's triangle:

   1 1   1 2 1   1 3 3 1   1 4 6 4 1   1 5 10 10 5 1

2. The raised powers (exponents) of H and T form patterns also. Say we toss a coin five times. The first term would be H^5T^0 (maximum H, minimum T) and each term after that would show that its exponents lose 1 if high or add 1 if low, until their order was reversed to H^0T^5 (minimum H, maximum T). Don't forget H^5T^0 is the same as H^5 since $T^0 = 1$ and H^0T^5 is the same as T^5 because $H^0 = 1$. We can use these superscripted exponents as our old head-count values. If you recall, we always counted only heads to keep things simple. The tails (T) were ignored. Here are examples of the simple translations: H^5 = five heads which is just like our old coin toss outcome of 5H; H^4T^1 = four heads, the same as our old 4H; H^3T^2 = three heads just like our old 3H; H^2T^3 = two heads or 2H; HT^4 = just one head or 1H; and T^5 = no heads or 0H.

    3. Each binomial expansion contains exactly $N + 1$ terms in it, a perfect match for the possible number of outcomes: never more, never less. Tossing five coins ($N = 5$) we expect and get six terms ($(H + T)^5 = H^5 + 5H^4T + 10H^3T^2 + 10H^2T^3 + 5HT^4 + T^5$) which perfectly identifies the six outcomes: 5H, 4H, 3H, 2H, 1H, 0H and gives their frequency of occurrence.

    No matter how many tosses of a coin we make, the theory will quickly give us a concise analysis. If we jump to 10 tosses of a coin ($N = 10$), you will quickly see the effectiveness of the binomial expansion and Pascal's triangle. For 10 tosses we expect 11 different outcomes, but 2^{10} possible paths (1024). We would be hard pressed to do all this work in several hours, but look at the quick results using a binomial expansion (in a vertical format):

Binomial Expansion	Coefficient (Paths or Frequency)	Coin Toss Outcome (Head Count)
$(H + T)^{10} = H^{10}$	1	10
$+10H^9T$	10	9
$+45H^8T^2$	45	8
$+120H^7T^3$	120	7
$+210H^6T^4$	210	6
$+252H^5T^5$	252	5
$+210H^4T^6$	210	4
$+120H^3T^7$	120	3
$+45H^2T^8$	45	2
$+10HT^9$	10	1
$+T^{10}$	1	0
	1024 total paths	

We used the binomial theorem to solve the question, What is $(H + T)^{10}$? The answer is the resulting 11 terms vertically displayed in the previous table.

Now let's imagine for a moment that we would like to toss a coin 100 times. This leads to an unbelievable 2^{100} possible paths. That might not *seem* unbelievable until you realize that $2^{100} = 1.26765 \times 10^{30}$! This is 1 million $\times$ 1 million $\times$ 1 million $\times$ 1 million $\times$ 1 million x 1.26765. A billion is only 1000 million. This is much more than Carl Sagan's "billions and billions" of stars. Starting to get the idea?

You couldn't finish listing and recombining all similar terms—for only 100 coin tosses—*within your lifetime*. The binomial expansion would get you an answer longhand in under a half hour. A computer using the expansion would be finished in a fraction of a second!

The option formulas we wish to learn about must analyze moment-to-moment price changes *for months*. They assume each price change is random, like a coin toss. If they assume one price change a second, there would be 3600 changes per hour or over 20,000 a day! So, it's like tossing 20,000 coins. The possible outcomes and paths become absolutely mind-numbing.

Developing and understanding formulas that can help simplify this is essential. We come to realize that the aggravation of learning the mathematics and formulas actually makes the impossible possible. It makes the work easier, and frequent familiarity can make the complex seem simple.

We will examine how to turn our coin tosses into a frequency and probability distribution in Chap. 4.

KEY CONCEPTS REVIEW

+ It seems coin tosses and binomials were born a perfect match for each other. And by a stroke of great fortune the mathematicians come to our rescue in the form of the binomial theorem.

+ The drudgery of analyzing a coin tossed 10 times leads to 1024 different paths with 11 outcomes which can take hours to sort through. But the binomial theorem can give us all the outcomes and count the paths within mere seconds. Knowing all the possible outcomes and the number of paths to each gives us their probabilities. Probability is the key to option analysis. We explain this in Chap. 4.

♦ Raising the binomial H + T to the power N gives us our answers. N is the number of tosses we make with our coin. For example, a coin tossed three times is represented as $(H + T)^3$. A coin tossed 10 times as $(H + T)^{10}$.

♦ The power tells us how many times the term inside the parentheses should be multiplied. For example, $(H + T)^3$ is the same as $(H + T) \times (H + T) \times (H + T)$. Mathematicians call this *expanding* the binomial. And the binomial theorem was born to do it, with no fuss and no bother.

♦ By expanding (multiplying out) the binomial $(H + T)^2$, we get $H^2 + 2HT + T^2$. We can interpret the powers to tell us the number of heads and tails for each outcome. H^2 translates as one path having the outcome HH (meaning two heads), 2HT means two paths have the outcome of one head and one tail, T^2 translates as one path having the outcome TT (meaning two tails and therefore zero heads). So, this easy binomial expansion clearly shows all four paths for a coin tossed twice.

♦ The number of paths are the coefficients (the leading numbers, e.g., the 2 in 2HT) and are easily known beforehand from Pascal's triangle. This repetitive pattern was discovered by the famous mathematician Blaise Pascal and gives us a wonderfully simple method to analyze coin tosses or other binomials.

THINGS TO THINK ABOUT

Computational Time and Error   We can all quickly figure out the outcomes and paths for a coin tossed two or three times. But beyond that things start to get a bit messy. A coin tossed five times has six outcomes and 32 paths. Can you list and enumerate them within 5 minutes without any errors or double counting? Probably you can.

Now think about this: a coin tossed 20 times has 21 outcomes and 1,048,576 paths. Do you think you can list and enumerate these within 48 hours and without error? It would probably take all the paper you've ever seen in your lifetime just to list them! The binomial theorem and Pascal's triangle can give us the answer in a few minutes, without a computer and without errors. Enumerating the possible outcomes and paths on a coin tossed 100 times would take *billions* of times as long! That's what we'd have to do without the binomial theorem and Pascal's triangle.

Basis for Option Models   The very binomial analyses we reviewed in this chapter, despite being very simple and straightforward, laid the groundwork for some of the most important option modeling attempts. The economist-professor William Sharpe developed an analysis of options based on binomials. Later it was expanded by John C. Cox, Stephen A. Ross, and Mark Rubinstein and quickly became the second most popular option formula after Black-Scholes. Their book *Option Markets* is a classic and should be read by all serious option traders. The ideas and math we have just covered and will continue to cover in the next few chapters will set you up nicely to understand the inner workings of their formula and analysis. Our studies in these opening chapters are preparing us to first learn about the simpler binomial distribution, which is the heart of the Cox-Ross-Rubinstein option model, and then, by extending the ideas a bit, to learn about the normal distribution, which is the heart of the Black-Scholes formula. It will be easier than you think.

QUESTIONS

1. What is Pascal's triangle?
2. What does *binomial expansion* mean?
3. How does the binomial theorem help us?
4. What is a coefficient? What is an exponent?
5. What are the coefficients for the following algebraic terms: A, $-H$, $3X$, $-2Y$, $256Z$?
6. What are the exponents (powers) for H^2, X, $(A + 1)^2$, $(H + T)^4$?

7. How do coefficients and exponents help us in our coin toss analyses?

8. The expanded binomial representation of $(H + T)^3$, which means H + T to the third power, multiplies out to be equal to $H^3 + 3H^2T + 3HT^2 + T^3$. Translate what this means in terms of paths and outcomes for a coin tossed three times?

9. The eleventh row (or tier) of Pascal's triangle is: 1 10 45 120 210 252 210 120 45 10 1. This row represents the coefficients for a 10 coin toss (the row's number is always one higher than the coin toss number). Since the coefficients tell us the number of paths to each of the 11 possible head-count outcomes, what are the total number of possible paths and can you associate these 11 coefficients with their 11 head-count outcomes?

10. In Chap. 4 we will begin discussing frequency of occurrence and show how it helps us analyze the probability of an event. We already discussed frequency a bit when we showed the number of paths to each outcome via Pascal's triangle. Based on the eleventh row of Pascal's triangle (see question 9) which event do you expect to happen more frequently: 10 heads or 9 heads? 7 heads or 5 heads? 6 heads or 4 heads? Write down the frequency of each event.

CHAPTER 4

Distributions Are the Key— What Are Distributions?

At their very core, option formulas depend on probabilities. These can be deduced if we count the appropriate *frequencies of occurrence*. And we can display a *distribution* of these frequencies in graph or table form. Understanding distributions is the key to options.

Distributions sound like arcane statistical secrets, but, in fact, we constantly run into them in everyday life. In math, a distribution is a "table of many answers." It has not one value or one answer, but many. That is, it is a whole array of potential answers, a spectrum, a spread, a rainbow of choices and possibilities.

The question, What is your favorite color?, if asked of many people, will generate not one answer, but a whole range of answers. And if we place numerical values on those answers, we would turn the answers from words like red, blue, green, into a spread of numbers that we could call a distribution. So a mathematical distribution is a matrix of numbers; in computer terms, an array.

This is a complicated concept. Let's put you at ease with a silly distribution first: the "peanut butter and jelly distribution." Imagine a kindly mom making two peanut butter and jelly (PB&J) sandwiches, one for each child. Two seconds later the screams and whines break out: "You got more jelly than me!" "You got more peanut butter than me!" Upon examining the sandwiches it is sadly clear that this is true. One sandwich has much too much peanut butter and the other has too much jelly—the peanut butter and jelly weren't distributed equally. Obviously this is grist for "repressed memory psychologists" in 10 years time and must be addressed now. The "spread" of PB&J was not smoothly allocated and so we have a "lumpy" *distribution*—too much in one place, not enough in another. In every case of making PB&J sandwiches, whether lumpy or marvelously smooth with just the right amounts in just the right places, a *distribution* will exist—it's just a question of what *type of distribution*. So a *distribution* is a spread of sorts, a peanut butter spread in this example. Not one lump, but a smooth continuous flow. This concept of smooth, continuous flow is very important.

Let's talk about another distribution that is nearer and dearer to the world of adults: the distribution of wealth. Who has it? How much? And where? Is it constant or changing? These are the questions we ask of distributions all the time. We know that wealth is not in only one place but *spread out* or *distributed* over many areas. And the spread (distribution) is not equal, for it is heavily concentrated in some areas and lightly concentrated in others. This is precisely the same meaning we wish to attach to frequency distribution and probability distribution.

Let's see how it relates to coin tosses. A *frequency distribution* can be developed by counting the number of occurrences for each outcome. Since tossing a coin four times can result in 16 possible paths, we could say it has 16 possible occurrences. We know that the 16 occurrences are distributed over the head-count outcomes as in the following occurrence, or frequency, distribution table.

Head Count	Occurrences (Frequency)
0	1
1	4
2	6
3	4
4	1
	Total = 16

The *frequency distribution* shows how the *occurrences* are *spread* out. The frequencies are usually listed in a table or drawn on a graph.

That's all we need to start deducing probabilities. The probability of something happening is defined as number of favorable occurrences/number of all possible occurrences. This ratio creates a fraction (or decimal, or percentage); it is always between 0 and 1, inclusive. Absolute certainty would be 1.00 (meaning 100 percent probability). And absolute impossibility would be 0.00 (meaning 0 percent probability). Therefore, the range is always 0.00 to 1.00. In our example of a coin tossed four times the head-count outcomes are the events we look for and can also be shown to be probabilities if we divide through by the number of all possible events (16 paths). Let's re-create the table and add probabilities:

Head Count	Occurrences (Frequency)	Probability (Relative Frequency)
0	1	1/16
1	4	4/16
2	6	6/16
3	4	4/16
4	1	1/16
	Total = 16	16/16

The last column in the table is the *probability distribution,* which can also be called the relative frequency distribution or relative occurrence distribution. Notice we find only one case each of 4H and 0H. Much more frequent were the cases of exactly 3H or 1H: four times each. And the most frequent situation was 2H: it occurred six times. We can easily show this whole example with a bar graph. In Fig. 4–1 we first graph the occurrences column of the previous table, which, of course, is also a listing of the frequencies (such a listing is usually called the frequency distribution). In Fig. 4–2 we show the relative frequency distribution (*also known as the probability distribution*), and you can see that the two graphs are essentially the same, adjusted by some simple math and a clever shifting of titles and labels.

Using this very simple example we can finally visualize the frequency distribution for a coin tossed four times that we have discussed in Chaps. 2 and 3. The bar graph in Fig. 4–1 shows *frequency* of occurrence, and the graph itself is a frequency distri-

F I G U R E   4–1

Frequency Distribution

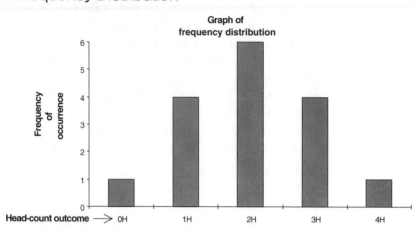

F I G U R E   4–2

Probability Distribution

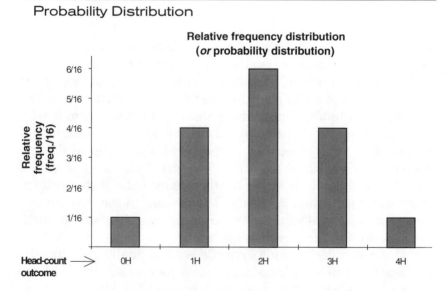

bution. *Relative frequency*, which is another name for *probability*, can be very easily computed from this data and is shown in Fig. 4–2.

Frequency is how many times an event occurs.

Frequency distribution is a listing in a table or on a graph of all the frequencies of occurrence of events.

Relative frequency is a comparison to determine how often a certain event occurs as a fraction of the total. Relative frequency thus measures probability of occurrence for that event.

Probability is the percentage (or fraction) of times an event occurs as compared to the total of all possible similar events. It is just another name for relative frequency.

$$\text{Probability} = \frac{\text{number of favorable events occurring}}{\text{number of all possible events that can occur}}$$

For example, the number of occurrences of exactly four heads (HHHH) was 1 and there were 16 possible results. Thus the frequency of that event was 1, the relative frequency was 1 out of 16 = 1/16, and the probability was the same: 1/16 (which equals .0625 or 6.25 percent).

We can turn our bar graph in Fig. 4–1 from a frequency distribution to a relative frequency distribution (*or probability distribution*) very easily. We merely divide the frequency of each event by the total possible, which is 16. This is seen in Fig. 4–2. The chart is the same. We merely adjusted the vertical scale (*y* axis) by dividing through by 16. Notice now, however, that the vertical values on the bars no longer add up to 16 but to a critically important number in probability theory—1 (1/16 + 4/16 + 6/16 + 4/16 + 1/16 = 1). Probabilities always run only from 0 to 1. Zero means no possibility at all, while 1 implies certainty. Since our total for the graph adds to 1, it shows that we are including *all possible results* which thereby implies a *certainty* that one of them must be the outcome. You can, therefore, focus all your attention on the graph since nothing should be hiding or missing from our analysis.

If our total came to .9 or 1.2 or anything but 1.0, you might surmise that something is missing or askew—in the absence of a perfect 1.0 total we would have uncertainty. Probabilities become the master key to unlocking the secrets of options.

SIX DIFFERENT COIN TOSS HISTOGRAMS

Let's see if some graphic representations can help us further develop the concepts of frequency, probability, and distributions. Figure 4–3 depicts six graphs of coin toss probability distributions: 1, 2, 3, 4, 5, and 10 tosses of a coin. We have graphed the probability of each different outcome in number of heads. The fancy name for this type of statistical graph is *histogram*. Each bar (or rectangle) in a graph represents one type of outcome for coin tossing. We put the six different graphs side by side to demonstrate a few critically important facts.

We graphed probabilities rather than frequencies since this is what we need to plug into options formulas. Also, we used decimals to familiarize you with the more typical graphs you will see in other books. Let's review two examples from the histogram (bar graph).

Example 1: When $N = 1$ (one coin toss), there are only two possible outcomes and paths. We could have valued the bars 1 and 1 instead of .50 and .50. They have a frequency of 1 and 1, but we wanted to show their relative frequency. If this were a pie cut into two slices, then each slice (path) would be $1/2 = .50$. The probability is merely a *relative* frequency, relative to the whole.

Example 2: When $N = 4$ (four coin tosses), there are five outcomes, but 16 paths (2^4). Therefore, each path is $1/16$ of the whole pie or .0625. Since the frequency breakdown is

One path of zero heads
Four paths of one head
Six paths of two heads
Four paths of three heads
One path of four heads

for a total of 16 cases or paths, each path gets $1/16$ relative frequency valuation (same as .0625). So we can restate the four-toss result as

	Frequency	Relative Frequency
1 path of OH	× .0625 =	.0625
4 paths of 1H	× .0625 =	.2500
6 paths of 2H	× .0625 =	.3750
4 paths of 3H	× .0625 =	.2500
1 path of 4H	× .0625 =	.0625
16 paths	× .0625 =	1.0000 total

FIGURE   4-3

Coin Toss Probability Distributions

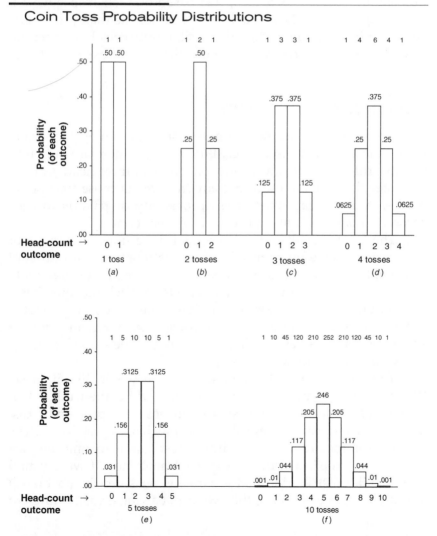

We see that the probability of getting exactly two heads from a coin tossed four times is 6 out of 16 which is .3750 (you could look it up). We now know how to assess the probability of each outcome.

Each of the six histograms (bar charts) in Fig. 4–3 is a distribution. Each separate distribution tells a story about the coin tossing event it represents. If the event is tossing a coin three times, Fig. 4–3c tells the following story: The number of different outcomes is 4 (zero, one, two, or three heads) and the probability of each depends on the frequency of occurrence. We calculated the probabilities at .125, .375, .375, .125 based on their respective relative frequencies of 1/8, 3/8, 3/8, 1/8. Since the total probability adds to 1.000, we know that all possible outcomes have been included. There is no room for events other than those described.

TELLING THE FUTURE

There is no single outcome that must happen when we toss a coin three times. It is kept to chance. But we know there are only four possible different outcomes (zero, one, two, or three heads). So we can foretell the actual outcome only in terms of those four possibilities. And we can only assess probability or payoffs to each based on mathematical expectations, never certainty.

The future result of tossing a coin three times is a range or spread of possible outcomes. We call this range a distribution of probabilities (or a matrix of probabilities). Graphed or made into a table it becomes a probability distribution. Each outcome has a chance, but some are more equal than others (i.e., more likely). Whenever you run into the term *distribution,* you can think "a spread of many values." A distribution is not one value but many, many values spread across a spectrum.

The world is not the simple place we would like it to be. While we view many events as black and white, the truth is that all sorts of shades of gray exist. The purpose of a probability distribution is to measure these shades as much as is practicable. The whole basis for predicting the future rests on analyzing the past to find the "true" measure of expected outcomes. If we can find a probability distribution that accurately measures the past (such as our coin toss examples), then we can, barring a vastly different environment, expect the same distribution to work in the future. We can, in this manner, describe probable outcomes with a mathematical expectation. *This is the basis for all option models.*

Economists have developed the efficient markets hypothesis. This basically says that despite zillions of hours of research by those who would predict the future, the future course of prices is unpredictably random. And this means that a coin toss model works very well in describing all past and future prices. The six histograms in Fig. 4–3 that we reviewed are the beginning of your entrée into the world of probability and distributions. But more than that, they are the life and breath of the theory behind options.

We can use what we've learned here as a very good start in understanding the more complex distributions. The very core of the option models springs straight from these probability distributions, and, therefore, being conversant in distributions is key to understanding option theory. When you clearly understand distributions, three-quarters of the difficult work is done. We expect you're still a bit hesitant, so let's see if we can't wrap up distributions with a few views from the lighter side.

A GAGGLE OF GEESE, A POD OF WHALES, . . . A FAMILY TREE OF DISTRIBUTIONS?

Mathematicians and statisticians are a busy, creative lot. Over the years they've discovered perhaps three dozen families of mathematical distributions that are very helpful in solving some very complex problems. But that's still about three dozen more than most of us want to deal with!

Luckily for us we only need to understand two families of distributions to get our hands around options: the binomial distribution and the normal distribution. By the time we're done we'll have discussed a few variations, but for the most part these two will suit us just fine. And, as a nice bonus, in many cases the binomial and normal distributions are so closely related that they are almost twins of each other, which makes learning to use them that much easier.

We've been describing coin toss distributions at length in this chapter and will continue to do so again and again throughout the book. It makes our studies easier. What you should realize, however, is that these coin toss distributions are not a separate family of distributions at all, but are part of the binomial distribution family. They are merely the simplest variation of the binomial distribution. The two events in coin toss distributions (heads and tails) each have the very same likelihood, 50 percent. This makes both the left and right sides of the graph nicely symmetrical. This is certainly not true of many other binomial distributions. Be thankful for small mercies.

And hopefully by now you've realized it wasn't purely coincidental that we've been endlessly discussing coin tosses while we beat you to distraction with the binomial theorem and Pascal's triangle. There is some method to our madness!

We've also harped on the phrases *frequency distribution, relative frequency distribution,* and *probability distribution* over and over so that you'd get used to them. What you should realize about these is that they are not names of families of distributions at all, but are simply generic phrases to describe the innards for each and every family of distributions, much like the terms *wood houses* and *brick houses* describe the inner makings of ranch houses, colonial houses, and split-level houses. When you tear down a ranch house or a colonial house, what you'll see is the wood or brick underlying each.

And, finally, here's an idea that might help lighten the load a bit. It has been our own experience that the term *distribution* doesn't bring to mind any imagery at all. That is, when we speak of a dollar bill or a bikini we get immediate (and sometimes colorful) mental images that help us visualize the discussion at hand. But the word distribution is so unspecific and can be used in so many varied ways that instead of visualizing it we draw a blank. This prevents us from "seeing" it as a physical object and stops us from identifying it properly as the key that unlocks the solution to our problem. Over the many years that it took to create and compile these distributions statisticians have grown dependent on them as the only way possible to sort out some of the most difficult complexities of science. They've learned to embrace distributions as the one and only Holy Grail that can provide solutions to many real-world problems. But this embracing is hardly universal as one student commented on his homework: "It may seem like the Holy Grail to some math monkeys, but since I keep flunking it sure don't seem to be no Holy Grail to me !" Perhaps what is needed is an image that pops up on our radar screens a lot more easily. Maybe we need a different name that is more concrete and tangible. We discuss this as the last item in the chapter.

THE DISTRIBUTION AS ANSWER TABLE

We've come up with an easy alternative phrase that works wonders for us. Hopefully it will work for you as well. Whenever we see the term *distribution* used in the technical, mathematical sense, we substitute the phrase *answer table*.

Technical Math Phrase	Easy Alternative Phrase
Coin toss distribution	Coin toss answer table
Binomial distribution	Binomial answer table
Normal distribution	Normal answer table

We've translated these technical phrases and turned them into far more understandable and descriptive names. And it's an accurate translation because answer table describes precisely what a distribution is. As we've learned by now, distributions are complex, so the only reason anyone in their right mind would use distributions is because they give us the fastest answers. Each distribution is a table of the answers we need.

Let's see if the translation works as well for our three descriptors: frequency distribution, relative frequency distribution, and probability distribution:

Frequency distribution	Frequency answer table
Relative frequency distribution	Relative frequency answer table
Probability distribution	Probability answer table

Using the phrase *answer table* reminds us clearly that this is where we should look for the answers to our problem. It helps us remember that distributions are in fact part of the solution rather than some obnoxious and hideous appendage that uselessly attaches itself to each statistics problem we encounter. Although they are not easy to learn, distributions are *not* the problem; they are the solution to our problems! So take them out of that taped

and tattered box in your car trunk and put them back by the
driver's seat where they belong!

KEY CONCEPTS REVIEW

+ Many questions do not have simple answers. They can
  only be answered by distributions. A distribution is
  mathematicians' talk for a "table of many answers."
+ By measuring the frequency of events that interest us we
  can make a comparison against all the possible events:
  this gives us the relative frequency. Relative frequency is
  the ratio of the two: the number of interesting events
  divided by the total number of possible events.
+ The relative frequency of an event is often called the
  probability of the event. They are one and the same.
+ If you ask, How many heads are likely to come up when
  we toss a coin four times?, there is never one single
  answer but a variety of answers. This variety of answers
  creates a distribution. It might be a frequency
  distribution, a relative frequency distribution, or a
  probability distribution. They are all closely interrelated.
+ Statisticians like to graph these distributions to allow an
  easy visual picture. Bar graphs of frequency distributions
  are known as histograms. We showed many in the
  chapter.

THINGS TO THINK ABOUT

Ask a Question, Create a Distribution   Let's say you
are traveling to Europe in February and you would like to know
the temperature and rainfall in Berlin so as to be properly dressed.
Should you look up the almanac's prediction for the day in
question and rely on that? Or would you prefer to see a graph of
the temperatures in February over the last 20 years on a bar chart?
And the rainfall also? That way you could see the extreme cases
and the likely *distribution* of all the temperatures and rainfalls in
between. You could also find the most typical temperature and

rainfall so as to make a clear and educated guess at what the future might hold. You see, most people automatically prefer to see the distribution via its histogram without even realizing that is what they are doing. Distributions sound like a tough concept in the abstract, but when you get real life practice with them you automatically seek their help in decision making.

It's Lonely at the Fringe   Suppose for a moment that you are a middle-class, upwardly mobile professional who likes to be different when you can. You need a new car but you are sick and tired of driving an SUV like everyone else. You want something different that will stand out. You go on the Internet and find websites that describe the tastes and proclivities of the American driving public. There at your disposal you find histograms showing the frequency of cars sold in your state by make and model. And further on you also locate car colors graphed by preference. Trying to be wild and crazy you look to the skinniest ends of the car and color spectrum to find what you are looking for. You order online and 6 weeks later you stun the neighbors as you pull into your driveway the proud owner of a brand new neon-orange Yugo (decorated with speed stripes and black flames). You've made your choice to stand apart from the crowd, and you now realize a lot of strange things are lurking way out there at the distribution's ends. You also have an additional insight into the events that help contribute to these unusual occurrences—you are now driving one of them!

QUESTIONS

1. What is a distribution?
2. What is frequency?
3. What is relative frequency?
4. What is probability?
5. What is a frequency distribution?
6. What is a relative frequency distribution?
7. How do relative frequency distributions differ from probability distributions?

8. Can you define probability by a formula?
9. What is a histogram?
10. Is a histogram a distribution?
11. When we toss a coin four times, is there one single outcome that must occur?

CHAPTER 5

Probabilities, Odds, and Payoffs

In Chap. 4 we showed how to begin turning frequencies of occurrence into probabilities. Now we can get into the fun part of figuring out how much we are going to get paid when we win a bet. Once we know the probabilities of an event we can massage the numbers with some simple formulas to generate the proper odds, payoffs, and returns. After we learn about these three, we will be able to get to the meat of option theory.

Odds and *payoffs* are inextricably linked together. They are versions of the same concept seen from a different point of view and, along with probabilities, they are the mathematical backbone of games of chance and gambling. They are also a wonderfully simple lead-in to the much more complex world of markets and finance where the preferred term for payoffs is *returns*. As such we can use them as stepping stones to an understanding of option theory math.

The first important concept in any gambling establishment is the "house take." Without it the show would not go on. In the casino or at the races, the overhead and infrastructure costs are huge, and the providers are far from being philanthropists. So, there is some amount that is automatically deducted from all wagers in the form of a "takeout" or "house edge." In mathematics these are known as *unfair games*. That is to say that *their payouts are not in line with the true chances of winning*. Over time it is a mathematical certainty that all the bettors, as a whole, will lose money and that the house will win money. Thus, their odds and payoffs are *biased* against all players.

It is structured differently in markets. The prices themselves have no house take built into them. The prices are considered fair and unbiased. (We are speaking about the insider market prices, not the slightly biased client's price a dealer will quote you.) Since we are trying to learn about markets here, the calculations we do will always be based on fair games and won't include provisions for house take as must be done for the unfair games played in casinos.

This makes the formulas simpler. We merely use the same formulas that the casino or track would use and set the house take to zero. In the math of games of chance this is sometimes called a *break-even analysis*. This means that the calculations for payoffs and odds will be based strictly on the true probabilities of an event occurring. No house take or markup is added into the formula. We will get to the formulas shortly, and you'll find the math very simple and straightforward. But first let's introduce two important concepts:

1. All option pricing formulas are built on the central concept of breaking even.
2. Breaking even implies a zero-sum game where all winnings equal all losses:

$$\text{Total winnings} - \text{total losses} = 0$$

The definitions of payoffs, odds, and returns vary widely from source to source. You might visit five different casinos or sports books and never find any in agreement on the definitions for payoffs and odds. Similarly, there are literally scores of Wall Street usages for returns. Furthermore, you will find dozens of variations on these meanings in the outside world, so before you lay down your hard-earned dollars it's best to learn the local meanings and translate them so that they make sense for the situation you're in. Here are *our* meanings and how we want you to think of them as we go through the book:

Payoffs

A *payoff* generally refers to the amount you will be paid for winning a single event. In coin tosses, where we typically suggest $1 bets, the usual payoff is $1 per winning event. If it varies from this, we say so. But the world is not always simple and the phrase "winning event" might mean different things at different times. Again we try to describe this as it happens. Game players seem to be gifted with an endless ingenuity for creating new bets. They can come up with a much larger variety of winning events than we could ever describe. Take a simple game where a coin is tossed four times. They might devise a bet that pays only when four heads arrives, or four tails. Or maybe payment is based only on the excess of heads over tails, that is, $1 per excess head (or tail). The possibilities are endless.

And, don't forget, payoffs can be negative also. In a $1 game where you settle up after each event, you might make a dollar (+$1) or lose a dollar (−$1), meaning the payoff can be +$1 or −$1. We describe this when it occurs.

Odds

Odds are merely payoffs dressed up in different clothes. The phrase "even money" means odds of 1 to 1. It describes the odds of, for example, a single coin toss that has payoffs of +$1 and −$1. You can win or lose an even (equal) amount. If the odds are quoted as "2 to 1," it means you can win $2, but can only lose $1 (for each dollar bet). It is also called 2 to 1 *against*, which means 2 against, 1 for. If you imagine a street fight with three people involved, you will note that there are always uneven odds, that is, 2 against 1.

A bettor assessing his chances often thinks in terms of the bad events *against* him versus the good events *for* him. You will find in our coin toss analyses that we constantly measure paths against and paths for. The comparison of these in the form of a ratio (*against* divided by *for*) is what creates the proper odds. The odds dictate the payoff. If we find the odds are 3 to 1, a $1 bet has a payoff of $3. If you are required to hand over your dollar before the game is played, you will also get this original dollar

back. So odds of 3 to 1 imply that, upon winning, you will be
paid three times the size of your bet *plus* you get your bet back.
(Some casinos get cute about sneaking the return of your original
bet into the portion they call the payoff by saying 5 *for* 1 instead
of 5 *to* 1. This is an example of why you must learn their rules so
you won't get suckered.) *Note:* You will often see 3 to 1 odds stated
instead as "3-1" which is merely an oddsmaker's shorthand with
the dash or hyphen substituting for the word *to*.

Returns

Return is the preferred term for an investment's payoff. If you
watch CNBC television enough or speak to a few investment
banker types, you will come to believe that returns are the only
things that matter in the universe. "Return on this" and "return
on that" and "year-to-date returns" are all that the stock and bond
market mavens focus on. In the end, returns are merely the sum
of all your payoffs over a certain time period.

While the investment and financial types might grow apo-
plectic at us discussing games of chance, odds, and payoffs in the
same paragraph as their beloved investments, the best investors
clearly understand the parallel and incorporate it into their strategies and thinking processes. When possible, they try to set the
stage so that they are the "house" and have the odds and payoffs
in their favor. Your results in any game, investment or otherwise,
will depend on how well you do in assessing the odds and payoffs
of the games you participate in.

Investment people generally speak about a particular return
over time, say, a 9 percent return over a year. To show a comparison of returns, odds, and payoffs let's look at the total return after
many events take place, such as after tossing 100 coins. For this
example each coin we toss will have a winning payoff of +$1 and
a losing payoff of −$1 (each toss is a $1 bet). The odds are 1 to 1,
which can be deduced from the payoff structure we just described.
The odds and payoffs stay the same throughout the 100 tosses,
but there is a huge swing in the returns from toss to toss. Note
that after the first coin toss the return is either +100 or −100 percent of the $1 bet. But after a series of 100 bets where you win 54
and lose 46, the net return would be only +8 percent. Here is the

calculation: (+$54 − $46)/$100 total = +$8/$100 = +.08 = +8 percent. As you can see, returns tend to describe the *sum of overall results* after many bets have been made and/or a long time period has run its course, whereas payoffs and odds tend to describe individual events. To convert the resulting return to a decimal or percent merely divide by the money at risk during the series of events.

As another example, if you put up $100 and get back $109, you would have a $9 profit or net return. This is pretty clear. But some economics books might say your *gross* return was $109, or they might say a return of 1.09 *times capital* (meaning 1.09 times your original investment). Or they could call it a net return of +.09 which is the same as +9 percent. Sometimes they neglect to say net or gross. The concepts of gross return and net return get confused and misused often, but when it's your money you'll know the difference! There's an old joke about how a fellow made a quick 50 percent return on his money: "My commodities broker was on a real hot streak trading cocoa and sugar futures. I gave him discretion to trade my account with orders to close everything out if he felt it had gotten too risky. I got back 50 percent in under a week—the 50 percent he hadn't lost yet!" Clearly that's not the same type of return you are hoping for. It should clearly say −50 percent when you lose half. There are plenty of hucksters who publish false advertisements about their great investment returns in order to get a shot at managing your money. The sad truth is that many, many published investment returns aren't even remotely close to reality. But you cannot depend on the SEC to protect you because it doesn't even have enough workers to keep its lists of flagrant abusers up to date, let alone stop them from lying. It's up to you to learn the rules of the industry and all the possible meanings and usages of returns before you send a penny. We'll try to be clear and specific whenever we mention returns or payoffs throughout the balance of the book.

HOW TO CALCULATE FAIR PAYOFFS

Finally, we have arrived at the point where we will show you the formulas and get down to concrete examples. All this talk of returns, payoffs, and odds is based on *probabilities* and *relative frequencies.* Let's create an example that shows how to calculate fair payoffs. **Pay attention here: Calculating fair payoffs is the key to all option analysis.**

Example 1: Suppose we toss a coin twice. What are the proper *relative frequencies, probabilities, fair payoffs* and *fair odds?*

We know you can do this in your sleep, but this exercise will illuminate the meaning of those four concepts. There are exactly four paths for tossing a coin twice: HH, HT, TH, TT. But only three different payable outcomes: 0H, 1H, 2H.

Here is a simple table of frequencies of occurrence for each outcome.

Head-Count Outcome	Occurrence (Frequency)	Appropriate Paths
0H	1	TT
1H	2	HT, TH
2H	1	HH

The frequency of outcomes are 1, 2, 1 for 0H, 1H, 2H respectively. The total of all frequencies is the same as the total of all possible paths: 4. Therefore, we divide by 4 to obtain the relative frequency of each outcome. Doing this yields the relative frequencies of 1/4, 2/4, 1/4 for 0H, 1H, 2H, respectively. This is also the probability of each, which we may, if we choose, change to decimals or percentages. That would result in .25, .50, .25 or 25, 50, 25 percent. It makes no difference whether we use fractions, decimals, or percentages, it merely depends on which is most helpful at the time.

Once we have the probabilities it is a simple matter to compute the fair odds and payoffs. For example, the outcome of 2H shows a probability (or relative frequency) of 1/4. That means 1/4 of the chances are *for* it to happen, which implies 3/4 of the chances are *against* it happening (the total of all for and against probabilities must add up to 1.00). Identical values could be found by saying .25 for versus .75 against or 25 percent for versus 75 percent against. The ratio of the probability against divided by the probability for gives us the odds. No matter whether you use fractions, decimals or percentages to do the calculation (division), you can plainly see that the true odds against it are 3 to 1. These are the fair odds we need to compute the fair payoff. So the fair payoff would be $3 per $1 bet. (The winning payoff would be $3, the losing payoff, −$1.)

Let's do a recap that includes all the possible outcomes:

Head-Count Outcome	Frequency	Relative Frequency	Fraction of Chances		Fair Odds	Fair $1 Payoff
			For	Against		
0H	1	1/4	1/4	3/4	3 to 1	$3
1H	2	2/4	2/4	2/4	1 to 1	$1
2H	1	1/4	1/4	3/4	3 to 1	$3
		Total = 4/4 = 1.00				

EXPECTED RESULTS (MATHEMATICAL EXPECTATIONS)

The final item on our list of phrases to learn is the *mathematical expectation*, also called the *average expected value*. It is a type of *average result* that is *weighted by probability*.

It is the result that you would *expect on average* if you repeated your test many times. You might run across the concept under the heading of many different terms that all mean the same thing, such as the *expectation*, the *average expected result*, the *mathematically expected value*. When mathematicians talk about an event having a certain *expectation*, they are not talking about hopes, hunches, dreams, or other such unspecific emotional feelings. They are talking about a mathematically proven result that has happened in the past and will recur in the future at the rate specified if you have the ability to try the event over and over again many times, say a thousand or more. For example, here is the *mathematical expectation* of the number of heads we will get when we toss a coin two times:

Computing an Expected Result (in Heads)

Head-Count Outcome	Frequency	Probability	Outcome × Probability
0H	1	1/4	0H × 1/4 = 0/4 H
1H	2	2/4	1H × 2/4 = 2/4 H
2H	1	1/4	2H × 1/4 = 2/4 H
	Totals 4	4/4	Average expected result = 4/4 H (= 1 head)

We computed the mathematical expectation of the average results by multiplying the outcomes in head counts (0H, 1H, 2H) by their probabilities (1/4, 2/4, 1/4). The sum total of these multiplied values is the average expected outcome or the mathematical expectation as measured in number of heads. It turns out to be one head. That is, one head is expected per game played (two tosses of a coin per game).

> *Example 2:* A slightly more involved question is, Given that this is a fair game, what is the expected profit or loss? Or, in a very similar vein, What is our *expected return?*
>
> Well, now we are starting to break away from abstract concepts and get down to the real nitty-gritty. We are evolving from expected outcomes to expected payoffs. As Cuba Gooding, Jr., said in *Jerry Maguire*, "Show me the money, Jerry!" That's what everybody really wants to know isn't it? How much money (return) can we expect given the nature of the two coin toss game we have just outlined?
>
> To analyze this we must align all the possible outcomes with their probabilities and their payoffs. This sounds more difficult than it is. We've already done most of the work.

Head-Count Outcome	Probability		Payoff		Expected			Individual Outcome Net Return
	For	Against	For	Against	Gain − Loss			
0H	1/4	3/4	$3	$1	(1/4 × $3 − 3/4 × $1)	=	($3/4 − $3/4)	= 0
1H	2/4	2/4	$1	$1	(2/4 × $1 − 2/4 × $1)	=	($2/4 − $2/4)	= 0
2H	1/4	3/4	$3	$1	(1/4 × $3 − 3/4 × $1)	=	($3/4 − $3/4)	= 0
							Total expected net return	0

The bad news is, Jerry, there is *no money* to show for all our efforts! By definition of a fair game we *expect* to break even! This might be a tough bone to chew on, but this is the way it really is in the big, wide world. Options are fair games, and so they closely parallel this process, albeit on a more complex level. It may not feel like it, but we are gaining knowledge very quickly, and this knowledge will allow us to begin solving the option puzzle.

We can use probabilities multiplied by payoffs to calculate any single event's *individual expected return:*

Individual expected return = winning probability × winning payoff
$$- \text{ losing probability} \times \text{losing payoff}$$

or using math shorthand,

Individual expected return
$$= \text{prob}_{\text{win}} \times \text{payoff}_{\text{win}} - \text{prob}_{\text{lose}} \times \text{payoff}_{\text{lose}}$$

Just remember, all our option analyses *will always require multiplying probabilities times payoffs.* Also, the individual expected return is but a small piece of any game. If we sum up each and every individual expected return, we can get the total expected return *for the game* as a whole:

Expected return for game
$$= \Sigma \text{ all } (\text{prob}_{\text{win}} \times \text{payoff}_{\text{win}} - \text{prob}_{\text{lose}} \times \text{payoff}_{\text{lose}})$$

The symbol Σ is sigma, a Greek letter that means *sum* in mathematics. We will explain its use in detail in Chap. 7. Don't get nervous about memorizing these formulas, just get the general idea of what they mean and how we easily created them from simple, but powerful and accurate, ideas. We will repeat it all again as we need it later.

Over the last few chapters we have become acquainted with all the phrases we wished to describe: results, paths, outcomes, frequency, relative frequency, probabilities, frequency distribution, returns, payoffs, odds, and mathematical expectations. In Chap. 6 we will put some of these ideas into play as we learn how to price our first simple option based on coin tosses.

KEY CONCEPTS REVIEW

- ◆ Odds, payoffs, and returns are all methods for measuring your winnings (if you're so lucky).
- ◆ Odds generally refer to the ratio of cases against versus cases for. For example, 2 to 1 means two cases against your cause and one case for your cause. Translated into payoffs: you get paid $2 for winning, but you pay $1 for losing (for each $1 bet). A losing payoff can also be shown as −$1.

- In the markets, investors discuss returns rather than payoffs. Same idea, fancier name. Returns refer to how much you get back on your original investment, usually measured as a percentage. While the concept is simple, the varieties and types of returns seem to go on and on.
- There are fair games and unfair games. In a fair game all players are expected to break even over the long haul. To be fair there must be no house takeout and all odds, payoffs, and returns must exactly reflect each event's true probability of occurrence.
- By knowing the probabilities in a fair game we can easily compute the fair odds, fair payoffs, and fair returns.
- By properly weighting (multiplying) a payoff by its probability we can compute an individual expected return for that particular case or event. Since we must break even in a fair game, the sum of all individually expected returns for the game should be equal to zero.
- Once we know the expected returns for all the possible events in a game we can assess the fair value for an option that is based on any event within the game. We show how in Chap. 6.

THINGS TO THINK ABOUT

Competition and Fair Payoffs   Fair payoffs are payoffs that, based on probability analysis, create a zero-sum winning/losing balance among all the players. In a casino there are *no* fair payoffs because the house must create more losers than winners in order to profit. The casino games are therefore unfair. If players were allowed to take bets as well as make bets, that is, act like the house while in the casino, what would be the impact? Would the average payoffs rise closer to fair payoff value or move further away?

Think of it this way. Allowing casino players to take either side of the bet is akin to a two-way market where players are allowed to invest for or against depending on their analysis of the situation. What happens in marketplaces is that the traders try to identify an edge on either side of an investment and then offer to cut the edge a bit so all others will trade with them. This competition can become cutthroat. In casinos the Big Wheel has some payoffs that can give the house a 16 percent profit. The first players might offer payoffs with only a 15 percent profit, and then the competition would offer 14 percent, and so on. Capitalists are a nasty, competitive bunch, aren't they?

Option to Never Lose?   Options give you the right to exercise (if you choose) or to walk away (and pay nothing at that point). Therefore, come expiration day options must have a value of zero, if not beneficial to exercise, or some value greater than zero (determined by how much is collected by exercising). Thus it seems that option owners should never lose, right? What do you think about this? In a very similar sense those who own insurance policies benefit from the same logic. Why then don't people sign up for an infinite amount of insurance or options? (*Hint:* Premiums are paid up front.)

QUESTIONS

1. What are odds?
2. In the newspaper sports section last Sunday we saw an "odds line" for a football game quoted as +7 and in a baseball game as −125/+115. These don't look anything at all like the odds described here in the book. Why not?
3. What is a fair game?
4. Option formulas are built on the central concept of breaking even. What is the simple formula that defines breaking even for a zero-sum game?
5. What is break-even analysis and how does it help us set up fair payoffs?
6. Tossing a coin three times leads to four outcomes (0H, 1H, 2H, 3H) with eight different paths. List all eight paths. How many result in an outcome of 0H, 1H, 2H, and 3H? What are the probability, fair odds, and fair payoff for 2H assuming a $1 bet?
7. Odds, payoffs, and returns are inextricably linked together. How are they linked?

8. We are playing a game where it is determined that our true chance of winning is .20 (same as 20 percent). What fair odds and payoff should we receive?

9. What do we mean by the phrase *mathematical expectation?*

10. Explain the formula: Individual expected return = $\text{prob}_{\text{win}} \times \text{payoff}_{\text{win}} - \text{prob}_{\text{lose}} \times \text{payoff}_{\text{lose}}$.

11. The symbol Σ is sigma, a Greek letter often used in math. In what context is it usually used?

CHAPTER 6

Writing Our First Option

In this chapter we will create our first option. Using the payoff analyses and probabilities of a four coin toss game we will deduce the value of a very simple option. The following table recaps work you've seen in previous chapters.

Four Coin Toss Game

Head-Count Outcome	Number of Paths	Probability (Relative Frequency)	
		Fraction	Decimal
0	1	1/16	.0625
1	4	4/16	.2500
2	6	6/16	.3750
3	4	4/16	.2500
4	1	1/16	.0625
	16	16/16	1.0000

There are exactly 16 possible different paths, and each has a distinct probability of $1/16 = .0625$.

We will discuss three variations of the four coin toss game and then compute the option value.

VARIATION 1: PAY FOR 4H ONLY

Suppose a friend wants to play a gambling game with you based on tossing a coin four times. The game will be fair to both of you; that is, neither you nor your friend has an *expected* advantage.

To arrange a fair game you must use random and unbiased equipment (such as a typical coin and coin toss method) and the payoff schedule must be arranged according to the true probabilities such that no one has an expected gain or loss over the course of many trials. Stated another way, no one's specialized knowledge will give an advantage and every player is expected to break even.

Your friend wishes to toss a coin four times and bet on getting four heads exactly. He doesn't care about the outcomes of zero, one, two, or three heads. He wants to go for the long shot only: four heads in a row in only four tosses.

You now know enough to deduce what the payoff should be. Let's review what we know from our earlier formulas and the previous table. There are five outcomes possible $(N + 1)$ and a total of 16 paths (2^4) to these five outcomes. Not all outcomes are created equal, and your friend has picked the lowest probability scenario of four heads:

Head-Count Outcomes	Number of Paths	Probabilities (Relative Frequency)
4	1	.0625
3	4	.2500
2	6	.3750
1	4	.2500
0	1	.0625
	16	1.0000

Some people inexperienced with probability analysis might think, There are five outcomes, so each one has a chance of 1/5 or .20. Therefore, they would assess odds against of 4 to 1. *They would get slaughtered* if they bet on getting four heads in a row and were only paid 4 to 1. Not *all outcomes are equal*, but an inexperienced person might not see this. It is the frequency and relative frequencies that properly determine probabilities, odds, and payoffs.

Pascal's triangle (1 4 6 4 1) for $N = 4$ is our guide to the paths and frequencies.

Since there are a total of 16 possible paths and only 1 path to the event that was favorable to the bettor (four heads), there are 15 paths against and 1 path for. The odds, therefore, should be 15 to 1. Receiving only 4 to 1 would be an obvious injustice.

Look at the probability column in the previous table. There is a value of only .0625 given for the outcome of exactly four heads. That implies that the cumulative total value of probability for the outcomes of zero, one, two, and three heads is .9375. You can add them: .0625 + .25 + .375 + .25 = .9375, or knowing that the total for all possibilities must be 1.000, you can subtract the value for you (.0625) to deduce the value against you (1.000 − .0625 = .9375). These are probability *complements*: .0625 + .9375. The complements are like offsets that always sum to 1.000. If one is .400, then the complement is automatically .600, for example. The odds could be figured exactly the same way using the probabilities instead of the paths: .9375 against, .0625 for. Divide: .9375/.0625 = 15. The ratio is 15 to 1, which we call odds against. The payoff should be $15 for each $1 bet.

The above probability analysis is a simplified version of what is computed by all the leading option models. The most popular is Black-Scholes. The Black-Scholes formula requires that we understand a probability distribution called the normal or bell-shaped distribution. This is where we are headed a bit down the road. Expanding and extending coin toss distributions until they mimic the normal distribution is the final endpoint we are pursuing, our Holy Grail of option understanding.

So, what have we accomplished so far with this example? We recapped how to deduce the fair odds (15 to 1) and probability (.0625) for the outcome of four heads in a row that your friend wanted to bet on.

Remember, these relationships hold only for that particular situation when we toss a coin exactly four times. The whole ball of wax changes if we toss 10 times or 100 times. (Getting four heads some time during the tossing of 100 coins is very easy, not a long shot at all.) We used the probability distribution (.0625, .25, .375, .25, .0625) for outcomes of (0H, 1H, 2H, 3H, 4H) which applies only for a coin tossed four times. If you toss a coin 100 times, then you must use that particular probability distribution or you are comparing apples and oranges.

VARIATION 2: PAY FOR 3H *OR* 4H

Let's add another possible payable outcome to our original version of the game. What would be the payoff and probability of getting three *or* four heads in a four coin toss?

We can use either of the two probability tables we used for Variation 1. There are four paths to three heads (THHH, HTHH, HHTH, HHHT) and one path to four heads. Since there are a total of 16 possible paths, this implies: 11 against, 5 for. So the odds should be 11 to 5. Dividing 11 by 5 shows that the ratio is 2.2:1, which is slightly easier to understand for most of us.

Instead of counting paths we can use an alternate method that involves only probabilities. In the previous table you can see that the outcome of three heads has a probability valued at .25 and that of four heads is .0625, giving us a total of .3125. This is for you, so against must be the complement, as they call it, which is the value 1.000 − .3125 = .6875. We can compute the odds against based on that: .6875/.3125 = 2.2. We hope that isn't a surprise. If you do it properly, either way gets the job done. Mathematicians prefer to work on the probability distribution values as the numbers of tosses get larger, because, as we showed earlier, the possible paths get astronomically huge, so formulas allow you to easily measure things that counting will not. Someone once said that the purpose of mathematics is to find ways to *avoid doing tedious computations.* Math formulas can simplify your life if you know how to speak the language.

VARIATION 3: PAY FOR 2H *OR* 3H *OR* 4H

In this final version of the game let's add one extra payable outcome and then we'll turn to creating an option. Suppose a friend says she'd like to win her bet if two or more heads come in? That means all the cases of two, three, and four heads. (There are five possible outcomes, and your friend has now picked three of the five possible sectors. This begins to mimic real life since options work in a similar way with sectors called *strikes.*)

Our table shows that 2H, 3H, and 4H have six paths, four paths, and one path, respectively, leaving the remaining two outcomes with one path and four paths. That adds up to 5 paths against you and 11 paths for you. This is more for you than against you! So the odds against you are only 5 to 11, which, after dividing 5 by 11, we find to be .4545 to 1. (This is a heavy favorite to win, since the odds are lower than 1 to 1.)

While this seems to be an unusual and peculiar payoff ratio, it is the only payoff ratio with which you will break even. When you lose on the five paths against you, your net loss is $5 \times -1 = -5$. When you win on the 11 paths for you, you will show a net profit of $+.4545 \times 11 = +4.9995 = +5$ (rounded). The net result of $-5 + 5$ is, of course, zero, so you break even. This is what we seek in a fair game. Our table shows probabilities of .375, .25, and .0625, for 2H, 3H, and 4H, respectively, which total .6875 for you. Against you must be the complement, 1.000 minus .6875 which is .3125. So the odds against are $.3125/.6875 = .4545$ to 1, the same as analyzed by path analysis.

We have brought you to the point where you are able to figure various payoffs and probabilities on simple distributions. Neither the 10 coin toss nor the 100 coin toss would be different in analysis. But getting the data off a table or bar chart histogram is awfully difficult since the numbers on it almost blend together to become unreadable. Organizing and summing up all these numbers is also horrendous work, so mathematicians have developed formulas to help. We'll show you their usefulness later as the need arises.

CREATING OUR FIRST OPTION

Finally, let's see how an option might be constructed and valued with the four coin toss model. Your friend says he'd like to bet so that he only wins! (Don't we all?) He really hates paying when he loses, but he wouldn't be against paying a little something up front before the game starts. If he loses, you keep his up-front money. If he wins, he gets paid appropriately.

Is there some small amount he can pay you before the tossing starts and not be liable for paying any more regardless of outcome, but if his ship comes in (he wants the long shot again, exactly four heads) he will collect exactly $1?

We can accommodate him, and you are probably already figuring out how. It turns out his request is identical to a simple option. This is the same long-shot bet we reviewed in Variation 1 of the four coin toss game. There are 15 paths against, with 1 path for. Said another way, for every 16 games your friend will win 1 and lose 15. So he must pay $1/16 before each game begins. After 16 games (on average), he will win $1 from you, but he will have prepaid $1/16 multiplied by 16 which equals $1. Therefore, he will be even, as will you. *You just created your first option.*

If you charge him any less, you will have an expected loss (not certain, just mathematically expected) each time the game is played. You must charge him a prepayment that equals his expected gain. This is it. This is what options are all about: *The buyer must **prepay** what his **expected gain** is.* This is the answer to every option valuation question you will ever have.

If you learn only one thing from our studies, learn this lesson: Every option formula you will ever run into is merely trying to compute the *prepayment required to break even.* Put another way, the option formulas are trying to calculate what the expected gain is and charge that amount up front.

If the option was free, your friend would never lose. You, on the other hand, could never win, but you would lose whenever the long shot came in. Charging a fair price up front ensures that both you and your friend will break even over many, many trials.

If you can figure out expected gain, you can easily price any option. (Notice that in our games everything takes place the same day, so there is no time delay in payment. Therefore, no discounting, present value, or interest rate factors enter this simplified picture. Unfortunately there is a need for these adjusting factors for real options. We get to them much later.)

CREATING OUR SECOND OPTION

There are many variations on the theme, however, and clever entrepreneurs are constantly revising the game strategies and outcome payoffs. Suppose the game changes to a payout of $1 for each and every head?

Your friend is not betting on a long shot anymore. He wants to be paid a dollar for any head. That means if zero heads arrive, you must pay zero dollars. One head, you pay $1. Up through four heads wherein you pay $4. Obviously your friend never risks a thing, so he must pay something up front. But how much?

Back to the drawing board. Your expected loss (his gain) can be reckoned by summing each payoff times its frequency of occurrence for every possible outcome:

Head-Count Outcome	Frequency	Payoff	Freq. × Payoff
0	1	$0	$0
1	4	$1	$4
2	6	$2	$12
3	4	$3	$12
4	1	$4	$ 4
	16		$32 Total

This table shows that over a series of 16 games you could expect (on average) to lose $32 in total. That is an expected loss of $2 per four coin toss event! *So, that is how much you must charge for this new option and payoff scheme.* That is, you must charge $2 per game up front which is $32 over 16 games.

Precisely the same result would have been reached by multiplying the probabilities (instead of frequencies) times the payoffs, as we did in earlier examples. The key is getting an accurate payoff schedule linked to an accurate probability distribution, and then multiplying the linked pairs (of payoffs and probabilities) and summing them all up.

As our friend's game designs change we must also change, but one principle always holds: *He must pay us an amount identical to his expected gain* (or our expected loss; it's the same thing). That means that sometimes he wins, sometimes he loses, but over a very long time we both should break even. This is the theory as based on fair games, break-even payoffs, and probability distributions.

To make these calculations we must first start by finding a reliable source of frequencies of occurrence per outcome. This allows us to create a probability distribution and compute a matching set of break-even payoffs (which correspond to the probabilities). The source can be empirical data (an actual history of a large number of occurrences) or theory (our coin analyses are all based on the *theory* that a coin comes up heads 50 percent of the time).

We require that these probability distributions will repeat in the future. Not on any given day, but over many, many cases and many days. If the past data or theoretic data do not repeat (to match our expectations), we will have an awful lot of surprises that math cannot help us with! This is precisely the business that insurance companies are in, and they are at substantial risk whenever the future diverges substantially from past patterns. Five big hurricanes in a year will put many out of business.

Several thoughts emerge about this. Casinos, bookmakers, insurance companies, coin tossers and options strategists are all kindred spirits. Their success depends on identifying the fair valuation of the products they deal in. They then must charge more than that to the user or consumer. It is merely the types of risks covered that separate the groups above. Some types of risk are considered entertainment, while others may be critical to economic survival. But, in the end, the mathematical processes of assessment are very similar.

Clearly, the analysis of tossing coins is very straightforward, at least for small numbers of tosses. But how does one develop a probability distribution for more complex events like the ups and downs of financial markets? And don't payoffs on financial assets like stocks and bonds differ greatly from coin toss payoffs? These are the questions we will answer in later chapters.

CREATING AN EXOTIC (PATH DEPENDENT) OPTION

One final concept for this chapter is *path dependence*. This refers to options that have payoffs that *depend on the path followed*. Many new exotic options factor this concept into them. Whereas we have only discussed final outcomes so far, like two heads or four heads, we can devise games that also pay out depending on *how* the outcomes occurred. That is, what also matters is what paths were followed to get to those outcomes. The two options we have analyzed so far are very straightforward and simple. Because they are so ordinary they are sometimes called "plain vanilla." Path-dependent options are a bit more complex and fit into the category termed *exotics*. Since understanding this path-dependent concept doesn't require any special knowledge beyond what we already know, it seems worth a short detour to explain it.

Falling back on our old standard, the four coin toss event, a friend wishes to bet on exactly two heads coming in as the final outcome. This is the most common occurrence and has 6 paths out of 16 possible. But here's the twist: your friend says that if *two tails happen in a row* during the four coin toss sequence, we don't pay her anything!

This result now depends on the paths followed to arrive at the final outcome. Both events (paths and outcomes) now have an effect on our calculation of the probabilities and fair payoffs. This wasn't true before, remember? We didn't care about paths until this "exotic" concept was created.

Of the six paths that lead to an outcome of precisely two heads (HHTT, HTHT, HTTH, THHT, THTH, TTHH) there are three with two tails in a row and three without. Therefore, there are only three paths that fulfill your friend's payoff requirements instead of six. (She requires payment only if exactly two heads arrive as a final outcome *and also* two tails didn't occur in a row.) So there are only three paths for her which implies 13 against her. The fair odds would be 13 to 3 against, which is the same as 4.33 to 1 after dividing.

Buying path-dependent options usually gives you less chance to win because of the extra things that must go your way, and, therefore, these exotic options are cheaper. Even though the formula to calculate their value is certainly more complicated, the essence is the same: enumerate the paths (or probabilities) for and against, weight them by their payoff costs, and then assess an average expected gain. This is fair value. You charge more if you are running a for-profit business! [*Note:* So what price should an option be valued at? If we assume your friend requires a payout schedule of $1 per success, then we would charge her $3/16 per game (3 payable paths out of 16 possible). Because it is an option, she never pays any losses after the fact. So, when the 13 cases against her show up, she smiles and pays nothing. But when any of the three cases for her arrive, we must pay her $1. Thus she has an expected gain of $3, on average, every 16 tosses. We recover her expected gain by charging an up-front premium of $3/16 for each of the 16 tosses.]

KEY CONCEPTS REVIEW

- ♦ The purpose of this chapter was to link what we've learned about coin tosses with the world of options.
- ♦ We did this by creating three simple variations of a coin toss game. In each version we used our standard game wherein a coin was tossed four times, but the payoffs varied game to game. Variation 1 paid off only when exactly four heads arrived. This is the long shot that occurs only 1 out of 16 times, and, therefore, the odds against were deemed to be 15 to 1.
- ♦ For Variation 2 we added a payoff of three heads, so you would be paid if 3H or 4H comes in.
- ♦ For Variation 3 we added a payoff of two heads, so you would be paid if 2H, 3H, or 4H comes in.
- ♦ Since the payable outcomes differ for each game, the payoffs should also differ. They vary according to which sectors or slices of the possible outcomes are included as possible winners. The more sectors included as winning events, the lower the payoffs will be. This is very similar to options where such sector selections are called *strikes*. In options our payoff and likelihood vary depending upon which strike we select. We'll run into this idea again in Chap. 7.
- ♦ We reviewed the simple computations involving fair odds and fair payoffs. At their simplest, fair odds are the ratio of probability against to probability for. Since the sum of all probabilities must always add to 1.00, the probabilities for and probabilities against are complements of each other. Know one and you automatically know the other. So, if you know that the probabilities for are .40, then the probabilities against must be .60.
- ♦ We can either count paths for and against or use probabilities for and against, whichever is easiest. The resulting answers for odds and payoffs are the same. But by learning to use probabilities and the probability distribution for coins we teach ourselves to prepare for much more complicated situations when it is almost

impossible to count the number of paths. For those situations we will turn to probability tables (distributions) that have been precomputed by mathematicians.

THINGS TO THINK ABOUT

Too Many Coin Tosses, So Little Time to Count Them By gradually including more coins in our tosses we are becoming aware of the fact that we had better learn to use the probability distribution for coins to help simplify things. All the answers we need are part and parcel of this probability distribution for coins. This distribution is directly descended from the far more famous binomial distribution. From there it is not much of a leap at all to learn to use the most famous and popular family member of them all, the normal distribution. Understanding binomial and normal distributions is our goal, and it will allow us to then easily understand the Black-Scholes formula. But this is all still a bit down the road for us.

QUESTIONS

1. What was the first option we created, and how much did it cost?
2. What do we mean by probability complements?
3. How does a probability distribution help us with coin toss analysis?
4. Which is a better way to calculate odds and payoffs: using paths or probabilities?
5. What does *expected gain* mean?
6. What does *expected loss* mean?
7. How are expected gain and expected loss linked?
8. What is a prepayment?
9. What is a premium?
10. How are insurance and option analysis linked?
11. Why must you prepay for an option?

12. What does it mean to say that options premiums are "prepayment for your expected gain"?

13. We said in the chapter, "If you learn only one thing from our studies, learn this lesson." What was that lesson?

14. In a four coin toss game we might use the following phrases for outcomes: four heads in a row, exactly four heads, more than three heads, and no tails at all. How do these outcomes differ?

15. In a four coin toss game if you select all tails, what are the odds and fair payoff? (*Hint:* It's the same as all heads.)

16. In a game where you will win .20 (20 percent) of the time and the payoff is $1, what is the price for an option to play the game?

17. In a game where your winning chances are .50 (50 percent) and the payoff is $1, what should you pay for that option to play the game?

18. What does *plain vanilla* mean?

19. We described path-dependent options and mentioned that they are sometimes called exotic options. What was meant by that?

CHAPTER 7

Sectors, Strike Prices, and Summation Signs

In Chap. 6 we created coin toss games and options. We discussed the value of an option for four heads only and also a different option that pays off for each and every head that comes up. We could also have designed other types of options such as "two heads or more" (all the outcomes of 2H, 3H, 4H cumulatively).

This last example, of cumulative sectors, is a much closer analogy to the real option market. It would be equivalent to a real option's strike price. In the old days when option traders would "strike a deal," they would argue over the price level at which the option kicked in. Thus they started to name the kick-in level the *strike price*. For example, you might strike a deal to buy IBM at $120 for the next 6 months, *at your option*. You would participate profitably if and when IBM reaches $120 or more. Your payoff would be cumulatively greater as IBM went higher and higher above $120.

If an option trader was to create real options for our coin toss examples, the options would be at the following five strikes or sectors: 0H (or more), 1H (or more), 2H (or more), 3H (or more), and 4H (or more). Such options would pay off if the outcome was equal to or greater than the chosen number of heads. In short, five different strike categories would be agreed to.

But all strikes or sectors are not born equal. If we examine the five sectors, we will find that the highest and lowest are very,

very different. The "four heads or more" category is clearly a long shot, only 1 out of 16 chances. At the other extreme is the "zero heads or more" category. This is the proverbial sure thing, because we will always get zero or more heads. The buyer of this option wants to get paid under every conceivable circumstance. Don't we all!

You will notice that as the option sectors (strikes) move from low (0H) to high (4H) the cumulative chances of collecting a payoff decrease sharply. The amount of money expected to be paid out by the option writer (sum of probabilities × payoffs), therefore, also decreases, which will lower the loss. The fair price of the options will thus fall accordingly.

We created brackets in Fig. 7–1 to reflect the cumulative probability of being right. The probability of winning on any option is the cumulative total from that bar through the rightmost bar, which is 4H. Include the starting and ending bars also.

$$\text{Cumulative probability} = \begin{cases} 16/16 \ (= 1.0000) & \text{for 0H or more} \\ 15/16 \ (= \ .9375) & \text{for 1H or more} \\ 11/16 \ (= \ .6875) & \text{for 2H or more} \\ 5/16 \ (= \ .3125) & \text{for 3H or more} \\ 1/16 \ (= \ .0625) & \text{for 4H or more} \end{cases}$$

This is interesting; in fact, it is terrific! We can just go with the sure thing option (zero heads or more) and retire to Tahiti. It always pays off, doesn't it? There are, however, two very large, black flies buzzing around our celebratory glass of champagne and begging for attention. They are named *payoff* and *cost*. What will the payoff be, and how much do these options cost to purchase? High probabilities, however wonderful, do not translate into retirement income. It is highly probable that the sun will rise each morning, but that tidbit of wisdom doesn't pay our bills. Now, if we could receive a nice payoff for each sunrise with no cost, well, that would be glorious.

Knowing about probabilities is a critically important step to solving the riddle of how to value options, but it is not enough. As mathematicians like to say, it is "necessary, but not sufficient." The valuation riddle includes two other elements: payoffs and costs. And, you will remember from previous chapters, in a world of fair values, where no one is granted a free trip to Tahiti, there

FIGURE 7-1

Brackets Show Cumulative Probability of Being Right

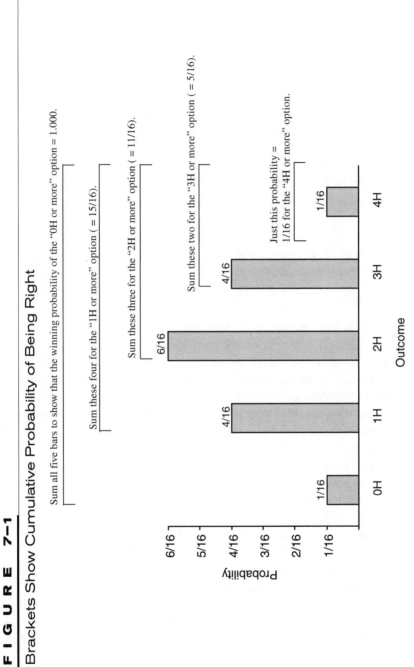

Sum all five bars to show that the winning probability of the "0H or more" option = 1.000.

Sum these four for the "1H or more" option (= 15/16).

Sum these three for the "2H or more" option (= 11/16).

Sum these two for the "3H or more" option (= 5/16).

Just this probability = 1/16 for the "4H or more" option.

Outcome

Probability

6/16
5/16
4/16
3/16
2/16
1/16

1/16   4/16   6/16   4/16   1/16

0H   1H   2H   3H   4H

is a strong mathematical link between probability, payoff, and cost. Roughly speaking, cost = probability × payoff.

The premier formula that equates these to option values is called the *Black-Scholes formula*. To work our way up to the option formulas we will develop another few elementary formulas and then piece them all together.

To add up all the probabilities multiplied by payoffs we need to be acquainted with a new and improved way to represent the summation of many things: the capital Greek letter sigma Σ. Sigma corresponds to the English letter S and is used by mathematicians to mean "sum."

Example:

$$\text{Cost} = \Sigma \text{ (probability} \times \text{payoff)}$$

This equation means simply that cost is equal to the *sum* of all the individual pairs of probabilities times their associated payoffs. For more specific uses of Σ, see the math tutorial in the next section.

[*Note:* We loosely used the term *cost* over the past few paragraphs. Cost has two possible meanings: one as seen by the option writer, the other as seen by us, the option purchaser. They both lead to the same identical calculation and thus have the same value. When an option writer sells an option she must recoup her expected loss if she is to break even and all our analyses are of the break-even type. Her expected loss is *her* cost. It must also be *our purchase* cost and our expected gain. In a break-even game, the sum of expected losses and expected gains is zero. In essence, each of the following six values are equal: writer's cost, purchasers' cost, writer's expected loss, purchaser's expected gain, the option's fair value, Σ (prob × payoff)].

If we can identify all the probabilities and payoffs within the coin toss sector we've chosen (or strike price zone), we can calculate the expected gain. We do this by taking each and every payoff, one at a time, and multiplying by the probability that corresponds to that particular payoff's likelihood. The sum of all these multiplied pairs is the expected gain for the sector or zone we've bet on. This expected gain, discounted for borrowing costs, is the fair value of the option.

Option fair value = expected gain (discounted)

We will cover this in more detail in Chap. 8. However, you may wish to browse through the following math tutorial. For those who need to understand the more intricate details of the options formulas, summations are a necessary item for your analysis tool bag.

MATH TUTORIAL: GEORGE FOREMAN AND SUMMATIONS*

Let's use a true (but silly) example to simplify the use of sigma (Σ). The champion boxer George Foreman has eight sons (or close to that), and he named each of them George! He decided that each one should be a namesake and thereby none could claim favoritism by dear old dad! This is an ideal case to show how and why mathematicians use various letters and symbols. Being exceedingly clever we have decided on a cute symbol to represent each of the sons—the letter G. To distinguish between the sons we add subscripts: $G_1, G_2, G_3, \ldots, G_8$. (Notice how quickly you recognized the "$\ldots$" as the mathematician's way of saying "and so on, through G_8.")

Now you also understand that since G_1 is a different son from G_2, G_1 is not the same as G_2, which is not the same as G_3, and so on. In fact no G is precisely the same as any other G, but there is similarity in that we recognize $G_1, G_2, G_3, \ldots, G_8$ all as sons of George Senior. So they have a lot of similarities by DNA inheritance, but also a lot of differences. There are no identical twins, but they all look somewhat alike.

Mathematicians need a way to group things that look the same but are different, and they invented subscripts. So we used subscripts and grouped them as $G_1, G_2, \ldots, G_8$. To talk about any specific son, we say "G_1 did this" or "G_5 did that." When we need to talk about them all generally, with no specific son in mind, we could say G, but we prefer the symbol G_i. The subscript i can be any number from 1 to 8 because we set those limits when we created it and we need to describe eight different sons of George. So, if we say "G_i" it means generally "one of the sons, but we are not specifying any one in particular."

---

* Optional reading.

Suppose we plan to name them in terms of their age; the eldest is G_1, the next eldest is G_2, down through to the youngest whom we name G_8. And suppose their ages in years are as follows (2 years apart):

$$G_1 = 15$$

$$G_2 = 13$$

$$G_3 = 11$$

$$G_4 = 9$$

$$G_5 = 7$$

$$G_6 = 5$$

$$G_7 = 3$$

$$G_8 = 1$$

To sum up *all* these values of G_i which are merely ages, we might use the Σ sign:

$$\Sigma G_i$$

This says, sum up all the individual Georges according to the values we assigned (their ages in this case). But it doesn't specify how many little Georges there are, when to start adding, or when to stop. The following terminology does this more precisely:

$$\sum_{i=1}^{8} G_i$$

This says, Sum up *all* the individual Georges starting at $i = 1$ (below Σ) and concluding at $i = 8$ (above Σ):

$$\sum_{i=1}^{8} G_i = G_1 + G_2 + G_3 + G_4 + G_5 + G_6 + G_7 + G_8$$

Which is quicker and easier to write: the left side of the equation which reads $\sum_{i=1}^{8} G_i$ or the right side with the eight $G_1 + G_2 + G_3$ . . . ? Imagine there are 100 or 1000 Georges! Obviously the terminology $\sum_{i=1}^{1000} G_i$ is much easier to write. After practicing a bit, you can become very comfortable with using and understanding this $\sum_{i=1}^{8} G_i$. It simply says, Sum up all the G_i, starting here and ending there.

If we wish to sum up all the ages (all the G_i), it would look like this:

$$\sum_{i=1}^{8} G_i = 15 + 13 + 11 + 9 + 7 + 5 + 3 + 1 = 64$$

The sum is 64. If we want to calculate the average (which we might need to do later in the book), simply divide by 8 (the number of Georges). This equals 64/8 which accidentally happens to be 8 also. So the average age, also called the *mean* age, is 8 years old. (There is no special reason to mention this except that we will later need to become acquainted with the mean value for a group of data. The *mean* is simply a type of midpoint. People more commonly call it the *average*. We'll run into it again much later in the book.)

Now let's advance to the next step. Suppose George Senior, the dad, says that each son will receive a weekly allowance of $0.50 times his age, providing the son does his chores. How much does dad owe each week? Let's start with the eldest. Well, $G_1 =$ 15 years of age and by multiplying times $0.50 we get $7.50. We could have said $\frac{1}{2} G_1$ was his allowance (since that is $\$\frac{1}{2} \times 15$) and been equally accurate. So the total paid by dad will be $\$\frac{1}{2} G_1 + \frac{1}{2} G_2 + \cdots + \frac{1}{2} G_8$ or $\Sigma_i^8 = 1 \frac{1}{2} G_i$. We can move the constant $\frac{1}{2}$ outside the summation (since every single G_i is halved) so that this is the same as $\frac{1}{2} \times \Sigma_i^8 = 1\, G_i$ (this restates it as $\frac{1}{2}$ times the same sum which we calculated before at 64). So, $\frac{1}{2} \times 64 = \$32$, which is what dad owes each week. You had probably already figured that out in your head.

One more fancy step and we are done. Suppose now that George Senior wants to set up an incentive payout for good grades in school. Each son George will receive a single grade point average (GPA) for each semester's report card. Best is 4.0 (straight A's) and worst is 0.0 (straight F's). The following incentive payouts will apply (rounding up GPAs).

Grade	Payout
4.0	$2.00
3.5	$1.50
3.0	$1.00
2.5	$0.50
2.0 and lower	0

But to adjust for age dad will multiply the age times payout. That is, G_1 at 15 years old will receive 15 × $2 for a 4.0 grade = $30. G_2 at 13 years old would only receive 13 × $2 = $26 for the same 4.0 grade average. So each payment due is age × payout. At this point the grades and payouts are unknown. We can easily abbreviate payouts as P. Let's call the grade payouts $P_1, P_2, \ldots, P_8$ for sons $G_1, G_2, \ldots, G_8$, respectively. Therefore, any individual payment due to a child is age (G_i) × payout rate (P_i) or $G_i \times P_i$.

Recapping, any individual payment can be shown by $G_i \times P_i$. The result of multiplying two or more things is called the *product*. The sum of all eight payments would be represented by

$$\sum_{i=1}^{8} G_i \times P_i$$

which is the sum of each and every one of the products $G_i \times P_i$. We must, of course, figure out what the grade payments $P_1, P_2, \ldots, P_8$ are or we can't get a real answer for any $G_i \times P_i$. But you can see the simple power of using the summation sign Σ to add up all the individual products $G_i \times P_i$. We will need to use this summing up process soon in our analysis of options.

In option analysis we need to find the products of all the individual probabilities times their payouts. We must then sum these products cumulatively (hence the need for Σ) to demonstrate the fair price for buying an option for a given sector or strike. Let's thank George for allowing us to use his sons as variables in our algebra lesson and bid him farewell. It's back to options for us.

KEY CONCEPTS REVIEW

+ In this chapter we made further progress on linking coin toss games to options by showing how coin toss sectors are very similar to an option's strike price.

- Coin options require that we select the sector that we wish to wager on, such as "more than 2 heads" in a four coin toss game (implying 2H, 3H, and 4H). We win when the outcome falls within the range of the sector we've chosen.

- Options in financial markets use a similar sector concept, but traders call the sector they've selected the *strike price*. This originated from the striking of a deal at a particular kick-in price, say, $120 for IBM. The kick-in price became known as the strike price.

- By selecting the sector with the largest range we would obviously win more often. But what would we win? The fair game analysis would tell the players that "sure things" have very high probabilities and thus demand extremely small payoffs. Whichever selection you make, the payoff will be adjusted to make it appropriate for its likelihood of occurrence. And then there is the cost of the option.

- The cost you pay to own an option (called the *premium*) exactly offsets the expected gain in a fair game (one where everyone is expected to break even). As we know from earlier studies, expected gains can be derived directly from the interplay of all the probabilities and payoffs.

- Thus, if we take into consideration the cost for borrowing money, the process of which is called discounting, we can tell you the fair value of an option: An option's fair value is its expected gain, discounted by the rate of interest for borrowing.

- Since we will need to add up many, many probabilities times payoffs later on, we introduced a math symbol to make it much easier: the summation sign Σ, which is the Greek letter sigma. In the optional math tutorial, we showed how to use it to sum up the ages of the eight little George Foremans.

THINGS TO THINK ABOUT

Circular Reasoning and Equations?   It may seem that we are going in an unending loop of circles because everything seems to equal everything else. In one sense this is true. But that is what happens when you set up equations to solve problems. By definition we are equating one set of values to another. But there is a method to our madness. Just like in a detective mystery we are setting out all the pieces that we do know so that we can figure out what we don't know. What we do know is how a simple game such as coin tosses works and how we can equate it to options. We also know that if we have all the probabilities and payoffs we can compute the fair cost of a coin toss option. What we don't know yet is how to translate that to the world of stocks and bonds. But we are getting closer.

Show Me the Money, Jerry! Another problem with our circular logic is that there doesn't seem to be any way to make money! Everything always breaks even. Yet it is clear that some people and firms make fortunes while others lose. What is going on here? We discuss making money in later chapters and point out the specific ways that traders and firms do so. But consider this: You and a friend sit down to a serious game of tossing coins. You bring big bankrolls and plan to stay until one of you is broke and the other is rich. Just because big money will eventually be won and lost does not change the fact that the game is inherently fair (over the long run) and that neither of you has an expected advantage going in. This means that even though we are describing a break-even game, as are all the formulas involving it, big money can still be won and lost if you play for big stakes. You just don't have any positive expectation of winning is all. Mathematically speaking neither of you has an expected gain or an expected loss at the outset. But if one of you can figure out an edge, a special tidbit of knowledge that swings the odds slightly in your favor, well then, that changes the whole ball of wax, doesn't it? There are no perfect coins and there are no perfect markets. Finding out what those edges might be, however, is no easy task.

QUESTIONS

1. The title for this chapter is Sectors, Strike Prices, and Summation Signs. What sectors are we referring to?

2. What is a cumulative sector when referring to coin tosses?

3. What is a strike price?
4. Why did we compare cumulative coin toss sectors to strike prices?
5. What is Σ, and what does it represent in math?
6. Why do we need Σ for our purposes?
7. Betting on a high probability event is not always the best idea. Why not?
8. What does the following formula tell us: cost = probability $\times$ payoff?
9. What do we mean by option fair value = expected gain (discounted)?
10. We've mentioned on occasion that expected gain = expected loss. Why does this make sense?
11. From the optional math tutorial: Here is a summation sign with several subscripts. What does each one mean?

$$\sum_{i=1}^{8} G_i$$

CHAPTER 8

The Fair Price of an Option

In Chap. 7 we learned that the strike price of an option was loosely analogous to the coin toss sectors we chose earlier (0H, 1H, 2H, etc.). We found that since an option typically kicked in across multiple sectors we would need to learn how to enumerate all such probabilities and payoffs, multiply them together, and sum their products. Over the previous chapters we have been laying the basic groundwork so that we might begin to understand real-world options. We have a great support structure in place, so it's time to slowly start expanding upward and outward.

Here is an important idea we broached in Chap. 7 and will develop further now:

> The fair value of an option is the mathematically expected gain for the price sector (strike) chosen.

Mathematically expected gain is the statistician's way to say "the average gain found over many past cases that would be expected again over the course of many new cases." We saw in Chap. 7 that the expected gain varies according to which strike price (or coin toss sector) we have chosen. Here is how we can calculate expected gain:

1. Select the price sector (strike) on which to base an option.

2. Create a complete distribution of possible payoffs for each outcome.

3. Create a complete distribution of probabilities that correspond to each payoff.

4. Multiply step 2 by step 3, one at a time creating products. Sum up the products.

Step 4 weights each payoff by its probability. You're done. These four steps are represented as follows in math shorthand: Σ Payoff$_i$ $\times$ probability$_i$. This is the same formula for summing the products covered in the optional math tutorial in Chap. 7. Now pay attention here:

> Calculating expected gain is the most important part of the option puzzle.

The result of the summing formula Σ payoff$_i$ $\times$ probability$_i$ gives the expected gain, which is the fair value of each option (before discounting). The list of how to calculate expected gain is very simple, but it is difficult to execute. Figuring out how to execute this list is what options are all about!

The first two steps are very easy. The difficulty begins with step 3: analyzing and describing the proper probabilities for each and every outcome payoff. Executing this in the world beyond coin tosses requires a lot more knowledge than we presently have; it is our goal to learn how to do this. By mulling over what we've learned about expected gains with coin tosses we can tinker a bit and slowly wend our way into the real world.

Let's review our simple four coin toss case and begin to see the adjustments necessary to link coin tosses to price moves.

Coin Toss Option	Sector of Payout	Probability	Cum. Prob.
0H or more	0H, 1H, 2H, 3H, 4H	1/16 + 4/16 + 6/16 + 4/16 + 1/16	16/16
1H or more	1H, 2H, 3H, 4H	4/16 + 6/16 + 4/16 + 1/16	15/16
2H or more	2H, 3H, 4H	6/16 + 4/16 + 1/16	11/16
3H or more	3H, 4H	4/16 + 1/16	5/16
4H or more	4H	1/16	1/16

Here comes a small curve ball. We can't value these coin toss options because payoffs have not been agreed on! We are familiar with tossing a coin for a dollar a toss, but we *could* design any number of payoff schedules instead: maybe a bonus for four heads or four tails or maybe a dollar for the first head, double for the second head, double again for the third head, and so on. The payoff schedule is crucial.

Another point is that since options allow for no further payment, the typical coin toss game payoff schedule has to be readjusted. The typical schedule of payoffs for tossing coins is based on no money up front and settling up after the event. Winnings and losses are based on the net heads or tails. We can't have the option buyer paying out $4 just because zero heads comes in. See the following table:

Typical Coin Toss Schedule of Payout

Outcome	Net Heads	At $1 per Toss
0H	−4	−$4
1H	−2	−$2
2H	0	0
3H	+2	+$2
4H	+4	+$4

Option buyers make no further payments after the initial upfront premium, so this payoff schedule is unacceptable to them. We must restructure the coin payoff schedule to appropriately fit an option. We will, for the sake of simplicity, pick a new payoff schedule of $1 per head (this differs from netting heads + tails as above). We repeat the coin option probabilities from the first table in this chapter, but add the new payoffs:

Coin Toss Option Strike	Sector of Payout	Cum. Prob.	Payout ($)
0H or more	0H, 1H, 2H, 3H, 4H	16/16	0, 1, 2, 3, 4
1H or more	1H, 2H, 3H, 4H	15/16	1, 2, 3, 4
2H or more	2H, 3H, 4H	11/16	2, 3, 4
3H or more	3H, 4H	5/16	3, 4
4H	4H	1/16	4

Notice that the Payout column has more than one choice except for 4H. This is because there are as many as five successful outcomes in some sectors, each with a different payoff. If, for instance, you select "0H or more" as your option, you would win if 0H, 1H, 2H, 3H, or 4H came in. Regardless of the outcome you will get into the payoff zone. We said the payoff will be $1 per head, so 0H has a payoff of $0, 1H pays $1, 2H pays $2, and so forth. We can't tell the payoff until the result comes in, but we now have a payoff schedule for each possible outcome.

The total probability of the "0H or more" option finishing in the payoff zone is 16/16 or 100 percent probability. We must now distribute that 16/16 appropriately to each individual result and then multiply them out. The sum of these products is the fair option premium. The following table analyzes the "0H or more" option premium:

Possible Outcome within Payoff Sector	Individual Probability	Individual Payoff	Prob$_i$ × Pay$_i$
0H	1/16	$0	$0
1H	4/16	$1	$4/16
2H	6/16	$2	$12/16
3H	4/16	$3	$12/16
4H	1/16	$4	$4/16
			Total = $32/16

Similarly we could have used our summing shorthand (Σ):*

---

*Note: We may switch the order of multiplying probability and payoffs in the formulas we use, because the order is irrelevant when items are multiplied. This apparent change merely reflects a convenient way to discuss the data as they happen to be laid out in the text at that time. Multiplication will not change the final result, or *product* as it's called in math. For example, 3 × 4 × 5 always equals 60 regardless of whether we multiply 5 × 4 × 3 or 4 × 3 × 5. As long as we understand that the summing up doesn't occur until each pair of payoffs and probabilities has been multiplied, we'll get it right. Also, if we use shortened names like *prob* for probability and *pay* for payoff, it doesn't change the formula at all; it might mean we didn't have enough space at the time.

$$\sum_{i=0}^{4} \text{Prob}_i \times \text{payoff}_i = (\text{prob}_0 \times \text{pay}_0) + (\text{prob}_1 \times \text{pay}_1)$$

$$+ (\text{prob}_2 \times \text{pay}_2) + (\text{prob}_3 \times \text{pay}_3)$$
$$+ (\text{prob}_4 \times \text{pay}_4)$$
$$= 0 + \$4/16 + \$12/16 + \$12/16$$
$$+ \$4/16 = \$32/16$$

Up-front premium = \$32/16 = \$2.00

The fair value premium is \$2.00, and this is what the buyer should be charged. Don't forget this is the "retire-to-Tahiti" perfect scenario. It pays off 100 percent of the time. It's just that *options aren't free*. An option buyer would expect to gain \$2.00 on an average result based on this game, these probabilities, and this payoff schedule. So any sane option seller must charge the buyer \$2.00 to stay solvent. Over any short-run series of results one of you will probably be ahead of the other, but over a long, long series you will both tend closer and closer to breaking even.*

Just as a point of trivia we might note that there is no difference in payoff between the "0H or more" option and the "1H or more" option. The only different outcome between the two is 0H which pays off at \$0. So excluding $\text{prob}_0 \times \text{pay}_0$ (which equals \$0) isn't excluding any payoff money. But we can change everything by increasing the payoff schedule as follows:

---

*Note: The math actually says that your expected gain or loss in percent will tend toward zero. But there is still a reasonable probability that you will be a tiny percent away from not breaking even, say 1/4 percent, for example. This *seems* negligible until you realize that you may have bet \$1 million by that long-run point and so you will be \$2500 away from breaking even. This is part of the gambler's fallacy wherein gamblers think they must get back to break even at some reasonable near-term point, according to the law of averages. The law of averages is a layperson's corruption of the law of large numbers, which talks about the tendency toward zero percent that we just described. Mathematicians see 1/4 percent as just one of many possible variations that will occur with reasonable probability. And they expect the fluctuation above and below zero percent to go on forever. In short, their understanding of the law says, "Don't hold your breath. It could be a few months, years, or decades before the dice, roulette wheel, or cards turn your way to break you even. You could be bankrupted a dozen times before it occurs. These are just typical fluctuations in the normal scheme of the way random systems operate."

Outcome	Individual New Payoff
0H	$5
1H	$6
2H	$7
3H	$8
4H	$9

Let's now calculate the "0H or more" option premium:

Possible Outcome (within Payoff Sector)	Individual Probability	Individual New Payoff	$Prob_i \times Pay_i$
0H	1/16	$5	$5/16
1H	4/16	$6	$24/16
2H	6/16	$7	$42/16
3H	4/16	$8	$32/16
4H	1/16	$9	$9/16
			Total = $112/16 = $7.00

The "0H or more" fair premium has now jumped from $2.00 based on the original payoff schedule to $7.00 based on this new payoff schedule. And the premium for the next option sector (1H or more) is no longer the same, but is $5/16 less because that's what 0H pays out ($prob_0 \times pay_0 = \$5/16$). The "1H or more" option excludes this event and so doesn't have to pay when it occurs. So, based on this new payoff schedule, the "0H or more" sector no longer equals the "1H or more" sector.

In the end, we must closely analyze the payoff schedule and assess the probability of each possible payoff. As the payoff schedule changes so will the expected gain and thus the fair value of the option. In Chap. 9 we will begin to wend our way from coin tosses to price moves.

KEY CONCEPTS REVIEW

♦ The fair value of an option is the mathematically expected gain for the price sector (strike) chosen.

- Calculating expected gain is the most intricate and important part of the option puzzle. This is the backbone of all option formulas no matter how complex they get.
- Knowing only the probability of an event or its payoff is insufficient to determine a fair value. Both are necessary.
- We've previously learned that calculating expected gain requires us to sum up all the possible payoffs times their probabilities. Thus we can show that the fair value for an option = Σpayoff$_i$ × probability$_i$.
- We showed a simple list of steps to compute expected gains, but the last steps are very difficult to execute. Figuring out how to execute these steps is what option valuation is all about.

THINGS TO THINK ABOUT

An Option's Expected Gains   Many times, if thoughts are isolated or taken out of context they lose their original sense or purpose. For example, let's review this quote from the beginning of our chapter: "We saw in Chap. 7 that the expected gain varies according to which strike price (or coin toss sector) we have chosen."

This statement could be very misleading to someone merely browsing through the book and alighting on that statement without understanding the bigger picture that is under discussion. The browser might reason: "How can there be expected gains, ever, if you are always talking about fair games where everyone breaks even? And, if such gains exist, then why bother to go further? Just bet on that sector and rake in unlimited profits! Right?" It is good reasoning, but is out of context to our discussion.

Our discussions concern options, and options are strange creatures for there are no negative payoffs with options, only winning payoffs or breaking even. As such there are many zones of expected gains because we must cumulate all the winning payoffs and neglect the losing payoffs. Since the sum of the winners and losers should zero out (which is what creates the fairness of the game), we are merely splitting the winners and losers into two separate piles and ignoring the losing pile (for the moment). That is one of the exciting things about options: you get a shot at sharing the winning pile, but you have no risk of sharing in the losing pile. In a sense we are stripping out the winnings from the losses in a manner similar to the stripping done by bond traders who create interest only and principal only bonds (called IOs and POs). When you buy an option, you are buying a piece of the winners-only pile. That's why you must pay a premium to buy it. Also, you only collect if and when the event bet upon finally occurs. And that's only a probability, not a certainty.

Options Are Specific Bets versus Average Outcomes

Here is an advanced thought worth considering. Options are a bet on the specific versus the average. As we develop our methods for valuing options you can see that, like life insurance mortality tables, the methods for valuing options depend on average results over many, many cases. The valuing is thus based on generic average outcomes. But a trader chooses an option today based on what he or she feels is a very specific outcome in the near future. To be worthwhile the trader's specific outcome must argue against what the generic, average outcomes are understood to be, or there won't be any profit to be gained.

This is more easily understood if we compare it to dice. Our ability to predict the next toss of the dice is poor, but over many, many tosses our predictive skills are great. For instance, we know with great accuracy how many 2s and 12s will be thrown over the course of a million tosses. But if you happen to know that the specific probabilities surrounding the next few tosses are substantially different than the average, then you can benefit from it. If, through some brilliant insight, you can recognize a bias, or see that special patterns indicate that the next tosses are less random than usual, you can make money over the long haul by wagering on such situations. Of course, you need to be right about the bias or it just won't work out well.

We are not agreeing that you *can* know these things, we are only saying that *if* you know the specifics are different this time, then you will be betting on information that the mathematical models do not account for. In the case of options, when you buy an option you are, in fact, saying that you feel this time is not an average occasion, it is special. How well you do will be based on how good your predictive knowledge is. If you have no special knowledge, then you will, on average, break even over many attempts.

QUESTIONS

1. We said the following in the chapter: "We can't tell the payoff until the result comes in, but we now have a payoff schedule for each possible outcome." What was meant by this?

2. We created a simple four-step list to calculate expected gains at the beginning of the chapter. We added, however, that the list was difficult to execute. Why is that so?

3. We repeated a statement from Chap. 7 that "the fair value of each option was equal to the expected gain (before discounting)." What has discounting got to do with it?

4. We showed the math shorthand: Σ payoff$_i$ × probability$_i$. This is the same formula covered in the optional math tutorial from Chap. 7. How would you translate it for a beginner?

5. Why is the following formula called the sum of the products: Σ probability$_i$ × payoff$_i$?

6. We switched the order of probability$_i$ and payoff$_i$ in a few of the formulas. How does this switching of order impact the results?

7. We mentioned in the chapter that "The payoff schedule is crucial." Suppose we doubled the payoffs in our example in this chapter. What would that do to the fair option value? Suppose we tripled the payoffs?

CHAPTER 9

Our First Stock Option: IBM

Valuing an option is all about our ability to describe the many possible future outcomes that prices can have. We need to be able to compute the probabilities and payoffs for each possible future outcome. This is our goal and the essence of the work we must cover.

If we could sum up all the possible individual payoffs and weight them in accordance to their individual probabilities, we could derive how much an option is expected to be worth at expiry, on average. Throw in a little . . . "present-value" . . . analysis (interest rate discounting) and you have the value of an option purchased today.

Let's get a more down-to-earth impression of what this means. We begin our transition into stock market examples now and gradually replace coin tosses. Many of these examples should look familiar. You will quickly realize that we are repeating many of the same ideas we've already covered in our preliminary studies with coin tosses.

AN OPTION ON IBM

IBM stock opens today at $100 a share. We will review the worth of an option that expires based on today's close. First let's consider the simplest of all scenarios, a probability distribution where there is only one possible outcome.

The probability graph shown in Fig. 9–1 has basically only one piece of information to impart: there is a 100 percent chance that IBM will close at precisely $110 today. Obviously, we can never have information like this for we will never know anything certain about IBM's closing price hours beforehand. And a $10 jump is really a far-fetched reality on most days. But if we did have this information, could we figure out a fair option price?

The answer is clearly yes. A call option on IBM with a $100 strike price, would be worth $10 at the close ($110 minus $100 strike price), a $90 strike would be worth $20 at the close, an $80 strike would be worth $30 at the close, and so on. Throughout this entire chapter we will deal only with the $100 strike price for the IBM call to keep things simple.

There is no uncertainty in the closing price for this overly simplistic scenario, and so the calculation is simple. If everybody knows the expected closing value of IBM ($110), then no one will sell the option for less than $10. And no one will pay more than $10. The price for everyone is fairly balanced at $10. In fact, it will probably never trade because there is no perceived benefit to buy it or sell it at $10. And that is the only price it could trade unless you can find a sucker who doesn't know that the close is already preordained.

F I G U R E   9–1

One Possible Outcome

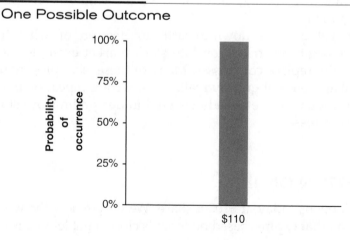

Today's closing IBM price

This is an easy scenario. Let's move on to the next simplest possible closing price situation depicted in Fig. 9–2.

Here there are two possibilities, each with a 50 percent likelihood: The price will close unchanged at $100 or else close at $110. This is a nice little investment. Half the time you break even, the other half of the time you make a $10 profit (provided, of course, you can buy it at the opening price of $100).

An option to buy IBM at $100 on the close is worth $0 in half the cases and $10 in the other half of the cases. This is not a simple one-case scenario, but we can easily figure out a fair price nonetheless. If we pay for each possibility according to its probability, we should pay zero times 50 percent and $10 times 50 percent. Summing these up, we get the following:

$$\$0 \times 0.50 + \$10 \times 0.50 = \$0 + \$5.00 = \$5.00$$

This is the fair value: the summing of payoffs × probabilities. We should be willing to pay exactly $5.00 for the call option to buy IBM at a $100 strike price.

Let's move on to a more complex closing scenario, depicted in Fig. 9–3. Notice how it resembles our four coin toss histograms. It should; we used the same probabilities.

We are getting a little closer to reality with each new scenario. Here there is no obvious bias to the upside as in the first two

F I G U R E   9–2

Two Possible Outcomes

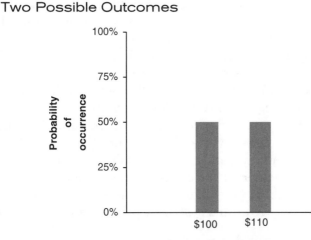

Today's closing IBM price

F I G U R E   9–3

Five Possible Outcomes

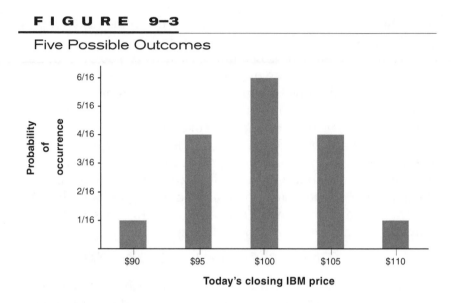

Today's closing IBM price

examples. And something new has entered the picture: IBM can go down! Having an option, however, allows us to *choose* whether or not we wish to actually buy IBM at $100 on the close. So, if it closes at $100 or less, we can just walk away, if we so choose, and we probably would.

Clearly, the option closing values are directly related to IBM's closing price as compared to the $100 strike price, but nothing was stated formally as of yet. This is a good time to cover the math for this concept. Mathematicians might call this trivial, but it can save us a lot of puzzlement later if we cover it now. The question at issue is, What is the value of an *expired* option? Or, in other words, What is the value of an option at *expiry* time? The mathematician's answer is max $[S - K, 0]$.

This looks complex, but it is actually very simple. It means we will receive the *maximum* of the two payoff choices: $S - K$ or zero. If the algebraic value $S - K$ has a positive value (that is, it is worth more than zero), we receive that positive value. In the alternative we pay nothing and receive nothing. This is because it is an option. The owner of an option is never required to pay anything at the end. In other words, in the worst-case scenario, you break even. $S - K$ means *spot stock* price minus strike price.

So, if IBM closes at $110 and the strike is $100, then $S - K$ is $110 − $100, which is +$10. You receive $10. If, however, IBM closes at $88, then $S - K$ is $88 − $100, which is negative $12. You, therefore, receive zero because $S - K$ doesn't have a positive value. The upside of an option is that you never have to pay extra at the end, even if the situation goes bad. So, when you see the math expression max $[S - K, 0]$ in option books, it won't look so forbidding any longer. And the Black-Scholes formula uses the expression $S - K$, so you'll do well to remember it.

Some confusion might arise because we have used $100 for several values. We show that IBM opens at $100, closes at $100, and the strike price is also $100. The strike price of an option is the cutoff or kick-in level. With a call option, like we are discussing, we receive *nothing* until IBM closes above that price. Below this we get zero. The strike price is never plotted in the graphs in this chapter. At the bottom of the charts (the x axis), we have been plotting IBM's closing price. We want to begin to show you how much the option is worth at expiration, and we can do this by plotting IBM's closing price minus $100. We show the positive value or zero otherwise. This is what the call option would pay at expiration, max $[S - K, 0]$.

We center all the graphs at $100 because that is where IBM starts the day. If today's opening price for IBM was $175, that would be the center of each graph. The most likely closing price for any stock is also it's opening price. Random walk and all that. On the histogram it's the bar in the center. As usual it represents the highest probability event. When we display what the option payoffs might be, the center is $100 − 100 = 0$.

The graph in Fig. 9–4 represents the probabilities of the option payoffs when IBM closes at $90, $95, $100, $105, and $110. To graph option payoffs on the x axis we must compute the IBM closing price minus $100. Therefore, any IBM closing price of $100 or less will show as an option payoff of zero. Some payoffs would show as negative if options could have a negative value, but they cannot since it is always your choice to exercise or not. Exercising your rights to buy IBM at $100 when it closes at $95 leads to a loss of $5, so you wouldn't do it. This limits the downside value of the option to breaking even, that is, zero. The data are shown in the following table.

F I G U R E   9–4

Five Option Payoff Outcomes

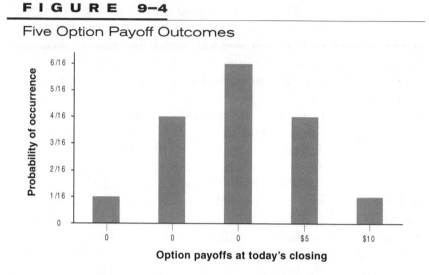

Option payoffs at today's closing

IBM Close	Probability	Option Payoff
$90	1/16	$0
95	4/16	0
100	6/16	0
105	4/16	5
110	1/16	10
	Total = 16/16	

We can use the data in this table to sum all the probabilities × payoffs:

$$\left(\frac{1}{16} \times \$0\right) + \left(\frac{4}{16} \times \$0\right) + \left(\frac{6}{16} \times \$0\right) + \left(\frac{4}{16} \times \$5\right) + \left(\frac{1}{16} \times \$10\right)$$

This simplifies to

$$\$0 + \$0 + \$0 + \$20/16 + \$10/16 = \$30/16$$

Since $30/16 = $1.875, that would be the fair price to pay given the probability distribution in the graph and table. A change to any probability or payoff we used will change the fair price.

Here's a more intuitive way to view the fair price we just calculated: If you pay $30/16 each time you buy this call option, you'll neither lose nor win; you'll break even. The reason why is that if you make this bet 16 times, you will pay 16 × $30/16 which equals $30. During these 16 tries you'll get back $5 four times (4 out of 16) and once you'll be paid $10 (1 out of 16). So, $5 × 4 + $10 × 1 = $20 + $10 = $30 total will be paid back to you. You've broken even on average over the 16 cases: a net expected gain of zero.

You may have noticed that we were really only interested in two bars on the last graph: the $5 payoff and the $10 payoff. Why? Because the others were payoffs of zero and thus added a zero amount to the option value. So we could say that in option valuation we will only be analyzing the piece of the graph that has a payoff greater than zero. This can cut down heavily on the number of computations we need to make.

We now make a big jump in complexity. Allowing for the fact that there are often many more than 1, 2, or 5 potential closing prices, we make the leap to 21 possible closing prices. Why 21? Because it fits nicely with a 20 coin toss event having 21 outcomes. In earlier chapters we discussed the 10 coin toss event in detail and showed how to work out the probabilities. Even though a 20 coin toss is certainly more complex, the process is identical. An added benefit is that histograms become smoother as the number of bars increase, which takes us closer and closer to viewing real-world scenarios.

We will use the following probability distribution table and the graph of Fig. 9–5.

Tossing 20 Coins

No. of Heads	No. of Paths	Probability (%)
0	1	0.00
1	20	0.00
2	190	0.02
3	1,140	0.11
4	4,845	0.46
5	15,504	1.48
6	38,760	3.70
7	77,520	7.39

Tossing 20 Coins (Continued)

No. of Heads	No. of Paths	Probability (%)
8	125,970	12.01
9	167,960	16.02
10	184,756	17.62
11	167,960	16.02
12	125,970	12.01
13	77,520	7.39
14	38,760	3.70
15	15,504	1.48
16	4,845	0.46
17	1,140	0.11
18	190	0.02
19	20	0.00
20	1	0.00
	1,048,576	100.00
	(total paths)	(total probability)

Translating coin toss payoffs into IBM prices requires some imagination. As we know, in a typical 20 coin toss game if the outcome is 10 heads, we have broken even. For the IBM stock, we

FIGURE   9–5

Twenty-One Possible Outcomes

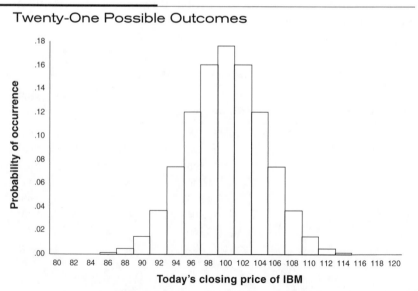

break even when the closing price is the same as the opening price, which is $100. On the histogram of Fig. 9–5 we are suggesting that each head greater than (or less than) 10 heads is worth $2 per share to IBM's closing price. In this way the maximum you can win or lose on IBM is $20 a share, just as we could win or lose a maximum of $20 if we were tossing for $1 a coin. This histogram gives us the best representation yet of the whole range of possible IBM closing prices. This is because it includes the largest number of outcomes so far (21) and begins to look a lot more like the real world. Also note that we can only see 15 of the 21 bars because some are too short to print, but they still have a probability value slightly greater than zero and cannot be ignored in our calculations. The shortest bars happen to represent the biggest winning and losing scenarios! What they lack in probability, they more than make up for in payoff. It is these extreme cases that make or break the average option trader.

The histogram in Fig. 9–6 is identical to the one in Fig. 9–5 except that it represents the option payoff values and so we subtracted the usual $100 from the IBM closing prices and omitted any results that were not positive. We shaded the bars that show profits.

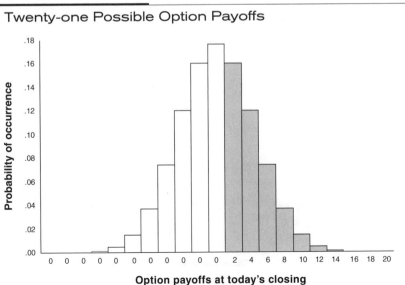

F I G U R E   9–6

Twenty-one Possible Option Payoffs

Option payoffs at today's closing

If we could get a probability value for each payoff greater than $0 and sum up all the probabilities × payoffs, we could create the fair option price for this probability distribution. To spare us the agony of all the math we will not do it here, but be assured it is the same step by step as the first three examples we did and, we hope you see, just as valid.

One final jump and we are done with this lesson. As we try to approach reality with our simple IBM example we must include more and more possibilities for IBM's closing price. You can see visually that what we are approaching is a probability distribution that is much smoother and more continuous than any of the coin toss histograms we have shown since the beginning. We are approaching the use of a probability distribution that can no longer be easily represented by skinny, rectangular bars on a histogram, but instead becomes a smooth curve that represents probability in height and payoff in width. Such a smooth curve is illustrated in Fig. 9–7.

The same curve representing option payoffs instead of IBM closing prices is illustrated in Fig. 9–8. The shading shows the area where the call option pays off. If (and when) we can evaluate the shaded area for individual probabilities and payoffs, we can give

F I G U R E   9–7

Smooth Curve Distribution

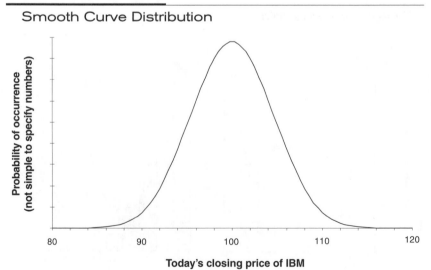

Today's closing price of IBM

F I G U R E   9–8

Smooth Curve Distribution of Option Payoffs

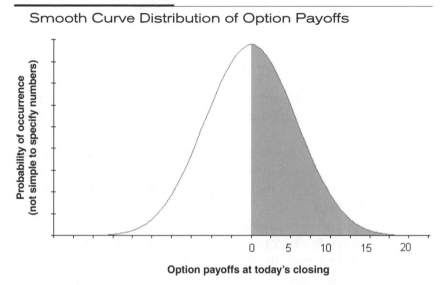

Option payoffs at today's closing

a value to this option. The problem is that this probability distribution is made up of an infinite number of extremely narrow bars, any individual one of which is invisible to the eye. We must multiply the height of each bar (its probability) times its payoff value and sum them all up—and there is an infinite number of them.

To mesh more properly with the real world we must determine a more realistic price range (based on a stock's volatility) for a more realistic time period (today's closing is too near at hand to be practical, but is nice to use and easy to see). If we then add a bit of interest rate magic (so far interest costs have been zero because we assumed everything happens in a few hours), we would have a workable option formula.

Anybody who knows how to adjust stock prices for volatility, divine the probability and payoff for each infinitely thin bar, multiply them out (an infinite number of multiplications), and then sum them up is light-years ahead of us. He or she can skip the next 10 chapters. For the rest of us, it's time to go back to the beginning, and we'll show you gradually how and why we can create a probability distribution for the future and how we can manipulate the infinite number of possibilities each distribution provides. We weren't kidding when we told you that we should think of distributions as our answer tables. Without them we couldn't work out the option answer in a million years.

KEY CONCEPTS REVIEW

* Valuing an IBM option is all about our ability to describe the many possible future outcomes that IBM stock prices can have.
* If we know all of today's possible closing IBM prices and can weight them in accordance to their probabilities, we can derive how much an option expiring today will be worth, on average.
* The payoff is easily figured if we know IBM's closing price. It's the difference between IBM's closing price and the strike price, but can never be less than zero.
* The formal payoff formula is max $[S - K, 0]$, which implies that the payoff can never be negative. It says you will receive the maximum of these two choices: (1) IBM's closing price minus the strike price or (2) zero.
* If IBM has a 50-50 chance of closing at $100 or $110 today, the call option to buy IBM at a $100 strike price is worth $5.00, on average: $0 × 0.50 + $10 × 0.50 = $0 + $5.00 = $5.00.
* Here's an intuitive way to view an option's fair value: The total you must pay to buy the option over, say, 100 cases will equal the sum of all the payoffs you'll receive over those 100 cases. You'll neither lose nor win, you'll break even. You'll be paid back precisely what you have laid out (on average) and will have broken even for a net expected gain of zero.
* A big jump up to 21 possible IBM closing prices improved the accuracy of our analysis. But as we'll see in Chap. 11, it still leaves far too much room for error. We need to add many, many more possible closing prices.
* As we try to approximate the real world we require an enormous number of closing prices. Each closing price must have its own bar on our probability histogram. We

need so many bars that we must make them skinnier and skinnier until they disappear from view. The histogram starts to lose its rectangular skyscraper shape and turn into a smooth curve called the normal distribution. It still maintains the same familiar meanings for us: probability in height and payoff in width.

◆ To determine a more realistic closing price range we must base it on how volatile our stock is. And today's closing price is too near at hand, so we must find how to use more realistic time frames, say, a month or a year. If we can manage this and also add a bit of interest rate magic, we will have a workable option formula for stocks.

THINGS TO THINK ABOUT

The Importance of S − K   We introduced the formal payoff expression max $[S - K, 0]$ in this chapter. This simply implies that the payoff at expiry can never be negative. It says you will receive the maximum of these two choices: (1) IBM's closing price minus the strike price, *or* (2) zero. Therefore, this expression represents the value of an option at expiry.

But other important option ideas are linked to the $S - K$ expression also, like the important concept of moneyness we discussed in Chap. 1. $S - K$ gives us a sense of whether an option is in-the-money (ITM), at-the-money (ATM), or out-of-the-money (OTM). Also, the Black-Scholes option formula uses the expression $S - K$. See if you can identify whether a stock is ITM, ATM, or OTM using $S - K$.

In Defense of the Littlest Bars   In this chapter we discussed the probability histogram of IBM's closing prices (which had 21 bars). We noted that 6 of the 21 bars were too short to print but that they still had a probability value slightly greater than zero and could not be ignored in our calculations. It turns out that the smallest bars happen to represent the biggest winning and losing scenarios because they occur so far from the center (which is the most recent price). What they lack in probability, they more than make up for in payoff. Why do you think these very few cases have such great impact on an option trader's profit and loss for the year?

QUESTIONS

Use the expression max $[S - K, 0]$ to help with questions 1 to 4.

   1. IBM closes at $109. The strike price is $90 for a call option expiring at the close. What is the option worth at expiry?
   2. IBM closes at $96.50. The strike price for a call option expiring at the close is $100. What is the option worth at expiry?
   3. IBM closes at $89. The strike price for a call option expiring at the close is $85. You had to pay $4 to buy the option. What is the option worth at expiry, and how much profit did you make?
   4. IBM closes at $115. You own two call options expiring at the close. Their strikes are $105 and $125. You paid $5 and $2 for them in the morning. What are the options worth, and what is your profit for the day?

Use the histogram in Fig. 9–9 to answer questions 5 to 7.

   5. If you buy IBM at $100 in the morning, what is your expected gain at the close? (*Hint:* You should sum all the probabilities $\times$ payoffs.)
   6. Assume you have a call option struck at $100 that expires at the close. What is its expected value at the close? How much should you be willing to pay for it before the close?
   7. In questions 5 and 6 we found there was no expected gain for IBM stock at the close but that the call option had an expected value at the close of $1.875. Why does the option have value if we don't expect the stock to gain (on average)?

For questions 8 to 12 we will ask you to evaluate a call option (strike price of $100) that expires at the close. For these examples we create overly simple probability distributions (there are only two possible closing prices, and each has 50 percent likelihood).

F I G U R E   9–9

Five Possible Outcomes

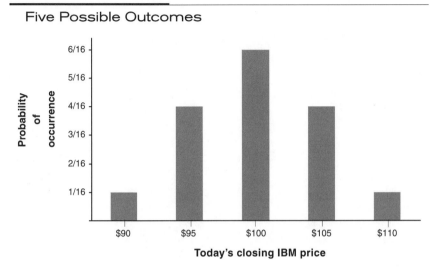

Today's closing IBM price

8. If the stock can only close at $90 or $110, what is the option worth?

9. If the stock can only close at $85 or $115, what is the option worth?

10. If the stock can only close at $70 or $130, what is the option worth?

11. If the stock can only close at $0 or $200, what is the option worth?

12. Now notice that in questions 8 to 11 we suggested a closing price range that kept getting wider (which is a measure of increased volatility). But the expected gain for the stock stayed steady at zero, since the downside offset the upside exactly. Despite this the worth of the options kept increasing more and more. What was happening? How did increasing volatility affect the option values?

CHAPTER 10

Statistics: The 15-Minute Cram Course

In this chapter we introduce a few of the basics critical to understanding statistics. You won't be a whiz on statistics after this very short introduction, but it might put you more at ease with the chapters that soon follow. We start with a far-out example that shows that when trying to predict the future, past data is *everything*. By the end of this chapter you'll become acquainted with a handful of new statistical phrases needed by every option trader.

WHERE PREDICTIONS COME FROM

The next example requires an affinity for science fiction and a playful imagination. You must suspend your disbelief for a few minutes as we detour into the "Twilight Zone."

You wake up in a dark, unfamiliar room with a whopping headache. (So far it sounds like a *lot* of Saturday mornings to us!) You can hardly think straight, but your last memory is distinct: bright lights, weird colors, aliens beaming you aboard their UFO. After shivering for a while, you make your first prediction: It was all a bad dream and you are merely suffering a hangover.

Why do you predict this? Because it is the most sensible, likely explanation in your repertoire of experiences. You have no real-life experience with UFOs and aliens, but you have had many experiences with nightmares, science fiction movies, and, unfortunately, with the flulike symptoms of a hangover. You're a regular Sherlock Holmes and not even proud of yourself for it. Without even realizing it you've automatically invoked Occam's Razor, that ancient maxim of logical thinking: choose the simplest story to fit all the known facts.

Unfortunately, your prediction is wrong. You really *have* been abducted by aliens! You are about to awaken on the planet Antares about a zillion light-years from the Earth. In fact, a huge alien has just entered your room. So much for your first prediction.

You are not harmed, but are treated like a guest. Your deep state of shock wears off gradually over the next few days—you think it is days, anyway. Slowly, over time, you become accommodated to your new surroundings. The aliens reveal themselves to you only a bit at a time as they let you slowly phase into their world. You come to realize that you must be jet-lagged worse than any human before you in history. But, being human, and therefore curious, you can't stop puzzling out the situation and making more predictions.

You decide it is daytime outside (even though you have no window). But when you are taken outside a short time later, you find it is nighttime, with a double moon hanging low in the sky. You predict, to yourself, that the sun will come up in a few hours. But it turns out that it is nighttime here for 2 weeks at a time. And the Antareans ignore day and night. They have a 36-hour sleep cycle. That is, 36 hours awake and 36 hours asleep. Clearly, you don't know anything about this world and all your predictions have flopped miserably.

After a while you begin to see some patterns of regularity. Every alien seems to be equal in height. They are twice the size of humans and look to be 12 feet tall. Trying to regain your confidence you predict the next alien you see will be 12 feet tall. And you are right. The same is true for the next half dozen aliens you see. The average alien is 12 feet tall; in fact, *every* alien is exactly 12 feet tall. There is no variance at all. This leads to perfect predictability.

Then you find out that there is a second type of alien on this planet. They are known as Betas, second-class citizens limited to menial jobs. Also, they are much shorter, only about 6 feet tall. Measuring them against yourself you realize they seem to vary from 5 to 7 feet tall. In fact, when you try to predict the height of the next Beta you meet, you are frequently off by a few inches. On average they are about your height, 6 feet tall, but the variance of 12 inches either way makes precise predictions very difficult. You start wondering, maybe there is some way to systematically improve your predictions.

But then you wake up back on the Earth with a really, really bad hangover!

Much later, long after the headache passes, you still vividly recall the dream and the embarrassment you felt when you failed miserably with every prediction made. Was it due to your total lack of knowledge about an alien society? Yes, that's it. Then, as if a light suddenly clicks on in your head, the epiphany comes. You see it quite clearly now: Our ability to make accurate predictions is based on having had many similar experiences in the past. Furthermore, we cannot predict an event exactly unless it never varies. The more variation that is possible, the less precise our prediction must be if we are to have any reasonable hope of it coming true. When variations exist, we may be able to assess probabilities, but never certainty.

THE PAST IS PROLOGUE TO THE FUTURE

If you are put into a strange world, you have no legitimate basis for making assumptions until you develop adequate experience. But it is in the nature of human beings, even those miserably lacking in the skills, to act the wise person, powerful and all-knowing. Ignorance has never stopped anyone from making assumptions and guesses, which is probably why there are so many darned problems in the world. As Amarillo Slim, one of the world's greatest poker players, has said: "Guessers are losers."

We can't be guessing if we are to accurately predict the future; we have to *know*. Every scientific endeavor should start with a concession to ignorance and then build a base of data by developing adequate experience. Otherwise even the smartest person in the world would be left clueless as to the probabilities of the likely outcomes.

Take the great Sherlock Holmes, as an example. If ever there was a case of a smugly cynical, all-seeing, too-big-for-his-britches know-it-all, he was the one. Far from being human, he was basically a supercomputer who had developed an encyclopedic knowledge of the sciences and all of humankind's experiences, along with instant recall. There seemed to be no problem that was insoluble to his enormous intellect. But here is an interesting tidbit: even he wasn't born that way. Without the encyclopedic knowledge and memories, gained from experience, he would be merely a brand-new supercomputer, fresh from the box with empty disk drives, whirring and clacking to no avail. Past knowledge and experiences are everything, even to geniuses.

So, when confronting a new environment or a new problem, we must collect data to assess what's going on. That which is regular and normal will become apparent only over time. And since most things have variations built into them, we must develop a methodology for dealing with these variations if we want to be able to predict the future. The methods that scientists and statisticians use revolve around finding out what is average and then finding out how much variation there usually is from the average.

The average is a midpoint. A sort of middle-of-the-road measurement. Because the average gives us no hint as to how much variation we can expect from all the other cases, it does not necessarily give us a terrific picture of the whole group. But since it is the center, it is not a bad place to start. If we then go a step further to develop ways to measure variation, we will have a far better system of representing our experiences. And if the same type of experiences are repeated in the future, as tends to happen often, we might be able to make predictions with some level of confidence. Thank goodness we are back on planet Earth where we have a base of knowledge and experience!

STATISTICS: MEASURING THE PAST

Statistics begins with the collection of data. Collect a ton of it and try to make sense of it later. The reason statisticians collect and measure data is because they are searching for patterns. Like engineers and scientists they are always trying to understand how things work. And when they can't find patterns, they feel they have wasted their time. It implies that they've failed to understand the data. They have gone to school for years in search of this type of knowledge. And while they may not even recognize it themselves, they long to do what others cannot: predict the future. To do this they have learned that they must unravel all the patterns that occur and then sort them into patterns that work. Finding patterns that repeat is everything to a statistician.

But most of us do not have the monklike fervor of statisticians, and so the study of statistics comes up a bit dry and indigestible, sort of like unfrosted shredded wheat or pancakes without syrup. But if we want to understand markets and options, a small dose is good for us, necessary even, no matter how distasteful.

There are two statistical methods we have touched on already: the binomial distribution and the normal distribution. We have spent time creating binomial distributions via coin tosses. We will describe the whys and wherefores of the normal distribution in the next chapters, as we need them. For now we will merely hit a few of the high points regarding distributions in general in as short a lesson as we know how. Where we point out how some of these factors relate to the normal distribution, it's just to give us a running start on Chap. 11, and we'll repeat it again later, so don't worry.

The First Pattern: Distributions Bunch Up in the Center

Centuries of collecting data have allowed statisticians to find many common patterns amid the data. One highly noticeable pattern is called *central tendency*. This means that after we plot the data on a sheet of graph paper we often find that it isn't wildly distributed all over the page, but has a tendency to clump together. In fact, the clumpiest point, usually at the center, is a very important part of statistical distributions. We call this central point the *average* in everyday language. Mathematicians call it the *mean*. They both refer to the same thing, the *center of the data*. So, the single most important measure of any group of data is the average or mean. Adding up all the data and dividing by the number of data points gives you the average or mean.

The average or mean is an easy statistic to calculate and understand, but it rarely tells the whole tale. We borrow the following silly, but brilliant, example from another book: A paid volunteer, possibly a very young and hungry university student, lies down on a bench in a laboratory. The experimenters arrange to stick his head in a subzero freezer at minus 100 degrees Fahrenheit (°F). At the same time, they stick his feet in an oven at 240°F. On average he is kept at a very comfortable 70°F (typical room temperature). Do you think he *feels* like he is at room temperature? Is it a surprise that he develops frostbite on one end and blisters on the other? Do you think he will volunteer again next week?

Obviously, extremes matter in this case. And they matter a lot in other sorts of data measurements too. After finding the average or mean, the next important question is, How far do all the data points stray from this central point (the mean)? Measuring the amount that data varies from the mean gives us the second most important fact about a distribution. This is called variance, or deviation from the mean. *Variance* is an important statistical term, and it measures deviation from the center. Statisticians have created a special formula for measuring variance which we will briefly discuss in a bit. There is another closely related formula that calculates another version of the variance called the *standard deviation*. We'll take a quick look at how that works too.

The mean and variance are the two most critical facts about each and every normal distribution. In fact, if you know those two facts, you have properly identified the whole normal distribution. You don't need to hunt around for other information because you have it all. The mean tells us where the center of the distribution is, and the variance tells us how wide the distribution is. Change the mean or the variance and you have an entirely different normal distribution. Mean and variance are the fingerprints of each normal distribution.

We discuss one last insight and then end the chapter with a simple example. If you know the variance, then you also know the standard deviation (it's the square root of the variance). So, knowing one means you know the other. You just have to translate by using the square root. We'll show you how in the next section.

This is very important since option formulas demand that we know the standard deviations of the stocks we want to analyze. In fact, the standard deviation has another name in option analysis: *volatility*. Without exaggeration it is the most important part of every option model. It's a measure of how far the stock price can be expected to move, based on experience. A pretty important measure if you are going to buy an option on that stock.

A Simple Statistics Example

Let's try an easy example to get a feel for mean, variance, and standard deviation. Let's say we have five test scores: 60, 70, 80, 90, 100. The average or mean of these scores is exactly 80. The first two scores are below the mean by 20 and 10 points, respectively, and the last two are 10 and 20 above the mean. To properly measure the typical distance from the center, the variance, we can't allow the points below to cancel out the points above, as they seem to do. If the points below are minuses, and the points above pluses, the sum will be zero. Zero won't describe how far the typical point falls from the center. It turns out, therefore, that we need each distance to always be positive (this way a negative distance won't cancel out a positive distance). One procedure is to work with the squares of the distance (multiply it by itself). Any negative number multiplied by itself becomes positive.

So, the variance is the average of the squares of the individual distances away from the mean. In our test example the mean was 80, so the distances away from the mean would be -20, -10, 0, $+10$, $+20$ in the order we first described them. The square of each would be 400, 100, 0, 100, 400 for a total of 1,000. Divide by 5 and the variance is 200. (*Note:* We divided by N, not $N-1$, here to keep our world simpler. If you are going to become a math wizard, you'll have to look into that esoterica on your own.)

A variance of 200 sounds kind of large for these scores, doesn't it? Not to worry. The standard deviation reverses our squaring and shrinks the size back again because it is the square root of the variance. The standard deviation in our example is the square root of 200, or 14.1. Notice that the distances away from the mean were -20, -10, 0, $+10$, $+20$, and you can see that the standard deviation is a lot closer to those original distances than the variance is.

That's enough statistics for our first pass. We merely wanted to acquaint you with the concepts of central tendency (average and mean) and variation from the center (variance and standard deviation). These are two key concepts in statistics, and we needed a feel for them before we discuss the normal distribution further. As we said earlier, these concepts play a critically important role in defining every normal distribution's dimensions and characteristics.

KEY CONCEPTS REVIEW

- When all data points are identical, there is obviously no variation from point to point. Statisticians would say the variance was zero. Under these conditions we can make perfect predictions, but it doesn't take a genius to realize this, does it?

- In the real world, data points vary all over the place. When we try to represent all the data with one point (the average), we get a middle-of-the-road value that tells us where the center of the data points is, but it doesn't tell us how far the typical data point can vary from it. For this we compute a statistical value called the variance.

- If we can provide a statistician with those two important items, the average and the variance, we can receive some reasonable predictions. For surer predictions we need to understand the world the data comes from (what type of distribution it fits).

- At this point the world we are studying nicely fits the normal distribution (the normal curve). By simply specifying the average (also called the mean) and the variance we can make a remarkable number of accurate future predictions.

- Variance has a direct descendant called the standard deviation. The normal distribution can be analyzed using either, but the standard deviation is preferred.

- The standard deviation is easily found: it's the square root of the variance.

- There's a happy surprise for us amid all this statistical mishmash: a stock's volatility and its annual standard deviation are one and the same thing.

- If we learn how to compute the annual standard deviation of returns, we'll know the volatility, by far the most difficult input for the Black-Scholes option formula. In fact, without the use of this annual standard deviation the formula would be a total flop.

THINGS TO THINK ABOUT

World Without Variation   Which would you rather live in: a world where everything was identically the same year after year and all predictions were guaranteed or a world of immense complexity where nothing ever repeats exactly and predictions were constantly a flop and you had to spend hundreds of hours learning statistics to understand how to make reasonable predictions? Gives a whole new meaning to the phrase "familiarity breeds contempt."

RMS: The Mathematician's Abbreviation Statisticians use RMS as an abbreviation for root mean square. Translated it means: take the square root of the average of the squared values. It's a mnemonic device to help them remember the procedural order for calculations. They, therefore, sometimes call the standard deviation by the name RMS deviation. You have to work backward to adhere to the correct procedure. First you find the deviations from the mean. That's the *deviation* part. Then you calculate the square of each. That's the *S* part. Taking the average or mean of all these squares is the *M* part. That gives you the variance. Taking the square root is the *R* part and that gives you the standard deviation. You didn't expect to find that mathematicians were as confused as you and also needed help, eh?

Going to Extremes
How important are extremes? Clearly the extreme temperatures we foisted upon our lab volunteer must have impacted him. How about another example of extremes, like skiing? Suppose you were told that the mountain you were visiting for the first time had a vertical slope of 32 degrees on average. That sounds pretty much like a very boring bunny slope to an experienced skier. If the terrain is perfectly flat, it has a slope of 0 degrees. If you look at the sun overhead at high noon (straight up in the air), it's 90 degrees. Then you find out they have only 10 slopes: 8 kiddie trails sloping just 20 degrees each and two quadruple diamonds and crossbones with an almost clifflike straight-up slope of 80 degrees! If you were blindfolded and taken to a random slope, doesn't the *extreme* matter a lot more to you than the *average?* As far as trading goes the extreme days make or break the whole year's profits. One top trader said that 95 percent of all his profits were in just 5 percent of the trades. Since he made a fortune throughout that period, they must have been pretty extreme trades, don't you think?

QUESTIONS

1. Why do we call the average a sort of middle-of-the-road measurement?

2. What is the average of these five data points: 23, 16, 19, 27, 15?

3. What is the mean for the five data points in quesiton 2?

4. What is the meaning of the term *central tendency* as related to clusters of data points?

5. Does the average or mean tell the whole tale? What do they leave out?

6. In our lab experiment the paid volunteer was kept on average at a very comfortable 70° F. Do you think the extreme temperatures averaged out in his opinion? What was the likely physical result of the extreme temperatures?

7. Can we make accurate predictions without noting similar experiences from the past?

8. What is the variance of the five data points we averaged in quesiton 2? Use the results to compute the standard deviation also.

9. What is the variance of these five data points: 22, 17, 20, 25, 16? Use the results to compute the standard deviation also.

10. What is the variance of these five data points: 18, 19, 20, 21, 22? Use the results to compute the standard deviation also.

11. Can we predict an event exactly if historically it often varies?

12. How does the variance and standard deviation relate to our study of the Black-Scholes option formula?

CHAPTER 11

Dow Jones versus Coin Tosses

This is where we begin our leap across the chasm that separates coin tosses from the world of stock prices and the Black-Scholes formula. It is time for us to start stretching the simple, workable concept of the coin toss binomial into the more complex world of stock prices. To that end we offer visual evidence that stock prices often bear more than a mild resemblance to coin tosses. Figures 11–1 and 11–2 are two graphs, from very different worlds, constructed in a manner that allows easy comparison. Make up your own mind.

Figure 11–1 shows 4 recent years of daily changes in the Dow Jones Industrials. It encompasses exactly 1000 days of data. Figure 11–2 shows a group of 1000 coin toss events. Each event is a coin tossed 20 times. We created both graphs with 21 bars and aimed to distribute similar percentages of their outcomes across the 21 bars. Some bars are too short to see, but they should never be ignored. While their number might be few, their huge payoffs guarantee that they will have an important overall impact.

Eyeballing the graphs, you can quickly see the overall similarities. Let's leave it at that for now. We wanted to show you the prima facie case for using the binomial distribution to represent stock prices. The complexities and difficulties of linking coin tosses to price moves are many. We'll deal with only a necessary few here and leave the rest until later.

F I G U R E   11–1

Dow Jones 1000 Daily Changes
(Dec 1997–Dec 2001)

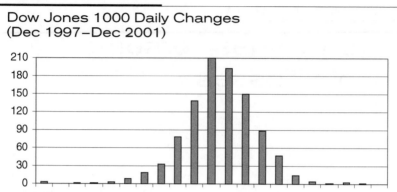

F I G U R E   11–2

Coin Tossed 20 Times
(1000 Cases)

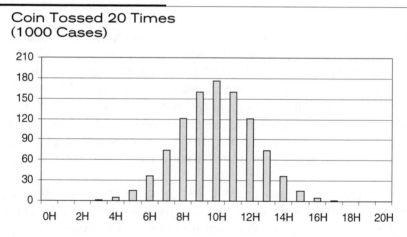

Two sticky differences are the type of math (discrete vs. continuous) and the type of statistical distributions (binomial vs. normal). The nature of the data with which we are working will determine this. Coin tosses use discrete math and binomial curves. Stock prices use continuous math and normal curves. Now what does this mean and why? The answers follow.

DISCRETE VERSUS CONTINUOUS

Coin tosses are simple events. You can see them, feel them, count them. The coin toss world is comprised of separate, countable events (together we've counted a lot of them). Mathematicians call such individually separate, countable events *discrete* and have developed a math just for such events. But the real world is much more nonstop and action oriented, more continuous.

Flowing rivers and falling rain are two examples of continuous real-world events. When a rainfall just begins, coming down in a slow pitter-patter, you might be able to count the drops and identify where they fall. But when it begins to come down steadily, we quickly lose track of location and count. And when it pours buckets there is no hope to measure individual drops. This continuous flow requires totally different measuring techniques and a different math.

Our world is full of many events that contain uncountably large numbers. Mathematicians learned to deal with this difficulty by starting small, as we did with coin tosses, and then expanding their logic to fit the faster, more continuous picture. They needed to develop a continuous math to help them deal with this.

BINOMIAL DISTRIBUTION VERSUS NORMAL DISTRIBUTION

Mathematicians use binomial distributions to help them with discrete (and countable), two-choice events. But when the numbers get too difficult to count, they move on to another distribution: the normal distribution. It is the most popular, widely used distribution in all of statistics. And, believe it or not, these are just two of the dozens of different types of distributions found to exist in the world. Even most mathematicians and engineers couldn't name them all. But they all know the binomial and normal distribution.

The normal distribution is known by many other names. It was first called the *gaussian* distribution after the great mathematician Karl Friedrich Gauss (1777–1855). It is also often called the *bell-shaped* distribution because it looks like a bell. Who said mathematicians have no aesthetic sense?

Many people refer to it as a *curve*, instead of a distribution. The normal distribution requires the use of many, many data points—uncountably many, actually. As more and more vertical bars get squeezed in to reflect this large increase in data, the bars become exceedingly skinny, until they seem to disappear. All you can see is the top of each bar. If you connect the dots at the top, you will get what appears to be a continuous line (or curve). Therefore, many people call it the normal curve, or the bell-shaped curve. Whatever the name, they are all referring to the very same normal distribution we speak of here.

When teachers say they are grading "on a curve," it is usually our bell-shaped, normal curve they are referring to. It is so common to use the bell-shaped curve for statistical purposes that it is considered the "normal" one to run to for any type of analysis that uses a distribution. People without long experience in statistics (educators, politicians, reporters) often claim the normal curve shows what normal should be in any population. This is certainly not always true. Nevertheless, although other distributions might be more appropriate at times, it is the vast and common usage of this distribution that eventually caused it to be named *normal*.

CUMULATIVE DISTRIBUTION FUNCTION: HOW TO GET PROBABILITIES FROM THE NORMAL CURVE

We can fall back on our studies of binomial distributions to help us get a leg up on clearly understanding the normal distribution. They are very similar in many ways. Let's start by using a key histogram (shown in Fig. 11–3) that we've seen in previous chapters. This histogram is simply a converted 20 coin toss binomial distribution. In Chap. 9 we made minor adjustments and turned it into a probability distribution of closing prices for IBM. If we want to know the probability of IBM closing at $100, we look at that bar (the tallest bar in the center) and find its height. That would be about .18 in this example, or 18 percent likelihood. If we wanted to know the probability of IBM closing at $100 or lower, we would need to add all the bar heights from the $100 bar through to (and including) the tiniest bar on the left (80). The 11 bars would add to .588 (58.8 percent). We couldn't eyeball this from the chart; we had to look up the table that accompanied the chart in Chap. 9.

We could also have used a formula. There is a cumulating formula for the binomial distribution that gives the same result. For example, Microsoft Excel offers such a formula as one of its math functions. We typed the name of the function and were prompted to enter three items: 10 heads, 20 coins tossed, and 50

F I G U R E   1 1–3

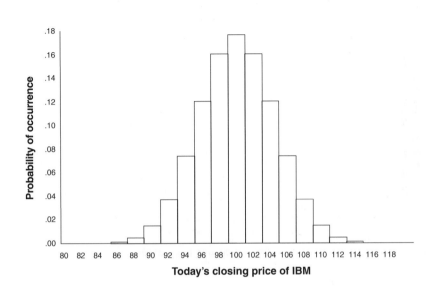

percent probability per head. Out popped the answer: .588 (the cumulative chance that from 0 to 10 heads would arrive in a 20 coin toss). The formula automatically used the 20 coin toss binomial distribution (per our choice) and accumulated the probabilities of all the bars until each headcount (0 through 10) had been summed up. This is called a cumulative distribution function (CDF). It adds from left to right.

The main function of a distribution is as a tool for analyzing probabilities. But adding up an enormous number of bars is a huge job. The CDF was invented to do the work for you. We can think of the CDF as a probability analyzer.

Without the CDF, option formulas couldn't exist. The CDF is the probability tool of choice, and there is a CDF associated with each distribution. The Black-Scholes formula uses the cumulative *normal* distribution function and the Cox-Ross-Rubinstein formula uses the cumulative *binomial* distribution function. All you need do is plug in a few important pieces of data and the cumulative probability gets spit out. To show this is less difficult than it seems. Let's take a look at the normal curve in Fig. 11–4 and try a few probability analyses with its CDF.

F I G U R E   11–4

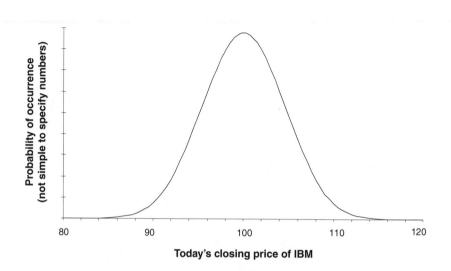

Today's closing price of IBM

    This is the normal curve version of IBM's closing price possibilities. Notice the bars (rectangles) of the binomial version have disappeared and been replaced simply by a curve, as we suggested is typical for the normal curve. If you can imagine a million razor-thin rectangles standing side by side, you might imagine how this normal curve could be created from the prior binomial curve.

    The concepts of measuring probability from coin toss histograms and binomial distributions which we studied earlier can be extended to the normal curve. But we can no longer count the rectangles and add their probabilities. As the number of bars becomes uncountably large the probability for any specific event must become very, very small. This makes the height of the curve very difficult to describe. So we measure probability, instead, by the accumulated area under the curve. This is the reason we need CDFs to do the measuring for us.

    In analyzing an option's value we might need to ask, What is the probability that IBM will close at $100 or lower? If we put $100 into the normal CDF, it would return .50 which is 50 percent. That is to say that the very center of the graph is at the halfway mark. That makes sense, right? But we tried the same thing with the binomial CDF and got 58.8 percent didn't we?

Yes, we did. Now pay attention: This is the reason we need to use a continuous distribution instead of a discrete distribution. We allowed ourselves just 21 bars in the prior binomial distribution to cover IBM prices ranging from $80 to $120. Therefore, we grouped the IBM prices into $2 ranges per bar. The very center bar represented not only $100, but the $2 surrounding it. That $2 range had 17.6 percent chance of occurring. But half of the prices fell below $100 and half fell above $100. That's 8.8 percent below and 8.8 percent above which is the overstatement difference.

The normal curve is much more precise and can hit the target price to within a penny, so it didn't include the 8.8 percent falling above $100. Our 21-bar binomial CDF was not able to hit a specific, narrow target price as structured. It would be able to pinpoint a much narrower target price if we made a huge increase in the number of bars and a huge decrease in each bar's width (the width is the price target). As we increase the number of bars the binomial distribution begins to look more and more identical to the normal distribution and will, if given enough bars, begin to return the identically same answers.

Such are the tribulations of discrete versus continuous math. Discrete is easier to understand and visualize, but it doesn't always do the job. For this reason we had to make the leap to continuous math and endure its complexities.

Next we are going to describe the normal curve and how to use the two important statistical concepts we learned earlier: the mean and standard deviation (which is the square root of its variance).

STANDARD DEVIATIONS AND THE NORMAL CURVE

Figure 11–5 shows a typical normal curve. Notice that we are no longer measuring price along the bottom axis, but simply distance from the mean or center. Or, more properly, deviation from the center. And we can't use just any old type of deviations that strike our fancy, but are required to use special units called standard deviations (SDs). There are many different ways to measure deviations, but statisticians over the years have developed a particular method of measurement that they find indispensable. And they gave it a very special name: the standard deviation.

F I G U R E   11–5

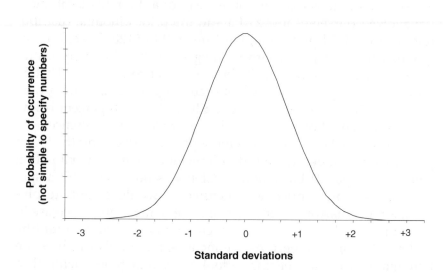

Now, let's take a closer look at the normal curve. Obviously, the center cannot deviate from itself, so it is located at 0 SD. The normal curve is designed to be six SDs wide, with three on either side of center. We describe right and left of center as + and −, respectively. In the normal curve the zone between + / −1 SD encompasses 68 percent of the whole area under the curve and, therefore, 68 percent of the data. The wider zone of + / −2 SDs contains 95 percent of the area. If we span + / −3 SDs, we have taken into account nearly the whole area, 99.74 percent of the area under the normal curve. So when someone describes a 3 SD move, they are implying an occurrence outside that zone. This is a real rarity because it occurs somewhere in the remaining 0.26 percent of the population, a long shot of almost 400 to 1.

Remember the 4 years of Dow Jones data in histogram format? Figure 11–6 shows what it would look like if we plotted it, instead, as a normal distribution with a mean of +0.024 percent and a standard deviation of 1.241 percent (the true values for the 1,000 days). Remember, we told you we only need those two facts to plot any standard normal curve.

There were 1,000 separate days of actual Dow Jones data. The days lose their individual identities as they merge into the overall gestalt of this normal curve. We can no longer pick out single days, but with help from the normal CDF we can more accurately

F I G U R E   11–6

Dow Jones Daily Moves
(Dec 1997–Dec 2001)

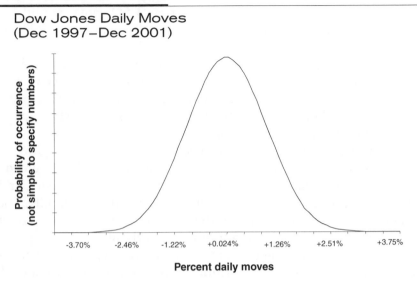

-3.70%   -2.46%   -1.22%   +0.024%   +1.26%   +2.51%   +3.75%

Percent daily moves

target price zones and easily compute their probabilities. We could never do this by hand.

Let's discuss the data a bit. The original data had a mean daily price move of +0.024 percent which is roughly 2.4 Dow points. This implies that, on average, each day throughout this 4-year period the Dow was up 2.4 points (assuming Dow 10,000). That's each and every day for 1000 straight days—a 2400 point uptrend! A huge bull market bias.

Also, we found the standard deviation of daily price moves was 1.241 percent or 124.1 Dow points (up or down). That means that although the average day was up 2.4 points there was wide volatility with frequent ups and downs. It wasn't a smooth ride.

The rules for normal curves and standard deviations help us translate as follows: The cutoff of $+/-1$ SD contains 68 percent of all the cases. Therefore, 68 percent of the days under review showed the change in the Dow to be between the following two points: the mean minus 1 SD and the mean plus 1 SD. Translated this means: on 680 days we expect that the Dow had a daily move somewhere between -121.7 points down and $+126.5$ points up.

For the other 32 percent of the days under review, the Dow had bigger moves than that! Remember, $+/-1$ SD describes the range of what happens only two-thirds of the time (68 percent).

The other one-third of the time wilder, bigger events are occurring. Let's calculate, then, how large the rare 3 SD move would be. Simply, 3 × 1.241 percent = 3.723 percent. That, at Dow 10,000, is 372 points. Now that's a memorable move!

We mentioned that there was wide volatility in the data. Whether it is "wide" or "narrow," or whatever descriptive phrase you might choose, is a relative matter. There are many arguments as to what volatility is and how to best measure it. The experts never entirely agree (nice to hear, right?).

The volatility used by the Black-Scholes formula is directly related to the standard deviation we just mentioned, 1.241 percent. The Dow Jones data we used was for daily moves, however, and thus its standard deviation measured only the daily volatility. The Black-Scholes formula requires the annual volatility, so we would have to adjust the daily volatility to properly fit.

Understanding the concept of standard deviation and relating it to the Black-Scholes formula's volatility is quite a handful, but it becomes second nature as you become more familiar with using it.

KEY CONCEPTS REVIEW

- To make the changeover from coin tosses to stock price movements we have to deal first with two sticky differences: the type of math (discrete vs. continuous) and the type of statistical distributions (binomial vs. normal).
- Coin tosses use discrete math and binomial distributions. Stock prices use continuous math and normal distributions.
- Mathematicians use binomial distributions to help them with discrete (and countable), two-choice events. But when the number of possible outcomes gets too difficult to count they move onto another distribution: the normal distribution.
- Whereas the binomial distribution has only 21 rectangles (in our example), the normal distribution uses an infinite number of rectangles. We can no longer count all the rectangles or add up their probabilities.

- The cumulative distribution function (CDF) is a mathematical function that enables us to add up any number of rectangles and quickly measure the probability under the curve. There are CDFs for both the binomial and the normal distributions.

- When using only 21 rectangles, as in our example, the binomial distribution is not nearly accurate enough to give us a good option value. That's why we had to shift to the normal distribution from the binomial distribution. Using the normal distribution we found a certain IBM probability to be .500 (50.0 percent), whereas the binomial distribution pegged it at .588 (58.8 percent). This substantial difference, caused by bracket inaccuracies, is the reason we must use continuous math and the normal distribution. It allows us to narrow the brackets immensely to get pinpoint results.

- The normal curve is designed to be six standard deviations (6 SDs) wide, placing three on either side of center. We find that $+/-$ 1 SD (either side of center) encompasses 68 percent of the whole area beneath the normal curve, $+/-$ 2 SDs contain 95 percent of the area, and $+/-$ 3 SDs hold 99.74 percent (almost the entire area under the normal curve).

- The volatility used in the Black-Scholes formula is directly related to the standard deviations defined by the normal curve. We used daily data, but the Black-Scholes formula requires annual data, so a time-scale adjustment needs to be made.

THINGS TO THINK ABOUT

The binomial and normal distributions we have examined so far have a perfect symmetry to them. They neither stretch too far left nor too far right, and they are not too tall or short at the center, and the same can be said about their extremities (tails). The tendency to overstretch left or right is known as *skewness* (no relation to the "skews" discussed by option traders). And the tallness or shortness of the center and extremities is known as *kurtosis*. These perfectly symmetrical distributions are the standards from which the option models' probability analyses spring. Would it have an important impact on our option valuations if real markets were found to be not nearly as perfect in their symmetry?

The Dow Jones data we used had a strong upward bias to it (+2400 Dow points over the 4 years). This just happened to be an extraordinarily bullish period for the stock market. Regardless, the amount of upward (or downward) bias is largely ignored by option theory. What is of more interest to the option theorists is the width of the distribution, that is, its tendency to stray from the center, which they translate as volatility. Can you see how recent results can color the views of traders and cause them to have certain expectations for the near future? If we went back a century and selected 25 different 4-year periods, would each show the same volatility? If every snapshot of the past volatility shows a large amount of variation, what does this say about our ability to predict the future of volatility?

Gauss and the Normal Curve

The normal distribution is sometimes called the gaussian distribution after the great mathematician Karl Friedrich Gauss who helped pioneer its creation two centuries ago. The story is that one day in Gauss's class the students got so out of hand that Gauss's teacher couldn't stand it any longer. The exasperated teacher gave the students a busywork assignment to add the numbers from 1 to 99 so that he might keep them quiet for a half hour (he hoped). Gauss solved the problem *in less than a minute*. He reasoned that if he made a vertical list of the numbers 1 to 99 (in ascending order) and right next to it listed the numbers 99 to 1 (in descending order) he would have 99 pairs of numbers with each pair always adding to 100! That means the two lists summed to 9900. Since the teacher only wanted one list summed, the answer was half, or 4950. Needless to say the teacher wasn't thrilled by Gauss's discovery. It's hard not to be awed by Gauss's natural genius for finding shortcuts to make computations easier. Therefore, if Gauss concluded, after many years of hard work, that there is no simpler way to analyze continuous probabilities than to use his normal distribution CDF, who are we to argue? Be happy he made it much easier for us.

QUESTIONS

Questions 1 to 3 refer to Figs. 11–1 and 11–2, at the beginning of the chapter.

1. Are there any noticeable differences in the bar heights of the two charts, and, if so, how would you describe the differences?

2. Assuming the typical trading market has a higher center and thicker tails than a perfectly symmetrical model, where does the difference get made up?

3. The far-out fringe data points (called outliers) are what the tails of the distributions are made of. Why are these data points much more important to a trader than the ones at the center?

4. Briefly describe the concepts of discrete math and continuous math.

5. Which uses discrete math: the binomial distribution or normal distribution? Why?

6. Which uses continuous math: the binomial distribution or normal distribution? Why?

7. What does CDF stand for? What does it mean? How does it help us? Is there a separate CDF for the binomial distribution and the normal distribution?

8. After spending a great deal of time learning about the binomial distribution, we are suddenly shifting to the normal distribution. Why?

9. How many standard deviations wide is the normal distribution?

10. Does each standard deviation measure the same percentage of the curve?

11. What is significant about three standard deviations?

12. When traders describe a move that has just occurred as a "three standard deviation move," what are they referring to?

13. Is there a link between standard deviations and the volatility used by the Black-Scholes formula?

CHAPTER 12

Turning Spot Prices into Forward Prices: $S \times e^{RT}$

What a Difference a Day Makes

"I will gladly pay you Tuesday, for a hamburger today!" Sound familiar? If you've ever watched Popeye cartoons, it should. A whole generation of kids chuckled with glee as the plump and rumpled Wimpy conned his way into borrowing money time and again. It was our first introduction to deferred payments— and deadbeats.

In this chapter we discuss deferring payment. This enables us to understand the cost of allowing Wimpy to pay on Tuesday rather than today. But instead of trying to adjust the price of hamburger we'll concentrate on price adjustments to stocks, like IBM.

When you read through the huge stock tables in your newspaper, the stock prices you see are all *spot* prices. This means the prices are based on the exchange of stocks and money on the third business day after the trade. Everybody trades stocks this way. But you could, in theory, make a special agreement to delay this exchange beyond the typical 3 days. If so, there would likely be a price adjustment required. This special agreement would specify a new forward delivery date and a new forward price.

Up until recently this was all theoretical, mind you, because it was a rarity in the stock business to trade individual stock forwards and there were no futures exchanges allowed to trade individual stock futures. This all changed in November 2002 as two exchanges began trading what are called *single stock futures*. So what was once a theoretical discussion has now become a real-world practice.

It's time for us to get acquainted with the pricing differences between spot, forward, and futures markets, and it will be much simpler than you think. We must understand these differences because option theory demands it of us. There is an important and elegant interplay between spot prices and forward prices in option theory that we can't discuss until you have more familiarity with the basics.

Right out of the box let's cut the workload in half. Because of the nature of competitive markets the forward price of any asset is substantially the same as the futures price for that asset. The option theorists, therefore, talk about forward prices and futures prices as if they are one and the same. This simplifies things a lot. If you know how to compute the fair price of one, then you also know the fair price of the other; it's the same. Furthermore, for sake of clarity we will refer to both as *forward* prices. If we need to discuss something specific to the futures market or specific to the forward market we'll say so. Otherwise we'll use the generic term forward prices for both, and anything we discuss has equal applicability to the forward or futures markets.

Here's the good news/bad news assessment. The bad news is that there are a half-dozen or so factors that can impact forward prices and, in keeping with good form, we need to run all of them by you. The good news is that we are studying options from the perspective of the Black-Scholes option model, and in the simplified theoretical world demanded by this formula, all but one of the factors drops out of the equation! The Black-Scholes formula requires but a single factor to turn spot prices into forward prices.

SPOT, CASH, FORWARD, AND FUTURES: WHAT'S THE DIFFERENCE?

If you are able to pay cash in 3 business days, you can buy almost anything you want in the cash markets (also called spot markets). The New York Stock Exchange and the NASDAQ are two of the world's largest cash markets, for example. The overwhelming majority of trades made are accomplished in the world's cash markets.

If you prefer to get a bit fancier and you have fair credit lines, you can sign up at many brokerage houses to trade futures. You'll have to keep a minimum balance of, say, \$10,000 and also pony up roughly 10 percent of the value of any positions you maintain.

But if you qualify as having sensational credit lines (tens of millions at a minimum), then the sales people from investment banking firms will be knocking down your doors, drooling on your rugs, and begging you to trade with them in the forward markets.

As you can see, this is a sort of financial caste system geared to your bankroll. Millions of ordinary people can and do trade in the cash and spot markets. But only a small portion of these, say 10 percent, trade futures or even understand what futures markets are. And far less, only an elite handful of traders, are ever allowed to deal in the forward markets. So, for the most part, the 11:00 business news every night is reporting on the cash or spot markets. The futures and forward markets are so specialized that most reporters barely know they exist. But the professional traders do, and they, of course, have the opinions and trading size to move prices. Sometimes it is quite apparent to even a novice that a futures market has strongly impacted its underlying cash market. When this happens, the newswire reporters break into a dialing frenzy. They call everyone on their rolodexes as they desperately dig for a quotable sound bite and end up with, "It's a case of the tail wagging the dog." Futures being the tail. But this is a pretty shrewd and powerful tail they're talking about. Futures impact the cash market each hour of every day, but it typically goes unnoticed by outsiders. They just don't get any respect.

One relatively easy way to identify spot, cash, forward, and futures markets is the delivery date. We say "relatively" because there are many, many markets in the world and every single one has different rules. Listing the exceptions might take 10 pages. There are no standardized delivery dates in global markets. What is considered normal delivery in one market often has exceptions in another market. So we must struggle more than a bit to properly define categories. Just realize that any definitions are very loose and that a calendar overlap of a day or two is always possible.

As a general rule of thumb, very short-term deliveries (up to 2 or 3 days) are the province of the cash or spot markets. We can consider the terms cash and spot to be identical and interchangeable for our purposes. In fact, we will more often use the term spot to refer to both. The concept of a spot market is actually very simple. In the stock market, for example, the delivery is "trade date plus three," which they call "T + 3." All trades on a Monday, let's say, are expected to be delivered and paid for on Thursday. The next day, Tuesday, all trades will be for Friday delivery and payment, and so on. If you are trading in a market where you must make or take delivery in a few days, this is a spot market. (Many commodity markets consider spot to be T + 2. As we've said, it varies from one market to the next, and sometimes a given market's reasoning for choosing certain delivery dates is quite inscrutable. Consider the stock market: until a recent change in 1995 the stock market had used T + 5 as their delivery date *for over a hundred years*. They couldn't be dragged kicking and screaming into the twentieth century until it was virtually the twenty-first century. The excuse was, in an era of electronic stock certificates, that brokers still needed 5 days to deliver or would fail!)

We can sum up the primary difference between spot markets and the more deferred delivery markets (forwards and futures) in one phrase: "Same stuff, later date." Deliveries further out in time than T + 2 or T + 3 (for spot markets) are considered forwards and trade only in forward or futures markets. The forward and futures markets are two distinctly separate market arenas that specialize in deferred deliveries and are as insanely competitive as Hertz and Avis. Since they evolved separately over many, many years and they serve different clientele, there are many subtle differences between the two markets. But the differences tend to revolve around highly technical issues like margin requirements, eligibility of participants, regulatory agencies, standards for delivery, and dozens of tiny issues of no consequence to the average investor. Thankfully, they closely agree on the issue which is most important to us: *price*.

There is virtually no difference in price between a forward and a future as long as it is for the same asset (say a bar of gold or a bushel of corn) with the same delivery standards (location, weight, form, grade, etc.). Almost all price differences between forwards and futures are due to differences in the products themselves, not because one is a forward and the other a future. To repeat an important concept discussed earlier: For our purposes here in creating a pricing formula, *we will consider forwards and futures to be the same thing*. We will only talk about forward prices from here on, but you should realize that the fair value of a futures price is calculated in precisely the same manner as a forward price.

THE CUTOFF BETWEEN SPOT AND FORWARD

There is a small dilemma: When does the spot delivery date end and when do forward dates begin for any given market?

Most traders would define forward dates to be delivery dates that fall *after* the standard spot date for that particular market, meaning it varies from market to market. For the stock market the spot delivery date is T + 3, and so delivery dates of T + 4, T + 6, and T + 100 would all be forward dates. Every market has its peculiarities and special rules. The key to determining a forward is to use that particular market's *normal* spot settlement date as *day zero*. Everything after the spot date in that particular market becomes a forward and accrues expenses and interest costs, regardless of whether it is a business day or not. Interest charges never sleep.

THE FORWARD PRICE CURVE

As you might imagine, there are just an enormous number of possible forward delivery dates, and each one carries its own special price. Every once in a while the prices for every date are the same. This is called a *flat market* because there is no curve at all to the price structure over time; it's just a flat, straight line. But usually there is a relatively smooth curve to the prices if we plot them against their delivery dates. This is called a *forward price curve*.

A forward price curve begins on day zero with the spot price and slowly curves upward (or downward) as it follows the path of prices for the many, varied delivery dates. And the shape of the price curve varies from marketplace to marketplace. In some markets the price curve doesn't have much curve to it at all; in fact, it might appear to be almost a straight line. At other times, especially when it curves downward, it can be quite precipitous because there may be a squeeze in effect wherein traders will pay absurd prices to own the spot but far less to own the distant forwards. Crude oil comes to mind as a market that can have spot prices that are much higher than deferred delivery prices. The prevailing shape of the price curve is due to the market preferences at that time.

It takes professional traders years to become conversant in the whys and wherefores of forward price curves. Certainly we could write chapters and chapters about such intricacies, but that would distract us from our original intent which is to study options. For the sake of brevity we will include a measured portion of what you might need to know, hitting the high points along the way. This will allow us to get back to our options studies reasonably soon.

If prices are higher for the later delivery dates, we call this a *normal*, or *contango*, market. Normal in the sense that this is the typical shape of many markets through recent history, although certainly not the case throughout ancient history. Markets tend to trade in this normal or contango mode when there are ample supplies available. The stock markets usually have plenty of shares available and thus most frequently trade in this normal, or contango, mode.

But when there is a nearby shortage of a given asset or commodity, then all bets are off. This shortage causes the market to invert or turn backwards with prices higher nearby than for the later delivery dates. This is called an *inverted* market or a *backwardation*.

Figures 12–1 and 12–2 are examples of the two types of forward price curves we just described. Gold is in a normal, or contango, market mode, while crude oil is in an inverted market mode, also called a backwardation. This says that there is plenty of gold available, but that inventories of crude oil are tight and that traders are very nervous about short-term supply. As a historical note you might consider that the 2003 Iraqi War began 2 weeks later, but it was the most prepublicized war in history, and so the markets anticipated possible oil shortages and the spot price shot up before there were actual shortages.

The forward price curve reflects the sum of the markets' opinions and valuations about market supply-and-demand expectations. It conveys more by this simple curve than the best traders could ever deduce, even if they had all the information in the world. It knows all and sees all, because it shifts from trade to trade and reflects the impact of continuous, up-to-the-minute

F I G U R E   12-1

Gold Futures Prices
(on March 01, 2003)

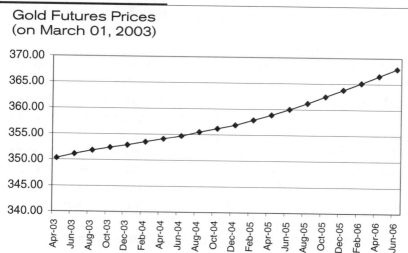

F I G U R E   12-2

Crude Oil Futures Prices
(on March 01, 2003)

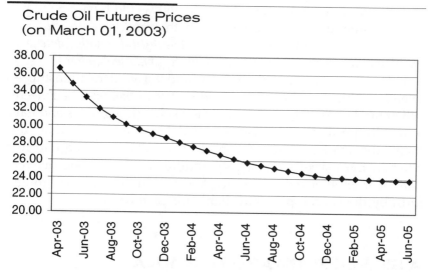

buying and selling pressure, which, of course, is a reflection of
new information and ever-changing opinions.

The forward price curve shows that the most attractive dates
are priced higher and the least attractive dates are priced lower.

This helps create an equilibrium in supply and demand. All delivery dates are considered equally attractive by the market after taking into account the adjusted price. Otherwise traders would switch to another date.

Of course, most traders have at least some small date preferences. They might prefer this date to that date for any of a thousand different reasons. If we view buying and selling activities as votes, we can see that the curve helps register these votes as the market's preferences. At some price it might become too expensive to hold on to your individual preference and you become ambivalent—and then indifferent. The market will compensate you for forgoing your initial date preference and switching to another date. It is these switches that move the price curve up and down as news and opinions change.

The concept of delivery date indifference is generalized and broad. It refers only to the marketplace as a whole (the sum of all buyers and sellers), not specifically to any one participant. You, as an individual, might desperately need a certain date of delivery and cannot do without it. In that case you would be happy to pay a hefty premium to get delivery on that special date. *But it is amazing how quickly you will find a way to substitute another date when the premium you must pay gets too high to comfortably afford.*

This is the nature of the spot and forward relationship—a relentless shifting of prices as traders try to balance their needs. When market participants are finished substituting dates and have optimally positioned themselves for delivery at a price that suits them, the market calms down. This results in an equilibrium wherein the market *in general* is indifferent to any one delivery date over another delivery date. And this indifference is brought forth by the special prices available for each date.

A SIMPLE FORWARD FORMULA

Despite the obvious complexities of measuring the delivery wants and needs of an entire marketplace we can build a simple formula that will help us. Our first scribbling of a formula shows the big picture, but it lacks usefulness:

Forward price = spot price + indifference spread

Spread is simply trader's lingo for the difference between any two prices. It could be wheat and corn, beer and champagne, or, in this case, the spot delivery price and the forward delivery price.

The problem is that we only know the spot price. We must work up a strategy to compute the indifference spread or we'll be stuck forever in a loop with two unknowns. It's like a line from the Three Stooges: "If I had some eggs, I'd have me some ham and eggs—if I had me some ham!"

As we pointed out earlier the forward price curve tends toward equilibrium when indifference sets in. Thus we've called the spread (between spot and forward) an indifference spread. The choice is between owning spot (in inventory) or owning a forward position (sort of a postponed inventory). If we can figure out the relative costs and benefits of holding spot, we are on the right road. The net of the two will dictate the indifference spread. Understanding this takes a few steps, but it is not as difficult as you might think.

COMPONENTS OF THE INDIFFERENCE SPREAD

The major unknown in our original formula was the indifference spread. Here is a start on how we are going to solve for it:

Indifference spread = carrying costs − carrying benefits

The *carry* is a term frequently used by traders who specialize in spot markets. It is a measure of the cost to maintain an inventory. If you trade only in forwards you never really maintain an inventory, because you keep delaying delivery. Only the market participants who hold the asset are incurring the costs and "carrying" the asset in inventory. Everyone else is *avoiding* carrying and its attendant costs.

What does it cost to carry an asset? The usual costs are the interest rate on borrowed money, storage fees, and insurance.* For

---

* Commissions, fees, and taxes are usually omitted. Large arbitrageurs can usually find ways to avoid or minimize these and other participants' costs can vary considerably, so we can't name one true number. These costs must, however, be included and considered where applicable. On rare occasions transportation and preparation to redeliver must be factored in.

commodities in exotic locations, the storage fees and insurance can be enormous. Coffee, sugar, copper, and crude oil come to mind as candidates. But most financial assets (stocks, bonds, and currencies) are *virtually cost-free* as far as storage and insurance are concerned. This limits the "cost of carrying" financial assets *to merely interest rate charges*. This is very, very important to our final formula as you'll see later.

Now, let's discuss the other side of the coin, the benefits of carrying. There are two components to this, and they are not necessarily straightforward because they can overlap a bit. First, there are cash flows accruing to the owners of the assets. *Cash flows* refer to dividends, bond coupons, or other monies received when you own the asset. If the asset is a currency, you can also deposit it in a bank and be paid the prevailing interest rate, for instance.

The second benefit of carrying is sometimes called the *liquidity premium*, which refers to any extra fees above and beyond the typical cash flows that must be paid to borrow the asset. When you borrow an asset, you owe the cash flows to the true owner. This liquidity premium is a little added extra that the market will pay to get possession of spot inventory either for business needs or emotional needs. Possessing the asset makes you liquid in that asset, meaning you can immediately use it or sell it if you so desire. That's why it's called a liquidity *premium*, because you must pay a little extra to stay "liquid" in the commodity or asset.

If an asset is in plentiful supply, no one will pay extra, and so there will be no premium paid for liquidity. This implies that the public and the industry professionals are unenthusiastic toward possessing the spot asset. Professionals try to hold only enough inventory for current needs. On occasion, however, the market develops an emotional need to hold extra inventory (called hoarding) which sends the liquidity premiums through the roof. Enough emotion can cause a minor panic or a "squeeze." When the public is screaming for an item, there are virtually no limits to the stupendous premiums that they will pay.

But there is another group that has a big impact on the liquidity premium: the "shorts." These are usually professionals who have sold the spot and must deliver, but they don't have the asset to deliver. So they borrow it. (Selling before you own an asset is known as being *short* the asset.) Most financial assets can be borrowed to cover delivery requirements when need be. On occasion the available supply is small relative to the number of borrowers. This will cause the liquidity premium to shoot way up as the traders who are caught short pay up to borrow it. Old Daniel Drew had a famous saying about this: "He who sells what isn't his'n, must buy it back or go to pris'n."

Putting it all together this is where we stand with the indifference spread:

$$\text{Indifference spread} = \text{interest} + \text{storage} + \text{insurance} - \text{cash flows} - \text{liquidity premium}$$

Now here is the fun part where everything gets easier. The Black-Scholes formula was created based on certain assumptions. The creators assumed that stocks have no dividends or liquidity premiums (no cost to borrow) and that there is no storage or insurance cost for holding the stocks. This is fantastic because it means that four of the five elements in the above formula have a zero value and drop out of the equation: storage = 0, insurance = 0, dividend cash flow = 0, liquidity premium = 0. This allows us to simplify the indifference spread to

$$\text{Indifference spread} = \text{interest}$$

This shows us that interest is the only carrying cost recognized by the Black-Scholes formula. We can now go back and easily finish our original formula for the forward price:

$$\text{Forward price} = \text{spot price} + \text{interest}$$

Let's see how it works with a simple example. We know that at, say, 6 percent per annum, the cost to carry inventory for 1 year would be $0.06 \times \text{spot}$. We can restate that as 0.06 spot. So the forward price in that case would be

$$\text{Forward price (1 year)} = \text{spot} + 0.06 \text{ spot} = 1.06 \text{ spot}$$

When we abbreviate spot as S, our result can be called 1.06S. Or simply put, the forward price equals an interest rate multiplier (1.06) times the spot price S. So we've solved our forward price formula. All we need is the spot price and the proper interest rate multiplier, which in this case is 1.06. One more twist and we're done.

THE ULTIMATE INTEREST RATE
MULTIPLIER e^{RT}

Economists have a much cleverer interest rate multiplier called e^{RT}. This is their very elegant formula for *continuously compounding* any interest rate for any period of time. They use this as their interest rate multiplier of choice in almost all advanced financial formulas. And, of course, so does the Black-Scholes option formula. While it looks bothersome, it is simpler to use than you would guess. Just raise the value e (2.718) to the power R times T. R is the interest rate and T is the time in years.

Consider this our fast-track, streamlined explanation for why it's okay to use e^{RT}. If simple interest is 6 percent for a year, your investment will return 1.06 times as much as you started with, right? The same values (0.06 for 1 year) plugged into e^{RT} show a return of 1.0612 times your starting amount. The tiny 0.0012 difference is merely the small extra return due to *continuous compounding*. In essence, the results are the same.

So, if spot is S, we can plug in the interest rate multiplier e^{RT} simply by multiplying, that is, $S \times e^{RT}$. This computes to 1.0612S, which is substantially identical to the forward price we arrived at by using a simple interest rate of 6 percent.

This, then, is the form that the Black-Scholes formula requires for our forward price calculation: $S \times e^{RT}$. We may have bitten off a little more than we could comfortably chew in this chapter, but we managed not to choke to death on it. In a nutshell the two main points in this chapter were to show how forwards get priced and why this weird e^{RT} variable appears in the Black-Scholes option formula. It was a long and tortuous story, but you'll be happy you paid attention to it because forward prices play a prominent role in our options studies. If you had no familiarity with our new forward price calculator ($S \times e^{RT}$), you would surely get lost later on.

As a final note we'd like to comment quickly on the Black-Scholes restrictions. Clearly, we live in a much more complicated world than any economist or mathematician can mathematically allow for. The original Black-Scholes option formula only works for stocks that have no dividends. Later modifications on the formula have been made by other mathematicians to embrace stocks that do have dividends. Still other modified Black-Scholes formulas adjust for commodities or currencies that have costs to borrow them (implying there is a liquidity premium). However, right now we are only studying the simplest basics of option theory as dictated by the original Black-Scholes option formula. You can check out the more advanced versions after you ace this course.

This topic of price curve and liquidity preferences is sufficiently arcane that it appears in John Maynard Keynes's major work *The General Theory of Employment, Interest and Money* (1935). In it he discussed a concept he called the "liquidity premium," and since then a few market aficionados have reused that term when referring to the forward price curve and cost of borrowing an asset. You can take the time to review Keynes' book and his complex style or take our word that we have simplified it and added some clarity.

KEY CONCEPTS REVIEW

- The typical stock prices in the papers are all spot prices. Delivery is in 3 days.
- You might arrange for delayed delivery in deferred markets called forwards and futures. You need special credit arrangements to do so.
- The primary difference between the spot market and the forward and futures markets can be summed up with a simple phrase: "same stuff, later date."
- Despite the many small differences between the two markets, the forward and futures prices for any asset are substantially the same.
- When we plot the prices for the various delivery dates, we create a chart of the forward price curve.
- If forward prices curve higher for the later delivery dates, we call this a normal, or contango, market. This happens in markets where ample supplies are available.
- Shortages, however, can cause prices to be higher for spot delivery than for the forward delivery dates. This is called an inverted market or a backwardation.

+ The forward price curve tends to reach an equilibrium when traders, because of the price differences, become indifferent to one delivery date over another. Thus some people have come to call the spread of prices an indifference spread.

+ This allows us to create the following formula: forward price = spot price + indifference spread.

+ The indifference spread can be computed by plugging in these two components: indifference spread = carrying costs − carrying benefits.

+ The carrying costs include such things as the interest rate on borrowed money, storage fees, and insurance. But most stocks, bonds, and currencies are *virtually cost-free* as far as storage and insurance are concerned. This limits the cost of carrying financial assets *to merely interest rate charges*. This is very, very important to our final formula.

+ The carrying benefits revolve about two complex components: cash flows and a liquidity premium.

+ In the Black-Scholes formula, storage = 0, insurance = 0, dividend cash flow = 0, liquidity premium = 0. This allows us to eliminate all the indifference spread components until we see that: indifference spread = interest costs.

+ This simplifies our original formula: forward price = spot price + interest cost.

+ We can build the interest cost into an easy-to-use multiplier. For instance, if we earn a 6 percent return on $1 for a year, we will then have $1.06 in total. The standard formula for simple interest is 1 + interest rate times the original investment (1.06 times $1). The 1.06 becomes our interest rate multiplier. We are investigating cases where the original investment is the spot price. We can abbreviate spot as S.

+ Multiplying S times our interest rate multiplier (1.06) yields $1.06S$. In other words, the forward price equals the interest rate multiplier (1.06) times the spot price (S). So we've solved our forward price formula—all we need is the spot price and the proper interest rate multiplier, which in this case was 1.06.

- Economists have developed the ultimate interest rate multiplier: e^{RT}. They use this as their interest rate multiplier of choice in almost all advanced formulas. It looks messy, but it's easy to use once you get the hang of it.
- They also use e^{RT} in the Black-Scholes option formula. Instead of a forward price calculation like $S \times 1.06$, they use $S \times e^{RT}$.

THINGS TO THINK ABOUT

Our new expression e^{RT} is an interest rate multiplier that shows the rate of growth on your original investment. It has an inverse function with a minus sign, e^{-RT}, that is also an interest rate multiplier, but, since it is inverse, it shows the rate of shrinking. Economists don't call this shrinking, they call it "discounting." When multiplied, the inverses cancel each other and equal 1: $e^{RT} \times e^{-RT} = 1$. Remember we spoke about the fair value of an option equaling the expected gain *discounted*? The discounting method used is this shrinking interest rate multiplier: e^{-RT}.

When you take delivery of spot material, you become a holder of inventory. All the traders who trade forwards and futures are trying to avoid holding inventory. Among the many reasons why they avoid holding inventory, a primary reason is cost. They are trying to avoid the cost. But the market is too clever for them. It builds this avoided cost into the forward prices so that, in effect, a buyer of forwards is paying the appropriate price to avoid holding inventory. So, in fact, a trader does not avoid the cost when buying forwards or futures. Traders who own forwards or futures tend to sell these contracts just before they come to delivery day and roll them out into other more deferred contracts. The accumulated extra price paid for this is known as the *cost of rolling*.

HOW TO DOUBLE YOUR MONEY

The Rule of 72 shows how to quickly estimate how long it takes to double your money (or what rate is needed for a certain time period). As examples, 8 percent takes 9 years ($8 \times 9 = 72$) and 6 percent takes 12 years ($6 \times 12 = 72$). The rule works based on our expression e^{RT} because when $R \times T = 0.72$, then e^{RT} becomes 2.00; that is, your original investment of 1.00 has doubled to 2.00 through compounding. It's a great rule of thumb and a time saver with more than reasonable accuracy. With a little practice you can compute doubles in your head like a regular Wall Street wizard.

WHEN FUTURES OR FORWARDS BECOME SPOT

Convergence is the term describing the collapse of time between spot delivery date and a future (or forward) delivery date. For example, say it is October 15 and the spot delivery day is October 17 and you are also looking at a December future contract scheduled for December 1 delivery. At that point their deliveries are 45 days apart. But a week later the deliveries are only 38 days apart and so on. When time passes and we've reached November 29, a strange thing happens: both spot and the December future are due to be delivered on the same day, December 1. The dates have converged. At that point there is no difference between the two markets, and so their prices must also be equal. This is called convergence of price. Essentially what was a price spread between the two has dwindled to zero when the delivery dates converge. A far more advanced question with no easy answer is, Does the spot price rise to meet the forward, or does the forward fall to meet the spot, or both?

INDIFFERENCE SPREAD EQUALS THE BASIS

One of the biggest headaches for hedgers is basis risk. Basis risk is an important aspect of a trader's life when he or she is active in both the spot and forward markets. Basis refers to the indifference spread we just described: spot versus forward. But it also implies a slight difference in the products that cannot so easily be dismissed. Cash, or spot, markets may require delivery of a product that is similar to, but not identical or fungible with, the futures product. As such, a nonconverging price difference may always exist.

QUESTIONS

Use the graph in Fig. 12–3 for questions 1 to 9.

1. What market type is represented by the graph in Fig. 12–3?
2. You have bought an April 03 gold future, and it is now March 27. You will get delivery if you don't get out in the next few days. You feel it is important to own gold,

F I G U R E   12–3

Gold Futures Prices
(on March 01, 2003)

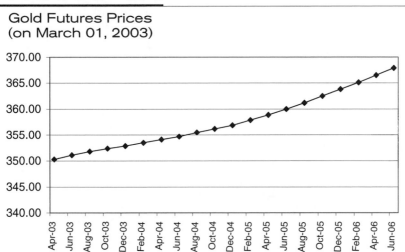

but you are afraid (or unable) to take delivery. What can you do?

3. April 03 gold closed today at $350.30 and June 03 gold closed at $351.10. How much will it cost to roll over?

4. The April gold contract trades until almost the last day in April. What will happen to the spread in price between April and June as time moves on?

5. What are the factors affecting how wide or narrow the April/June spread is?

6. At this point in time short-term interest rates are at very low levels (1.45 percent). If gold storage costs 0.3 percent a year and the liquidity premium is a low 0.4 percent, how would you calculate the annualized return for carrying gold?

7. What does it mean when we say "a 1.37 percent annual return for carrying gold"?

8. What is your guess as to the typical price curve for individual stocks like IBM or AT&T? Does it look similar to the forward price curve for gold in Fig. 12–3?

9. What is your guess as to the typical price curve for U.S. government long bonds? Does it look similar to or different than the forward price curve for gold in Fig. 12–3?

Use the graph in Fig. 12–4 for questions 10 and 11.

Crude Oil Futures Prices
(on March 01, 2003)

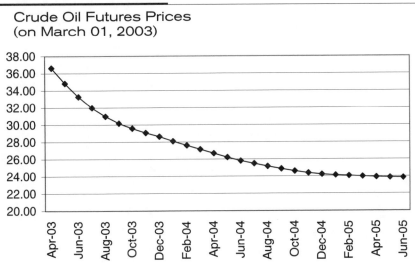

10. What type of market is displayed by the crude oil
    market graph in Fig. 12–4?
11. What rational explanation could there be for such a
    steep price curve in oil (see Fig. 12–4)?

The Formula

PART TWO

SECTION

CHAPTER 13

Skeleton for an Option Formula

At this point we are familiar with the basic math of options. We aren't expert in this math, mind you, but you can now nod wisely when various concepts are discussed. Throughout the book our studies have uncovered important pieces to the option puzzle. We would like to see now if we can somehow pull the pieces together into the simple framework of a formula that would show us how an option might be priced.

We expect this is sort of like tinkering in the garage with spare parts trying to build a car engine. The engine might not be very elegant or functional at first, but we will be better mechanics for our efforts. And when we open up the hood of any car afterward, we will know at a glance where everything fits and what it does.

We are not looking to build a finalized, polished version here, but merely a generic framework. Taking this broad brush approach will exempt us from resolving the intricate subtleties that the original option modelers had to deal with. Rather than being forced to prove every concept in excruciating detail we will be allowed to merely try to get the big picture right: what a workable option model might look like at first sketching, rough and unfinished.

In the 20 years before Black and Scholes cracked the code there were dozens of teams of mathematicians separately racing forward on similar projects. Most were caught just a tad short when Black and Scholes published their results, having been hung up on an unsolved detail or two. Because most of the researchers tended to view the option problem similarly they were limited to rummaging through the same box of statistical formulas and mathematical tools. This accounts for why many of the models look like clones of each other. Many option formulas, even today, have the same basic look as the Black-Scholes formula, which was finalized 30 years ago. This makes it simpler for us to become familiar with the various components and remember them later on. When you've seen one, you've seen 'em all.

All we have to do is develop our makeshift option formula in a simplistic, logical fashion and it comes out mimicking the Black-Scholes formula. Since we wanted this to be a quick, painless course in sketching, we will not rigorously prove the merits of each detail. This allows us to speed things up a lot. You will clearly recognize the blueprints we're about to draw up when you see the Black-Scholes formula.

THE KEY TO ALL OPTIONS: PROBABILITIES AND PAYOFFS

As we've said many times throughout the book, the key to all option pricing is the ability to sum up all the payoffs $\times$ probabilities. Easy to say, but hard to do. Here is the mathematician's way of saying it:

$$\Sigma \ \text{Pay}_i \times \text{prob}_i$$

Remember discussing the option payoff at expiry $(S - K)$ in earlier chapters? This says that, at expiration, the IBM spot price (S) minus the option's strike price (K) gives us the option's final value. Technically speaking this can be shown as max $[S - K, 0]$, meaning you get the bigger payoff of $S - K$ or zero. If $S - K$ is a positive number, it is profitable and we exercise the option. But if the value $S - K$ is negative, then we would choose *not* to exercise (unless we like losing money) and our option would simply expire. In that case we get nothing and pay nothing. Therefore, each option payoff must be zero or higher, always.

It's helpful to note that the strike price (K) is always constant throughout the calculation and never changes (for the $105 call, say, K always stays at \$105 throughout the calculation). But the final IBM spot price S is uncertain and can vary all over the place. We use S_i in place of S to show it can have many, many values. The tiny subscript i can have a million different values (or more) if needed. This is what makes multiplying the payoffs and probabilities impossible for discrete mathematics. So, instead, we use a continuous math (built into the normal distribution) to evaluate all these zillions of tiny calculations. Don't forget, each possible spot price S_i has an associated probability of occurrence (called prob_i).

We started this chapter with the simple summation: $\Sigma \text{ pay}_i \times \text{prob}_i$, and we are now going to build our model from that. Since the payoff values are also equal to $S_i - K$, let's put that into the expression in place of payoff_i. This gives us a new expression:

$$\Sigma(S_i - K) \times \text{prob}_i$$

So far we've used the summation symbol sigma (Σ) to help us recognize that we must always add up a zillion tiny values to compute the expected gain. Now that we are learning to use the continuous math of the normal distribution we should try to use the symbols it requires and drop the sigma (Σ), which is used in discrete math only. We'll add the normal distribution symbols later. So far the new formula looks like this:

$$(S_i - K) \times \text{prob}_i$$

Also, we can split the two values S_i and K apart if we make sure we continue to properly multiply each by prob_i. All option formulas do this, for a reason that we will discuss later in the chapter. Let's split them apart, which doesn't affect the value at all:

$$S_i \times \text{prob}_i - K \times \text{prob}_i$$

To make the expression a bit easier to read we can rely on an alternative multiplication symbol used in many books. This change allows us to use a dot "•" instead of an "×". Whenever you see the dot "•", it simply means "multiplied by," same as an "×".

$$S_i \bullet \text{prob}_i - K \bullet \text{prob}_i$$

All our option examples so far have taken place based on today's closing prices. But in the real world of options it is often many days before the option expires, and thus the payoff is really based on a price that exists many days in the future. In essence, the price is a forward price. It turns out, then, that we are more accurate in using the forward price of IBM rather than the spot price.

Sounds complicated, but just in the last chapter (Chap. 12) we discussed an amazingly simple expression to relate spot and forward prices. We told you there was an important and elegant interplay between spot and forward prices in option theory that we couldn't discuss until you knew some more of the basics. Well, we're ready. This is where we disclose a few of the magic tricks that the option creators used to make the formula so short, sweet, and effective.

In Chap. 12 we showed that IBM's spot price S_i can be made into a forward price merely by applying the interest rate multiplier e^{RT}. That is, if S_i is the spot price, then $S_i \cdot e^{RT}$ is the forward price. Don't forget the dot "•" now replaces our usual multiplication symbol "×". Let's change the spot into a forward (that is, S_i into $S_i \cdot e^{RT}$):

$$S_i \cdot e^{RT} \cdot \text{prob}_i - K \cdot \text{prob}_i$$

We are almost done. This formula gives us the value of a call option at expiration. But expiration might be months *or years* away. The question is, since we won't get paid this expected gain until some time in the future, how much should we pay for it today? To calculate this we must discount the future expected gain into what it is worth today. This is also known as present valuing. Happily for us, since e^{RT} is a growth factor, its inverse function e^{-RT} (notice the minus sign), is a shrinking factor. Since the whole formula represents the future expected gain, if we multiply the whole formula times e^{-RT}, this will tell us the appropriate *discounted present value* that we should pay today. This is like the clever sleight-of-hand part of a magic trick. By multiplying through with e^{-RT} we make the original e^{RT} disappear and then reappear elsewhere, but as its inverse! This happens because multiplying *inverse functions* makes them cancel each other out, returning the value 1 (and it's unimportant to show 1 as a multiplier, so it disappears). To recap, $e^{-RT} \cdot e^{RT} = 1$. Let's walk through it:

1. Multiply: $e^{-RT} \cdot [S_i \cdot e^{RT} \cdot \text{prob}_i \quad - K \cdot \text{prob}_i]$
2. Expand: $e^{-RT} \cdot S_i \cdot e^{RT} \cdot \text{prob}_i \quad - e^{-RT} \cdot K \cdot \text{prob}_i$
3. Reconfigure: $(e^{-RT} \cdot e^{RT}) \cdot (S_i \cdot \text{prob}_i) - e^{-RT} \cdot K \cdot \text{prob}_i$
4. Simplify: $1 \cdot (S_i \cdot \text{prob}_i) \quad - e^{-RT} \cdot K \cdot \text{prob}_i$
5. Final formula: $S_i \cdot \text{prob}_i \quad - e^{-RT} \cdot K \cdot \text{prob}_i$

If you didn't go through these five steps and merely glanced at the starting and ending points, it would seem that e^{RT} simply moved from next to S_i to next to K. But, in fact, the first e^{RT} was canceled out through multiplication and its inverse, e^{-RT}, is now part of the second piece.

We've done what we set out to do. We've created an option formula (of sorts) from scratch, and we call the result our final formula. It tells us the price we can pay *today* for the call option even though we won't reap the harvest until the expiration date in the *future*. What it doesn't do, however, is show us how to evaluate our unknowns, S_i and prob_i and how to tie our formula into the Black-Scholes formula. With a little help from the statisticians and the normal distribution we can do both.

Over the past few chapters the going has gotten tougher, but we are now over the hump and things will start to lighten up shortly. We're going to wrap this up real soon, but for the rest of this chapter we need you to wake up and pay attention here! The economists throw one more sleight-of-hand magic trick at us. It explains how Black and Scholes cleverly solved for $\Sigma \, \text{pay}_i \times \text{prob}_i$ while we could not. The finish line is looming directly in our sights. If you stick it out, you'll get your first look at the Holy Grail of option markets, the Black-Scholes formula. And there are another few bonus goodies right at the end of the chapter.

GETTING DOWN TO PROBABILITIES

The option mathematicians had a problem that was unsolvable with discrete math, so they turned to the continuous math of statistics. Their problem was how to evaluate all the possible final IBM spot prices S_i and their individual probabilities prob_i. They recognized that the normal curve formulas called CDFs enabled them to cumulate each and every tiny probability under the curve. As we've discussed in detail in Chap. 4, these cumulative distribution functions (CDFs) are the key to tapping into the probabilities of the normal curve.

Having said that, it finally makes sense to discuss the symbols that go hand in hand with using the normal curve. A normal curve CDF is represented by the symbol $N(D_1)$. N stands for, you guessed it, the normal curve, and D_1 stands for the point we want to cumulate through. Put less precisely, the symbol $N(D_1)$ means "we are going to split the normal curve into two probability zones: more than D_1 and less than D_1".

How Many Probabilities for an Option:
One or Two?

During our tinkering process in arriving at our final formula we used only one probability which we called prob_i. But Black and Scholes (and others) seem to display *two probabilities* in their formulas, even though they agree that there is only one true probability! In an effort to perform computational magic they use both $N(D_1)$ and $N(D_2)$ although only one of them, $N(D_2)$, is a true probability as we've come to know it.

This sounds pretty confusing, right? Why did they do this? And, to use an old quip from Saturday Night Live, "More importantly, what does it mean to me, Al Franken?" To answer these questions we need to compare the Black-Scholes formula with our final formula, item for item. Here, then, is our first peek at the Black-Scholes formula. We hope it's everything you thought it would be!

Black-Scholes formula: $S \cdot N(D_1) - e^{-RT} \cdot K \cdot N(D_2)$

Our final formula: $S_i \cdot \text{prob}_i - e^{-RT} \cdot K \cdot \text{prob}_i$

The two are so similar that we can readily compare them. But, of course, that's what we were aiming for, to make you sufficiently familiar and comfortable with the Black-Scholes formula that you could begin to really dig in and learn how to use it, rather than being overwhelmed and intimidated by it! If we think of $N(D_1)$ and $N(D_2)$ as simply probability 1 and probability 2, we can see that the Black-Scholes formula uses two different probabilities, whereas we use only one. That is the crux of the difference between our homemade final formula and the Black-Scholes formula, so let's see if we can reconcile this difference.

Each formula has two pieces: a left side and right side. Let's take a closer look at only the right sides of the formulas:

Black-Scholes (right side only): $- e^{-RT} \cdot K \cdot N(D_2)$

Our Final Formula (right side only): $- e^{-RT} \cdot K \cdot prob_i$

They look identical except for the probability pieces. Where we use $prob_i$, the Black-Scholes formula uses the normal curve probability $N(D_2)$ instead. We are actually in total agreement with Black and Scholes here. There is only one true probability for a given option, *and this is it.* Though we give them different names, we agree that our probability $prob_i$ can be precisely computed by $N(D_2)$ and that both represent the *one and only* true probability.

Notice that neither $N(D_2)$ nor $prob_i$ are linked to possible payoffs. That's because we broke payoffs into two pieces, remember: $S_i - K$. Since the strike price K remains constant and never changes, it presents a simple calculation. Splitting it out and separating it to the right side of each formula at least makes one piece of the puzzle clear-cut and easily solvable. The difficulty lies in the millions of possible final spot prices S_i and their individual probabilities. That has been pushed to the left side of each formula:

Black-Scholes (left side only): $S \cdot N(D_1)$

Our final formula (left side only): $S_i \cdot prob_i$

On the left side, it seems, all four expressions are different. And they do not look too easy to reconcile. But, by using an old math trick we can reconfigure our final formula to make it more similar to the Black-Scholes formula and help clear up the differences.

Here is the trick. Any number multiplied by 1 is still the same number. But there are an infinite number of clever ways to represent 1. For instance, the fraction 4/4 is 1, 99/99 is 1, and S/S is also 1. If we multiply S/S times our left side, $S_i \cdot prob_i$, it turns into $S/S \cdot S_i \cdot prob_i$. With multiplication and division, any order sequence of calculation gives us the same final answer. So we can reconfigure the order in which we do the calculations any way we choose. We choose this way: $S \cdot S_i/S \cdot \text{prob}_i$. Inserting parentheses doesn't affect the calculation at all, but does help us more clearly see the relationships, as follows: $S \cdot (S_i/S \cdot \text{prob}_i)$. Let's recap our new look:

Black-Scholes formula (left side only): $S \cdot N(D_1)$

Our reconfigured formula (left side only): $S \cdot \left(\dfrac{S_i}{S} \cdot \text{prob}_i \right)$

We can now clearly see that Black and Scholes' $N(D_1)$ is equivalent to our newly reconfigured probability piece ($S_i/S \cdot \text{prob}_i$). This new probability piece leans heavily on the one true probability (our old prob_i) which is modified by the multiplier S_i/S. If you recall some of our earlier lessons, you'll recognize that S_i/S is simply a distribution (because S_i has not one value, but many possible values) of all the possible returns on IBM's stock price. Study this table of returns for a moment:

Possible Final IBM Spot Prices S_i	Possible Final IBM Returns S_i/S
$100	1.00
$101	1.01
$102	1.02
$103	1.03

This table is short and sweet and, therefore, omits the zillions of possibilities that exist in between and beyond the few numbers we've included. But it exemplifies nicely the point we need to make, which is the very simple relationship between all the final possible spot prices S_i and final possible returns S_i/S. Remember, we keep S, today's spot price of IBM, constant at $100. Therefore, we are always dividing S_i by $100.

What you see in the returns column of the table, represents just part of the long list of all the possible returns. These are the weights we must assign to each and every prob_i if we want to properly create the expected gain, which is what the formula represents. This weighting was not done on the right side of the formula (we only had prob$_i$ there), so it must be done on the left side. The problem with the formula we've created from scratch is that we've got the right idea, but no way to implement it in the real world. Black and Scholes do have a way to make it work, however, by using the normal curve CDFs and employing an elegant trick or two.

Black and Scholes' trick for applying the appropriate payoff weights is to take the true probability from the right side of the Black-Scholes formula, called $N(D_2)$, and modify it by S_i/S (the possible returns on IBM). This shows up as $N(D_1)$ on the left side. This is not the option's true probability, but is a pseudoprobability, in other words, a *modified version* of the true probability (even as 6 year olds we knew about *modified versions* of the truth). This modified (pseudo) probability $N(D_1)$ is the one that gives payoff weightings to each probability and thus solves the last and most difficult part of the puzzle.

To recap, the Black-Scholes formula looks very much like our final formula, but it uses the normal curve probabilities to actually compute what, for us, was only a concept. The expression we originally theorized was Σ pay$_i \times$ prob$_i$, and Black and Scholes turned our theory into practice. Here is a last look at the two formulas that will help you see what matches exactly and what had to be *modified* to turn theory into reality:

Black-Scholes formula: $\qquad S \bullet N(D_1) - e^{-RT} \bullet K \bullet N(D_2)$

Our reconfigured formula: $\qquad S \bullet \left(\dfrac{S_i}{S} \bullet \text{prob}_i \right) - e^{-RT} \bullet K \bullet \text{prob}_i$

The classic option formulas, such as the Black-Scholes formula, are laid out in two pieces due to the need to split the famous $S - K$ payoff value. Each piece requires a slightly different probability. The true probability $N(D_2)$ had to be modified for the left piece. This is because the left piece involves the extra complexity of calculating payoff returns. The need for two different probabilities is the reason for splitting the $S - K$ payoff value.

BONUS TIDBITS

All this may seem real far-out and esoteric. So let's see if we can give you a reason or two to be happy we traveled this far. The two normal curve CDFs, $N(D_1)$ and $N(D_2)$, actually have some down-to-earth, real-world uses. It turns out that $N(D_1)$ is widely recognized by traders as the single most popular hedging factor: it's the *delta*. It's also known to mathematician's as the *hedge ratio*. That sounds pretty impressive doesn't it? And it should, because if there is a single piece of information that every option trader wants to know, it's the delta.

Now you realize, of course, that traders never call it $N(D_1)$, and they certainly never call it the modified true probability or the pseudoprobability, because they haven't got a clue what any of those mean. What they do know is that the risk they see and feel every minute of every trading day is largely related to the delta. Some vaguely know it's based on the normal curve and a probability such as $N(D_1)$, but traders can only focus on what they need to know at the moment (that's your first trading lesson). If it doesn't make or lose them money, they can't be bothered. So you can see how important delta is because that's all they chatter about all day long. "I'm delta long this, but I'm delta short that as a hedge." We discuss delta in plenty of detail in later chapters on risk and hedging.

And what about $N(D_2)$, which we termed the true probability? It may not be as popular or as widely referred to as the delta, but mathematicians had a name for it years before they could calculate it or could write the first option formulas. They were searching for it desperately because it is clearly the core of the option formula. Their name for it is "the probability to be called." Let's translate that into English: in a call option there is a certain probability that the strike price K will be reached at maturity. If reached, the option will be exercised, implying you will be called to deliver IBM shares. Thus $N(D_2)$ is the probability of having the IBM shares called. That's why we renamed it the true probability. It is the probability that the mathematicians needed before they could begin to write the formulas. And, more importantly to us, it is the probability that your option will be *worth anything* at expiration (i.e., get in the money), which is a pretty important probability to anyone who trades.

You can clearly see now that our tinkering has led us to develop a powerful formula with the same basic framework as the Black-Scholes formula. Other major formulas such as the Cox-Ross-Rubinstein binomial model look remarkably similar. Given the preparation we've just gone through, we are more than ready for Chap. 14 where we start using the formula to figure out option premiums on stocks. Afterwards, we teach you a snappy acronym that ensures you will always remember the five factors that are needed to calculate the Black-Scholes formula. With a little practice you can begin to look much smarter than you are! And as Billy Crystal says: "It's not how you feel, dahling, it's how you 'rook'. *And you 'rook' mahvelous, dahling!"*

KEY CONCEPTS REVIEW

- In this chapter we pulled together all the many pieces we had learned and built a simple generic framework of a formula to show how an option might be priced. Because we skipped many of the rigorous steps necessary for a valid proof we only expected to create the shape and form for a reasonable formula, not derive a new one.

- As we've said many times, the key to all option pricing is the ability to sum up all the payoffs × probabilities. Therefore, we started with

$$\Sigma \, \text{Pay}_i \times \text{prob}_i$$

- We know that option payoffs are linked to whatever the final spot price of IBM is less the strike price: $S_i - K$. We put that into the expression in place of payoff$_i$, which gave us a new expression:

$$\Sigma \, (S_i - K) \times \text{prob}_i$$

- We dropped the summation symbol sigma (Σ) because it is used in discrete math and we are switching to the continuous math of the normal distribution. With "Σ" out, the new formula looks like this:

$$(S_i - K) \times \text{prob}_i$$

- We split the two values S_i and K apart, which is okay if we make sure to continue multiplying each by prob$_i$. Let's split them apart, which doesn't affect the value at all:

$$S_i \times \text{prob}_i - K \times \text{prob}_i$$

♦ We changed the multiplication sign "×" to a dot "•". Both mean the very same thing. This gives us

$$S_i \bullet \text{prob}_i - K \bullet \text{prob}_i$$

♦ It turns out that we are more accurate in using the forward price of IBM rather than the spot price S_i. We can make S_i a forward price by applying the interest rate multiplier e^{RT}:

$$S_i \bullet e^{RT} \bullet \text{prob}_i - K \bullet \text{prob}_i$$

♦ So far our formula gives us the value of a call option at expiration. But expiration might be months or years away. How much should we pay for it today? We can calculate the present value by using the inverse function e^{-RT} (notice the minus sign). We multiply the whole formula times e^{-RT}. This will tell us the appropriate discounted present value and create our final formula:

$$S_i \bullet \text{prob}_i - e^{-RT} \bullet K \bullet \text{prob}_i$$

♦ Here is the Black-Scholes formula; you can see they have a lot in common:

$$S \bullet N(D_1) - e^{-RT} \bullet K \bullet N(D_2)$$

♦ It turns out that the two formulas are identical if we can show that the Black-Scholes' $N(D_2)$ = our prob_i and Black-Scholes $N(D_1)$ = our $\text{prob}_i \bullet S_i / S$. We make a case that this is true in the chapter and suggest that our jury-rigged formula runs along similar lines of logic used by Black and Scholes. Our purpose in doing this is to show that not only can we understand what goes into the Black-Scholes formula, but that we built something that looks just like it from spare parts in our garage!

♦ A reward for going the distance: It turns out that Black and Scholes' two probabilities $N(D_1)$ and $N(D_2)$, actually have some down-to-earth uses. $N(D_1)$ is widely recognized by traders as the single most popular hedging factor; it's called the *delta*. And $N(D_2)$, which we termed the true probability inside our formula, is known to mathematicians as *the probability to be called*. It is the probability that your option will be worth anything at expiration. Most traders think that's pretty important.

THINGS TO THINK ABOUT

We've Come a Long Way, Baby   There are an awful lot of option books and option formulas out there that only Ph.D.'s in math have any shot at understanding. Despite this we have rummaged around and put a bunch of spare parts together to make a formula that looks tantalizingly like the famed Black-Scholes model. This tells us that we are close to the level of technical knowledge necessary to understand the inner workings of options. We've finished almost all the hard work of becoming acquainted with new and difficult math concepts. From here on we have to focus on how to cleverly use what we know to deepen our understanding of the formula vis-à-vis the markets.

The second most popular option formula is the Cox-Ross-Rubinstein model. Despite the fact that it is based on the binomial distribution and uses slightly different symbols, if you compare it to the Black-Scholes formula and our final formula, you will be amazed at the similarities. There is a perfect piece-by-piece correspondence among all three formulas. In short, they all have the same shape, form, and logic for arriving at an option's value.

All that tinkering around in our garage with spare parts must have taught us some pretty useful stuff if our generic formula fits perfectly with the two most important models in the world. You should be proud of yourself—very few traders know as much as you do about the inner workings of options. If we can learn how this technical mumbo-jumbo can be translated to the real world and get some market savvy, we are heading in exactly the right direction.

QUESTIONS

1. The key to all option pricing is the ability to sum up all the payoffs $\times$ probabilities, which can be shown as Σ $\mathrm{pay}_i \times \mathrm{prob}_i$. Why is this easy to say, but hard to do?
2. In $\Sigma\ \mathrm{pay}_i \times \mathrm{prob}_i$ what does the subscript i mean?

3. We replaced pay_i with the expression $S_i - K$. What does $S_i - K$ mean, and why are we allowed to substitute this expression?

4. Using $S_i - K$ calculate the payoff at expiration for an IBM \$90 call option if IBM's spot price S_i closes at \$80, \$90, \$100, and \$104.

5. Assume the interest rate is 10 percent, IBM spot is \$100, and you need to compute a 6-month forward IBM price. How would you do it? (*Hint:* Use e^{RT}.)

6. We talked about discounting and present valuing in the chapter. Take the 6-month forward IBM price (the answer to question 5) and reverse the process to show how this discounting process works. (*Hint:* Use the inverse of e^{RT} which is e^{-RT}.)

7. We split apart our payoff $\times$ probability expression, $(S_i - K) \times \text{prob}_i$, into two parts: $S_i \times \text{prob}_i$ and $-K \times \text{prob}_i$. Why is this okay?

Getting Comfortable with the Black-Scholes Formula

In Chap. 13 we built a generic option formula piece by piece and then introduced the Black-Scholes formula for the first time to show how remarkably similar the two formulas were. In this chapter we will begin to familiarize ourselves with the Black-Scholes formula by working a few examples in detail, step by step. Here is the Black-Scholes formula as it is typically shown in most option books:

$$C = SN(D_1) - KN(D_2)\, e^{-RT}$$

This formula may look odd to you because our multiplication dots (•) are missing. Let's include the dots again, spread the formula out a bit, and comment on it piecemeal:

$$C \;=\; S \cdot N(D_1) \;-\; K \cdot N(D_2) \cdot e^{-RT}$$

Call Premium	Spot Stock Price	Probability @ D_1	Strike Price	Probability @ D_2	Discounting Factor

We learned how to decipher each piece in Chap. 13, but let's do a quick recap. Like they say about chicken soup for a cold, "it might not help, *but it couldn't hurt.*"

C = call premium (the fair price of the option)
S = spot stock price
$N(D_1)$ = probability 1 from the normal curve CDF (evaluated at point D_1)
K = strike price of the option (the kick-in exercise level)
$N(D_2)$ = probability 2 from the normal curve CDF (evaluated at point D_2)
e^{-RT} = discounting factor (the value e to the power "minus $R \times T$")
R = interest rate, risk free
T = time, portion of a year

We must figure out the value of each of the five components on the right side of the equation [S, $N(D_1)$, K, $N(D_2)$, e^{-RT}] and insert them. Then, after some simple multiplication and subtraction out comes the call premium. As we've said before, the dots are simply math symbols for multiplying. Most formulas don't show where multiplication is implied, which can be confusing when you don't know the formula well.

Finding the values of S and K is a snap, and the value of e^{-RT} is simple enough to determine after a little practice, but finding $N(D_1)$ and $N(D_2)$ is much more complicated.

The symbols $N(D_1)$ and $N(D_2)$ do not require multiplying $N \cdot D_1$ or $N \cdot D_2$. N means nothing by itself nor does $N(\ )$. We need both N and D_1 together in the format $N(D_1)$ to have it make sense. It then represents the normal curve's CDF evaluated through the point D_1. This is clearly the most complex part of the formula. Without it the formula might be fully explained in a few chapters instead of a book. We described CDFs in Chapter 11 specifically to help prepare us for learning to use $N(D_1)$ and $N(D_2)$. They are cumulative distribution functions, the summed up probabilities from the normal curve. We've already done a lot of preliminary work with summed up probabilities for the binomial distribution. We'll get back to $N(D_1)$ and $N(D_2)$ again at the end of the chapter.

We can get comfortable with all the pieces by working some simple examples and putting the Black-Scholes formula to some practical use. Let's figure out the value of a call option on IBM.

Black-Scholes Analysis of a Call on IBM

Let S = 100 (That is, IBM spot is trading at $100 right now.)

K = 100 (strike price = $100 means the call option grants the right to buy IBM at $100 at expiration, no matter how high it actually is then.)

R = 10% = .10 (annual riskless rate of interest)

T = 1 year (time to expiry, in years)

Probability 1 = $N(D_1)$ = .72575 }
Probability 2 = $N(D_2)$ = .65542 }

For probabilities 1 and 2, we are merely giving precalculated values rather than getting into the complex explanations needed.*

So, how much is this IBM call worth? Let's go to the formula and compute the call premium C:

$$C = S \cdot N(D_1) - K \cdot N(D_2) \cdot e^{-RT}$$
$$= (100) \cdot (.72575) - 100 \cdot (.65542) \cdot e^{-(.10) \cdot (1)}$$

We have four of the five components already calculated, but not e^{-RT}. Use the following table to see how we turn rate and time into a discount factor. To simplify things, we let T remain steady with a value of 1 year in each calculation.

R(%)	e^{-RT}	Discount Factor
0	$e^{-(0.00) \cdot (1)}$	= 1.000
2	$e^{-(0.02) \cdot (1)}$	= 0.980
4	$e^{-(0.04) \cdot (1)}$	= 0.961
6	$e^{-(0.06) \cdot (1)}$	= 0.942
8	$e^{-(0.08) \cdot (1)}$	= 0.923
10	$e^{-(0.10) \cdot (1)}$	= 0.905

The value of e by itself is always 2.718. But e^{-RT} changes according to the values we place on R and T. You can see the e^{-RT}

---

* For those "in the know" already, we used a volatility of 20 percent for IBM stock.

values vary inversely with R due to the minus sign. As the interest rates rise, the discount factor grows smaller.

In our IBM option example R is 10 percent (same as .10) and T is 1 year. If you look in the table at the 10 percent row, you'll see that it reads across: $e^{-(0.10)\cdot(1)}$ and 0.905. That is, e^{-RT} at 10 percent for 1 year implies our answer is $e^{-(0.10)\cdot(1)}$. This is equal to 0.905, which is called a discount factor. [We substituted 2.718 for e so that the value $e^{-(0.10)\cdot(1)}$ translated to $2.718^{-(0.10)\cdot(1)}$. We simplified it further to $2.718^{-0.10}$ which equals 0.905.]

The discounting can be translated as follows: One dollar in a year is worth 90.5 cents right now (if the continuously compounded interest rate is 10 percent). This methodology determines today's present value for money that will be received at a future date. Present valuing is a critical step in the financial analysis of cash flows.

The two values e^{RT} and e^{-RT} are very important to us in options analysis and are polar opposites. The first creates forward value and the second creates present value. We originally met e^{RT} in Chap. 12 when we turned a spot price into a forward price using $S \times e^{RT}$. In that situation we computed the forward value. To do the opposite, that is, compute the present value, we multiply by the discounting factor, e^{-RT}. With a little practice this becomes second nature even if it seems complicated right now. For our purposes here just recognize that at 10 percent for 1 year e^{-RT} is worth .905. Back to the formula:

$$C = S \cdot N(D_1) - K \cdot N(D_2) \cdot e^{-RT}$$
$$= 100 \cdot (.72575) - 100 \cdot (.65542) \cdot (.905)$$
$$= 72.575 \quad\quad - 65.542 \cdot (.905)$$
$$= 72.575 \quad\quad - 59.305$$
$$= \$13.270 \quad \text{(the premium per share of an IBM \$100 call)}$$

This \$13.27 is the fair value for that specific IBM option under the conditions we specified. *As each condition changes, the fair value will change.* Don't forget, option traders *cannot make money by trading at fair value.* They must sell higher and buy lower. This is not always easy to do, as many have found out. In fact, as the competition has increased over the last 20 years, it is always very difficult to buy low and sell high compared to fair value.

Using the formula is not too difficult, as you can see from our practice example. It is the deeper understanding of the pieces to the formula that is difficult. We have outlined the basics here and hopefully this will pave the way to enable you to achieve a greater sophistication and knowledge. As such you will be able to join in the search that has become an obsession for many other traders: the search for mispriced options.

Let's try another example.

$$S = 100 \text{ (IBM spot} = \$100 \text{ right now)}$$
$$K = 130 \text{ (Strike is far away this time.)}$$
$$R = 10\%$$
$$T = 1 \text{ year}$$
$$N(D_1) = .23829$$
$$N(D_2) = .18093$$

$$C = S \bullet N(D_1) - K \bullet N(D_2) \bullet e^{-RT}$$
$$= 100 \bullet (.23829) - 130 \bullet (.18093) \bullet (.905)$$
$$= 23.829 - 21.283 = 2.546$$

Wow! What happened? We had an option value of $13.270 a minute ago and now it's dropped to $2.546! The only real change was the strike price (*K*) which moved from $100 to $130. And the probability values $N(D_1)$ and $N(D_2)$ also changed dramatically. Their change was due solely to the change in *strike price*.

When IBM spot is trading at $100 now, the 1-year option to purchase it at $100 is worth a lot more than the 1-year option to purchase it at $130. Clearly, there is a much larger chance to make money with the $100 option than with the $130 option. The lower strike price ($100) translates to higher probability and higher pay-offs per final IBM value. Say IBM closes at $134. The lower strike will pay off at $34, while the higher strike pays only $4. Therefore, $N(D_1)$ and $N(D_2)$ have much larger values at the lower strike ($100).

So now you have a mild working familiarity with the Black-Scholes formula. Clearly, the spot stock price (*S*) and the strike price (*K*) are simple to find and input. The discounting factor e^{-RT} is certainly more complex, but if you think of it as a simple interest rate multiplier (worth .905 at 10 percent for a year), it is easy to deal with.

The key difficulty to deeply understanding option formulas is the meshing of probability distributions with payoff distributions. We've noted this often. Without a good approximation for all the *possible future outcomes*, the party would be over and options would be totally unpriceable.

It just so happens that Black and Scholes have found a good method for approximating this, and it is expressed as their components $N(D_1)$ and $N(D_2)$. Unfortunately these components are about as simple as four-dimensional Rubik's cubes.

Options traders come to intimately know $N(D_1)$ and $N(D_2)$ by their more common names. $N(D_1)$ is also called the *delta* or the *hedge ratio*. $N(D_2)$ is less well known but just as important; it is the *probability to be called*. The concept of the delta, or hedge ratio, is very important to all of us, and we will cover it again later when we discuss the topics of risk and hedging. Familiarity with the detailed math underlying it is not critical for the first pass through on this elementary tour. In Chap. 15 we reveal an acronym that will make this complicated mish-mash far easier to remember. It's such a good memory aid, in fact, that we have students telling us they remember it 15 years later.

KEY CONCEPTS REVIEW

+ In this chapter we got up close and personal with the Black-Scholes option formula.
+ We described each and every piece of the formula so that the reader could get more comfortable with it.
+ We reviewed many facts learned earlier such as the normal curve probabilities, CDFs, $N(D_1)$ and $N(D_2)$, and e^{RT} and e^{-RT}.
+ While doing this we also solved for two call option premiums step by step.

THINGS TO THINK ABOUT

Most traders have far less acquaintance with the Black-Scholes formula than what was reviewed in this chapter. And, for the most part, you already knew all this material. You are now far more familiar with the Black-Scholes formula than the average trader. The typical option trader plugs some inputs into his or her computer and out spits the option premium. He or she never really considers taking apart the "black box" that generates all the magic answers.

Where they excel, and we are naïve, is in real-time trading. If they aren't keenly experienced, canny, and shrewd, they soon get blown out of the markets. If you trade in the markets every day and survive for a few years, you have what it takes. Then it's just a question of how good your skills are and at what level you can play the game. We will work further on our technical skills in the coming chapters and also try to prepare you for some of the realities of the markets. If you want to become a good trader, you'll have to have a strong and deep understanding of all the things we discuss and absorb a lot of real-time experience as well.

Twenty years ago we had an impatient junior trader corner us and demand, "I really want to learn everything there is about trading and everything you can teach me. I can't wait. How long will it take me to become a full-fledged trader who knows everything?" Put on the spot and knowing how impatient this fellow was we said, "Two years. In 2 years you should know how to trade and be smart enough to realize how much more you need to know." He said *"Two years! I can't believe it. No way."* Two years went by and we asked him whether he had learned everything he needed to know about trading. He said, "I feel I learned a real lot, but only about half as much as I need to know." Twenty years later we asked him if he learned everything he needed to know about trading, and he told us "I think I'm getting there!" This is a very shrewd trader. When he does certain types of arbitrage trades, everybody in the pit follows him. You can never say you've learned everything the markets have to teach you. There is a new situation to learn about every day. Surviving counts for a lot more than you might think, and the true measure of discipline is the ability to thrive in different types of market environments. Experience is measured in decades not in the number of tickets you've time stamped this month or the coups you've pulled off recently. Some of the hottest traders are here today, but gone tomorrow. Don't let that happen to you.

QUESTIONS

Questions 1 to 5 relate to the Black-Scholes formula:

$$C = S \cdot N(D_1) - K \cdot N(D_2) \cdot e^{-RT}$$

1. We must figure out the value of the five components on the right side of the equation and insert them to compute a call option premium. Name the five components.
2. Briefly describe each of the five components from question 1. Also describe C.
3. In the chapter we said finding the value of S or K is a snap. Why is that so?
4. We mentioned that the value of e^{-RT} (the discounting factor) is simple enough after a little practice. Let's get a little practice now. Compute e^{-RT} for two time periods (6 months and 1 year) and three interest rates (0, 5, and 10 percent).
5. As we said, finding $N(D_1)$ and $N(D_2)$ is much more complicated. For our examples here we'll provide them as needed. We want you to calculate the fair value of the following five IBM call options using the information provided. Assume IBM is trading at $100 now and that interest = 10 percent.

$80 call, 3-month expiry: $N(D_1) = .9581$, $N(D_2) = .9429$
$90 call, 4-month expiry: $N(D_1) = .8126$, $N(D_2) = .7625$
$100 call, 6-month expiry: $N(D_1) = .6337$, $N(D_2) = .5516$
$110 call, 6-month expiry: $N(D_1) = .4572$, $N(D_2) = .3746$
$120 call, 6-month expiry: $N(D_1) = .3023$, $N(D_2) = .2327$

Introducing Volatility and SKIT-V

The Five Black-Scholes Inputs

In Chap. 14 we discussed the Black-Scholes formula and broke it down into its component parts. In this chapter we will take one final step down to arrive at the formula's most basic level: the very inputs that make up the component parts. We have created an acronym for these inputs called SKIT-V. If you can remember that simple mnemonic, we guarantee you will be able to recall the five inputs of the Black-Scholes formula long after you've forgotten the formula. Better yet, it will help you instantly recall and connect all the inputs in your mind so that you see them as the inseparable pieces of the option jigsaw puzzle that they are.

The Black-Scholes formula, as we learned in Chap. 14, can be broken down into five separate pieces which we called its five components. Each component requires one or more inputs. The five Black-Scholes components from Chap. 14 were S, $N(D_1)$, K, $N(D_2)$, e^{-RT}. We are now going to describe the inputs that are necessary to create the components. By coincidence, there are five of them also. They are S, K, I, T, and V. We can easily remember them as SKIT-V.

The five inputs described by SKIT-V are

S = spot price of stock
K = strike price of option
I = interest rate

$T = $ time to option maturity
$V = $ volatility of stock

These are the five inputs required by the Black-Scholes formula. A computer program can be set up to take these five inputs, derive values for the five components $[S, N(D_1), K, N(D_2), e^{-RT}]$, and use the formula to get the call premium. We've covered the relevance of the first four of these SKIT-V inputs in previous chapters. Our intention here is to put them all together and show how they fit as a whole.

In Chap. 14 we used R for interest rate. But I makes for a far better acronym, so we switched. And you did not see V in Chap. 14 either because we avoided the pain of showing you the inner workings of $N(D_1)$ and $N(D_2)$ which is where V shows up. We'll gently introduce V here and try to keep away from being too technical.

If you know where to look in *The New York Times* or the *Wall Street Journal* and use a little deductive reasoning, you can quickly find yesterday's values for the first four: S, K, I, T. But volatility V is far more difficult to get a handle on. That's because *everybody knows S, K, I, and T, but nobody knows V.*

The spot price S for a stock like IBM, the strike price K, the time to option maturity T, and the risk-free interest rate I are all easy to get. But nowhere in the papers is the volatility discussed or published. V is a very slippery character.

You see, no one is ever sure that they've got V correct! It's a moving target that is rarely hit. Even if you manage to hit it dead on at any given moment, it keeps changing shortly thereafter, anyway.

"How can this be?" you ask. Why is V more difficult than the others to determine? If it is so slippery, how is it that upstairs traders can have matrixes of option values instantly available to them?

To understand this we should first consider Black and Scholes' definition of V, which is the *future* volatility of the stock. And most people try to measure it with *past* data! The *past* volatility is easy enough to compute if you are conversant with elementary statistics. But unless history repeats exactly, this *past* volatility is only one of many possible *future* volatilities.

This begs the question: Is the future a constantly repeating stream of past events? Many people might think so, but market data does not support it. And academics who support the efficient market hypothesis say the past is irrelevant to the future. They say that the patterns of stock prices and their volatilities are not stable, constant, or repeating. So the elegant assumptions of the Black-Scholes formula are nice, but not necessarily related to the real world.

The reality is that volatilities are ever-changing and basically unpredictable. Is there any hint at all from past data? The answer is a tentative and guarded yes. But it is only a hint, not a bankable certainty.

Black and Scholes assumptions essentially say: *If you can input the volatility for a future period, our formula will compute the fair price of an option for that period.* Otherwise, the formula will be in error. But no one knows the *future volatility*. It is this uncertainty that leads to a lot of confusion about volatility. In trying to get a handle on the confusion, traders have developed different names for different types of volatility.

Traders talk about three different categories of volatility: historical, implied, and future. We can best explain them by categorizing them into their time frames: past, present, and future (not unlike the three ghosts that visited Scrooge).

Historical volatility is simply a measure of the past, a statistical analysis of what has already happened. To calculate it we take recent data, say 30 days worth, apply the formula that computes standard deviation, and then annualize it. Traders *always* look at this data to get a feel and make up their minds as to what should be happening today and what might be happening tomorrow or next week. Some technical analysts go so far as to create systems that use this historical data to try to predict the future. They then suggest trades based on these predictions. You're on your own for that research. We believe it has potential, but it is beyond the scope of our discussions here.

Implied volatility is what the market is implying right this minute, the present. To calculate it we take today's call premium (C) and apply the Black-Scholes formula backwards. If we include C as an unknown, there are then six unknowns in the formula. If we know any five of these, we can readily compute the sixth. Normally we input the five we call SKIT-V and receive C (the call premium) as our answer. Alternatively, we can input SKIT-C and derive the value for V instead. This will tell us the volatility that the market is presently trading at. That is, the market is presently implying this volatility, which is why we call it implied volatility. Clever, eh?

Future volatility is the volatility that will occur over the coming weeks and months. It is the volatility required by the Black-Scholes formula in order to give the correct call premium C. To calculate it you need a crystal ball. Nobody knows how to calculate future volatility (or if they do, at least they are not sharing the knowledge). Anyone knowing a future volatility for certain could make some awesome trading coups. In fact, the best option traders are those who understand the ways of volatility movements. They exert their edge by being right about certain volatility patterns of the public. They aren't even close to always being right, but they have a tradeable advantage that nets a profit at year end over many plays. No one knows the future for sure, but knowing a coin is biased 52 percent for heads can make a big difference—casinos have grown rich on similar edges.

The Holy Grail of option trading is the Black-Scholes formula and a knowledge of future volatility. If you have these two, you can become the world's greatest option wizard. In the search for this Holy Grail many very clever analysts and traders massage the historical and implied volatility information trying desperately to get insight and a glimpse of the future and of future volatility.

Future volatility has a sort of legendary, mythical status. It's often discussed, but never uncovered. The search for the correct volatility to use has led to dozens of very well thought out, highly technical research papers by people with Ph.D.'s in economics. *None agree on the best way to predict future volatility.* A general consensus of the research would be that the market's implied volatility (the opinions of the smartest players) is as good as it gets. And it has been shown again and again that implied volatility is a far better predictor of the future than any simple historical volatility measure.

KEY CONCEPTS REVIEW

- ◆ In this chapter we got down to almost the microscopic level to discuss the basic inputs that go into calculating the component pieces of the Black-Scholes formula.

- There are five basic inputs. We created an acronym called SKIT-V as a simple mnemonic device to remember them. These five most basic inputs are

  S = spot price of stock
  K = strike price of option
  I = riskless rate of interest
  T = time to option maturity in years
  V = expected future volatility

- We already had a working familiarity with the first four, but the fifth (V) was only peripherally discussed until this point. V represents volatility.
- The Black-Scholes formula assumptions require that we input not any old type of volatility, but the future volatility. Interestingly, no one knows the future volatility!
- In their scramble to make sense of this, traders have separated volatilities into three categories: historical, implied, and future. We suggested they are best understood by the time frames they represent: past, present, future.
- The Holy Grail of option trading could be thought of as having two parts to it: a formula to compute fair option value (Black-Scholes) and the correct volatility to input. Now that the formula has been discovered, the Holy Grail and fortune await those who can decipher the proper volatility to input. Therein lies the challenge.

THINGS TO THINK ABOUT

The reason market prices move is because of differences of opinion. The biggest cause for differences is the uncertainty of what the future will bring. Opinions wouldn't matter if all the future facts were already known. It's stupid to bet against a sure thing. That being said, no one knows for sure what a share of stock is worth because its value depends on future outcomes as yet unknown. In options, however, the only unknown is the future volatility. If we knew the future volatility, then all five inputs would be known and *very little argument would exist as to the fair value of the option.* Thus an IBM option's premium would trade up and down exactly in line with the IBM shares of stock. The option market would become a boring extension of the shares of stock and lose all its mystery. As it is, there is a tremendous ongoing argument as to the correct future volatility and thus the option market is alive and kicking. So, it's not so bad that there is a mysterious unknown in the equation.

On the same point, if everything was already known about the future, then any attempt at researching or deciphering the path of future volatility would be pointless, because everybody would already know it. But now it offers tremendous possibilities of fame and fortune. And just to give a little fuel to the flame, we believe that it is doable at least to a small degree.

QUESTIONS

1. What does SKIT-V stand for?
2. Name the five inputs that comprise SKIT-V.
3. Which inputs are easy to find? Which are hard?
4. What are the three types of volatilities that traders use?
5. How can we compute historical volatility?
6. How can we compute implied volatility?
7. How can we compute future volatility?
8. Why would you be able to make big money if you knew the future volatility?

CHAPTER 16

Pros and Cons of the Black-Scholes Formula

The Black-Scholes model is the preeminent formula in the options market. It was the rocket fuel that helped launch the derivatives markets in the 1970s. In October 1997 the creators were granted the Nobel prize for their formula and the changes it wrought in the world of finance.

Discovering the first accurate options model was a major breakthrough. There are a mind-numbing number of economic factors that could possibly impact an option's value, but through hard work and insight the possibilities were narrowed and harnessed. During the late 1960s and early 1970s many top mathematicians and economists joined the battle to be the first to find the solution to pricing options. The atmosphere was superheated; success or failure meant academic credentials were either raised to glory or demolished forever. The competition included several who won Nobel prizes for other pursuits. Paul Samuelson, for example, said he was right on the cusp of finding the answers, but fell a tad short. Close, but no cigar. The Black-Scholes formula got the gold.

What went into the formula and what was left out was one key to success. Answers come quickest for solving the least complex problems. With focused simplicity Black and Scholes got to the line first. But the first version of any software often leaves many problems unsolved. This, it turns out, is true for the Black-Scholes option formula as well. In the search for simplicity many assumptions had to be made that are not accurate reflections of the real world. We now discuss the pros and cons.

Positive Attributes of the Black-Scholes Formula
  * First available formula
  * Universally accepted by traders
  * Fast and easy
  * Elegant mathematics
  * Easily modifiable
  * Clean derivatives

Problems with the Black-Scholes Formula
  * For spot stocks without dividends
  * Only calls
  * No early exercise
  * Requires modified versions
  * Assumes unreal conditions
  * Inaccurate log-normal model

Let's discuss these points, one by one.

PROS OF THE BLACK-SCHOLES FORMULA

First Available Formula to Price Options Accurately

Prior to the publication of the Black-Scholes formula in 1973 there were other formulas used in the marketplace, but they were lacking in completeness on a variety of pricing issues. And there were many competitors simultaneously vying to publish when the Black-Scholes formula appeared in a financial journal. But Black and Scholes got there first. They were the first to break the 4-minute mile in their field. Many runners have run 4-minute miles since Dr. Roger Bannister ran his, but he was the pioneer.

Universally Accepted by Traders

The Black-Scholes formula is so well-known and accepted that it has become the standard in the trading industry. Traders accept it as the universal valuation method. If they trade volatility at 10.75 percent, they can hang up the phone without discussing the premiums at all. They just plug the 10.75 percent volume into their computers under Black-Scholes formulation and the premiums pop out automatically. Everybody in the business recognizes the importance of the Black-Scholes formula. But that doesn't mean they believe it is infallible or even accurate in every case. It is simply a standard that they can all agree on, a starting point. We will broach the issue of the accuracy and inaccuracy of the Black-Scholes formula at the end of this chapter.

Fast and Easy to Use in Calculators

Speed counts, as does ease of use. The Black-Scholes formula is easier to program into a computer than many alternative formulas. And the inputs required by the formula are easier to find than those needed for other option models. Floor traders in the pit have the formula programmed into their handheld calculators. Some option models, such as those that use binomial methods, require a much longer time to calculate a single premium.

Elegant Closed-Form Mathematics

Mathematicians and engineers use differential equations to describe the physical motions of complicated systems. The Black-Scholes model was developed using stochastic differential equations (SDEs) that describe the complicated dynamics of an option within the financial system. The Black-Scholes formula is called the *solution* to these SDEs. In that sense it has a far prettier pedigree than most other models, including the binomial methods we've learned about. Closed-form solutions like the Black-Scholes formula are very quick computationally and less messy to program. They are the tidiest answers to any engineering problem.

Easily Modifiable (Many Versions Exist)

The many assumptions required by the Black-Scholes formula imply that it can only thrive in its own overly simplistic world. This is a bit of a problem, which we'll cover later. There is a positive aspect to the formula that helps solve this problem. Because of its elegant, closed-form mathematics, economists have found it relatively easy to modify the basic formula to allow adjustments for the real world. There are probably a dozen versions of modified Black-Scholes formulas in present usage. The economist-mathematicians home in on a deficiency and find a way to solve it with modifications to the basic formula. The ability to allow for easy modifications is one of the things that keeps the Black-Scholes formula at the top of the class. While many of these modified formulas have been given other names (such as Garman-Kohlhagen), they still trace their lineage to the Black-Scholes formula.

Clean Partial Derivatives (for Risk Measures)

In Chap. 17 we will discuss option risk and what can be done to hedge it. The path to understanding option risk and learning to manage it runs straight through the Black-Scholes formula and its partial derivatives. These partial derivatives come from applying the math of differential calculus. The mathematical symbols used are Greek letters, and option traders have come to call them "the Greeks." The primary Greek option tools are named delta, gamma, vega, and theta. We later show that these are the first and second derivatives of the Black-Scholes formula.

Mathematicians using differential calculus can easily and cleanly derive these risk measures from the Black-Scholes formula. This cannot be done as easily with other option models. In fact, without computers there might be no reasonable way to get risk measurements for other option models. At the beginning of the option model revolution, the 1970s, there wasn't enough computer power to calculate risk measures other than those for the Black-Scholes formula. This left traders in the dark. And good traders can't trade confidently without knowing their risk.

CONS OF THE BLACK-SCHOLES FORMULA

Created Only for Spot Stocks without Dividends

In the 1970s option researchers were battling to design a model for stocks only. While it would be nice to create a model for all assets, only stock options were actively traded at the time and that was their focus. By limiting the scope of the formula they simplified matters greatly. It would take a very long and complex formula to simultaneously provide solutions for all possible asset classes. The basic Black-Scholes model works for stocks in the spot market only and the stocks must have no dividends. Thus bonds, foreign exchange, commodities, and futures and forwards are not handled properly by the basic Black-Scholes model, nor was that ever intended. If you have a spot stock without dividends, the Black-Scholes does a good job of generating the fair value for a call option. Modified Black-Scholes formulas now exist for all the other assets and derivative assets we mentioned a few sentences ago.

Generates Only Call Premiums (No Puts)

The Black-Scholes formula is solved for calls only. If you want to compute the value of the put at the same strike, you can calculate the call and then use conversion valuation methods. This is not too difficult to do, as we'll see in Chap. 20, but not as elegant as the call computation either.

No Early Exercise Allowed (European Style Only)

In Europe the typical option is not allowed to be exercised before the expiration date. Thus, such options are called *European-style options*. In the United States we frequently allow exercise before the expiration date. This is called *American-style* or *early exercise*. The basic Black-Scholes formula works *only* for European-style options. Some modified Black-Scholes formulas have been created to allow for early exercise.

Assumes Many, Many Unreal Conditions

There are many assumptions of the Black-Scholes model which don't make sense in the real world. Here is a list of the assumptions which we haven't already commented on elsewhere:

- Constant volatility
- Constant interest rates
- Infinitesimal trade size
- Infinite rehedging
- Continuous trading (24 hours)
- Continuous compounding

+ Infinite trading liquidity
+ No fees or commissions
+ No bid/ask on prices or interest rates
+ No cost to borrow stock

None of these assumptions are true. On the other hand, many of these assumptions are generally accepted by economists as normal constraints necessary to build models. In other words, Black and Scholes didn't create these assumptions to cheat the competition. Most competitors used simplifying measures similar to these. We won't get into the details here, but you should recognize that all models are based on idealized and simplified versions of the real world. When we try to explain the real world with simple models, there are always difficulties and flaws to be dealt with.

The questions are, Does the model help increase our ability to understand the real world dynamics that we could not get a handle on before? How well does it do this? What are the flaws and how costly are they? These are very advanced questions and all of the results are not yet in. Ongoing research may give us the answers in the years to come.

Requires Many Modified Versions

Researchers worked very hard to find ways to remedy some of the overly simplistic assumptions of the basic Black-Scholes formula. They created a whole slew of modified Black-Scholes formulas to solve various deficiencies. There is no single Black-Scholes formula that works in all cases, but there are many modified formulas that work reasonably well under different assumptions.

Uses Inaccurate Log-Normal Model

Black and Scholes used the log-normal distribution as their model for stock price movements. The problem is that there are no statistical models that perfectly match stock price movements, but the log-normal distribution fits closest. So Black and Scholes opted for the closest approximation available. Unfortunately, if the statistical method you choose does not properly foretell the true future probabilities, then there will be errors in the option values. This leads to errors in Black-Scholes valuations.

"WHAT'S LOGS GOT TO DO WITH IT?"

There is frequent confusion involving the applicability of the normal curve and the log-normal curve to stocks and options. While the two may appear to be entirely different statistical distributions, it is simpler to think of them as transformations of each other before and after the logarithmic function is applied. For instance, if we run across a group of data (like stock prices) that has a log-normal shape to it, we can easily change its shape into that of a normal curve by taking the natural log of each piece of data. As long as we remember we are working with a translation of the original data and have a valid reason for doing so, we can then apply normal curve analysis to it (we should retranslate it after the results are in). This allows us to more easily analyze difficult data.

Assorted past stock prices happen to look much more like a log-normal curve than any other statistical distribution. Since our job is to make an educated guess at what the stock might do in the future, it makes sense to expect such a distribution (log normal) to continue for future prices, also. Black and Scholes decided to translate all price data from log normal to normal so that they could use the easier normal curve analysis inside their formula. They did this by taking the natural logarithm of each "price relative" to translate log normal to normal. Notice that economists care far more about price relatives (such as percent rate of return or percent growth rate) than they care about the prices themselves. If IBM at $100 moves to $110, it has a positive 10 percent growth rate. Falling from $100 to $90 is a minus 10 percent growth rate.

No one is quite sure why stock returns look log normal. Economists try to explain it by suggesting that the markets expect continuously compounded returns. That is, every time a stock trades (even tick by tick) investors are expecting to get a certain continuous rate of return measured from the moment the trade takes place. It turns out that if we continuously compound a group of simple interest rates, we will generate a group of final returns that mimic a log-normal curve. Taking the log of these will translate them back to simple rates of return, once again producing a normal curve. This translation trick involves our old friend the continuously compounding growth factor e^{RT} and the fact that it is easily manipulated by the natural logarithm (ln). We can take the natural log of e^{RT} like this: $\ln(e^{RT})$. This quickly reveals the power that e is raised to (RT in this case). Then, we can easily figure out R (the continuously compounded rate of interest) if we plug in T (time to maturity). In

(Continues)

"WHAT'S LOGS GOT TO DO WITH IT?"
(*Continued*)

the following example we show that a continuously compounded rate of 9.531 percent gives the very same final return as a simple interest rate of 10.000 percent.

Example: Let's suppose IBM grows from $100 to $110 in 1 year. The growth rate is easily calculated as $110/$100 = 1.10. The continuously compounded growth rate is defined as e^{RT}, which implies that $e^{RT} = 1.10$. We can solve this by taking the natural log of both sides: $\ln(e^{RT}) = \ln(1.10)$ which simplifies to $RT = \ln(1.10) = 0.09531$. Since $T = 1$ year, then $R = 0.09531$. It isn't necessary for us to do all this analysis since it is done automatically inside the Black-Scholes formula. This sidebar merely explains why the terms *log normal* and *normal* are sprinkled throughout the whole of option literature.

CONCLUSION

Any reasonably long-term study shows that stock prices and the log-normal curve differ in two main areas. There are far more sleepy, quiet days in the stock market than the log-normal curve would predict. That is, the number of days when the market is hardly changed are more frequent than theory says. Nothing too exciting about that discovery. But there are also found to be more wild and crazy days than predicted by theory. The market goes bonkers more often than statistics would allow for. This doesn't happen often, but when it does, the moves are sensational and make the evening news.

For example, a three standard deviation range should cover 99.74 percent of all the cases in a normal distribution. In a sample of 1,000 days, 997.4 should fall within this 3 SD range. Let's say, then, that 2.6 days can be expected to fall outside the range. In our 4 years of Dow Jones daily price moves we included exactly 1,000 days. Instead of 2.6 days outside the range of 3 SD, there were 11 days with huge moves, four times the expected number. The profits and losses during these crazy days are huge and can affect a trader's whole year.

So, the Black-Scholes formula does not properly account for these extra outliers (price moves that are "off the charts"). But the market is not blind to this. These rare events are priced into the marketplace by pumping up the valuations of the "wings," those deep out-of-the-money lottery options. This causes the implied volatility of the wings to be much higher than the at-the-money options. There is always more than one way to skin a cat.

Studies have been made for almost 30 years now on the efficacy of the Black-Scholes model in the real world. There is a great deal of arguable evidence and lots of academic contention. We would summarize the findings by saying that, on the whole, the Black-Scholes formula is very good at what it does. It isn't perfect, but even given its shortcomings and limitations it is an effective measurer of fair option premiums.

Only the most sophisticated traders can understand the subtle cases where one type of modified formula is more or less valid than the Black-Scholes formula. Most arguments about the Black-Scholes model versus other models, such as the Cox-Ross-Rubinstein model, come down to pennies per share difference. And this bias is not consistent, that is, always too high or too low, or we could make some money trading on it. But you cannot take advantage of a difference measured in pennies per share unless you are a pit broker. For the rest of us it is untradeable and unnoticeable. The Black-Scholes formula has stood the test of time. It's a very good model. Its advantages far outweigh its shortcomings.

KEY CONCEPTS REVIEW

- ◆ The Black-Scholes model is the preeminent formula in the options market. In this chapter we reviewed many of the pros and cons of the formula.
- ◆ Discovering the first accurate options model was a major breakthrough.
- ◆ The Black-Scholes formula is now universally known and accepted by traders.
- ◆ It's fast and easy to use, which is nice today, but was far more important 30 years ago when only corporate

mainframe computers were available (and very expensive).

+ The formula uses elegant mathematics that allows for easy modification and an easy derivation of risk measures. Remember, we know the delta right away—it's $N(D_1)$.

+ In developing the formula there were many hurdles to overcome. Sometimes reality has to take a backseat if certain problems are too hard to solve smoothly the first time. In a similar vein, the 1910 Model-T Ford didn't have an electric starter, automatic transmission, or cruise control. But it was a pretty nice car for the money!

+ Black and Scholes couldn't yet deal with dividends, so they restricted the formula to stocks that had no dividends.

+ The formula only calculates call options. If you want puts valued, you must do a few tricks with our CPL.PCS conversion methods in Chap. 20.

+ Many years ago most options were only exercisable on the expiration day. These came to be known as European-style options. Americans wanted the ability to exercise whenever it suited them. These came to be called early-exercise or American-style options. The Black-Scholes formula cannot handle early-exercise options.

+ To successfully complete the model, Black and Scholes had to make a whole slew of conditions and restrictions that were not necessarily realistic, but this is not unusual for other models either. We listed 10 of the additional conditions and restrictions in the chapter.

+ The last problem of note is the distribution used by the Black-Scholes formula. There is no distribution which accurately reflects the markets, but the closest is the log-normal distribution. This is what Black and Scholes used, and we discussed its limitations.

+ Summing up, the Black-Scholes formula is not perfect, but on the whole it does a darn good job and effectively measures fair option premiums. These days whenever a researcher claims to have found a better method, the whole of the academic and financial community sits up and pays attention. That's how high a standard the Black-Scholes formula has set!

THINGS TO THINK ABOUT

Universal Acceptance   To show how universally accepted the Black-Scholes formula is, option traders in some upstairs markets can make deals based on volatility rather than the option premiums themselves. For example, let's say you want to buy the $350 call option on 1-year gold. A dealer quotes you 14.8%/15.0%. The same quote in terms of premiums would have been $22.30/$22.60 under the prevailing conditions. But as gold moves up or down the quote in dollars can change every 2 seconds, while the quote in percent will not.

QUESTIONS

1. Name three things that are positive about the Black-Scholes formula.
2. Name three things that make the Black-Scholes formula less than ideally perfect.
3. What modifications, also called "relaxing of restrictions," would you think might be required for someone to create the perfect formula?
4. Some studies say that the Black-Scholes formula slightly misprices the at-the-money and deep out-of-the-money options. Does this sound right, and if so, why?
5. Some traders worry a lot about the Black-Scholes formula's assumption of constant volatility. What does this assumption mean and why is it flawed?

PART THREE

Trading

CHAPTER 17

A Primer on Risk and Hedging

MARKET RISK

Where uncertainty resides, risk follows. Few places demonstrate this principle more spectacularly than the stock, bond, and commodity markets. In this chapter we will discuss price risk and some techniques traders use to try to deal with it.

As investors blow hot and cold they can cause the markets to quickly rise and fall, flapping like windsocks in an airport breeze. These fluctuating prices create gains and losses for those with positions, putting them at risk. The greater the price movements, the greater the risks.

It is in the nature of all traded markets to behave like this; none are exempt. If we could predict these price moves, we might be able to devise a way to protect ourselves, but that is the problem: market prices are notoriously unpredictable. This causes uncertainty in the final outcome and, thus, risk.

Because of this uncertainty every market position, whether deemed an investment or a speculation, has risk associated with it. Of course, investments are deemed less risky than speculations, but neither of them is remotely close to being risk-free. Thus all market positions, regardless of type or name, have risk associated with them. The only sure way to eliminate the risk is to completely close out (liquidate) the position. In the jargon of the trade a fully liquidated position is termed a *closed* position. Therefore, by our

logic every *open* position contains risk and the only riskless position is one that has been closed, that is, fully and completely
liquidated.

To lessen the risk associated with open positions traders often
try to hedge by adding a counteracting position to the portfolio.
For example, if the trader owns London Gold he or she might sell
New York Gold against it. The portfolio now has a two-legged
position (bought London/sold New York), where one leg will
serve as an offset to the other, hopefully. We say hopefully because
hedges do not always work as planned. The variety of trading
assets chosen as hedges by traders is enormous. Some work much
better than others. And some end up as disasters.

FINDING A HEDGE

In the search for a hedge, a trader must find a hedging vehicle
that mimics the price moves of the asset owned. The potency for
risk control is directly related to the correlation between the two
assets. A hedging vehicle that perfectly duplicates (replicates) the
price moves of the original asset will allow you to hedge away all
your risk. We call this the *Perfect Hedge*. Traders find out the hard
way, after years of experience, that Perfect Hedges do not exist.

When you buy one asset and later sell a hedging asset against
it, you have created a two-legged position called a *spread*. Some
traders prefer to call this two-legged position an *arbitrage* or any
of a half dozen other names. Regardless of the name, all two-
legged positions change the nature of your exposure. It no longer
matters that the market has a volatile move up or down; only the
difference in price moves of the two assets counts. Let's say you
bought shares in computer company A and decided to sell shares
in computer company B against it as a hedge. If A goes up $3.00
a share and B only goes up $2.75 a share, your gain is only the
net difference in the two, $0.25 a share. If the price between the
two, the spread, had remained exactly unchanged, you would
have had no gain or loss. If the two always move in lockstep, then
your risk has been eliminated. But even the best hedged positions
tend to have fluctuations in the spread, and thus the risk can never
be entirely eliminated, but it can be reduced. Instead of a $3.00
gain or loss (in our example), you had a $0.25 gain or loss. That's

how most good hedges work; they put a muzzle on the exposures. While a muzzled dog might still give you a painful nip, at least the dog can't bite your whole hand off!

A valid hedge must reduce exposure consistently, day after day, month after month. If the hedge you choose suddenly fails to parallel your asset's price action, its usefulness as a hedge has disappeared. Sometimes traders find an attractive, predictable short-term correlation between two assets. They proclaim this pair as hedgeable because recent price moves prove it, even if cause and effect are uncertain. When the recent relationship of parallelism disappears, the traders awaken from their trances; a little wiser, but much poorer.

Circa 1987, the whole of Wall Street was hedging mortgage-backed securities versus the 5-year treasury notes. It was a very nice hedge for a long while (which is why so many got sucked in). It turned into a blood bath when the prices diverged instead of remaining parallel to each other. Hedged portfolios lost much more than unhedged portfolios, which is the tip-off that the traders weren't really hedging. Instead, they were betting on a convenient short-term tendency for the two assets to track each other. But a profitable correlation over a recent period of low volatility does not truly qualify a trading vehicle as the perfect long-term hedge. As often happens in such cases, the tendency for the two to track each other abruptly reversed. The divergence accelerated when those with long-term views, but short-term pain thresholds, panicked and dumped their portfolios. The entire street was stuck with the same bad hedges. We discuss this concept further under cross-hedging a little later in the chapter. Let's discuss a few more practical examples.

HEDGING 1000 SHARES OF IBM

For simplicity's sake let's say we have purchased 1000 shares of IBM in the spot market, the market most people trade in. We are, therefore, long 1000 shares of IBM in our account. *Long* is when you've bought something and are now an owner. The market weakens and we get uncomfortable. We decide to lessen our exposure to IBM shares. What are our choices? We can liquidate our shares in the spot market which will fully eliminate any further risk. Or, if available, we can hedge our position by selling IBM derivatives: futures, forwards, or options. (For these examples we may discuss hypothetical derivative markets not yet available to us.)

If we sell 1000 shares of an IBM forward or futures contract against our long 1000 spot shares, then we have created a two-legged spread position called a *carry:* long spot, short forward (*short* is when you've sold something you don't own). This is pretty good as hedges go, but it still leaves us open to exposure if carrying costs should change and/or other minor travesties occur. For ease of comparison we could say we were roughly 95 percent protected against any price moves in IBM. Not quite perfectly hedged, but still one of the best hedges possible.

Weak traders pretend they are now 100 percent perfectly hedged. Rather than owning up to the fact that they still have some exposure and learning to manage the risk, they pretend it is risk-free and ignore it. These newly opened spread positions usually have limited exposure, but they do not always harmlessly self-dissolve at delivery time. When problems arise, the weak trader doesn't have the discipline to liquidate the position at a small loss and instead loses a big chunk of money in a seemingly riskless position. Hoping doesn't work in trading, only disciplined action does.

If, instead of forwards or futures, we sell 1000 shares of IBM call options, then we have opened a whole new world of complexity. Traders often call this a *buy-write:* long IBM stock, short call options. We have only partially hedged by doing this. Depending on which call option we sell, our protection would vary widely. For example, if we sell an at-the-money call, we would have only 50 percent protection. A deep out-of-the-money call would hedge us far less, granting only a tiny 10 to 20 percent protection. And even worse, as you will see in Chap. 18, the 50 percent protection from the at-the-money option might be only 45 percent tomorrow. It is not a constant, unchanging thing. Option hedges are always in a state of continuous flux.

Let's look at a hedging scenario that's a bit more offbeat. Suppose we decide to sell some IBM bonds to hedge our long IBM shares? If so, we are moving even further afield and find ourselves less hedged. Clearly, the price of an IBM bond is very dependent on the overall creditworthiness of IBM and on the abil-

For sake of simplicity we've made a concerted effort not to discuss put options as yet. We have a later chapter (Chap. 20) that shows how a call option and a put option can be converted into one another under the right conditions. You will begin to see the interrelationship between the two at that point. We should mention, however, that put options are just as valid a hedging vehicle as call options are. In fact, in some cases they might be the better of the two. They can offer us downside price insurance on our IBM shares for a fee (their premiums). But just like call options, they only hedge away a portion of our risk. That is, on a moment-to-moment basis we will only have partial hedging benefits. For example, the at-the-money put option will only protect us against 50 percent of the daily price moves. This is because the delta is -0.50. When we learn more about deltas, you'll see this more clearly.

ity of IBM to continue paying off its debts. The relationship that exists between the corporate profitability of IBM and the prices of its stocks and bonds is a complicated and tenuous one. No one, as yet, has been able to predict how one affects the other on a daily basis. The IBM shares could be up or down $20 and the bonds might not move a penny. What kind of hedge is that? Not much of a hedge, we can tell you. Only the most clever and experienced professional traders should even consider this as a viable hedge. They also need an exit plan when all heck breaks loose and the hedge goes into the toilet!

As a last hedging scenario let's create this hypothetical situation: Intel surprises everyone by offering to buy all IBM shares in a takeover attempt. They propose exchanging three shares of Intel for every share of IBM. We might hedge by selling 3000 shares of Intel against the 1000 IBM we are long (if we can borrow the Intel shares). The relationship between IBM and Intel shares was always tentative before this, but now a more strongly defined relationship exists *as long as the merger talks continue*. If the talks collapse, it's every man for himself. This new proposed relationship of 3 to 1 can disappear in a twinkle. What was a good hedge can turn into a disaster. That's why Wall Streeters have a special name for this type of hedge: *risk arbitrage*. This Intel versus IBM hedge is far more tenuous and unreliable than classic textbook arbitrage allows.

ARBITRAGE IN THE REAL WORLD

Normal textbook arbitrage is supposedly risk-free and highly predictable. But, as is usual for theory, that is a vast oversimplification. The risk-free arbitrage concepts written about in textbooks are like quarks and muons with a life span of nanoseconds. No risk-free arbitrage stays available for long unless it is hidden from the traders who specialize in such things.

Risk-free arbitrages are typically created when normal spread relationships get bent or broken due to an excess amount of business that can't wait and must be done immediately. What causes the risk-free arbitrage to disappear is the countervailing action of professional traders. Perhaps only a handful of specialists can see the profit at first. They will buy the cheap leg of the arbitrage and sell the expensive leg of the arbitrage until they have reached their limits. This usually absorbs all the available arbitrage and returns the spread to normal. But if this does not narrow the arbitrage (and erase the profit), then the spread will continue to widen and this will attract other, less efficient traders who may not be as quick as the first group but may have lots more money. This second flight of arbitragers may even be pointed in the right direction by those in the first group (who are completely loaded now and want the arbitrage to narrow so they can take profits). It is exceedingly rare that a sure-thing arbitrage exists for more than a very short while on Wall Street. The traders are fast and their pockets are deep.

What more normally exists for the real world to see in the newspapers are various forms of risky arbitrage. But there is a bit of a problem here. The further a trader gets away from buying and selling precisely the same asset, the less the phrase *arbitrage* should apply. But these days every two-legged trade under the sun is being called an arbitrage. The term *arbitrage* has been degraded to the point where it often means no more than "something bought versus something sold, and we hope they offset, somewhat."

These so-called arbitrages can and do run the gamut from nearly risk-free all the way to insanely risky. Many of the very risky ones are really cockeyed arbitrage concept trades created by nutty traders. Some of these arbitrage concepts are so weird that normal humans are precluded from fathoming the logic behind them. But, for the most part, a believable cause-and-effect story is part and parcel for every reasonable arbitrage. Buy NASDAQ and sell the Dow because the recession is over and technical stocks will ascend more quickly. Buy gold and sell bonds because inflation is beginning to rear its ugly head again. The possibilities are truly endless. Don't forget, though, that after all the fancy ideas are put aside, an arbitrage that is not of the famous risk-free sort has risks and exposures similar to every other two-legged spread. A good arbitrage begins, then, with a good hedge.

Finding a good hedge, however, is not a matter of simply culling through the many new and exciting stories you hear each trading day and choosing one that strikes your fancy. Rather, it requires finding a steady and reliable historical price interdependence. Replication (duplication of price moves) and correlation are the keys. If you hedge with assets that are far different than your original IBM shares, you are opening Pandora's box of demons and maladies. In many cases you might be adding risk rather than reducing it. It is far safer to stick with proven historical hedges and their strong correlations. When it comes to hedging, steadiness beats flashiness every time. Or as one trader says, "discipline beats conviction, every time." You might be absolutely convinced that some new concept arbitrage should work out to be wonderfully profitable, but it is far better and safer to keep to the old and proven disciplines of using hedges that always work.

Whether we call a two-legged position a spread, a hedge, or an arbitrage is moot. The great majority of all such two-legged positions are not classical risk-free arbitrages, but they do bear *some* resemblances thereto. For our purposes we expect that the two assets involved will parallel each other pricewise. The more perfectly they match one another, the better the hedge. But as we pointed out earlier and will be reiterated, there aren't any perfect hedges.

NO PERFECT HEDGES

To get a handle on the degree of price protection offered by any two-legged spread, hedge, or arbitrage you need to measure the correlation between the two legs. Perfect correlation gives you a perfect hedge and no residual exposure. None of the IBM hedge scenarios we suggested was a perfect hedge, and each had a distinctly different risk profile. Some might hedge you 95 percent, while others might hedge you hardly at all, say 10 percent. We are not going to get into mathematical formulas here, but merely relate several ideas and concepts so that you can become better equipped to understand how traders view the world of hedging and risk control. Almost all traders use gut feelings and very few pay any attention to mathematically precise measures, anyway. [The exception is when their back offices provide daily option risk reports which are required reading. Five minutes later the average trader has tossed the sheets aside and is back in the markets trading by gut instinct.]

If we say someone has a *hedged* position, the reader might think we mean perfectly hedged and we do not want any misunderstanding on this: for all intents and purposes there are no perfectly hedged positions except those that have been fully liquidated. You may not appreciate this until you have been in the business for 20 years, so take our word for it.

Any position that remains *open* has some exposure and possibility of unexpected loss. The manner in which such losses can occur may seem, at times, to be excursions into the Twilight Zone. Following are two such occasions when the surreal became real. These are examples of markets which were expected to provide perfect hedges, but which ended up providing something far more bizarre.

Starting in 1973 two huge waves of inflation swept across America, and they surprised the heck out of everyone. They began in the commodity markets and continued, on and off, until 1981. Most people are aware that oil prices had skyrocketed through the 1970s, but so had almost every other commodity price. Against this background many previously perfect hedges came apart and scared the bejeezus out of the markets. We'll tell you two stories here, one about the potato market and another about silver.

About 1974 the potato market started to really take off. While there are more than a few varieties of potatoes in America, only two types of futures were traded: Maine Potatoes and Idaho Potatoes. The Maine Potato futures were traded in New York. The prices started to rise day after day. Reports in the press hinted that these price updrafts were an aberration and that the market had to come back down. Also, the Maine Potato prices were going up much faster than those in the Idaho Potato market, which many considered to be a superior quality potato. One day rumors started circulating that there was a massive short squeeze in progress. Just like a turn-of-the-century story out of a Jesse Livermore book it was rumored that the Rocky Mountain Potato King had sold more Maine Potatoes than he could deliver!

As it turned out, there was merit to the rumors. The King soon came forward in the press to say, in essence, that Maine Potatoes were absurdly high and their price couldn't be maintained. He had every confidence that the good people of New York and the East would see this soon and come to their senses. Well, as delivery time approached it became apparent that there were not enough contracts in deliverable position to fulfill his obligations. The exchange pressured him to cover his shorts, roll them forward, or come up with the deliverable receipts. The response of the King was essentially: "I'm not gonna buy at these stupid prices and I'm not gonna deliver. So how do you like them potatoes?" Well, the exchange freaked out and, fearing a massive default, they froze all trading and declared a delivery settlement in cash (rather than in receipts). They picked a price to settle all the contracts and that was that—all open positions were liquidated. The price they chose made very few people happy although it was in line with recent prices. They also assessed a fine against the Rocky Mountain Potato King.

No one was happy with what transpired. Everybody started suing everybody else. The moment the price freeze took effect all perfect hedges immediately became unhedged (the futures legs essentially became useless as hedges), and it ended up a disaster for everyone. Remember, just because the futures market stops trading does not at all mean that the cash market stops. Anyone who had a cash market position and had hedged with the futures got tremendously hung up with uncertainty and exposure. Prices in the cash market kept going up and down like a roller coaster despite the fact that the futures market price was frozen. When two markets stop paralleling each other, the hedge relationship has been destroyed. There were a lot of broke and unhappy hedgers after this debacle. The potato futures markets never recovered and ceased trading soon afterward.

Here is the second example of perfect hedging gone awry. About 5 years later the silver market went absolutely bonkers. Prices rose from a historic norm of $4.00 an ounce all the way to

$51.50 an ounce by January 1980. One of the world's largest mining companies decided to sell its future production of silver in the futures market. This was a very legitimate procedure by a very legitimate industrial producer. The selling of future production is a critically important component of any successful futures market. Producers are key in keeping prices in line with reality. Unfortunately, not all the intricacies of hedging with futures are obvious, even to professionals. Sometimes it takes unusual circumstances to prove that small risks, which once seemed unimportant, can become critically important. One such unusual circumstance, which was not considered possible, was that silver might quintuple in price before the producer could arrange to deliver the piles of silver. But the impossible happened.

As the company sold its silver in the futures market the price kept rising and rising. The managers were happy at first because the company has untold silver reserves underground and this paid to keep the mines running day and night. Given enough time the company could pump out silver faster than a fire hose can pump water. Unfortunately, time ran out. As the futures prices soared, the managers received margin calls on their short positions every single day. Now, they are bona fide hedgers and so receive first-class rates for original margin requirements. But this wasn't original margin that was being requested, it was variation margin. And *all* traders, regardless of stature, must pay cash for any variation margin calls. At first they used bank lines and then cash reserves to pony up the margin. But the calls got bigger and faster as silver prices went absolutely crazy. In the end they had to buy back their hedges at prices far higher than they had originally sold them at. They had a huge loss, but at least they could resell their silver at great prices now, right? Wrong. By the time everything was unwound the price of silver had crashed and they had never rehedged. This episode became just one more in a long line of perfect hedge horror stories.

These are extremely rare cases where the whole market structure was shaken. But we chose them to make a point. The best hedges, just like the best laid plans, often go astray. Legitimate, skilled hedgers can create what they believe are perfect hedges, but outside forces can change everything. These examples are very unusual, but they help you understand why we keep reiterating our warning against perfect hedges—there are far too many things that can go wrong. It is best to believe that perfect hedges do not exist, and then, if you work really hard at it and you're lucky, you'll find a very good hedge that does a great job for you. But if you're smart, you'll still sleep with one eye open, anyway.

FROM PERFECT HEDGES TO CROSS HEDGES

If there are no perfect hedges, then what kind of hedges are there? The answer is a wide variety ranging from very, very good to really bad and totally ineffective. If we assume our mythical perfect hedge would have a rating of 100 percent effectiveness, then we can say there are some very, very good hedges that rank at 98 percent or so, and many slightly lesser hedges that come in at 80 percent, 70 percent, and so on. When we go lower than that (and we admit these rankings are very subjective), we are starting to deal with what are called *cross hedges,* that is, hedging with vehicles that may be related but are only somewhat of a match.

At one extreme we have the perfect hedge with total correlation and a rating of 100 percent, and on the other end of the spectrum we have the nonhedge with no correlation whatsoever and a 0 percent rating. In between we have the cross hedges which have only fair correlations and middling ratings of, say, 40 to 60 percent on our subjective hedging scale.

As we move away from perfect hedging we get more and more into cross hedging. When the reliability gets worse than that, we aren't really hedging at all and we can consider them nonhedges. Of course, there's not much reason to hedge then, is there? And so, nonhedges represent very little of the legitimate hedging activity that goes on. This means that the vast majority of hedging activity involves a mixture of very good hedges, that have various mismatch problems (or else they'd be perfect), and cross hedges which are less reliable, but still fairly effective as hedges.

Our example of hedging our spot shares of IBM by selling them in the forward delivery market is a mismatch, of sorts. We would be largely hedged, but not perfectly hedged, because small things can still go awry before delivery. And they do, believe us. The two-legged position (long spot IBM/short forward IBM) has a slight mismatch in terms of delivery date and carrying costs. As a trader allows the mismatches of the hedges to get bigger, risk increases and certainty of outcome falls. Additional profits (or losses) begin to enter the picture. Mismatching and cross-hedging open the door to extra profits if you get it right and extra losses if you don't.

Therefore, traders use mismatches and cross hedges to try to enhance profitability. They experiment. While trying different trading vehicles as hedges, a trader might reject a perfect match with 100 percent correlation (like selling spot IBM shares which would fully liquidate the position) and substitute a mismatch like selling a forward or future with 95 percent correlation. Reaching for extra profit opportunities next time the trader might try a cross hedge with only 60 percent correlation, and so on. At an extreme, a wild and crazy trader might be buying apples and selling oranges because he or she is making a ton of money doing so, and then one day they carry the trader out of the trading room in a strait jacket when the hedged position finally blows up. And all such undisciplined traders do self-destruct, it's just a matter of time.

GETTING SUCKERED INTO CROSS HEDGES

Less-than-clever traders often put on hedges for all the wrong reasons. Rather than take a loss on a trade, which is the most important thing for traders to force themselves to do, many traders will turn the loser into a two-legged position by hedging and then hold on and pray. Liquidating the trade locks in the loss, whereas a hedge keeps it alive for another day and another chance. Bad traders love this trick. Sadly, it earns them a ton of pain over the next few days as the losses begin to grow and grow. The rule of thumb is: Bad positions get worse far more often than they get better.

At other times the trader might be trying to liquidate a position, but can't quite get the desired price. A parallel market beckons with ample liquidity and a very nice price. The parallel market is only a slight mismatch, and the trader figures "What the heck." It's as if a mildly magnetic force seems to pull the trader toward this hedge mismatch. Naturally, the ability to unwind this mismatched position worsens over the next few days, which makes the final liquidation excruciatingly painful and far more costly.

At other times the trader might not even have a position at all, but the price difference between the trader's main market and the parallel market starts to look very tempting indeed. It appears that there is a more than normal profit potential in the arbitrage. The trader feels that opportunity is far too good to pass up. In fact, this is the market's way of attracting traders and, like a Venus Flytrap, eating them alive. We warned you earlier that sure-thing arbitrages don't last longer than a few moments. The only reason that an attractive trade like this becomes easy to execute is because the best traders are full up and choking on their positions. Our inexperienced trader is about to get another lesson in market dynamics. The sucking sound that follows is the trader being swallowed into the vortex of ex-traders.

Inexperienced traders get suckered into these bad trading practices all the time. They don't want to take their losses when due and figure that as long as they keep dancing, the piper might leave unpaid. The piper always gets paid. The reality is that they should be taking the opposite side of the trades they are making. Trades that are easy to make often turn out being hard to take. Experienced traders know that the market promises many, many things—but the market often lies.

Following is a walk through on a typical hedging strategy, albeit slightly more exotic than most.

CRUDE OIL: HEDGING LIBYA VERSUS NEW YORK

To be a successful trader you must know what you want to do long before the market allows you to do it. Making spur-of-the-moment decisions almost always ends in grief. If you are going to do a successful hedge or arbitrage, you need to have your reasons thought out well ahead of time and your execution plan must be ready to launch.

Let's use crude oil for an example. Suppose you just purchased a tanker of crude oil sitting in a Libyan seaport in the Mediterranean. You might be able to sell that very same tanker, in exactly the same place and take a small profit. Effectively your exposure is over and you are almost perfectly hedged.

On the other hand you might hedge by selling a tanker of crude in Amsterdam for 1-month forward delivery and make a bigger profit. If you have computed all the angles and can make the delivery on time and afford the extra costs and international paperwork, then you have a good deal in the making. There are extra problems in terms of timing and physical delivery, but the profits are, hopefully, greater. You are doing a deal that you understand and have prepared for, not one you got suckered into due to unpreparedness or desperation or hope. Hope kills traders.

Every good trader tries to find the optimal match between profitability and hedge reliability. Say the Amsterdam/Libya crude oil trade offers a $1½ per barrel profit and the more difficult New York/Libya trade offers a $2 per barrel profit. The big question is, Which trade is the most profitable given the risks involved? Only an experienced trader can give you the right answer, which is not one simple answer but a whole distribution of possible answers: payoffs versus probabilities. And some of the possible payoffs will be losses due to the occasional bad scenario that can unfold (wars, storms, embargoes, backed up harbors, delay penalties, etc.). The key is that you know, as an experienced oil trader, that the profitable cases far outweigh the occasional losses.

Part of what defines a good trader is knowing precisely how to hedge a trade's risk using an appropriate hedging vehicle, in an appropriate quantity, for an appropriate location and date. Each decision is discretionary and is based on profitability and risk parameters as understood by the trader at that time. What is appropriate for today's conditions may not be appropriate next week. Managers must depend on their trader's astuteness in these areas of expertise—or find a new trader.

The most important thing learned by all traders is: There is no such thing as a perfect hedge. After enough experience, you will come to understand that every hedge has some sort of mismatch associated with it. The object is to understand when the mismatches are acceptable relative to the profitability offered. The larger the mismatches, the greater the exposure. As exposure increases, and therefore risk increases, the profitability must also increase to compensate. It's always a matter of payoffs and probabilities.

AVOID GOING BANANAS

Here's our favorite example of the silliest cross hedge ever. It happens that a professional homebuilder is in business during the great inflationary period in the United States (1973–1981) when every single commodity price is going up day after day, year after year. Somewhere near the end of the period the homebuilder becomes frantic. Every day the price of nails he uses is going higher and higher and he can't afford it any more. He becomes terrified that the price increases are putting him out of business. Try as he might he can't find anyone to make him a forward market in nails. Finally he learns that there is a local market in banana futures that has been steadily going higher along with the price of lumber and nails. In desperation he buys a contract—and promptly loses his shirt. When a friend asks him what the heck he was thinking, he replies, "Everything was going up. I just had to buy *something!"*

Obviously hedging nails with bananas is, well, bananas! Whenever you hedge with a low correlation vehicle, you end up with a *great deal of risk.* Knowing that perfect hedges can't be found, traders often put on blinders and pretend that every conceivable offset, however bizarre, can be considered a valid hedge, especially if they can point to a recent correlation of profitability to justify it. Traders need to have guidelines set by management to keep them on track with corporate objectives. Without reasonable guidance and oversight, which requires hands-on management, more than an occasional trader has been known to go bananas.

MANAGERS AND TRADERS, LIMITS AND LOSSES

You must be able to answer the following question before entering a new position, What are the risks and can they be controlled? Unless the risk can be measured and managed, you are dealing with a potential fiasco. When risk can't be measured, you haven't a clue as to the size of your liability. Every single company involved in the billion dollar trading scandals over the past decade could have measured their exposure if they chose to do so. And at some point, far short of disaster, they could have stemmed the losses. We can only guess as to why they continued down their paths of destruction. Our best surmise: It is human nature to ride out losers. And big losers will become huge losers if you roll the dice often enough.

This is the prime rule of trading: Always understand your risk and know the worst-case possible loss. You must be able to measure your risk under all possible conditions. You must feel it, breathe it, live with it. This is what traders do for a living—good traders, anyway. You then must find ways to manage this risk like hedging. But managing risk also means devising position and loss limits beforehand and exit strategies when the loss limits are reached.

Corporate management must set up limits. Within these limits it is the trader's decision to micromanage the moment-to-moment or day-to-day choices. The limits should be set up in such a fashion that each trader or desk has a limit compatible with other trading areas within the firm. For example, it would be foolish to grant each of 20 traders a position limit of, say, 100 contracts of bonds when the whole firm would be uncomfortable with a net position of 1000 or 1500 contracts.

Even though there is a high probability that each independent trader would not be at his or her limit every day and that all would not also have the same market view (long or short), there is a disaster lurking here. It is precisely when every trader seeks to press his or her belief to the limit that the overall market is polarized in one direction. A market like that is ready for a major shift in volatility and/or price. In short, you would be shocked how often 20 traders will all be fixated the same way just at the moment the market is preparing a blood bath!

When limits are exceeded (and given traders' aggressive natures they often are), immediate action must be taken. No discussions, no meetings, no memos—just a preplanned strategy that is executed. You would be amazed at the indecision that is created when risk limits are found to have been exceeded. What was unthinkably against policy just moments before discovery is suddenly open for discussion by nervous managers, and they often allow the excess risk positions to stand.

We can smirk and judge such things from afar, but a closer look will shed a different light on it. The managers must make decisions under the added emotional pressure of fear or greed. They are in fear that the moment they liquidate the excess positions (and report losses) the market will reverse (as the traders keep warning) and they will look like fools. On the other hand, they are guilty of greed when they see the excess trades are profitable and conclude they will miss out on profits needed to "make the quarter." What manager wants to be the one to end a profitable situation? And what manager wants to be the one to report losses that would have been recouped? The managers are now viewing trading limits through the eyes of desperate traders. They feel they are embracing a new, "more logical" rationale than the original policy allowed for. This is precisely why it shouldn't be open for discussion or rethinking. Just liquidate the positions and put the traders on warning. This must be automatic, or you are lost.

Limits tend to be overstepped during market periods when traders have strong opinions. This means that the traders involved have a very strong opinion that the market is right (and will continue) or that the market is wrong (and will reverse). These situations present optimum periods of profitability, or so the traders argue. It is just at such times that price volatility is likely to be increasing rapidly and may continue long enough to swamp the highly opinionated traders.

Another very important aspect is that the *discovery* of over-the-limit positions usually goes hand in hand with losing positions, not winning ones. This is because no one ever investigates or argues with excess profits. Investigations are set up when losses start occurring. The investigated trader or team usually swears it is accounting's fault for mispricing the positions or failing to recognize certain important income. Sometimes it is, but more often the trader is making excuses while hoping for a reversal of fortunes.

Also, traders rarely come forward voluntarily to admit excessive positions if things are going well. But, if they have any tendency toward self-preservation, they usually volunteer an admission when things have gone sour and they are in over their heads. Surprisingly, these are not the guys who sink you. The traders who sink firms are the ones that have no sense of fear or self-preservation. Their strategy is to keep control of all the information and hide everything from management, because they can turn this losing situation around by themselves. They never show management a loss until they are finally overwhelmed and don't know where to turn. At that point it turns out that they have lost more money than is stored in Fort Knox.

Everyone knows that you can't get out of a hole by digging deeper, but bad traders are rarely thinking straight when they start losing. They just keep on digging until someone takes the shovels away. It is up to the managers to set a reasonable policy and then adhere to it. If it were up to traders, there would never be any limits on their activities because they always expect to be right.

Many people don't realize that most of the huge trading firms that were wiped out by losses were profitable traders for years. They showed large profits at first, but they were unreasonably large profits. And this was their downfall. That may sound strange, but consider human nature. No manager will allow a trader to vastly increase his or her position unless the trader shows a string of impressive results. But the risks involved may not be well understood. In fact, the risks are often ignored. Since traders are expected to make money, most managers don't look closely into the matter of how the profits developed. The methods of traders are considered mystical, magical things by many managers who are unclear as to how the money is being made. And as long as the profits continue to show up they don't care. But sometimes the profits are figments of creative imaginations. At other times the profits are the vagaries of highly volatile swings of good fortune. When the trades go sour and are doubled up again and again, the volatility can blow the traders right out of the water—and the company with them.

The key is to have managers who are closely communicating with the traders and the back office. Aside from processing trades the back office should be monitoring risk and providing daily insights into how the money is being made or not being made. The magic and mystique vanish quickly if you'll just take the time to look behind the curtain.

KEY CONCEPTS REVIEW

- ◆ Market prices are notoriously unpredictable. This is the primary cause of investment risk.
- ◆ Every open position contains risk. The only riskless position is one that has been closed, that is, fully and completely liquidated.
- ◆ To lessen the risk associated with open positions traders often try to hedge by adding a counteracting position to the portfolio.
- ◆ A hedging vehicle that perfectly duplicates (replicates) the price moves of the original asset will allow you to hedge away all your risk. We call this the perfect hedge.

- Traders find out the hard way, after years of experience, that perfect hedges do not exist.
- Hedges are created when the owner of an asset sells a different asset against it. This creates an open two-legged position sometimes called a spread, a hedged position, or an arbitrage position.
- Entering into a two-legged position changes the nature of your exposure. Now the only thing that matters is the spread in price between the two. If the two always move in lockstep, then your risk has been eliminated. But even the best hedged positions tend to have fluctuations in the spread and thus the risk can never be entirely eliminated, but it can be reduced below what it was before hedging.
- A valid hedge must reduce exposure consistently, day after day. If the hedge chosen suddenly fails to parallel the original asset's price action, its usefulness as a hedge has disappeared.
- If we own spot shares of IBM, the only way to remove all risk is to liquidate our spot shares of IBM in the spot market. This closes out the position and the risk entirely. This is not a hedge.
- Alternatively we can hedge 95 percent of our risk by selling IBM shares in the futures or forwards market.
- If we sell 1000 shares of IBM at-the-money call options, we'll get about 50 percent protection. Selling a deep out-of-the-money call would hedge us far less, granting only a tiny 10 to 20 percent protection.
- If we try to get esoteric and sell some IBM bonds to hedge our long IBM shares, we will find ourselves less hedged. No one, as yet, knows how bond prices and stock prices interact on a daily basis. The IBM shares could be up or down $20 after a month and the bonds might not move a penny—not a hedge at all.
- Normal textbook arbitrage is supposedly risk-free and highly predictable. But, as is usual for theory, that is a vast oversimplification. What exists in the real world, instead, are many types of risky arbitrages.
- Sometimes it takes hectic market conditions to shake and break our theories. When the commodities markets went

crazy in the 1970s, many previously perfect hedges came apart and scared the bejeezus out of the markets. We cited two stories, potatoes and silver. The potato futures markets ceased trading, making hedging impossible. In silver a major hedger couldn't meet its margin calls and had to buy back its hedges at prices far higher than it had originally sold them. The company took a huge loss.

♦ To try to get a handle on hedging we give subjective rankings of effectiveness. The perfect hedge would have a 100 percent rating and the nonhedge would have a 0 percent rating. Somewhere in between are what we call cross hedges which have only fair ratings of 40 to 60 percent on our subjective hedging scale.

♦ The vast majority of hedging activity involves either very good hedges, that have small to medium mismatch problems (or else they'd be perfect), and cross hedges which have far more mismatch problems, but can still manage at times to be reasonably effective as hedges.

♦ A perfectly hedged position ceases to have profit and loss swings. Thus it is the mismatching and cross-hedging that keeps the door to extra profits open if you get it right or to extra losses if you don't. Traders are almost always in favor of trying new and different cross hedges in order to enhance their profitability.

♦ Inexperienced traders often find themselves putting on far more hedges than they should, and for all the wrong reasons. Rather than closing a position and taking a loss, which is the most important thing for traders to force themselves to do, many traders will turn the losing trade into a spread to keep it open. Hope springs eternal that tomorrow might turn this loser into a profit. It rarely works out that way.

♦ Our favorite example of stupid cross-hedging was the banana trade. A homebuilder tries to hedge nails with bananas because he couldn't stand watching prices go up day after day for years; he just had to buy something! Immediate pain is sure to follow. It is also a metaphor for market emotions. When a trader's pain tolerance level has been pierced, the market is overpriced (for that trader). When all the traders get the powerful, screaming urge to do the same thing, at the same time, the "greatest fool theory" is in play. In our banana example the greatest fool was about to buy (he couldn't stand the pain). Market tops are made at such time.

♦ Every single company that had a billion-dollar trading fiasco over the past decade could have measured its exposure if it chose to do so and could have limited its risks to much lower levels. At some point the company had lost the thread of what good trading is all about.

♦ The prime rule of trading is: Always know your risk and forecast the worst-case scenarios. You must be able to measure your risk under all possible conditions. You must feel it, breathe it, live with it. This is what traders do for a living. Good traders, anyway. Bad traders let the market carry them out to sea and have its way with them. Story has it when George Soros was losing a fortune on Crash Day October 19, 1987, he said, "When I go out of this market I'm going to be walking, they're not going to be carrying me. Sell out our position now!" Only the best and toughest traders can hold to such iron discipline, and it is part of what makes them great. Praying has no place for the best traders. All the trading companies that have gone bankrupt found themselves on their knees praying in the last weeks of their existence—the gods of the markets may have been amused, but they weren't forgiving. Thou shalt not take more risk than thou canst afford. Inscribe it on a stone tablet and put it on the trading turret or save it as an epitaph below RIP. As a trader it's your choice.

♦ A manager's responsibility is to liquidate excessive positions immediately and advise the traders that they are on probation. This must be automatic, or eventually you will be lost.

♦ The key to risk management is to have managers who know how to control risk! The managers should be as knowledgeable about traders and trading as possible. They should be in constant touch with the back office and be receiving daily reports into how the money is

being made or not being made. It's not acceptable for a
risk manager to be a mild-mannered clerk who scrapes
and kowtows to the traders. That is quite simply a recipe
for disaster.

THiNGS TO THINK ABOUT

Traders who make and take delivery frequently are often called
spot or *physical* traders, meaning they buy and sell the actual physical assets. The term is most frequently associated with the commodities markets, but applies also to those who maintain inventories of bond or stock receipts. It takes years of experience for a
physical trader to learn the ins and outs of market interrelationships. As we pointed out in our crude oil trading example, each
arbitrage decision is based on the profitability and risk parameters
as understood by the trader at the time of the trade. What is appropriate for today's conditions may not be appropriate next
week. What worked last year may not work at all this year. It is
up to the trader to stay on top of all the fine points and nuances
of his or her marketplace. A trader, much like a small store retailer,
is always trying to figure out where the demand is coming from
and where it's going to be down the road. Managers must depend
on their trader's astuteness in these areas of expertise because they
cannot keep up with the information flows or the intuitions
required—as managers they may have many other duties to perform. At the same time, however, they must still determine viable
risk parameters that both encourage the business and protect it.
The trader is the pit mechanic who fine-tunes the cars, the manager is the pit boss who oversees the whole crew and makes sure
they optimize their efforts to keep the car on the track.

The most important thing learned by all arbitrage traders is
that there is no such thing as a perfect hedge. They spend years
developing the experience to understand the various forms of mismatches that cause hedged positions to go awry. Their job is to
learn how to optimize profitability versus exposure. The larger the
mismatch, the greater the exposure, but the greater the potential
for profitability. As exposure increases, and therefore risk increases, the profitability must also increase to compensate. It's al-

ways a matter of payoffs and probabilities. One of the great investors of the last 50 years is Sir John Templeton. He was one of the first to heartily recommend looking into global markets. His thesis is: You can get a better edge in value where the knowledge is most difficult to come by. If you do your work and develop a superior knowledge base in seemingly backward and underappreciated areas, the opportunity is the greatest. The best arbitrage traders are constantly trying hard to uncover edges in their areas of expertise; it's just that their expertise is in areas that have been well understood and heavily picked over for years. Sir John Templeton says go to the lush and forbidding jungles to prosper, but most traders are hoping to find a free and bountiful harvest on the rocky slopes of their overworked local farms. Which is much like the joke about the guy looking for his lost car key late at night. His friend sees him cursing up a storm as he walks round and round under the street lamp looking at the ground. His friend says, "Why are you looking here? You lost your key about 50 feet over there." The fellow replies, "Yeah I know, but the light is much better over here!" Just because something's *convenient and there* doesn't mean it has *what you need*.

QUESTIONS

1. Oftentimes traders find an attractive, predictable, and profitable short-term correlation between two assets. Is this a good start for a hedging operation?

2. A trader has a fully hedged portfolio. Soon the daily profit and losses start to become larger than that of a similar portfolio that is unhedged. What does this tell us?

3. A trader owns spot shares of IBM and decides to hedge in the futures market. He now has a two-legged spread position known as a *carry*. On our subjective hedging scale, how well hedged is the position and what types of things can go wrong with a carry position hedged with futures?

4. A trader owns spot shares of IBM and decides that she can write call options against the shares to earn a little

money and also protect against the price of IBM going lower. How much is she hedged, is this a good idea, and, if not, what's wrong with it?

5. Assume the trader in question 4 sold at-the-money call options and was hedged 50 percent at the time. Will the percent protection be the same tomorrow and next week?

6. In the chapter we proposed a crazy takeover attempt: Intel offered to buy all IBM shares by paying three Intel shares for one share of IBM. Before the announcement Intel was trading at $25 and IBM was trading at $60. After the announcement, Intel went down to $23 and IBM went up to $67. Explain the buy/sell dynamics that made Intel go down and IBM up. What might some reasons be?

7. Referring to question 6, why does there still seem to be a guaranteed profit in the present prices ($23 and $67)? What would you do to arbitrage these guaranteed profits? What problems would you run into?

8. When a management begins to investigate trader activity, it seems that the traders are often over their limits and are losing money. The discovery of over-the-limit positions usually goes hand in hand with losing positions, not winning ones. Why is this?

9. Everyone knows that you can't get out of a hole by digging deeper. Why does it seem, then, that traders keep digging deeper? That is, why do they hold onto the same losing positions and often add more?

10. Many people don't realize that most of the trading firms that were wiped out by huge losses were very profitable traders for years. They showed large profits at first, but they were unreasonably large profits. And this was their downfall. Why does this make sense, and to what degree is this a simple example of human nature in action (greed and fear)?

CHAPTER 18

Option Risk: Finding It and Hedging It

EVALUATING A TRADER'S OPTION PORTFOLIO

In Chap. 17 we began a preliminary discussion on risk. We discussed hedging a spot market position of 1000 shares of IBM stock. The most efficient hedge is to sell the very same asset (IBM shares) in the forward or futures market (if available). In this chapter we discuss the risk associated with options; how to measure it and how to hedge it. Options are more complex to monitor and understand than spot, forwards, or futures. This leads many people to feel that option analysis lies beyond their abilities. If they spent just a little time becoming more familiar with the tools of the trade, however, they would find their fears were overblown. Very few traders are knowledgeable enough to calculate all the required hedges on their own; the tools do all the work for them and simplify things immensely. Don't forget our motto: What one fool can do, another can.

Simply stated, options are multidimensional, and so they require multidimensional accounting and risk-management procedures. Thankfully, we do not have to reinvent the wheel to do this. Mathematicians have already laid out the proper procedures for us. It's just that their instructions are written in a Greek alphabet soup. We'll introduce and translate the Greek symbols shortly.

A trader's "book" or a firm's portfolio can be huge at times, but we can simplify matters by breaking a massive position into its component parts. They can be deconstructed and then summed again later. The tools we use remove the shrouds of mystery by methodically analyzing each and every single asset. Understanding a portfolio's risk presents no difficulty if we are able to do a full breakdown and analysis of its components. The total sum of the individual exposures reveals the portfolio's risk.

Take the case where a new manager comes on board and inherits a large unhedged portfolio. Strange things seem to be happening to the portfolio's profits and losses (P&Ls) day after day. After a few bad weeks, the manager instructs traders to reduce the risk. They enter all sorts of hedges. But it appears as if the portfolio has taken on a life of its own and doesn't respond to the new hedges. It seems the old rules cease to apply. Huge unwarranted gains and losses appear and then disappear. Projected P&Ls and hedging techniques fail miserably. The portfolio seems to be unhedgeable and the losses unstoppable. The portfolio gives the appearance of being haunted. While this is the way it feels, it is all nonsense. The rules still apply, but the people making hedging decisions just aren't measuring all the risks.

A large portfolio can often look like it is perfectly hedged and has no risk, but there are no perfect hedges as we pointed out in Chap. 17. Every open position, even when hedged, has some risks. A large portfolio has that many more. A portfolio may seem to have no risk because the daily P&Ls are small, for a time, and never seem to amount to anything substantial. They move up a bit one day, down the next. Then a quiet market comes to an end with a minor explosion. After a surprising jolt of volatility, things are suddenly aswim. Positions that looked riskless now kick in with huge daily P&L swings. Traders make position adjustments and new hedges are added, but the big P&L swings continue nonetheless. What is going on?

Here's a hint: this never happens in quiet markets. In a dead market you can be woefully underhedged and never get spanked for it. But volatile markets shake and break things until they come apart. The core of the problem is unhedged risk. The positions appear hedged, but they have absolutely, without doubt, not been fully and completely hedged. We must unveil every risk that exists in the portfolio. Options have many dimensions of risk. And each dimension of risk is correlated to the six components that create an option's value.

The Components of Options Analysis

Let's start with the components we know from the acronym SKIT-V:

S = spot stock price

K = strike price

I = interest rate

T = time to expiry (in years)

V = volatility, defined as 1 SD of annual price moves

There is one additional component that was assumed to be zero by Black and Scholes, but shouldn't be. It's the stock dividend, which we'll call D. Over the next several pages we'll review the ways option experts measure these six important components (SKIT-V-D).

There are three phases to risk management of derivatives:

1. Identify and measure every knowable risk.
2. Create hedges that offset all hedgeable risks.
3. Continuously monitor to catch surprises early and readjust.

Here's the deal: Many Greek names that you've heard, but may not have understood, are the traders' names for risk measurement tools in options trading. Delta, gamma, vega (kappa), theta, and rho are by far the most important names. We will acquaint you with each of these shortly. Traders and risk management people spend their days worrying about the P&L impact of these on their option book. The names won't sound so strange when you get more comfortable with the whys and wherefores of each.

How to Measure Option Risk

For our purposes here we define option risk as any unhedged change in an option's value. The change in option value is always caused by changes in the components. Change is the only thing that matters. If everything remains constant, then there is no risk, no exposure. But, of course, things do change. There are three key questions in our analysis: What risks show up when things change? What is their rate of change? How can we hedge this?

There are math tools that can help us with this. But to use these tools we must come face to face with the nightmare of most math students: calculus. If you go get a drink and relax a bit, we guarantee that it will be far less painful than you fear, for we will spend only a few pages on it and touch on the highlights only. (If you gut it out, by the end of the chapter you'll be able to talk option Greek with the best of them.)

Measuring rates of change is something calculus does spectacularly well. Calculus is a branch of continuous math developed specifically to deal with very, very small changes. Consider it the mathematics for things under a microscope.

Basically there are two types of calculus: differential and integral. They perform opposing (inverse) operations. If used together, they would cancel each other. They are like the pills that Alice took in Wonderland: "One pill makes you smaller and one pill makes you large."

Differential calculus specializes in making things so large that we can see what is happening on a microscopic level. It works by putting formulas and curves under a microscope, selecting a tiny area, and measuring the rates of change in that specific area. Mathematicians discovered how to dissect and understand the curve of an option's value using these tiny changes. We can do it, too, by looking at tiny segments of each curve and investigating how the pieces vary from point to point. Differential calculus has the tools we will use to help us analyze and measure option risk.

The other type of calculus, integral calculus, does the exact opposite. It specializes in stepping back away and focusing on the big picture. If we are a doctor examining a patient's eye through a magnifying glass, we will see only tiny veins and even the cells that create the inner eye. But if we put away the magnifier and step back we will see the whole eye and then the face of the person. This is what integral calculus does. It reverses the magnifying process and shows us what the big picture looks like when summed together as a whole. The tiny component parts become the whole organism again. Mathematicians use this methodology to add up an infinite number of tiny things and give us the proper totals. Remember the infinite number of exceedingly thin bars in the normal curve? Integral calculus allows us to sum them up easily. We can accurately calculate any area under the normal curve that we want (see Chap. 9 on calculating an option on IBM). Very advanced options books thrive on integral calculus. We are already past the point where we would need it.

We are not going to turn you into calculus wizards here. Instead we will merely hit the high points so that when your local math genius starts babbling about "first and second price derivatives" you are not in a fog. You'll know he is referring to deltas and gammas, which are the same thing. And, since three-quarters of all option speak comes down to mumbling about deltas and gammas, after a short while you'll begin to feel right at home.

Differential calculus allows us to ask simple questions such as, How much will the option value change as the spot price of IBM changes a tiny bit? Or, in a slightly different vein, how much will the option value change as a tiny bit of time passes?

These rates of change are called *first derivatives* in calculus. They measure the rate at which two items are changing compared to one another, their relative "speed." Each of the six components has its own rate of change, its own speed.

Let's use a familiar example: driving your car down the road at 45 miles per hour. To change your speed you must either accelerate or decelerate. In the calculus of motion, speed is the first derivative while the acceleration is the second derivative. For traders, the only second derivative normally used is called gamma. Traders say the option's speed is its delta and the acceleration is its gamma. Just as a car's power is measured by its ability to accelerate, so too, is an option's. Traders who don't pay close attention to gamma are often in shock when they get whiplashed right out of their seats.

LEARNING TO SPEAK THE GREEK

Let's get into the nitty-gritty of what the standard risk tools are.

Delta $= \dfrac{\partial C}{\partial S}$ Computes the change in C (call premium) per tiny change in S (spot stock price)

Theta	$= \dfrac{\partial C}{\partial T}$	Computes the change in C (call premium) per tiny change in T (time)
Vega (kappa)	$= \dfrac{\partial C}{\partial V}$	Computes the change in C (call premium) per tiny change in V (volatility)
Rho	$= \dfrac{\partial C}{\partial I}$	Computes the change in C (call premium) per tiny change in I (interest rates)
Gamma	$= \dfrac{\partial^2 C}{\partial S^2}$	Computes how fast the delta is changing per a tiny change in spot stock price. It measures acceleration. This is the only second derivative.

The symbol ∂ represents the Greek equivalent of our lower-case letter d. In calculus it denotes a tiny change. So $\partial C/\partial S$ computes the tiny change that will occur in C (call premium) for each tiny change in S (spot price). The division symbol shows it is the ratio of the two. The symbol $\partial C/\partial S$ is very important in options and has a far more familiar name. It is called the delta.

Delta is the single most discussed options tool. Basically, people trade IBM options as a substitute for owning IBM stock. The delta puts a simple number on the relative speed of the two. If the delta is 0.45, it means the option moves 45 percent as fast as IBM stock. Deltas always run between 0.00 and 1.00.

The analysts took it a step further and wanted to know how fast the delta was changing. They used calculus to take the second derivative and named it gamma. You can see the relationships clearly in the following table.

Simplified Deltas and Gammas

Price of Stock	Option Prem. C	Delta (Prem. Change)	Gamma (Delta Change)
103	3.60	0.30	0.10
102	3.30	0.20	0.05
101	3.10	0.15	0.03
100	2.95	0.12	0.02
99	2.83	0.10	
98	2.73		

Delta and Gamma

The previous table is an oversimplified example of how deltas and gammas are computed. Notice the column titled Option Premium C (in the Black-Scholes formula, C stands for call premium). Each pair of premium values generates only one delta value. Now look at the Delta column. Each pair of deltas generates only one gamma value.

Notice that when the stock price is trading at $101 the option premium is $3.10. However, we expect this $3.10 to become $3.30 if the stock pops up a buck to $102. This $.20 change per $1 spot stock move is the delta. A delta of 0.20 means the option moves 20 percent as fast as the stock between those two points. That's it! That's about all there is to the way the average person under-stands and uses delta. Traders, however, spend all their waking hours trying to control and hedge their ever-changing delta ex-posures. The expected up move *or* down move of any option pre-mium should be *almost* identical over a small stock price move and not as represented in our table. Also, then, the deltas and gammas should be changing more gradually than in our table. We wanted larger changes than reality usually gives for purposes of the example.

From $102 to $103 there is a bigger move (0.30) in option value. This change in delta, from 0.20 to 0.30, must be protected against. Note the gamma between those two deltas. It is 0.10 which represents the delta move we just identified. That's why we need gamma, to point out the risk of potential changes in delta.

The measurements of all the other multidimensional types of option risk require similar analysis. Whether we wish to measure volatility risk* (vega $= \partial C / \partial V$) time risk (theta $= \partial C / \partial T$), or in-terest rate risk (rho $= \partial C / \partial I$), we are always measuring the option premium *change*, which is ∂C, per small move of the component.

---

* Volatility risk is also sometimes called kappa because vega is not really a Greek letter, but a word starting with V is nicely fitted to *volatility*, isn't it? If called kappa, it still equals $\partial C / \partial V$ because the V in the bottom means volatility.

Theta

Analysts love to point out that options are wasting assets. The clock is ticking, day by day, minute by minute. Every passing day lessens the value of the option to some degree. But by how much? If we want to know how time affects our option, we use theta to get a measurement. In theory we could measure our theta exposure every hour, but the typical trader's report measures theta in terms of days. Usually a trader wants to know his or her daily time-value loss, also called the *bleed*, as premium value slowly bleeds away. Traders also like to project what the position will look like, everything else equal, if a week or a month of time goes by.

Vega (Also Called Kappa)

Volatility exposure is usually measured in terms of 1 percent volatility moves. Traders speak of each 1 percent as a *vol*. "The market moved up three vols today," means that the market's implied volatility rose 3 percent (from 25 to 28 percent perhaps). If there is one secret to understanding options, then volatility is it. The only unknown in the Black-Scholes formula is volatility. The longer you trade options, the more you will realize that the whole structure of the options market is keyed to volatility.

Vega is the name of the measuring tool that tells us how changes in volatility impact an option's value. The following table shows how each 1 percent volatility move can change option premiums. It is the relative change in premium that determines an option's vega (the premium change of a call per 1 percent vol move). Put more mathematically it's the amount of ∂C per amount of ∂V. The standard change in anything is one unit. In volatility, one unit means a 1 percent volatility move (from 32 to 33 percent, for example). Now let's look at the following volatility analysis table.

Volatility Analysis
(Very Rough Values)

Volatility (%)	Premium on Option	Vega
30%	3.50	0.18
29%	3.32	0.17
28%	3.15	0.15
27%	3.00	0.14
26%	2.86	0.13
25%	2.73	

As volatility goes up, the premium goes up. But how much does the premium increase or decrease per a 1 percent volatility move? The answer is it is constantly changing. In our table the vega is 0.13 for the 25 → 26 percent volatility jump. The vega is 0.18 when volatility levels move from 29 → 30 percent. In both cases it's a 1 vol move, but the vega is different for both (don't forget vega is also called kappa by some analysts).

Let's say you owned $100,000 of premium in this option. It closed at 27 percent volatility and $3.00 premium. If there was a 1 vol up-move next day, that would impact you by $0.15 on $3.00 which is a 5 percent shift. On your $100,000 position this means a $5,000 move. This expected move in your P&L proves you have vega risk (volatility exposure). Exposure reports for the trading department highlight volatility as one of the most important risks.

The same idea of measuring exposure holds true for all six components (SKIT-V-D). Happily, one of the six components is easy as pie to analyze because it usually doesn't change: the strike price K. Once you have created an option portfolio your strike prices are locked in, aren't they? Since they don't change, there is no risk from that component. There are, however, exotic options which allow for variable strike prices. But our discussions here are limited to plain vanilla calls only.

Next up is Fig. 18–1, a little visual aid that pulls it all together for you. If you think in these terms, you'll be able to see the big picture at a glance. We call on our old friend SKIT-V-D for a helping hand.

Exposure to the spot stock price S is monitored by delta and gamma. The strike price K presents no exposure and is not mon-

F I G U R E   18–1

Recap of Risk Tools

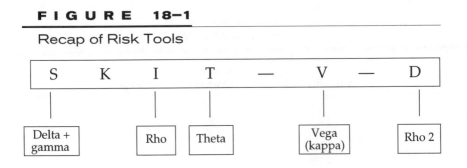

itored. The exposure to interest rates I is measured by rho. Time T is monitored by theta. Volatility V is looked after by vega (or kappa as some people prefer to call it). The final component of the six is the dividend of the stock, D, a sort of second interest rate. We use another rho to measure that; we'll call it rho 2.

An exposure report is created every night for most trading operations. Sometimes it is updated hourly when things are a bit hectic. Traders usually log in their trades, moment by moment, on computers which update their exposures instantly. It takes more than a little practice to translate all the exposures that are measured. In the end they all say the same thing, however: If this component moves, you will experience a P&L change of this amount. Perfectly hedged positions do not experience P&L shifts. Therefore, expected P&L shifts tell you instantly that risks do exist and where they exist. Since all trading has risk, there must be a corporate policy as to what is an acceptable exposure to risk. As long as the company's risk limits are being observed, everything is under control.

Traders consider the big three exposures to be spot price, time, and volatility (*STV*). We measure spot price risk with deltas and gammas. We measure the exposure to time passing with theta. And exposure to changing volatility we measure with vega (kappa). If you keep the big three in mind, all the other risks will fall into place for you. Traders don't worry about the multidimensional exposures all day long, they worry about the big three, *STV*.

AN INTRODUCTION TO OPTION HEDGES

So, we've introduced the standard measurements of option risk. Now, how do we eliminate the risk after we've identified and measured it? The answer is that, we must offset the risk with an appropriate hedging vehicle.

We define hedging vehicles as any and all tradable assets in the spot, forward, futures, or options markets. It is up to us to find the best asset to neutralize our risk. Remember our silly banana futures hedge from Chap. 17? Obviously, banana futures would never be the appropriate hedging vehicle. But we must stay on the alert, because all nonperfect hedges have a bit of banana flavor to them. When choosing our hedging vehicle, we must beware of the residual risks that remain. And all hedges have some.

The hedging vehicle must offset the driving force of the risk you have. Clearly, all option risks are not driven solely by the spot price. Traders worry not just about S, but about the big three, STV. Hedges must be selected for their ability to offset T (time) and V (volatility) and the lesser risks (rhos), too. If we fail to hedge all the multidimensional risks, there is some market movement that will ambush us in the end.

Risk Factor	Appropriate Hedging Vehicle	Greek Tool
Spot IBM price S	Spot, forward, or futures in IBM	Delta, gamma
Interest rate I	Borrow/lend money	Rho
Time T	Buy/sell similar options	Theta
Volatility V	Buy/sell similar options	Vega (kappa)
Dividend D	Borrow/lend the asset or stock	Rho 2

Delta and Gamma Hedging

Let's start by talking about delta exposure. Imagine you have bought 1000 call options on IBM. This represents the right to call 100,000 shares of IBM stock. The option delta happens to be 0.15. Your exposure is calculated as delta $\times$ underlying shares, which is, $0.15 \times +100{,}000 = +15{,}000$. This means your exposure is identical to owning 15,000 shares of IBM right now. Said another way, your daily P&L will move up and down in value as if you were the proud owner of 15,000 shares of IBM. To offset this risk you must sell short 15,000 shares of IBM against it. If you did this, your portfolio would show a position of long 1000 IBM options/ short 15,000 shares IBM stock. For the time being your risk would be neutralized, vis-à-vis IBM's spot price.

This is called being *delta neutral*. That's how traders hedge their delta risk. They buy or sell IBM shares in spot, forward, or futures markets trying to stay flat. But as various SKIT-V components change, the delta of 0.15 will shift relentlessly up and down, say to 0.20, then to 0.17, and so forth. This makes the portfolio longer or shorter IBM without the traders doing any tinkering at all. If the traders run a new exposure report, it will indicate the equivalent shares of IBM that they are long or short as of that moment. To stay delta neutral the traders must sell excess long positions or buy back excess short positions. This is known as *dynamic hedging* (also called rebalancing or rehedging). The traders hope everything stays quiet and they won't have to rehedge very often.

But the various components of SKIT-V never seem to keep still very long. It reminds us of the comic Dave Barry's description of the layout of Tokyo streets. He was on a tour using a Tokyo street map. It was full of incomprehensible detours, construction, and road work. He said his map didn't so much resemble a street map as a photograph of a rectangular box of live, squirming fish bait. That pretty much describes a snapshot of option risk. For a fleeting second you think you understand exactly what must be hedged, but then minutes later the whole thing has slithered off into an entirely different risk profile. So don't get too frustrated in trying to grasp what's going on with all the changes. We've said it before: Options are complicated. Only experience can help you put it all in perspective.

After we've neutralized the delta, what do we do about gamma? The purpose of gamma is to foretell potential moves in delta. That is, it helps you anticipate the increases and decreases in delta as IBM spot prices move. There are two trading approaches to gamma.

The first approach is simple and passive: You ignore the gamma and simply rebalance the delta hedge as needed. Any cost to your P&L is chalked up to the contrariness of options. The second approach is more aggressive: You try to neutralize the gamma to make it go away. But you cannot make gamma go away by buying or selling shares of IBM. This is a perfect example of an inappropriate hedge. You must hedge with other options to lower your exposure to gamma.

Here are a few quick hints about hedging gamma. At-the-money options have the most gamma. As you move away from being at-the-money, in either direction, the gamma falls toward zero. There is very little gamma to deep in-the-money or deep out-of-the-money options. So, at-the-money options are best hedged with other at-the-money options, and so on.

Typically, a portfolio that is long options has positive gamma risk. So you would need to sell other options to lower this risk. Conversely, a portfolio that is net short options tends to have negative gamma risk and you must buy other options to reduce the risk. Hedging gamma is a relatively advanced concept which we can't do justice to here. Suffice it to say that only the more experienced option people are knowledgeable on the topic. The others avoid it completely using the first approach (benign neglect), but their ostrich-like tendencies do not make the risk disappear. They try to hedge their gamma risk by constantly readjusting their delta neutral positions and are surprised when they can't ever keep up.

There is a cost for constantly rebalancing the hedge when you are gamma negative. You must buy some IBM every time it rallies and sell it out when the price goes lower. You are at risk in choppy markets. But you are being paid to render this service to the market, if you think about it. The reason you are gamma negative is that you have sold options to the marketplace. Therefore, you have already been paid the premiums for taking on this risk.

Think of it like this: you are wearing a new fashion creation for traders, the option hedging poncho. It's one of those hooded pullovers with a single-pocket pouch in front to keep your hands warm (it's continuous and goes all the way through). When you sell options, you immediately earn money and you stuff this cash into the pouch. But you must pull it out later in dribs and drabs as you gradually lose money from delta neutral hedging because you are always buying high and selling low. On average the sum of the dribs and drabs will exactly offset any money you earn from selling options—if you sell at fair prices. After thousands of cases, the poncho will be empty. Any interest earned on the money is included in this calculation.

The reverse is true if you are gamma positive. Because you start by buying options you must pay the money up front, so you will have to borrow it at first. You will regain this money in dribs and drabs as you sell high and buy low while delta neutral hedging. The sum of all the dribs and drabs you are able to stuff into the poncho will allow you to pay back your borrowings and any interest due. On average, after many cases, you will break even and the poncho will once again be empty.

This break-even philosophy requires, as the Black-Scholes formula does, that we can hedge without fees and bid/ask spreads, and so forth. In the real world, however, we will lose any such expenses when we try to dynamically delta hedge to stay neutral (flat).

Hedging Interest Rates (Rho and Rho 2)

Interest rate risk (rho) is measured by analyzing how much your portfolio will move for each 1 percent change in the cost of money. Let's use T-bills as an example. If T-bills move from 4 to 5 percent, we call that a 1 percent change in interest rates. Suppose you find that for each 1 percent up-move in the T-bill rate your option portfolio will increase in value by $55,000. This is equivalent to having overborrowed $5,500,000 for 1 year (if your options have 1 year to expiry). To hedge this you could lend $5,500,000 for a year. You must identify your overborrowing or underborrowing and offset it for an appropriate length of time.

Dividends (rho 2) are far more difficult to hedge. There are no easy, straightforward hedging vehicles. There are some convoluted methods that can work with limited success, but this is advanced stuff which we won't spend too much time on here. The dividend generates a cash flow, and this is an important carrying benefit. It has an important impact on the total charge for borrowing or lending the asset. A really sophisticated trader might develop a borrowing/lending strategy around this concept to help as a hedge. Also, there are specialized derivatives that strip a stock's capital gain (its price move) from its dividend. Such derivatives might also be used as hedging vehicles for rho 2. As you can see it's very complex. Luckily, dividends have one of the smallest impacts on risk. This is just one more example of how hedging can become very complex and further mitigates against the possibility of finding a perfect hedge.

Hedging Time (Theta)

The remaining two risks involve time and volatility. We use theta and vega to measure them. Theta and vega risks are unique to options. Therefore, they can only be offset by hedging with other options.

Let's discuss theta and time decay first. Aside from science fiction, time passes in one direction only: At the end of each day a little more time has disappeared. There are very few surprises with time. If we bought an option this morning and it had 200 days to expiry, it can't abruptly turn into a 187-day option. That would happen only 13 days from today. Any change in time takes place at day's end when all options lose 1 day. The standard unit for time change is 1 day.

So, in simple theory, you could buy one option, sell another against it as an offset, and be risk-free. But simple theory fails us, yet again. Time is not simply additive when it comes to options. One day's theta on a 5-day option is not equivalent in value to one day's theta for a 365-day option.

We will mention one rule of thumb, briefly, so you can say you've heard of it. Mathematicians have a quick and dirty measure for comparing two options with different maturities. They use the square root of time rule. For example, let's compare a 12-month option with a 3-month option.

Divide the long maturity by the short maturity and take the square root: $\sqrt{12 \text{ months}/3 \text{ months}} = \sqrt{4} = 2$. This is the magic ratio (for this case) and gives us two important pieces of information. First, everything else being equal, the premium on the 12-month option will be two times as expensive as the 3-month option. Even though it intuitively seems like the ratio should be closer to four times, the relationship with time is not simply linear and the square root rule computes a far more accurate ratio for us.

Second, the daily time decay (theta) will work the opposite (that is, inversely). The 12-month option will lose time value at one-half the rate of the 3-month option. It's a bit surprising that time decay is so much higher for the shorter option. But think of it this way: if the 365-day option is $36.50, it is worth 10 cents a day. If the 91-day option is $18.20 (half the price), it is worth 20 cents a day. So, when a day passes, the 365-day option loses only 10 cents due to time decay, while the 91-day option loses 20 cents.

So the thetas are 10 cents versus 20 cents, and one will not easily hedge the other. You would need to sell twice as many 1-year options as 3-month options to offset the theta. And this ratio changes slightly again tomorrow. That's why the best hedge for your theta risk will be options that have the same maturities.

Hedging Volatility (Vega)

Our last component is volatility. Volatility is the bugaboo of option traders—an enigma wrapped in a mystery. The volatility required as input to the Black-Scholes formula is the future volatility. To properly value an option you must be able to foresee the future and predict how volatile the stock will be during the life of the option. This can only be guessed at. So, volatility is the wild card in trading options.

No one knows the proper volatility to plug into the formula, but they all have opinions about it. The market's best volatility guesses are reflected in the cheapness or dearness of today's option premiums. As volatility opinions swing up and down, the option premiums likewise move higher and lower. We can use this relationship to figure out precisely what volatility the traders are implying by putting the values into the Black-Scholes formula in reverse. Traders call this the *implied volatility*.

Stocks fluctuate up and down on a daily basis. Some days are quiet, other days wild. When the range is small, the options traders start to think that maybe their volatility guesses are too high and they begin to sell options, edging the implied volatility lower. Conversely, if the stock has a hectic day, the options traders start to buy options, thinking maybe they underestimated the true volatility. This pushes the implied volatility up again. This battle goes on day after day. Traders with option positions are under constant threat that implied volatility will go against them during these battles. That is why traders measure vega—to try to understand the risks of implied volatility.

Suppose you have purchased options and laid out a total of $100,000 in premium. You calculate your portfolio has a vega exposure of $5000 for each 1 vol move (each vol = 1 percent). To eliminate this exposure you must find a set of options with a matching $5000 exposure (for 1 vol) and sell those. That would, for the moment, zero out your vega risk. A portfolio with zero vega risk is considered to be vega neutral.

Just remember that every time you add extra options to try to neutralize risk you are adding some delta, gamma, theta, vega, and rho which might cause other imbalances. And minutes later a movement in the SKIT-V components can once again throw the whole portfolio out of balance (don't forget, a snapshot of a box of squirming bait is inaccurate the moment you look away). So you must constantly monitor your portfolio (including the hedges) to see what further hedging action is required. Traders must learn to live with risk because it is impossible to hedge away all exposures entirely. It's like solving a four-dimensional Rubik's cube. *Remember*: The only option portfolio with zero risk in every category is a fully liquidated one.

A CAVEAT ON THE FORMULA

Now that you are acquainted with option hedging we can discuss a problem with option theory that would not have made sense before. The Black-Scholes theory requires many of the formula's inputs to remain constant throughout the whole life of the option, but they are not constant. The theory also expects the trader to be able to execute many, many hedges to protect the arbitrage assumptions, but it is not possible to execute these hedges the way the theory demands.

Black and Scholes determined that the fair value of an option should be based on the risk-free rate of return. This is because there is no risk to a trader who follows their hedging strategies and rebalances his or her option portfolio every moment. Since they have likened option hedging to doing risk-free arbitrage, they believe that such a portfolio should return the same as a portfolio of risk-free bonds. That's why they use the risk-free interest rate in their formula.

But their hedging strategies require rehedging the portfolio every nanosecond. Obviously this is impossible. Real traders rehedge once a day, on average. So, a prime tenet of the theory is impossible to execute. Another big discrepancy is Black and Scholes' assumption of constant volatility throughout the life of the option. This is never true. There are a slew of other impossible assumptions, some of which are painful, others less so. We covered them in Chap. 16.

This leads to the classic conflict of real life versus theory. If the Black-Scholes theory is flawed and not executable, doesn't that make it worthless? No, not at all. What it means is that you cannot employ the formula and naively expect the same results that the theory propounds. Consider this: A line, according to theory, is one dimensional and has no thickness to it at all. If the lines in our geometry books were accurate, then we could not see them on the page because they would be invisibly thin. We have never seen what is described by theory. For similar theoretical reasons no one has ever been able to draw a perfectly straight line or any other perfect geometric shape, for that matter. There is always some tiny flaw. That doesn't stop us from using geometry and trigonometry to build bridges or accurately propel satellites into space. While theory might never be perfectly matched in the real world, we have used it, nonetheless, to create many powerfully important systems.

The Black-Scholes theory has defined an option's fair value for the case where costs don't exist and certain hedges are executable. Given their world you will break even by buying and selling options at their fair values and hedging as they suggest. Clearly, you will not do as well in the real world. So, any trader looking to become a profitable option dealer must be able to sell for prices above the fair value, and buy below. If you can find prices above and below fair value, then theorists would say you have found "mispriced options." The object of all option trading is to find such mispricings and trade on them. This is much easier said than done. But the Black-Scholes formula gives us a place to start by establishing the fair break-even price for an option. We must locate mispriced options if we want to construct a profitable portfolio.

Here is a surprise for most financial people: The average trader running a delta neutral portfolio will lose money over time. A trader trafficking in fairly priced options will merely break even over time if he or she can hedge for no cost. But since commissions, bid/ask spreads, and slippage are part and parcel of every transaction, the trader will lose money. To make up for this the trader must buy cheap enough and sell dear enough to overcome expenses and make a profit. Very few traders can manage this without customers who are comfortable paying them a little bit extra every trade.

KEY CONCEPTS REVIEW

+ Options positions are far more difficult to analyze than spot, forward, or futures positions. Even the simplest option has layers of complexity to it. Simply stated, options are multidimensional and so they require multidimensional accounting and risk-management procedures.
+ Measuring option risk and neutralizing it requires special tools. Mathematicians have already laid out the math tools we need. Traders know them as "the Greeks" (i.e., the math symbols are Greek letters). The most important are delta, gamma, theta, and vega. They are derived directly from the Black-Scholes formula.
+ No matter how large or how complex a portfolio is we can easily analyze its risk if we are able to do a full breakdown and analysis of its parts. The sum of the exposures for each individual position in the portfolio reveals the portfolio's total risk.
+ Our studies show us that the proper start is an analysis of how our five SKIT-V inputs impact an option's value. To these five we add dividends, even though the Black-Scholes formula presumes they don't exist. Dividends (or their equivalents) crop up so often in option trading that we include them as an active part of the risk profile. This makes six important inputs that must be analyzed. We abbreviate them as SKIT-V-D.
+ The three phases of risk management are (1) identify and measure every knowable risk, (2) create hedges that offset all hedgeable risks, (3) continuously monitor to catch surprises early and readjust.
+ In measuring risk the only thing that matters is change. To be more precise, what matters is the rate of change. Differential calculus gives us the tools we will use to measure these rates of change. They are known as first

derivatives. They measure the rate at which two items are changing compared to one another—their relative speed. Each of the six SKIT-V-D inputs has its own rate of change—its own speed.

- The symbol ∂ represents the Greek equivalent of our lowercase letter d. In calculus it means a tiny change. So, $\partial C/\partial S$ translates as the change in C per change in S, where C = call premium and S = spot stock price. The division symbol shows it is the ratio of the two or the rate of how the two move. Ratio and rate are similar in meaning and in etymological derivation.

- The expression $\partial C/\partial S$ is very, very important in options. And it has a name that you will find far more familiar: the delta. The delta puts a simple number on the relative speed of the option versus the stock's spot price. If the delta is 0.45, it means the option moves 45 percent as fast as IBM stock. Deltas only run between 0.00 and 1.00 (calls positive, puts negative).

- Because delta is so important to traders, the cleverer traders decided it was important to learn how and why the delta moves. They created gamma to help measure this.

- Options are wasting assets. As each day ends, the option has one less day until expiration and thus one less day for potential gain. Traders measure this loss in time value with theta. Traders also call this loss of time value an option's time decay.

- Volatility exposure is measured by vega. The longer you trade options, the more you will realize that the key to the whole structure of the options market is volatility.

- Exposure to S (IBM spot price) is monitored by delta and gamma. The strike price K presents no exposure and is not monitored. The exposure to interest rates I is measured by rho. Time T is monitored by theta. Volatility V is measured by vega. The dividend D is a sort of second interest rate. We use rho 2 to monitor it.

- Traders consider the big three exposures to be spot price, time, and volatility (STV). If you keep the big three in mind, all the other risks will fall into place for you.

Traders don't think about the six input exposures all day long, they worry only about the big three, *STV*.

♦ How do we eliminate the risk after we've identified and measured it? The answer is that we must offset the risk with an appropriate hedging vehicle. Hedges must be selected for their ability to offset *S* (spot price), *T* (time), and *V* (volatility) as well as the lesser risks we call rhos. If we fail to hedge all the multidimensional risks, there is some market movement that will ambush us in the end.

♦ Here's a quick example of delta exposure. If you've bought 10 call options on IBM, this gives you the right to call 1000 shares of IBM stock. If the option delta is 0.15, then your exposure is calculated as 0.15 × 1000 = +150 shares of IBM. To offset this risk you must sell 150 shares of IBM against it. This is called being delta neutral.

♦ Delta neutral means maintaining your delta at zero. That's how traders hedge their delta risk. To stay delta neutral the traders must sell excess long positions or buy back excess short positions as things change. This is known as dynamic hedging (also called rebalancing or rehedging).

♦ Hedging gamma is much more difficult. The best way to neutralize gamma exposure is to hedge it with other options. At-the-money options have the most gamma, while deep in-the-money and deep out-of-the-money options have almost zero gamma (so they are less helpful as hedges).

♦ Theta hedging can only be done with other options. At the end of each day every option loses 1 day of theta, but all thetas are not born equal. One day's theta on a 5-day option is not equivalent in value to one day's theta for a 365-day option. The thetas are related by an inverse square root of time rule.

♦ Similarly, vega hedging can only be accomplished by using other options. Suppose you calculate that your portfolio has a positive vega exposure of $500 for each 1 percent move in volatility. To eliminate this exposure you must find a set of options with a matching $500 exposure (per 1 vol) and sell those.

♦ Using other options to neutralize your risk is a lot trickier than it looks. Every time you add options to a portfolio you are also adding positive or negative delta, gamma, theta, vega, and rho which will cause other imbalances. It's like playing a game of three-dimensional chess; it's very hard to visualize what's going on and every new move affects every other previous move. The only option portfolio with every risk perfectly hedged is a portfolio that has been fully liquidated.

♦ The Black-Scholes formula assumes staying delta neutral is cost-free. But in the real world staying delta neutral through dynamic hedging costs money. Therefore, the average trader running a delta neutral portfolio will lose money over time.

THINGS TO THINK ABOUT

Don't Let It Overwhelm You   At this point you might be feeling a bit overwhelmed by the many issues involved in option risk analysis. But just remember, there aren't any option traders, including the geniuses who created the formulas, who could get their arms around all the complexities of options on the first try. Without a lot of practice and experience no one can understand all that has to be learned or get a clear-headed perspective on what is important and what is not. Few traders are knowledgeable enough to calculate all the required hedges on their own; the tools do all the work for them and simplify things immensely. They simply plug the inputs into a computer and play with the results until they can develop a risk profile that suits their style of trading. It takes hours each day for good traders to review their trades and strategies until they feel they understand their exposures and profit potentials. That's the only way anyone can fully learn options. Slow and steady we make progress; little by little does the trick. If the average trader can do it with constant review and hands-on practice, then you will be able to also. Don't forget our motto: What one fool can do, another can. The average trader is very bright and aggressively confident, but is far from being a math whiz. We know this from first-hand experience; believe us, it's true.

Weekends and Theta   Researchers have kept up a long-running argument for years: Are all days of the year equal in the eyes of theta? Clearly the markets don't trade on weekends and holidays. And studies show that Mondays often have bigger moves due to the accumulated news that can occur over the weekend. So, one camp believes we should only measure trading days (252 per year), while the other camp says use the 365-day calendar. Which is more accurate? The jury is still out. Both arguments have pluses and minuses. We lean slightly toward the 252 trading-day year. With enough hard work you might develop an edge in this area. Wherever there is argument or confusion there is opportunity to make trading profits.

QUESTIONS

1. What are the three phases of risk management?
2. How do we eliminate the risk after we've identified and measured it?
3. What are the names of the most important of the Greek risk tools?
4. What risk tool monitors spot price movements? How is it expressed mathematically?
5. What risk tool monitors strike price movements? How is it expressed mathematically?
6. What risk tool monitors interest rate movements? How is it expressed mathematically?
7. What risk tool monitors time decay? How is it expressed mathematically?
8. What risk tool monitors volatility movements? How is it expressed mathematically?
9. What is gamma, and how is it different than other risk tools? How is it expressed mathematically?
10. How many option premiums do you need to calculate the delta?
11. How many deltas do you need to calculate the gamma?
12. Theta is the risk tool that measures time loss. Why do traders only measure theta one day at a time? Why not each hour?

13. Vega measures volatility. If your position has positive vega, it means that rising volatility will be profitable for you. Volatility tends to move in the same direction as option premiums (higher volatility means higher option premiums). If you have positive Vega, are you more likely a net owner of options or a net seller of options? Why?

14. Perfectly hedged positions do not experience P&L shifts. Therefore, what do you know about a position that shows varying profits and losses every day?

15. You are a trader and you receive your daily P&L breakdown. You essentially broke even for the day, but it turns out you made $10,000 in vega profits and had $10,000 in delta losses. What does this mean in terms of risk, and where are the risks coming from?

16. What does *delta neutral* mean?

17. What is delta neutral hedging? What other names is it called?

18. What is a gamma positive position?

19. What is meant when we say that the hedging vehicle must offset the driving force of the risk you have?

20. We have said that traders worry not just about S, but about the big three, STV. What does the expression STV mean and how can traders hedge against it?

Even though all options lose 1 day of theta at the end of each trading day, all theta is not equal in value. Thetas between two options are related by an inverse "square root of time" rule. Questions 21 and 22 refer to this.

21. Assume a 90-day IBM option is worth $3.60 and the same option for 360 days is worth $7.20. At first glance it seems that the first option's time value is priced at 4 cents a day and the second option's time value is priced at only 2 cents a day. Assuming for the moment that they will lose 4 cents a day and 2 cents a day, respectively, how does this relate to the inverse "square root of time" rule?

22. Options do not, in fact, lose time value at the same flat amount every day. option time decay accelerates

rapidly as the last days of an option's life are approached. We assumed that the two options might lose time value at the flat rate of 2 and 4 cents a day. Calculation shows, however, that the 360-day option would lose 1.1 cents the next day and the 90-day option would lose 2.1 cents the same day. How does this fit with the inverse "square root of time" rule?

23. Why is staying delta neutral much more expensive than the Black-Scholes formula suggests?

24. How can a delta neutral trader manage to become profitable given the costs of hedging?

CHAPTER 19

How Traders Make Money

Whether one trades upstairs for a banking/broking operation or downstairs on the exchange floor, every trader has the same goal: to make money every day. But how can this be if, in fact, the markets are random and the future is unknowable and if even the most sophisticated option traders are at the mercy of an unpredictable future volatility?

There are only two ways to make money in any business. You make it from the other professionals in the market or you make it from your customers. While there are many, many variations on how it is done, there are only those two categories to choose from.

The vast majority of traders and trading operations benefit and prosper solely because they have customers. They fail to thrive when they are without clients. That's just the way it is in the business world—all businesses included, financial or industrial.

Only a tiny handful of traders are good enough to out-think the market over a long period and take significant money from the other pros. While falling just a bit short of having ESP they, nonetheless, can see things that lesser mortals cannot. There are very few traders that can survive without customers. When we say a tiny handful, we aren't kidding. Even if these guys told us everything they believe, we couldn't follow it anyway. Look at

George Soros. He wrote a book on his trading philosophy, and it's as difficult to fathom as Stephen Hawking's book *A Brief History of Time*. There's no doubt they both understand their topics exceedingly well, it's just that their knowledge may not be translatable into a common language for us. Thought processes and use of language come from a person's individual experiences. Theirs are far different than ours, and it is possible that their thought processes cannot be readily passed on to others.

There is another group of successful traders who seem to know what they are doing, but have enormous runs of being hot and cold. When they are lucky enough to stay hot for more than a year or two, they give the impression of being wizards. Typically they make money by being strong believers in some market phenomenon or another. When the trend disappears, as most trends soon do, they keep believing and lose a huge chunk back. It is impossible to pinpoint who is a wizard and who is just riding a hot streak. There were many thousands of individual daytraders in the stock market in the past 10 years. Many made fortunes up until March 2000. Almost all of them flamed out and disappeared as the NASDAQ spiraled lower by 70 percent. What does that tell us? And Enron supposedly made billions and billions trading energy in the California electricity crisis of 2000–2001. Where did all the trading profits go? Not for office overhead, we can say for sure. They lost it back in other ill-advised trading ventures.

By far the lion's share of consistent and dependable money made by traders is from their customers, not from other trading professionals. By becoming expert in the needs and wants of their customers, traders can make money in the markets year after year. That's why the trading firms are willing to pay their brokers so much to keep the customers' business coming in. The commissions generated by the customers are nice, but profits obtained from *trading* with customers put the icing on the year-end bonuses.

Those not affiliated with trading firms will find all this news disheartening. And rightfully so. But the reality of all competitive games is that you must have an edge to win. Most professional traders have found it by mining their customer base. An individual trader without a customer base is at a tremendous disadvantage. But that is not to say you cannot find other advantages. It's just that the easy ones are already taken. Without clients you have to work harder and smarter to get an edge. It's impossible for all of us to be George Soros and take a zillion dollars out of the markets. But it is also impossible for George Soros to understand everything that is happening and to fully assimilate all the information available. No one is all-knowledgeable. If you can develop a niche where you understand more than the market in general, you will have an edge.

We now discuss how trading profits can be categorized for most firms. This will help you understand how corporate traders view the market as well as show you what to look for in any department's trading P&L.

THE CATEGORIES OF PROFITABILITY

Clearly, commissions charged for executing and clearing business are a huge positive revenue stream for Wall Street. We state this as a given. We are only interested in profits that are less clear-cut and identifiable, that is, in how traders make money aside from such brokering and clearing fees.

Here are the categories where traders make their money:

1. Bid/ask
2. Markups (pipping)
3. Scalping
4. Spreading
5. Arbitrage
6. Borrowing/lending money
7. Going with order flow
8. Proprietary speculation
9. Pricing private products

These categories apply equally well to all types of trading in all markets. Whatever angle is learned in one market eventually passes to all the other markets.

Bid/Ask

A dealer is a trader who makes markets, that is, two-way markets, with a buying price and a selling price. You call for a quote and he or she makes a bid and offer simultaneously. Let's say volatility is trading 25 percent on a certain IBM option. The dealer might quote 24.5/25.5 (or whatever bid/ask spread is competitive). If the dealer has an active client base that is constantly buying and selling, he or she will be lucky enough to buy at 24.5 percent and sell at 25.5 percent within minutes. Guaranteed profits ensue. So, if you have a niche market with an active clientele and your bid/ask spread is wide enough, you can make low-risk profits continuously.

The world of trading is far too ferocious for that scenario to play out unchallenged. Competition comes in, bid/ask spreads get slashed, the market gets choppy, and your edge gets watered down. The real world rarely allows for easy profits. A much more likely scenario is where the dealer keeps quoting, but acquires a ragtag assortment of positions that neither perfectly offset each other nor allow free money to be made by sitting still.

Having clients trade on your bid/ask spread is an edge. But quoting often leaves the dealer with unhedged positions which can and do wipe out the small bid/ask profits if the market starts to run. If the dealer is a shrewd trader, then he or she finds a way to shade the quote to protect against a market that is running and to avoid piling up a position that continues to worsen. Whole books could be written about the appropriate strategies. Reading your client as a buyer or seller and then shading your quotes higher or lower is strenuously denied by management. But every dealer must do it to survive. The dealers who do not move instinctively with order flow don't last the year.

Clearly, the bid/ask spread is an edge for most dealers who make markets. But an edge can quickly disappear in cutthroat competition. A trader without a wary eye will end up broke as the cleverer traders pick his or her pocket.

Which brings up another point. Unless you are shrewder than your clients, you will surrender your profits to the sharks among them. A dealer must be more knowledgeable and sophisticated than his or her clients to prosper. You cannot make quotes to other dealers and rightfully consider them customers unless your information sources are better than theirs. Traders are an aggressive bunch and a profit is a profit, wherever they can get it. No one looks more self-amused than a trader smiling slyly after ripping off another dealer. Only the best trader with the best information can make money quoting other professionals.

The bid/ask spread is an edge, but it must be allied with great trading instincts and talents if you expect to be profitable. And the special talents that make a great dealer might be of little use in other areas of market trading. About a dozen years ago there was a floor trader in the Chicago bond pits who became quite successful and thus famous. He specialized in making a dealing market in the pit to other floor traders. That is, other brokers executing T-bond business would come to him in the pit and he would make a two-way market for size. He was such a wizard at this that he did a tremendous volume of business and made a fortune from the bid/ask spreads. He became the biggest individual trader of U.S. treasury bonds in the world. But the story isn't over.

He tried to branch out into upstairs trading, that is, trading other peoples' money in T-bonds and other financial futures from a desk upstairs. He was given a huge amount of money and infrastructure, but the fund failed from the start. He was a genius in the pit because his reflexes were ideally suited to reading and responding to the instantaneous flows of market information he received as a dealer. And these skills allowed him to keep a good portion of the bid/ask spread he was earning. But he gave up those edges when he went upstairs and was immediately on the outside, looking in. His highly specialized skill sets weren't being fed with the information flow that had made him successful, and he wasn't entitled to the edge of the bid/ask spread any longer since he wasn't a dealer. He went back to the pits after a while and was again very successful.

Bid/ask spreads paid to dealers are an edge, but do not assure automatic profits. Successful dealers probably have specialized talents that are not necessarily transferable elsewhere. The basketball great Michael Jordan desperately wanted to be a major league baseball player, but he couldn't break out of the minor leagues.

Markups (Pipping)

If a trader is given orders to fill by clients, he or she is often allowed to take a markup. Taking a pip here and a pip there adds up nicely at the end of the month. But how large or how small should the markup be? What is fair? This is an eternal bone of contention between customers, traders, and the customers' representatives.

Some traders are extraordinarily frugal and thus generous to clients, taking tiny markups and depending on client loyalty for return business. Their bosses might even get annoyed because they are not making enough money on the clients. At the other extreme are the "rip-your-lungs-out" type of guys. They believe that a good client will sit still for anything, and if they don't, well, they weren't very good clients anyway. The sales force and relationship managers are in a constant battle with these rapacious traders to knock it off. Most traders fall somewhere in between the generous and rapacious types. Markups can be a significant profit center for a trader and the trading department.

Scalping

Some traders are adept at spotting small discrepancies in the market that disappear in an instant. These guys are like hawks that can spot a mouse from 200 yards away, swoop down, and make the kill. Everyone else blinks and it's gone. Quick reflexes and nerves lend a small edge.

Most scalping, however, is a bit longer term. The market might be 24.5/25.5 for hours when the trader hears a 25 bid and jumps on it (sells it). He now becomes the best buyer by bidding 24.75 and gets hit after 10 minutes. He nets 0.25 in 10 minutes. Most scalping is like that.

There are risks, but a good trader is in and out in minutes or is looking to "scratch" the trade (break even). He or she rarely has positions for very long. Scalping is easier to do on the floor where you see more order flow than an individual upstairs dealer. A trader who doesn't get out of losers quickly is apt to blow up as a scalper. A scalper must remain cool, calm, and collected at all times. It takes a lot of control and discipline to knock out many small winners and keep the losers from getting out of hand. Scalpers learn not to hope and pray, but to get out when the trade turns sour. Despite this, scalpers still have more losing days than most would want to admit. But good scalpers make a living and sleep better than many others because they don't take positions home, so they start off square every day.

Spreading

Spreading requires an added dimension of market knowledge and trading ability. Instead of focusing only on the most actively traded asset, as most traders do, the spreader pays attention to all the related assets in the marketplace. All the strikes, all the expirations.

Spread traders come to understand not only the $100 strike price calls, but the $80, $90, $110, and $120 calls as well; not just the June expirations, but also the Septembers and Decembers. Spread traders learn how and why the various strikes and maturities interrelate. They learn what is a cheap price to pay for the spread between any two and what is an expensive price. They become expert in all the ins and outs of swapping one for another.

Because it requires special expertise, there are fewer traders capable of quoting spreads and thus the spread market is a bit less competitive. While it is true that the odd month or strike has less trading activity, spreaders can quote a bit wider to allow for a small extra margin per trade.

It is best for traders to avoid positioning a large number of spreads for a long period of time. Market interest wanes as old positions age. It is ideal if they can keep the inventory moving off the shelves, but customers typically continue buying one strike or selling another for days or weeks at a time, forcing traders to take on a position. Spreaders have to work off this inventoried position before it becomes stale and unprofitable.

One trick is that the nearby month (the one about to expire) often has peak interest and huge volume just before expiration day. It is important to get rid of positions when the market allows you the liquidity to do so. It is always cheaper to get out of positions when the volume is there.

There are the occasional rollover biases that repeat from one expiration cycle to another. This suits spreaders very nicely. They might take on a position in anticipation of such a rollover bias. Playing on the habits and tendencies of traders who don't understand the ins and outs of deliveries enables the spreader to have a profitable edge.

Years ago one large option firm was very successful at all types of spreading and did it massively. They were heard to say, however, that sometimes they felt they were trying to "pick up dimes in front of steam rollers"! Most successful spread traders, however, choose to look for the loose change fallen at the side of the road rather than get run over by the steam roller. They pass up a few dimes, but tend to live longer that way.

Arbitrage

There are many possible ways to get involved in arbitrage and even more ways to pretend you're doing arbitrage when in fact you aren't. For our purposes here let's assume a trader is doing legitimate arbitrage. The opportunities for decent arbitrage do not arise nearly as often as many people would like to believe. Whether you're down in the pit fighting for an extra dime on an option conversion or upstairs doing massive risk arbitrage between two takeover stocks, the easy money always disappears very quickly. What is usually available are the somewhat riskier deals where patience, sophisticated knowledge, and financial wherewithal are essential to success. This is tailor-made for professional traders backed by large amounts of capital. Traders might have to acquire a position over a period of months and sit on their hands while awaiting the opportunity to make a profit. But these deals, which are certainly not always winners, can be very profitable, especially because they are done in size and with conviction. Good traders know the interrelationships of all the products in their market and can on occasion hit a home run when the relationships become skewed by the wrong players for the wrong reasons.

Borrowing/Lending Money

All clients, even the most creditworthy, run into occasional cash-flow problems. In particular this happens at the end of reporting periods: month-end, quarter-end, and year-end. They might need to roll a purchase forward or backward. They might need to re-arrange their incoming or outgoing cash receipts. The customer will approach a trader to do a repo of sorts. *Repo* is short for repurchase agreement. The largest repo market is for government securities. It is really just a method for financing the client's inventory of government bonds. But any asset can be used in a repurchase agreement, if it has an easily established market value.

Regulations and mandated guidelines exist for brokerage firms that limit what percentage can be loaned against various asset classes.

For the trader it is strictly a financing transaction and has no market risk. The trader lends the client money at, say, 6 percent for a week and borrows it elsewhere at, say, 5.9 percent. The margin of profit can be larger or smaller depending on a dozen circumstances. But traders must make money on repos or the boss will kill them. Tying up valuable borrowing lines to break even is a corporate sin.

Going with Order Flow

One of the least appreciated, but most important, aspects of having a thriving customer base is seeing their order flow. This refers to the flow of their buying and selling activities. Order flow tells you the trend up to that moment. While no one can be certain what tomorrow will bring, if order flow has been strengthening of late, then merely expecting continuation doesn't require the wisdom of Solomon. Thus, customer order flow is, in many respects, inside information. The movies refer to *inside information* as huge chunks of secret business that move markets. But the real day-to-day inside information is the ebb and flow of the whole market's business, the customer business. The insiders in any market are the consumers and producers. Without their participation a market would cease to function. Speculators, traders, and brokers can add liquidity to a market, but they ultimately depend on those who consume the products and those who produce them.

Suppose you were granted every trader's wish: all the customers in the world had to trade through you. You alone, then, would be privy to the most important information any trader could ask for: who was buying, who was selling, what the quantities were, and when their opinions changed. And, of course, everyone is happy to "talk their book," that is, discuss why they think they are right about their trading views. You would learn an awful lot about what was really happening in the market.

When Joe Oddlot buys the equivalent of one or two futures contracts through you, that is a tidbit of interesting trivia, but it does not affect the market. At the other extreme is the information that governmental giants such as the Federal Reserve or the Bank of England are in the market. Since no one has deeper pockets than they, they attract an instantaneous market response.

The stature of the buyers and sellers and how their business affects the marketplace is critically important information. And it is unknowable to all but a few people in the know. Good traders can survive under most conditions, including being outsiders (i.e., not being privy to important information). Give these same traders some bona fide information on market flow and they will prosper very nicely. If a reasonably fair trader was given all the information and orders, he or she would become the most powerful marketmaker in the world, almost overnight. Making money in markets is all about edges.

So, when traders see the order flow of customers, they have valuable information if the flow is sufficient and the clients are marketmovers. Going with the order flow of winning clients is an edge that helps over time. Knowing when it's over is also an advantage. And there are some clients who can from time to time be negative indicators, so opposing them can also be an edge. There is a great deal of information to be gleaned from customer order flow, and good traders know how to arrange their positions so as to maximize the benefit.

Proprietary Speculation

Many big dealing firms take large positions for their own accounts. It is not at all clear that they make worthwhile money from these activities. At any given time one of their big shooters can be making a score in the Japanese yen and be losing his or her shirt in the Aussie dollar. Many top managers believe that you must trade proprietarily for the sake of attracting and encouraging client business. They believe that if you are uncomfortable positioning a large inventory that you will be unable to quote large size to customers and thus won't be in the running for their business any longer.

Given the enormous positions and losses at Enron and Long Term Capital Management (LTCM) it seems that in most cases what the Lord giveth, the Lord taketh away. Both firms had brilliant traders, as much market information as anyone could hope for, and made billions of dollars in the early years. They gave it back, plus much, much more, and ended bankrupt. There are a handful of spectacular speculators who haven't given it all back and aren't likely to, but even they can have huge downdrafts (witness George Soros and Julian Robertson getting burned in 2000).

Taking big positions with longer-term market views can lead some firms to have huge P&Ls. One day up, the next day down. The problem is that even if you have inside information each trade is still only a probability, not a certainty. You can never know all the forces in the world that are working for you and against you. Without perfect information there is no predetermined outcome. As such, there is a possibility of loss, which translates into huge risk. If you have no edge whatsoever, you are playing a 50-50 proposition. With good information you move to 60-40 or even 70-30. Even then there is still a very high probability of loss (unless you consider 30 percent a low probability). Most big players have to expect the occasional disaster. *If you bet the ranch, you will, on occasion, lose it.*

This doesn't stop firms from taking positions or from believing they are invincible. If they have an edge in information, which they might well have, then they will win more often than not. And in the right circumstances they can have good runs of luck that allow for many terrific periods of profitability.

A word of caution: It is extremely naïve to believe that a good run of profitability is proof certain of trading shrewdness or future invincibility. Typically, after a good long run a trader is elevated in stature and encouraged by management to increase trading size. When the inevitable bad turn of events takes place, the bet size has been increased substantially. And, if doubling down is allowed during this bad turn of events, you are facing a potential disaster. Many trading disasters have followed this path. Hubris in markets is tantamount to laughing at the gods. *The gods always get the last laugh.*

Pricing Private Products

The pricing of large private deals for special clients can often be one of the biggest contributors to any trading department's bottom line. A customer requests a tailor-made investment product, and the trading department creates it. The fewer competitors vying for the business, the higher the profitability. A few big deals can make the whole year.

Special long-term financing arrangements, including borrowings and little cash up front, are the most profitable. When a firm wants financing on a deal for a long period of time, they are not shy about paying up a little. This might double or triple the profitability to the dealer. And a 10-year deal is 10 times more profitable than a deal struck for just 1 year.

What we are discussing is sometimes called *off-market* pricing. The client doesn't want the whole market to know its business, so it limits its inquiries to a single investment banker. The investment banker, being no dummy, recognizes that the pricing of the deal need not be as competitive as it would be in the open market and hopes to make a few extra bucks for the value added. Some of these deals are so big that the client would probably save a lot of money by hiring a whole in-house trading desk. But since it's a special, nonrecurring deal, the client doesn't want this continual overhead. Relying on the close working relationship with the banker is frequently the preferred course of action. This is a big transaction for the client and who better to share it with than old, faithful friends. After all, loyalty does have a value, doesn't it?

KEY CONCEPTS REVIEW

+ There are only two ways to make money in any business: you make it from the other professionals in your market or you make it from your customers. While there are many, many variations on how it is done, there are only those two categories to choose from.

+ Very, very few traders or trading operations prosper without clients. You shouldn't get the impression that this situation only describes traders and trading firms; it is the same throughout the entire business world. Every business whether it be financial or industrial, educational or medical, recreational or spiritual suffers without a solid customer base. Customers make the business.

+ The business world is highly competitive, and the reality of all competition is that you must have an edge to win. Most professional traders have found their edges within their customer base. Traders without a customer base are at a tremendous disadvantage.

♦ Without customers a trader must turn to the other alternative: making money in the marketplace from the other professionals. This is far more difficult to do. Without clients you have to work harder and smarter to get an edge. If you can develop a niche where you understand more than the market in general, you will have an edge.

♦ We state as a given that the commissions and fees charged to clients for executing and clearing business are hugely profitable for Wall Street. Our discussions focus, instead, on the methods used by traders to make money outside such brokering and clearing fees.

♦ The first concept we discussed was the bid/ask spread that a dealer (trader) quotes to others. With an amply wide spread and a highly active, two-way order flow this is a terrific winner.

♦ Next we turned to customer orders that are away from the market. It is typically accepted that it is okay to take a small markup of a "tick" or a "pip" or two. This doesn't mean ripping off the customer, it literally means the smallest possible differential. Big markups get big complaints. These are guaranteed profits unless the customer happens to pick the high or low and you are waiting for the extra tick that never comes—but your customer deserves a fill.

♦ Some traders have immensely quick reflexes and can move in and out quicker than the flicker of a lizard's tongue. These traders find they are able to lay in wait and then scalp a market for a small profit before anyone knows the trades were even there.

♦ Other traders work hard at learning the more esoteric facts about rollovers and back-month differentials. They become successful spreaders by developing skills far more specialized than their brethren.

♦ Arbitrages can, on occasion, be done in size to generate very good profits. These are not the risk-free blink-and-you-miss-them types, but the longer-term, somewhat risky market anomalies that take place for the wrong reasons. They can also entail the potential for delivery of

huge positions and sitting with large positions over
relatively long time periods.

♦ Some trading desks are run like banking operations and
have more than the occasional opportunity to borrow or
lend money to their clients.

♦ Going with order flow is a very large edge that is often
underappreciated. Knowing which way the market
orders are flowing leads to a multitude of positive edges
for a trading desk. Seeing this flow before the rest of the
world recognizes it is a decided advantage.

♦ Proprietary speculation is the catch-all phrase we use for
any trade types we haven't been able to categorize
separately, any outright price bets on assets where the
trading desk or management "has a hunch and wants to
bet a bunch," and any arbitrages that aren't really
arbitrages but are in the portfolio, nonetheless, and stay
long after the bloom is off the rose. Some very smart,
sophisticated traders such as the brainy group at LTCM
positioned themselves in arbitrages of all sorts (they
weren't true arbitrages though) and went from geniuses
to morons as billions and billions went from their
pockets to the pockets sitting on the other side of the
table.

♦ Occasionally firms get the opportunity to privately price
products for clients who want to keep their business
away from the eyes of the world. Such opportunities can
be extraordinarily profitable.

THINGS TO THINK ABOUT

Customers, Customers, Customers Think of all the
businesses that you use often and know well. The newspaper store
on the corner, the supermarket, the Wal-Mart and the K-Mart, the
car dealer, the corner gas station. Don't forget the diner and res-
taurants you frequent and even the insurance agent, travel agent,
and pharmacist. They all have to make a living and overcome the
expense of running a business. Where does their revenue and
profit come from? It always comes back to the same basic premise:
Selling products that they can mark up to their customers. If they can't

do that, they have to find another line of business. In this fashion Wall Street is not so very different from Main Street. Remember, very few businesses are able to prosper without customers. Just because Hollywood loves to portray high finance as complex deals executed by brilliant, well-dressed executives doesn't mean they have the picture right. The real Wall Street is an aggressive, work-aholic atmosphere full of down-to-earth hardworking people look-ing for how they are going to earn their next dollar. They know they are not exempt from the basic rules of business and the most basic is that without customers a business fails to thrive.

QUESTIONS

1. We suggested there are only two ways to make money in business. What are they?
2. How important is a client base to the profitability of a company?
3. What's the difference between a dealer and a trader?
4. How does a dealer make money from the bid/ask spread? How important is the width of the spread and the active, two-way order flow?
5. What are the dangers of being a dealer?
6. What does it mean to take a pip or a tick as a markup on a trade? Why do some traders take a single tick while others seem to take far more than that?
7. Some quick traders scalp the markets. What is meant by this?
8. We've described many different categories of trade types and styles. Must they always be separate, or do they sometimes overlap between the types?
9. What are rollovers, and how can they be profitable for traders?
10. What are back-month, differentials, and how can they lead to profits for traders?
11. Why are some traders able to be successful at spreading, more so than others?
12. Suppose you have important clients come to you and request that your trading desk price a special product

for them. They describe the product and the large quantity needed and tell you this is all very hush-hush and yours is the only desk that they are interested in dealing with. Do you think that you could find a way to make a profit on this? Do you think your margin of profit would end up better or worse than most of the competitive deals you've worked on all year?

13. Lately in the news there have been some trading scandals involving the possibility of *front-running*. This is a form of going with order flow where the client never gets a chance for an execution. The trader involved in front-running a buy order, for example, tries to buy the market ahead of the customer's order and doesn't fill the customer's order unless the market breaks down. If the market keeps going up, the customer gets nothing and the trader reaps the benefits. How is this advantage different from the edge of going with order flow that we've described?

CHAPTER 20

How to Convert Puts and Calls: CPL.PCS

Up to this point we have dealt exclusively with call options and avoided discussing puts at all. This was a conscious decision; we wanted to simplify our studies, which were complex enough already. But in the real world puts can be even more actively traded than calls. While traders usually buy calls to play the upside of a stock and buy puts to play the downside, a put can be converted into a call, or vice versa, under the right conditions. And, under conditions allowing such conversions, traders will forsake one for the other to save a dime. We will discuss some of the simple maneuvers traders use when they try to substitute puts for calls or vice versa.

Everything we learned about calls applies to puts, but we must make adjustment for the fact that they are mirror images of each other. When calls go up, puts go down. Since they move in opposite directions, we must learn how to deal with this confusion. And, as we delve into the put-call conversion relationship we will begin to better understand how puts and calls are tied to the shares of stock they represent.

We can view shares of IBM as having a dual nature: potential gains in good years and potential losses in bad years, upside versus downside. Thus, an owner of IBM stock has both positive upside (same as a call option buyer) and negative downside (same as a put option seller). Every long IBM stock position can, therefore, be thought of as synthetically equivalent to buying a call on IBM and simultaneously selling a put on IBM. Option traders can use this equivalence to create synthetic portfolios. That is, choosing any two of the three (puts, calls, shares of stock) traders can create a synthetic version of the third. We describe this in the following formulas.

TWO SIMPLE FORMULAS: CPL.PCS

Here is a six-letter acronym to memorize the put-call relationship: CPL.PCS. We have created a silly name that makes it easy to memorize: *Corporal Paces*. He is our military advisor for option conversions. He used to be a captain, but was demoted for too many 007-like antics.

CPL.PCS is our abbreviation for two formulas:

$$C = P + L \quad \text{or} \quad \text{Call} = \text{put} + \text{long}$$

$$P = C + S \quad \text{or} \quad \text{Put} = \text{call} + \text{short}$$

The first shows how to create a synthetic call, and the second shows how to create a synthetic put.

Long means we own shares of stock; *short* means we have sold shares of stock and must deliver them. You should understand that we really only have three symbols to play with (C, P, L), but when the algebraic manipulations created $-L$ (a negative long position) we simply replaced it with S (a short position). This makes it easier to explain and understand and is also algebraically correct.

Deriving These Simple Formulas

Where did these formulas come from? We started with the well-known equivalence that we described in our opening paragraphs: a long position in stock is identically equal to buying a call and selling a put. Let's repeat that in a slightly more formal manner: Long = +call − put. This is our starting formula. The other two formulas are just reworkings of this starting formula.

With a few simple algebraic moves [adding +put to both sides, letting the + and − puts cancel each other, and reversing the sides (all legitimate)], we can rearrange our starting formula to obtain: Call = put + long. That's how we got CPL, the first part of Corporal Paces.

From this we subtract a long from both sides, cancel the + and − longs, and reverse the sides again to get: Put = call − long, but we prefer to restate this in the following way: Put = call + short (since a negative long is the same as going short, to a trader). This is where PCS, the second part of Corporal Paces, comes from. So, that's the origin of CPL.PCS, two different versions of the same starting formula. Let's recap:

Call = put + long   (abbreviate as CPL and pronounce it as "Corporal")

Put = call + short   (abbreviate as PCS and pronounce it as "Paces")

There is really only one basic formula with the three symbols (C, P, L), but we have manipulated it into several versions to help us. Essentially we are using the formulas to give us clear-cut mathematical definitions on how to create synthetic puts and calls.

DOING CONVERSIONS IN THE PIT

In an active option market there are pit traders who specialize in keeping the puts and calls in line for a tick or a pip. That means that if conversion specialists in the pit see the put or call trade a tick or two out of line, they will try to arbitrage the two. The traders want to keep a zero position, so, if they buy the call, they will sell the put immediately *and* sell shares of stock. Conversely, if they buy the put, they will immediately sell the call and buy shares of stock. Essentially, the traders take our simple formulas and rearrange them so that the final position equals zero. For example,

Corporal ($C = P + L$) is the same as $C - P - L = 0$.

The rule of thumb for traders doing conversions and reverse conversions is, Whatever you do with the put you do the same with the stock. (If you buy the put, you must buy stock as an offset.) This makes the hedging process automatic and helps them avoid costly mistakes while trying to scalp for dimes. There's precious little time to think in the pit and no room for error. When the trade is there, you've got to jump on it. Those who hesitate are lost, and snoozers are losers.

SIMPLE RULES

Traders have other limitations while doing conversions, if they want to get it right. Here are some simple rules for assuring equivalence:

1. Put and call strikes must be the same.
2. Put and call expirations must be the same.
3. Stock hedged in the spot market is a match only for spot options, and so forth.
4. The number of shares must offset precisely; one put or one call = 100 shares.
5. All legs must be placed simultaneously at prevailing market prices.

The strikes must be the same. A $90 call can only be converted to a $90 put, not a $100 put or an $80 put. The expirations must be the same. An April put cannot be converted to a March call. If the options are for spot shares of IBM, then any IBM hedges must be made in the spot stock market. Hedging in the forward or futures markets can cause the arbitrage to misfire. And finally, when you enter a conversion or a synthetic position, if you fail to execute all legs immediately, you add extra risk exposure to the position. The technical analyst types call this an error of nonsynchronicity. Traders call it lifting a leg. We can imagine many descriptive adjectives for a trader with one foot on the ground and the other dangling in midair, but conservative and low-risk do not come to mind.

EXAMPLES OF CPL.PCS

A few examples can help make Corporal Paces more familiar.

We want to create a synthetic IBM $110 call option. From CPL we realize that the IBM call = IBM put + IBM long. So, we can create an IBM $110 call option if we buy an IBM $110 put option and buy 100 shares of IBM stock *right away*. That's simple enough, isn't it?

Let's try another. We want to create a synthetic IBM $90 put. From PCS we realize that the IBM put = IBM call + IBM short. So, we can create an IBM $90 put option if we buy an IBM $90 call and sell 100 shares of IBM stock *right away*. If you don't have it in your portfolio, you will need to borrow the stock to deliver it; thus you owe it and are short.

Synthetic positions are identical in terms of risk and exposure. So it really doesn't matter whether you have a natural position or a synthetically created one. When analyzing a portfolio, it sometimes helps to simplify two- and three-legged positions into a simpler synthetic equivalent. Suppose you run into a portfolio with long AT&T calls, short AT&T puts, and short AT&T stock? You can show that these three (if the strikes and maturities match) might be offsets of each other. If so, this would make the portfolio almost flat with little or no exposure despite having an apparently complicated open position. Such joining together of offsetting positions can help you more easily visualize what is really going on. Lots of complex positions can be broken down into simple spreads with easily defined exposures and hedges. It's a neat trick, so keep an eye out for it.

KEY CONCEPTS REVIEW

+ Puts and calls of the same strike and expiration can be easily converted into one another. When such conditions exist, traders will swap one for the other to save a dime.

+ Everything we learned about calls applies to puts, but we must make adjustment for the fact that they are mirror images of each other. When calls go up, puts go down. Since they move in opposite directions, we must expect to be confused in visualizing the outcomes until we have enough experience to regain our sea legs.

+ IBM shares have a dual nature: an upside potential for gains with a downside potential for losses. This can be shown to be equivalent, in terms of risk, to owning an IBM call and selling an IBM put (you don't *own* the put or you would *benefit* from the downside). All put/call conversions depend on this equivalence.

* Option traders have, therefore, learned to think of IBM shares as the synthetic equivalent to buying a call and selling a put. Option traders use this equivalence to figure out how to set up synthetic portfolios.

* We created a simple acronym, CPL.PCS. (pronounced Corporal Paces) that helps us understand the synthetic put/call relationships and remember the synthetic formulas to create a call or put: $C = P + L$ and $P = C + S$.

* The first formula shows how to create a synthetic call: Call = put + long.

* The second formula shows how to create a synthetic put: Put = call + short.

* These two formulas are derived from the first equivalence described earlier: a long stock = buying a call + selling a put. This is the basic formula. The others are simply reconfigured versions that allow us to show more clearly what a call equals and what a put equals.

* Some pit traders specialize in keeping puts and calls in line to make a profit of a single tick or pip. They want to keep a zero position, so, if they buy the call, they will sell the put immediately and also sell shares of stock.

* The rule of thumb for traders doing conversions and reverse conversions is that whatever you do with the put you do the same with the stock. (If you buy the put, you must buy stock as an offset.)

* The first two conditions that must exist to make a conversion doable are that the strike and expiration of the put must be identical to the strike and expiration of the call.

* Several other conditions must exist for a perfect conversion. The underlying asset must match the option; for example, spot options match spot stocks, and futures options match futures stocks. The number of units must offset precisely: one put or one call = 100 shares. And all legs must be placed simultaneously at prevailing market prices (no waiting and praying).

* Creating a synthetic IBM $110 call option: From CPL we realize that an IBM call = IBM put + IBM long. So, we can create an IBM $110 call option if we buy an IBM $110 put option and buy 100 shares of IBM stock *right away*.
* Creating a synthetic IBM $90 put option: From PCS we realize that an IBM put = IBM call + IBM short. So, we can create an IBM $90 put option if we buy an IBM $90 call and sell 100 shares of IBM stock *right away*. (If you don't have it in your portfolio, you will need to borrow the IBM stock to deliver; thus you owe the shares and are short.)
* Synthetic positions are identical in terms of risk and exposure to natural positions. It really doesn't matter, then, whether your position is natural or synthetic.
* When analyzing a portfolio, it often helps to simplify two- and three-legged positions into a simpler synthetic equivalent. Long AT&T calls, short AT&T puts, and short AT&T stock in a portfolio can be shown to offset one another (if the strikes and maturities match). If so, this would make the portfolio almost flat with little or no exposure despite having an apparently complicated open position.

THINGS TO THINK ABOUT

Put/call conversions require the strikes to be identical. What would happen if they weren't? Let's suppose we are buying the $80 IBM call, selling the $70 IBM put, and selling shares of IBM at $72. If the market runs up to $79, we have no protection since we don't have the right to call the shares until $80. We sold the $70 put which will earn us a little premium, but it is far less premium than we should have received had we sold the proper $80 striking price. This split strike conversion leaves us improperly hedged between the two strikes of $70 and $80.

Put/call conversions also require the expirations to be identical. What happens when they are different? Just like the split strike conversion, a difference in the expiration dates will leave us improperly hedged because one of the options will outlive the other. For example, we buy the June $80 IBM call, sell the September $80 put, and sell shares of IBM at the market, say at $72. Everything looks okay until about the third Friday in June when the price of IBM is, say, $85. We exercise the call at $80 to get the shares of IBM we are short and we repay them. Suddenly we realize that the call has been used to cancel out the short shares of IBM, but we are still short the September $80 put and no longer have any downside protection. If IBM falls to $75 or, gulp, $65, we will lose a fortune. So much for split expiration trades!

QUESTIONS

1. What is the basic relationship between owning shares of stock versus puts and calls?
2. What does Corporal Paces mean to us?
3. What does CPL.PCS stand for?
4. How did we derive the two formulas in CPL.PCS ?
5. What are the two main conditions that are required before puts and calls can be converted into each other?
6. How are puts and calls kept in line on the floor of the exchange?
7. What is meant by a synthetic position? How does this differ from a natural position?
8. How would you create a synthetic AT&T $20 call if you could only trade the AT&T $20 puts and the AT&T shares?
9. Suppose the AT&T $20 calls are trading at $9.00, the AT&T $20 puts are trading at $5.50, and the AT&T shares are trading at $24.00. Is there a profitable arbitrage to be done, and, if so, how would you do it?
10. How does a synthetic position vary in risk from a natural position?
11. How does understanding synthetics allow us to better understand a complex portfolio?

CHAPTER 21

The Best
Option Strategies

WHAT IS THE BEST OPTION STRATEGY?

We've covered a lot of ground; from coin tosses and probability distributions to deriving the formulas for options pricing. By now even the most patient would-be option traders are apt to be cranky and anxious for some answers. "All this theory is very illuminating," they say, "but how does it help us make money?" Or, stated more specifically, which option strategy makes the most money?

Sad to say, the perversity of the markets precludes any easy answers. The option theories tell us how to make money *only* if we can identify *mispriced* options (that is, options priced too low or too high). But it is strictly a surreal catch-22 situation because proper option pricing demands that we input *future* volatility, which can only be found in a crystal ball that no one possesses. So, locating mispriced options is not the simple task that many option books would blithely lead us to believe.

But year after year professional traders and trading firms manage to extract big money from the markets, in spite of their legendary failings as soothsayers. How can this be? We discussed these tricks of the trade in Chap. 19. It turns out that although traders are able to consistently prosper, their methods of doing business have little to do with predicting the future. They have edges in trading not available to outsiders.

We turn now to the big question, Which option strategy makes the most money? There is a clear-cut answer, but it may not be very satisfying. It turns out that there isn't any one strategy that is preordained to make the most money. Or more accurately, there aren't any strategies that can automatically be deemed winners or losers. Regardless of how complex or clever your strategy is, over the long haul you will win just often enough to break even—before expenses. The flip side is that, shockingly enough, no matter how simplistic or idiotic your method, you will still win just enough to break even before factoring in expenses. The worst methods, it turns out, are the ones which incur large expenses, usually by overtrading. This adds losses from bid/asks, slippage, and commissions (not by accident, this is the way professional traders *make* money).

That, anyway, is the theory behind the efficient market hypothesis as well as the Black-Scholes formula. Both theories depend heavily on markets being unbiased and unknowably random. However, if you see something that the market does not, such as a future that is ever so slightly more predictable, then you can make some money. You must develop an edge, the unearthing of a small bias, say. If you can develop such an edge, you can use option theory to profit from it. The strategies that follow are used by traders who believe they know a bit more about the future course of the market than others. They are trying to take advantage of biases they believe will exist in tomorrow's markets. If they get it right, these strategies will make money. When they get it wrong, these methods will lose money. None will automatically make money time after time. Once again, there is no free lunch.

PAIRED STRATEGIES

The most popular strategies come in pairs; that is, each strategy has two legs (one long and one short), which oppose and offset each other to some degree. Traders who discuss such strategies may variously call them positions, strategies, spreads, hedges, or arbitrages. To traders, any one of those names is interchangeable with any other. It would be erroneous, therefore, to believe that a

trader's description of a hedge or an arbitrage means he or she
thinks it is safer than if it was called a spread, position, or strategy.
An apparently safer name is no protection whatsoever: *all* trading
strategies have risk until liquidated.

Paired strategies require a touch more sophistication and are
a bit more complex to understand. The offsetting nature of the
two legs creates a summed risk profile that resembles neither individual leg. Some risks are lessened, while others might be mag-
nified. Each of these trading strategies has strengths and weaknesses. Each works wonderfully at times and fails miserably at
other times.

There are dozens of strategies. For the sake of simplicity and
to better grasp the issues at hand, we have narrowed the list to
the eight most common strategies. Each strategy has a reverse
position, often popular in its own right. The total is 16 if we include the reverse positions (and grows larger still if we substitute
puts for calls wherever pure call strategies are discussed). Here
they are:

Stock versus Calls
1. Covered writes

Calls versus Calls
2. Vertical spreads
3. Horizontal spreads
4. Ratio spreads

Calls versus Puts
5. Synthetic stock positions
6. Straddles
7. Strangles

Calls versus puts versus stocks
8. Conversions

Note: All the above call strategies have corresponding equivalents
for puts. The table that follows adds more information to this
outline.

Category	Typically Called:	Description	Reverse Position Called:
Stock vs. calls	Covered write or buy-write	Long stock/short calls	Delta neutral hedging
Calls vs. calls	Vertical spread or bull spread	Long low strike/short high strike	Bear spread
	Horizontal spread calendar spread (for a debit)	Short near month/ long far month	Calendar spread (for a credit)
	Ratio spread ratio write	Long 1 ATM/short 3 OTM	Back spread
Calls vs. puts	Synthetic long	Long calls/short puts	Synthetic short
	Long straddles (same strike)	Long calls/long puts (*both* long)	Short straddles (same strike)
	Long strangles (different strikes)	Long calls/long puts (*both* long)	Short strangles (different strikes)
Calls/puts/stocks	Conversion	Short call/long put/ long stock	Reverse

Each category is discussed separately.

1. Covered Writes (Buy-Writes)

Market view: Neutral to slightly bullish

Selling an option is akin to "writing" price insurance. Option sellers are thus known as *writers*. If you write an option with no protection it is called a *naked write*. If you have protection, it's called a *covered write* or a *buy-write*. The two legs are very simple: *buy* shares of stock and *write* a call option on the stock.

Covered writing (buy-writing) is the most popular option strategy and is often the first option strategy that neophyte investor-traders are introduced to. The offsetting nature of the two legs makes it a bit less risky than owning stock, and thus it is acceptable to everyone from the SEC to the Pope. That doesn't mean that it is riskless, however, and it doesn't mean it is a better strategy than others. As it turns out, it is no better and no worse than any other option strategy. It just happens to suit the risk/ reward profile of more investors and thus has become the most popular. Many investors like to think they are earning free money on their portfolios. They are not.

Covered writing is less risky than merely owning stocks outright because the second leg (writing a call) is a hedge, of sorts, and slightly reduces the risk of the first leg. But like all strategies it excels in one type of market and fails in other types of markets. Buy-writes and covered writes are known as neutral-to-slightly-bullish strategies. That means that if you are predicting a flat-to-slightly-higher market, this is a good strategy to employ. Covered writes are quite possibly the best strategy of all for that type of market scenario. But they lose a chunk of money in bear markets and woefully underperform all your friends in raging bull markets.

Let's spend a moment analyzing why this is. In a manner of speaking we can say that stock ownership has two exposures: upside and downside. Call options can be thought of as encompassing all of a stock's upside. Put options can be thought of as encompassing all of a stock's downside. Like yin and yang they complete each other. If mixed properly, a put and a call can create a synthetic share of stock (see strategy 5, synthetic stock positions, and Chap. 20).

When you own stock and sell off the call portion (i.e., enter a buy-write), you have effectively sold off the upside and are left holding only the downside. That sounds pretty gruesome, but the fee you receive for selling the call portion creates an added cushion to your profit margin. It effectively lowers the purchase price of your stock to below the market. Thus, you won't start losing unless the market falls below this new effective purchase price. And you can participate a little on the upside (until the call level—strike price—is reached).

So, you have transformed all the upside possibilities (that you once owned) into a higher certainty of profit in the middle. And you have a bit less downside. If the market stays here or rallies a little, you will be very happy with the outcome. You have used derivatives to transform your risk/reward profile into a new shape and distribution.

Example: Covered Write (Buy-Write)

IBM stock is trading at $100 and a $105 call option (3 months) is $4. Buy IBM at $100, sell the call at $4. This means you are effectively long IBM at $96 a share (which is below the market), but you have an obligation to deliver IBM at $105 for the next 3 months, if the option buyer calls the shares from you.

If IBM closes at $90 in 3 months, you are net down $6, but you would have been down $10 without selling the call. If IBM closes at $100 in 3 months, you have a profit of $4, where you would have only broken even without selling the call. And if IBM closes at $110 in 3 months, you will have made $9 (paid $100, lost it at $105, got $4 call premium), whereas you would have made $10 without selling the call. Your maximum profit is only $9 no matter how high IBM goes because *you've given away the upside,* remember? But giving away the *upside* helps cushion the *downside* with the $4 call premium you receive.

This strategy shows a profit as long as IBM closes above $96 and benefits dollar for dollar until it gets to $105, at which point you reach the maximum profit, $9.

If you are correct that a neutral-to-slightly-bullish type of market will prevail during the life of the buy-write strategy, you will earn returns that are superior to your friends. You have structured your position to augment your return for such market performance. If you are wrong, you will do far worse than your friends in big bull markets and slightly better than your friends in big bear markets. The random markets theory says that there will be up and down markets occurring at unknowable intervals. If such a mix of good and bad markets occurs, you will end up over a long period doing just as well as everybody else. That is, just as well as the stock market does during that long period.

Remember, it requires specific, accurate knowledge about the future to outperform the market. If you have only general feelings and no specific knowledge you will do as well as the market does.

The Reverse Position

To take a reverse position you would sell a stock and buy a call against it. We discussed a similar concept (long calls vs. short stock) under the topic of delta neutral hedging in Chap. 18.

This is slightly different, however, because in delta neutral hedging you are required to sell only the number of shares needed to keep your position neutral (i.e., flat). But someone doing a reverse buy-write (buy one call, sell 100 shares) will be oversold a bit and slightly bearish, not neutral. For example, an IBM call with a delta of 0.45 has the same spot price risk as 100 shares × 0.45. This is equivalent to a long position of 45 shares of IBM. If the call is equal to 45 shares, then selling 100 shares of IBM against this will make you oversold (net short) 55 shares.

Since the typical buy-write puts you in a slightly bullish position, the reverse of a buy-write puts you in a slightly bearish position.

A Variety of Spreads: Vertical, Horizontal, Ratio

The big plays for most option traders revolve around the three most active inputs to an option's value: spot price, time, and volatility (STV). As you may recall, these correspond to the big three risk measures: delta, theta, and vega.

The Big Plays: STV
Vertical spreads   = spot price plays
Horizontal spreads = time plays
Ratio spreads   = volatility plays

Vertical and *horizontal* are descriptive of the *relative directions* in options tables. When options first started being reported in the papers, the print layout was typically something like this:

IBM Call Options

	Jan	Apr	Jul
$90	10.60	13.25	15.40
$95	6.60	10.00	12.40
$100	3.50	7.30	9.80
$105	1.70	5.10	7.60
$110	0.70	3.60	5.80
$115	0.30	2.30	4.40

Notice that the strike prices are listed vertically while the expiration dates vary horizontally across the page. This typical newspaper layout has had an important impact on the names given to many option spreads. When you hear talk of vertical spreads, horizontal spreads, and diagonal spreads, you can figure out the meaning by recalling this layout diagram.

2. Vertical Spreads: Bull Spreads

Market view: Bullish on spot price of IBM

If you buy the $90 strike and sell the $95 strike within the same vertical column (that is, with the same expiry), you have created a vertical spread. It doesn't matter which two strikes you pick, only that the same expiration month is chosen. This particular spread (buy $90 /sell $95) is also called a *bull* spread. Bull spreads win if IBM goes higher.

Here is an important trick to help you keep this straight: Bull has two L's in it. If we take them to stand for "long the low" strike price, we have a terrific memory aid. Every time you find a spread where the trader is long the lower strike (and short the higher strike), it's a bull spread. You can't go wrong with this trick, and it will enable you to quickly grasp the trader's mindset for any call spread. And here is a remarkable and surprising bonus: It's also true for puts. So, it doesn't matter whether the spread is comprised of puts or calls, whenever a spread is long the low strike, it is a bull spread. Any two offsetting puts (or calls) can be easily classified like this. Believe us, this is a sanity saver of the first magnitude and will, at times, protect you from utter confusion.

Here is another hot tip about vertical spreads: The spread can never fall below zero or rise above the difference in the strikes. Let's use our earlier bull spread as an example: we buy the $90 call/sell the $95 call. At expiry time the spread can only be valued from $0.00 to $5.00. If IBM closes below $90, the spread is always worth $0. But if IBM closes above $95, the spread will always settle at exactly $5, no matter how high IBM gets.

But what about in between? If IBM closes between the strikes, then you must calculate the famous $S - K$ value, with S being IBM's spot price on expiration day and K the lower strike ($90). For example, if IBM closes at $91.50 on expiry day, then the spread set.les at $91.5 - $90, which is $1.50. The spread can close between zero and $5.00, never higher or lower. So the risk is limited and easily calculated at the time of entry.

Based on our previous table of IBM call values the January 90/95 spread is worth $4.00. If you buy it at $4.00, that would be your maximum risk because it can only go to zero. But your upside is only $1.00 because the most the spread can ever be is $5.00. Why would anyone take this risk/reward? Because the probability of closing at $5.00 is four times greater than the probability of closing at zero. Vertical spreads convert the market's opinion of the odds and probabilities into a neat little answer: the spread premium. Since the price of IBM is $100 right now, if nothing happens, i.e., the market stays unchanged, you'll make the maximum $1.00 profit on the spread. IBM has to drop $10 to $90 or lower for you to lose the full $4.00 net premium you paid up front.

The Reverse Position
Bear spreads are exactly the opposite, winning if IBM goes lower. Taking the other side of our bull spread would put you in a bear spread. You can use the memory trick "LL" in reverse. If it's *not* a bull spread, it is, by definition, a bear spread.

3. Horizontal Spreads: Calendar Spreads (for a Debit)

Market view: As time passes, the nearby option value will waste away faster than the far out option values (a play on time decay).

   If you move horizontally across the table and find a pair of expiry dates to spread, we would call that a horizontal spread. Perhaps you might sell the nearby January $100 and buy the far out April $100. Keeping the strike the same makes it a horizontal spread. This is also called a time spread or a calendar spread.

   Calendar spreads are traded actively by those who are looking to profit from the wasting assets theory. That is, options are assets that waste away day by day, and so there must be a clever way to take advantage of this. If IBM undergoes a quiet spell, the options will lose value day after day and expire worthless. Passing time deflates option premiums. Meanwhile, highly volatile markets inflate option premiums. Time and volatility are opposing forces in any option's valuation. It's a yin-yang thing. Clearly, the nearby option has a higher time decay than the further out months. This would make a nice spread trade with automatic profits, then, if only the market complied with an appropriately subdued level of volatility until the nearby expiration date. But the market never complies nicely—not ever.

   Typically, some traders will make bets that there will be no volatile market activity in the near-term. To benefit from this they would sell the nearby option expiry and buy a deferred expiry as a calendar spread. If they are correct, the nearby expiry will become worthless as time runs out and they will be left holding a bargain-priced long position in the deferred option. Thus, as time goes by they expect to earn money daily.

Two problems can creep in. First, if the market gets really deadly quiet, the deferred option that you own can have its value quickly wither away, far beyond your expectations. On the opposite side, if the market suddenly erupts, the value of the nearby option can gain dramatically on the deferred option causing a loss on the spread. There are no free lunches here, or anywhere else on Wall Street, for that matter.

The nearby option must, by definition, be cheaper than the deferred month option, and so you must pay money out of your account to enter this spread. Your account will be hit with a debit. So, if you are short the nearby option, we call it a calendar spread with a debit.

The Reverse Position

The calendar spread with a credit simply implies you must buy the nearby option and sell a further out month. You will get money paid into your account, a credit, but you have the risk that the market will stay quiet just long enough to destroy your nearby option and then come to life, putting you at danger of infinite loss if your deferred option runs up against you. You have no protection after the nearby expires.

Diagonal Spreads

Market view: Not completely clear what type of market is most profitable

Mix a vertical spread with a horizontal spread and you'll get a *diagonal* spread. Pick one from column A and a different row from column B or C. For example, if you buy the $110 July and sell the $90 April, that's a diagonal spread. Different strikes, different expiries. This is a bit more complex than either the vertical or horizontal spreads.

Let's use this diagonal spread to test the LL memory trick. Buying the $110 July/selling the $90 April is a bear spread and a calendar spread. It's bearish because you are *not* long the low strike. You are, in fact, long the high strike, right? So, to that extent the spread has a bearish bias. But the calendar portion complicates the issue since time and volatility are now involved also.

Some traders think diagonal spreads are like mixing two flavors of ice cream: it worsens the taste of both. Things get muddled with diagonals; it's not completely clear what market view will lead to the best results. We prefer vertical or horizontal spreads.

4. Ratio Spreads: Ratio Writes

Market view: Volatility will move sharply lower

Here is a typical ratio write: buy one ATM call/sell three OTM calls. This is only one version of the many possibilities that might be created and is actually just a variation on the covered write (or buy-write). Traders usually vary what is bought (not necessarily shares of stock anymore) and how many calls are sold (not necessarily a ratio of one call per 100 shares any longer). Our example is a 3-to-1 ratio write, but traders often use 2-to-1 and 3-to-2 ratios. And they often buy an ATM (at-the-money) option as a substitute for 100 shares of IBM stock.

The ratio write is essentially a play on future volatility. Think of it as owning a portfolio loaded with shares of IBM and then selling a great many options against the portfolio. If the market suddenly goes dead, that is, the price of IBM stays unchanged every day, the volatility will fall sharply. Your shares of IBM will not move in price, but the options will collapse in value as they parallel the volatility move. You can buy back any options you sold and make a huge profit. And in this example all that happened was that volatility fell; an ideal outcome for ratio writes.

Let's take a small fantasy break to help you visualize volatility better. Imagine yourself way up in the sky in the hot-air balloon from Jules Verne's *Around the World in 80 Days*. Your life depends on the balloon's ability to continually hold hot air and your ability to keep replenishing this hot air. There is a gas burner on board with an adjustable flame that can superheat air and pump up the balloon. The hot-air balloon is the option. The flame used to heat the air and pump up the balloon is the volatility. Volatility is the key; it is the fire in the belly of the market needed to continuously pump up the option.

Every balloon loses some air every day, just like options waste away. Without a continuous stream of new air the balloon will slowly deflate. When the flame is off, it will deflate much faster. But when the flame is turned way up, the balloon will expand and expand until it seems it might burst. Volatility is the mechanism that pumps a continuous stream of new hot air into options. Traders are constantly betting on whether the flame, along with the flow of hot air, will increase or decrease over the next days and weeks.

A ratio write involves the overselling of options; it is thus a bet that the flame is flickering and may soon go out. Of course, nothing in options is quite that simple or unambiguous, but this visualization gives you a good overview of the most important force at play.

The Reverse Position

The opposite of a ratio write is called a back spread. Rather than *sell* three times as many OTM calls, you must *buy* three times as many OTM calls. For example, sell one ATM call/buy three OTM calls. Frequently the calls purchased are deep out-of-the-money, far away in the back strikes. Thus traders call these *back spreads*. This is a play on volatility going higher and pumping up the back strikes faster than the ATM strike. If the market doesn't have a big move (causing volatility to head higher), your three OTM options will end up worthless and you'll still be stuck short the ATM, which may still have substantial value. It won't be pretty.

5. The Synthetic Long: Long Calls versus Short Puts

Market view: Bullish

As we described in Chap. 20 on converting puts and calls, a position that combines a long IBM call and a short IBM put (at the same strike) is identical to being long shares of IBM stock. This is called a synthetic long IBM position. The two derivatives (options) have been pieced together to re-create the original underlying asset: shares of IBM stock. Thus it is considered a bullish position since your profit and loss will be identically the same as owning IBM shares.

The Reverse Position

We can create a synthetic short in IBM shares by buying an IBM put and selling an IBM call (at the same strike). This will yield the same exact profit and loss in your account as being short shares of IBM.

6. Long Straddles: Long *Both* Puts and Calls (Same Strike)

Market View: Higher volatility and/or big price move soon

Unlike our other paired strategies long straddles do not have legs that offset each other. Both legs are long. This means you buy both a put and a call. Double your pleasure, and double your exposure. Straddles require using the same strike for both puts and calls. The ATM strike is most frequently used, but any strike is acceptable. [Strangles are very similar, but use different strikes, so we describe them as a separate strategy (strategy 7).]

Straddles have double the exposure because you are buying twice as many options and have no protection with an offset. They are also double the price. To overcome this costly purchase you need a big move in IBM's price or you need volatility to soar. Let's work an example using the following table to help you get a feel for what is going on.

IBM Puts and Calls
(IBM Spot Price = $100)

	Jan Calls	+	Jan Puts	=	Straddle
$90	10.60		0.70		11.30
$95	6.60		1.70		8.30
$100	3.50		3.50		7.00
$105	1.70		6.60		8.30
$110	0.70		10.60		11.30
$115	0.30		16.00		16.30

We've developed this hypothetical table for puts and calls. It's based on the same IBM call values table we used earlier in the chapter. In it the $100 straddle (ATM) is trading at $7.00 (puts and calls are each $3.50). IBM is trading at $100. If we buy this straddle at $7.00, we will make money if IBM closes below $93 or above $107 on expiration day in January. The more IBM moves away from $100 (the strike price), the better off we are. So, we are betting on a big move in IBM's price. Alternatively, if volatility gets pumped up long before then, the put and the call will naturally increase in value, allowing us to exit early.

The Reverse Position

The short straddle requires us to be short puts and short calls (same strike). We are betting that IBM will not move much and that we will benefit as the put and call expire worthless. So, if we are short the $100 Straddle at $7.00, a close of IBM between $93 to $107 at expiry will benefit us.

7. Long Strangles: Long *Both* Puts and Calls (Different Strikes)

Market View: Higher volatility and/or big price move soon

The strangle and straddle are very similar except that strangles require the use of different strikes. The term *strangle* comes from the image of a market mysteriously stuck in a narrow trading range as if it is being choked or strangled by invisible forces. The long strangle is a bet that it will break out of the narrow range, soon. To benefit from this you buy an OTM put and an OTM call which must be at two different strikes (by definition of out-of-the-money).

For example, using the previous IBM Puts and Calls table, IBM is trading at $100 and the most active strangle would be the $95 put and the $105 call. The put is $5 below the market ($5 out-of-the-money) and the call is $5 above the market (also $5 out-of-the-money). They cost $1.70 and $1.70, totaling $3.40 for the long strangle. If IBM closes below $91.60 or above $108.40 at expiry, then you have a profit. That's a wider range to break even than the straddle required ($93 / $107), but you are only paying $3.40 whereas the straddle cost $7.00. You get what you pay for.

The Reverse Position

The short strangle is often the more popular version. Traders seem to feel they can tell when a market is quieting down and will stay that way. Those who think the market for IBM will remain quiet can short the IBM $95/$105 strangle and make money if correct. They sell the $95 put and also sell the $105 call getting a credit of $3.40. IBM is trading at $100 now, and they earn money as long as IBM stays between $91.60 and $108.40 at expiry. This looks so inviting that it sucks in lots of sure-thing players who scamper in panic when those end zones are approached near expiration time. If you can tell when large volume is transacted in short strangles, you can also tell when their break-even, panic points are approaching. Do traders pay attention to this and try to squeeze the shorts? You better believe it.

8. Conversions: Short Call/Long Put/Long Stock

Market view: Totally neutral, no opinion whatever

A few categories ago we described synthetic short positions. A conversion is a synthetic short position accompanied by a purchase of stock to zero it out. That's it. It's really no position at all. It's as close to a perfectly hedged, riskless position as you can get. Essentially, a conversion is a completely hedged and neutralized three-legged position. But keep reading because we'll show, once again, that there are no perfect hedges.

Active traders may have many conversions open on their books because they find it more economical to lessen exposure through a series of protective hedges and offsets rather than liquidate the original trades. Say you are a pit trader. You sell a call and later want to get out. It might make sense, if it is cheaper, to buy a *synthetic call* rather than a real call like the one you are short. To buy a synthetic call you would buy the put and go long the stock. The three together give you a conversion. Technically speaking it is a closed-out position that remains open on the books until the expiry date.

As we have pointed out many times before, however, there are no perfect hedges. Come expiry day there are rare occasions when the position does not self-liquidate and you are stuck long or short, much to your surprise. Only professionals should ride conversions all the way through expiry day. The rule of thumb is if IBM will settle far from the strike, then it will automatically self-liquidate and everything will be fine. If, however, IBM is very close to the strike at expiry, you cannot be sure that the clearinghouse will exercise you automatically or that your counterpart won't call or put you at the most disadvantageous time. It pays to get out before expiry if there is any question of uncertainty.

The Reverse Position

If you are synthetically long (long call/short put) and go short stock to zero it out, you have done a *reverse conversion*, often called a *reverse*. Everything we said about conversions applies here. There is no risk until expiry day which you might prefer to avoid. But, otherwise, it is a totally flat position with no hope of gain (or loss).

KEY CONCEPTS REVIEW

+ The option theories tell us how to make money *only* if we can identify mispriced options. We cannot easily do this because it demands that we input future volatility which no one knows (or at least if they do, they're not telling). Locating mispriced options, then, is far more difficult than we are led to believe.

+ Professional traders, those in the pit and those who trade from upstairs, make big money from the markets year after year, but almost all do it with tricks of the trade not available to us outsiders. We described these methods in Chap. 19. Very, very few professional traders are successful at predicting the future, but they prosper nonetheless. And they have no magic option strategies that automatically crank out money.

+ So, which option strategy makes the most money? The sad truth is that there isn't any one strategy that is preordained to make money. Whether a strategy makes or loses money over a short period is simply due to the type of market that exists during that period. If all options are fairly valued, then any single option or any combination of options will break even over the long haul—before expenses. And the worst methods are, therefore, the ones which incur large expenses (which is where professional traders take our money and gain their biggest edges).

+ If this gives you a headache and we seem to be going in circles, then you are understanding everything just fine. The theory behind the efficient market hypothesis as well as the Black-Scholes formula depends heavily on markets being unbiased and unknowably random. No matter what we do, they tell us, it will break even—before expenses, of course.

♦ The theories do allow, however, that if you see something that the market cannot see, such as a future that is ever so slightly more predictable, then you can make some real money. If you are able to develop an edge or unearth a small bias, you can use option theory to profit from it. Almost all traders who ever opened their mouths to trade believed, at the time, that they had an edge. Reality would argue against them. But that could not stop them from plying their favorite strategies in their efforts to display their superiority over the markets and rake in the big bucks. Each trader has a favorite, special, secret strategy, and each of these strategies is about as secret and special as last Saturday's meat loaf special. But hope lives on, especially in traders.

♦ We described in the chapter the more popular strategies used by traders who believe they know a bit more about the future course of the market than others. They are trying to take advantage of biases they believe will exist in tomorrow's markets. When they get it right, these strategies will make real money. But when they get it wrong, these methods will lose real money. None will automatically make money time after time. Once again, there is no free lunch.

♦ The single most popular strategy (which must certainly give contrarians pause) is the covered write also known as the buy-write. Buy some shares of IBM and protect yourself by selling some call options against it. Thus you are buying stock and writing options. This strategy is best suited to a market that stays flat or has a slightly upward bias to it. It is in the nature of hardened market professionals that "popularity breeds contempt." This means that if a strategy is very popular then the smart money is waiting for the open wallets of the suckers who are making it popular. Unfortunately for the pros, on rare occasions a popular trend can outlast their smart money bankrolls, sometimes by years.

- When a strategy becomes as popular as the covered write, it is abused and overused by every inexperienced option strategist. The weight of all the option selling causes the call premiums to shrink until they are underpriced. This tends to make the strategy less rewarding. As it turned out, however, the steady upward bias of the stock market throughout the 1990s helped many covered writers to prosper anyway. They've come to think fondly of this strategy as an automatic winner. Their warm and cuddly feelings have dissipated quite a bit during the recent bear markets.

- The second strategy we discussed, vertical spreads, acquired its name because of the old newspaper layouts for option prices. In such newspaper layouts the first vertical column showed only the strike prices. Thus we can create a vertical spread by choosing two of those many strike prices (buying one, selling the other). We further categorize these as bull spreads or bear spreads. Here is the hottest memory trick of all: since bull has two L's in it, think of the L's as standing for long the low strike. Bear spreads are simply the reverse.

- So, a bull spread is a vertical spread where you are bullish (upwardly optimistic) on the price of the underlying. An example would be to buy the $90 call and sell the $100 call against it as a spread. Amazingly, this trick works just as well with puts, even though you would think everything would be reversed and upside down. A bull put spread would be to buy the $90 put and sell the $100 put just like with the calls. Remember, if you are long the low strike, it is a bull spread! There aren't any option quick tricks better or more helpful than this for simplifying a complex position quickly; believe us—we've done it a lot.

- Horizontal spreads refer again to the old newspaper layout. Running horizontally across the page in the first row were the option expires (the months). So, a spread created horizontally would be a buy of one month and the sale of another month. For example, you might buy the March $90 call and sell the June $90 call. This is obviously a time spread, also called a calendar spread. The earlier month is always cheaper than the further out month, and thus we can deduce which month is bought by identifying the spread as a debit or credit. If you must lay out money, your account will be debited that amount, and this implies you must be buying the further out month (which is more expensive). The reverse is true if you receive a credit in your account. So horizontal spreads are often spoken of as debit or credit calendar spreads.

◆ Ratio spreads merely mean you are not doing the typical one-to-one spread, but in fact are doing some multiple such as 3 to 2, 2 to 1, or 3 to 1. This adds extra exposure and complexity, but might make sense under the right circumstances and certain market views.

◆ We covered synthetic longs and shorts in detail in Chap. 20. Simply said, buying a call and selling a put is identical to holding a long position if both strikes and both expiries match.

◆ Buying straddles is the fun part of options: double your pleasure, double your fun, and double your risk. You buy both a put and a call and pray the market moves violently so that the double premium you just laid out will be worth it. If you want to buy or sell a lot of option premium quickly, trading at-the-money straddles is the way to go. There are a variety of straddles to choose from, but to qualify as a straddle the strikes must match (be equal).

◆ If you can't afford to trade the expensive straddles, then you might consider it's poor relation the strangle—poor because the premiums are much cheaper. Just like the buying of a straddle, the buying of a strangle means buying both a put and a call, but they are typically both out-of-the-money and, therefore, much cheaper. Since both are out-of-the-money, it also means that the two strikes must be different: if IBM is $100, the $20 out-of-the-money strangle is the $80 put and the $120 call.

◆ Rounding out our eight most popular strategies is the conversion which we also discussed in Chap. 20. The conversion is essentially a perfectly hedged position with no risk, or as little risk as can be found in an open position. We may buy an IBM put, for example, convert it into a call by buying some IBM shares of stock, and then hedge it by selling the IBM call against it. We have thus included all three legs, and they perfectly offset each other. This is very popular with professional traders for hedging up their loose ends and risks. It also allows them to take an ungainly portfolio of dozens of various puts and calls and make diverse positions far more controllable.

* There are many other strategies that we haven't discussed such as the min-max (or fence), boxes, butterflies, and condors. They are often just combinations of the strategies in this chapter or variations on the same themes. There's more than enough material here to get you started and on your way. It's important to note, however, that we haven't deprived you of all the really good strategies by failing to re-create a mini-encyclopedia of methods. No strategy, regardless of its complexity or advanced nature does anything other than try to focus on a given market view and profit from correctly predicting the market. If the market view is wrong, every strategy, no matter how advanced or complex, will lose money.

* To succeed as a professional trader you've got to know a little bit about a lot of strategies and then be on the lookout for the bending and stretching of the norms. This tells you that the market is pushing or pulling in a certain direction. What you've got to worry about is not the option strategies, but the ways that investors use and abuse the option strategies. It's not the equipment used that makes a great athlete, it's his or her ability to outplay and outthink the competition.

* Throughout this chapter we described many of the most popular strategies, which you can see aren't as mysterious or as impressive as you once thought. If the need arises to review any complex portfolio of options, these strategies (and their reverses) will stand you in

good stead. They allow you to quickly sort out and pair off many positions that would otherwise seem unconnected. They also enable you to more clearly understand the nature of the risks being taken in the portfolio and the mind-set of the trader taking them.

♦ After some experience and a great deal of practice with the strategies in this chapter, you'll start to see the logic used by traders and learn to develop your own methods. There are no certainties or sure winners to depend on in trading, only our hard-earned experiences that allow us to develop educated opinions about the future. Market prices are always based on investors' opinions of the future. Educated opinions born of experience will tend to fare slightly better on average. In markets, ignorance is not bliss.

THINGS TO THINK ABOUT

Good News, Bad News   At the beginning of seminars we often tell classes that the good news and bad news about options is the same news: there are only puts and calls. It's good news because everyone knows they can easily buckle down to learn about just two things and quickly become an expert, right? It's bad news because the apparent complexity and creativity needed to understand options must have been a sham if there is only one choice to make (a put or call). And, anyway, all those high-finance, guaranteed-type arbitrages can't be possible if that's all there is, right? Well, you now know a bigger truth: there *are only* puts and calls, but you also know we can be long or short, use not only options but also underlying shares, choose from 15 different strikes and 5 different expiries, and create strategies from a seemingly infinite number of weird ratio combinations and permutations. There's a lot to know and understand about the trading and strategizing of options. It's certainly more than just puts and calls. On the other hand, would you start a class out on day one by telling them they might have to learn to come to grips with a countless number of possible positions and variations on a theme? Markets aren't the only place where hope is more constructive than fear.

QUESTIONS

Use this table to help answer questions 1 to 15:

IBM Call Options

	Jan	Apr	Jul
$90	10.60	13.25	15.40
$95	6.60	10.00	12.40
$100	3.50	7.30	9.80
$105	1.70	5.10	7.60
$110	0.70	3.60	5.80
$115	0.30	2.30	4.40

1. Assume IBM shares are trading at $100. If you wanted to write a naked $10 out-of-the-money call expiring as soon as possible, how would you do it?
2. Assume IBM shares are trading at $100. How would you create a covered write using the nearby at-the-money call? What type of market scenario would benefit this position the most?
3. What's the difference between a covered write and a buy-write?
4. What is a vertical spread?
5. What is a bull spread?
6. What is a bear spread?
7. How much would it cost to put on the April $90/$100 bull spread, and how would you do it?
8. What would be the optimum IBM closing price at April expiry for the $90/$100 bull spread?
9. What is the maximum profit for the scenario in question 7?
10. What is the worst-case scenario at expiry for the scenario in question 7?
11. What is the loss for the worst-case scenario at expiry in question 7?
12. What is a horizontal spread, and what are two other names for it?

13. How does defining a horizontal spread as a debit or credit tell you which option was bought and which was sold?

14. What is a diagonal spread?

15. Suppose you believe IBM shares are not going to budge over the next few months and wish to do a 3-to-1 ratio write with the Jan $105 call. If IBM is at $100 now, how would you do it and what are the possible outcomes at expiry?

Use the puts and calls in the following table to help answer questions 16 to 21.

IBM Puts and Calls
(IBM Spot Price = $100)

	Jan Calls	Jan Puts	Straddle
$90	10.60	0.70	11.30
$95	6.60	1.70	8.30
$100	3.50	3.50	7.00
$105	1.70	6.60	8.30
$110	0.70	10.60	11.30
$115	0.30	16.00	16.30

16. We want to create a synthetic long IBM position using the January $100 put and call. What should we do, and what price would we be long the shares of IBM at?

17. What is the difference in risk and cost for this synthetic long position versus a natural long position in IBM shares?

18. We decide the market is going to be very volatile for the near future, and we want to buy the $95 IBM straddle. How would we do it, what would it cost, and what are the possible outcomes at expiration in January?

19. What is the difference between a straddle and a strangle?

20. How would you buy the $95/$105 January strangle? What are the possible expiry outcomes?

21. What is a conversion, and why would traders do them?

CHAPTER 22

Market Insights and Edges

A BRIEF RECAP

Today's financial markets are more complicated than ever. This is due, in large part, to the spectacular growth of derivatives. In this book we studied the three most basic derivatives in detail: forwards, futures, and options. It is from these three that the more complex derivatives, such as swaps, emanate. And, of the basic three, options are far and away the most difficult. That is why 90 percent of our time was spent in a detailed analysis of options. We studied how to price options, how to measure their risk, and how to hedge this risk. We even went so far as to discuss the basic strategies involved in trading options.

As we graduated from pricing options on mere coin tosses to pricing options on shares of IBM stock, we ran smack into the perversity and slipperiness of the markets. Mathematically describing the future price movements of stocks is far more difficult than describing future coin toss outcomes. Although academics talk glibly about the delightful similarities between the two, analysis of market prices requires the use of math and statistics more complicated than that needed for analyzing coin tosses. Even our greatest mathematicians have been unable to solve fully the mysteries surrounding stock price movements.

RANDOM PRICE MOVES
AND BLACK-SCHOLES

The random nature of price movements was first described in 1900 by Louis Bachelier, but didn't gain in acceptance or popularity until more than 50 years had passed. It wasn't until the 1950s and 1960s that mathematicians began the battle to develop the math needed to describe the random actions of prices. Economists entered a frenzied contest to be the first to formulate a successful option theory. The Black-Scholes option formula was an extension of such theorizing and was first published in the early 1970s. Before the Black-Scholes formula, no one was able to explain options fully. There were a lot of partially complete theories and ideas, but no one could fully and accurately describe why option values changed, how they moved, or how to compute *fair* value. The Black-Scholes model pulled it all together. In one spectacularly small formula they managed to compile all the many factors that matter.

So when someone is looking to learn about options there isn't a tighter, more complete explanation than that implied within the inner workings of the Black-Scholes formula. Since you cannot fully understand options until you can see all the forces at play, we used the Black-Scholes model as a window to observe such interactions. The Black-Scholes formula became our guiding light; understanding it became our goal.

Good trading requires that a trader properly manage risk/ reward scenarios, but before the Black-Scholes formula options risk could not be calculated. Nowadays, option traders live and die with Black-Scholes valuations and no reasonable options trader enters trades without consulting the formulas. Black-Scholes was the first formula to give traders the ability to make sense of the immensely complex world of options.

Unfortunately, most options traders have only superficial knowledge of the formulas. To most traders the models are merely "black boxes" that quietly generate unlimited numbers of option pricings and evaluations. They are invisible pieces of computer software, unseen and poorly understood.

Surely, then, there must be some advantage for us to have spent so much time ripping apart the option formulas and studying in detail what goes on under the hood. And there is. Following is a list of insights from our studies that go far beyond the average option trader's understanding and thus can help you become a far better-than-average trader.

No set of rules or insightful thoughts can guarantee success; only hard work, superior knowledge, and discipline can do that. But here are some of the guideposts you might consider following on your way. How far you take these insights is up to you.

MARKET INSIGHTS AND EDGES FROM STUDYING BLACK-SCHOLES

1. There are no automatic winning option strategies that will blindly generate profits.
2. Option models are not crystal balls, nor are they ever bullish or bearish on the market.
3. Delta neutral option positions are rarely profitable.
4. Option mispricings are phantoms.
5. Without an accurate opinion of the future you can't make money in options.
6. If there is a *single key* to beating options, it is understanding volatility.
7. Market prices are not stationary statistics; they do not repeat themselves.
8. People make the prices and people are often emotional.

There Are No Automatic Winning Option Strategies

We have learned that, regardless of which option strategy you choose, there is no method that magically provides automatic profits (see Chap. 21). This is true, but it is not the same as the grim academic theories that say no one can outsmart the markets. Hardly any of those gloom and doom academic types ever got up close and personal with trading. They all tend to project their academic theories onto the real world from far away. This does not work. As a poet said "East is East, and West is West, and never the twain shall meet." Just as there is no perfect hedge, there is no perfect theory. Theory and real-world practice rarely agree.

There is a much more optimistic message if you read between the lines. While the average investor cannot expect to make better than an average return, superior investors can. And inferior investors can expect to do poorly. That sounds about right for the world we live in, doesn't it? And it is also a lot less forbidding, too. If you plan on being an average investor, putting in an average effort, developing an average market knowledge with only average information, you have no shot of making better than an average return. So the key is to be better than an average investor. To do this you cannot blindly follow simple strategies or you will put yourself right back in the category of being average. You must develop original points of view that are proven valid over time. *This is certainly not easy to do, but it is far from impossible.* We discuss this topic further below when we consider how you might develop more accurate opinions of the future.

Another angle to consider: If no strategy is an automatic winner (or loser) and none is automatically superior (or inferior), then perhaps popularity might impact the final results. This means that since all people have a tendency to follow the leader, some strategies might come in and out of fashion over time. The most popular strategies will work well *while the masses are accumulating their positions* and then disappoint tremendously *when they all rush to dump their losers.* This is one angle played by some of the shrewdest traders. It takes a lot of work to get a handle on and a stony discipline to follow through, but it is an edge. We never said this was simple, did we?

Option Models Are Not Crystal Balls, Nor Are They Ever Bullish or Bearish on the Market

Option formulas and theories are not linked to crystal balls; they can provide no amazing insights into what will happen next in the markets. The models themselves are never bullish or bearish, even when the options market seems to be (we discuss this soon). Unlike some egomaniacal newsletter writers, the models never predict the future of the markets with daring boldness. They are more akin to the oracles at Delphi, cloaked in the shadows, uttering generalities about the mysteries of the future. Instead of making exact predictions, the theories and formulas use the science of statistics to tell us how old stories may *possibly* replay themselves.

This is key . . . they look only to past market data for drawing their portrait of the future.

Statistics are like that old joke about the doctor who is analyzing his patient's condition: "Hmmm . . . this is very interesting. Tell me, did you ever have this before?" The patient says "yes" and the doctor cheers up and nods sagely: "Well, I can definitely tell you . . . you've got it again!" The option formulas look to *yesterday's market activity* to fashion a statement about what tomorrow is likely to bring. Statistical theory always concludes: "Today is the same as yesterday, just a day later."

If the markets have been deadly quiet for 10 years there is hardly a statistical measure in existence that will predict an eruption of excitement. Whereas there are always market soothsayers ready to predict huge rallies or crashes, statistics will rarely allow for any such possibilities unless the recent past is peppered with similar tumult. Statistics depend on samples drawn from a past population to make their predictions for the future. If the samples were drawn from a strictly sleepy market, then that is the story that statistical methods will project as their expectation of the future. *The projection is always for more of the same.* Some economists tell us that predicting with statistics is equivalent to driving your car by staring out the rear window. Everything is fine until the road starts to turn!

Option formulas *do not* take into account the ebb and flow of investors' opinions and expectations. In fact, ignoring investor sentiment (risk preferences) was a key assumption that allowed Black and Scholes to finish their formula first and ultimately win the Nobel Prize. Investors may get emotional, but it is not an "input-able" factor for the formulas. If everybody is stark raving mad about the telecommunications market, let's say, the option formulas are unaware of it. To the formulas a trading day in 1965 is much the same as a trading day in 2005. The formulas make a cold, statistical analysis of recent price moves. The formulas expect that all price moves are independent of each other and totally random in nature. They believe that every day exists in ignorance of every other day and the price moves are akin to water molecules randomly bombarding each other as they continue streaming down a busy river.

But there is no disputing that markets often take on a bullish or bearish turn of mind. People tend to act based on their beliefs

of how safe or unsafe their investments are, given the world at
that moment. This is an emotional process and can vary greatly
from day to day. If you factor in the two infamous market emotions, fear and greed, you can see this can get very complicated.
So while the models might be suggesting, say, a 25 percent volatility for IBM, the investors might be optimistically going bonkers
buying calls and selling puts in total disregard to recent valuations. This furious trading leads to a higher implied volatility for
calls and a lower implied volatility for puts. A distortion or
"skew" takes place in the volatility curves. Emotional investors
can push values far from levels that calm theories might suggest.
So options markets can reflect bullish or bearish sentiments even
though the models are unable to account for this. *Studying this
phenomenon is very important to the option trader who hopes to do better
than average.*

Delta Neutral Positions Are Rarely Profitable

Black-Scholes is founded on the thesis that a portfolio of options
can be kept free from risk by constantly keeping it delta neutrally
hedged. Since such a portfolio has no risk, a trader should only
expect to earn the risk-free rate of interest. Black-Scholes further
suggests that traders will break even during such hedging because
both their borrowings and lendings are done at the risk-free rate.

We opposed this notion in our chapter on hedging when we
said that the average option trader running a delta neutral portfolio *will lose money over time.* We contend that Black-Scholes's assumptions fail to mesh with the real world. According to Black-
Scholes, the trader should earn the risk-free rate (T-Bill rate) on
any money invested in options or hedges during the process of
maintaining delta neutrality. But in the real world traders must
pay *above* the T-Bill rate to borrow money and so they will lose
on that basis alone. Additionally, Black-Scholes assumes no commissions, no bid/asks, no slippage, 24-hour trading, infinite liquidity, and an ability to rebalance the portfolio constantly, among
other things. All these assumptions fall far short of the real world.

In short, no trader can abide by the assumptions of Black-
Scholes. Therefore, there is a real cost to staying delta neutral and
it is not small. As such, the only way a trader can expect to break
even with delta neutral hedging is if the original option positions

have an excess built-in profit (i.e., they are "mispriced"). The most likely source of such "mispricings" is from customers who are given "off-market" prices. We discuss "mispriced" options as our next topic.

A trader given a portfolio of "fairly priced" options (if such a portfolio could be found) will not prosper *on average* if required to remain continuously delta neutral through expiration. Since the future path of prices is random, we can never say on any short series of bets what the outcome will be. On a few occasions the trader might make big profits or losses, but most often will win or lose only a little. This is because even delta neutral positions have risk; any that are not rehedged every instant become *path dependent*. That means their profitability is based on the path of prices that occur until expiry. On average, the delta neutral position itself will break even, but transaction costs will turn it into a losing proposition. Over a thousand cases the trader will net lose expenses, which can add up to quite a bit.

Can we find an edge here? Yes, there might just be a small advantage to those who trade in a special way. Assume that fairly priced options are too cheap relative to real-world costs (per our arguments above). A trader who has a strategy that embraces buying rallies and selling dips (as trend followers do) can cheaply buy an option that includes all such activities in the fair price but doesn't charge extra for slippage, commissions, or execution services. Options might well be a systems trader's dream vehicle, automatically doing what the trader has to do with painstaking care minute to minute.

Option Mispricings Are Phantoms

The concept that "mispriced" options are freely available in today's markets is a myth started by economists and option book writers. "Assume a mispriced option" is economist talk that assures us, for the sake of argument, that mispriced options do exist. They might just as well have said, "assume an abominable snowman" or "assume you've climbed Mt. Everest" for all the proof they offer.

If mispriced options exist at all, they are well hidden and difficult to ferret out. It is the job of professional traders to scour the markets relentlessly in search of such mispricings and pounce on them immediately. Don't pass Go, don't ask your boss, just jump all over them and smile like the cat who ate the canary. Mispricings last about as long as $100 bills lying on a New York City sidewalk. And these types of mispricings are only *relative mispricings*, meaning that traders can use other strikes or maturities to hedge the risk and capture the relative difference in the over- or under-pricing between the two strikes or maturities.

The mispricings that most investors long for, however, are not these relative mispricings, which are usually out of line only a tad, but the outright, egregious type which we'll call *extraordinary mispricings*. Such extraordinary mispricings occur, in theory, when IBM stock continues to trade at a volatility hugely different from that implied in the IBM options. You know the dream. All other investors have lost their wits and are totally clueless about the correct volatility for IBM. Meanwhile, *you know* that IBM stock will steadily trade at a 25 percent vol for the foreseeable future, but everyone else thinks differently and continues to pay 40 percent for the options. They will lose their collective shirts as you are proven right. You alone will reap the windfall, for you alone are omniscient. Nice dream, huh?

Unfortunately, those dreams don't come true very often. And there is a good reason why they don't. It has to do with the inability of humans to predict the future with any type of ironclad certainty. To know that an option is extraordinarily mispriced we must be able to show it differs substantially from the *true distribution of all possible future volatilities*. No one knows how to do this. This is a complex idea and it's worth our while to spend the few moments needed to discuss it.

The volatility priced into an option today is called its *implied volatility*. This is the market's collective "guesstimate" of the future volatility of the stock. Suppose the options are trading at 25 percent vol (implying the market's guess for future IBM volatility is 25 percent). Now here is the complicated part: even if IBM stock has a volatility over the next three months of 32 percent (or 19 percent) *this does not mean that the 25 percent options were mispriced.* The market is evaluating the future in a probabilistic manner. This means that the 25 percent volatility guesstimate is expected *on average* if we were able to bet on many similar cases. Traders do not expect 25 percent each and every time. They realize that a prediction of 25 percent implies not just one outcome, but a range of possible outcomes: high expectations that future volatility will

range from 20 to 30 percent and much lower expectations of extreme volatilities such as 10 percent, 15 percent, 35 percent, 40
percent, and so on. But even these extreme possibilities will arrive
on occasion as they are part and parcel of the distribution implied
in a guesstimate of 25 percent. The center of the distribution is 25
percent and the extreme results are long shots that shouldn't occur
too often. If they do, then we most likely have an error in our
estimation methods. And losses to show for it.

So, to know ahead of time that the 25 percent guesstimate is
clearly wrong we would need a printout of the future proving
that over many cases the *average future volatility* turns out to be
far different than 25 percent. No one has such knowledge of the
future and so any statement that an option's volatility is extraordinarily mispriced is merely an opinion without corroborating
proof.

The idea that it is easy to make money from mispricings is
an immensely appealing concept. What could be nicer than believing that mispricings are waiting there for the few of us in the
know, the cognoscenti? We've worked hard studying options and
deserve it, right? Unfortunately, it is just a lot of academic dream-
ing, possibly attributable to "ivy tower fever." Too much time
cooped up in dim, dusty rooms, away from the sun.

No one has yet published a method that will clearly point
out which options are mispriced and which are not. Until then
the concept of mispriced options has much in common with the
proverbial needle-in-the-haystack; it exists for purposes of discussion, but is there really a needle-in-the-haystack if no one can ever
find it?

Without an Accurate Opinion of the Future You Can't Make Money in Options

Vague opinions will not place you above the average investor.
Market prices reflect average investors' opinions about the future
values of assets. Beating the market is all about having opinions
better than the average of the great masses. If your opinion is
identical to the *average* of all investors, then you will obtain no
better return than they will, that is, an *average* return.

You need to differentiate yourself from them, do something
differently, and not think with a like-mindedness. And your opinions of the future must be more accurate. There are a lot of crazy

opinions out there and lots of crazy people willing to explain them, but this will not make you a better investor. The price for listening to others can be steep indeed.

During the extraordinary stock markets of the 1990s, we were deluged with crazy opinions from dreamers and scam artists paraded in front of us daily on the stock market "sell-a-vision" programs. Hour after hour we were exposed to overly confident money managers, crowing CEOs, and the pathologically glib I-can-sell-iceboxes-to-Eskimos types. They told us compelling stories, but after a while their predictions failed to mesh with reality. While the "revelations" given by the talking heads on TV may seem like inside info, we are here to tell you it isn't so.

You cannot depend on such biased information to make calm, rational judgments about the future. Remember, just as there are no easy-to-follow option strategies that always perform well, *there are no advisors who will always perform well*. Being able to ignore the rantings of advisors and prognosticators is a major step in your education as a trader. This revelation alone is enough to save you a fortune in bad trades.

Here is an idea on how to proceed with your quest to become a better trader, straight from the mouth of a bona fide maestro. Twenty years ago the great hockey player Wayne Gretzky told a reporter the secret that gave him an awesome advantage: "I skate to where the puck is *going to be*, not to where it already is." Believe it or not, this very idea is *the secret to beating the markets*. You need to figure out how investors will be feeling in the future, not how they are feeling right now. Every reporter and commentator will let you know how the investors felt today, hours after it's too late. Your job is to predict how their feelings will change tomorrow and next week. Being able to see the future slightly better than your opponents is the key in any competitive area of human conflict.

Gretzky's idea is a great idea, but it sounds a bit like magic. Somehow he managed to do what others could not and the rest of us are left without a clue as to how he did it. But now, many years later, he has revealed his secret in a TV biography interview. Gretzky described in detail the way he learned to predict where the puck was going to be. It goes back to his early teenage years, when he sat hour after hour in front of a television watching replays of that day's hockey games. He had a yellow pad and a pen in front of him. With pen on pad he robotically traced wherever the puck was during the game and never took his eyes off the screen. He saved all the sheets. When he reviewed his many evenings of work, he found that most of the sheets had been worn completely through *in certain key areas*.

He recognized that these were the areas where the puck went over and over and over again. Regardless of the teams, the situations, or the players' intentions, the puck kept coming back to these same vital areas. He began to be able to predict repeatable patterns . . . which is the first step in any scientific analysis. He had developed a *statistical analysis of the puck*. And he plied it to become one of the greatest players in NHL history.

So, if you need a hint on how to get an edge in the markets, you now have one. You must develop *your own trading philosophy* of the markets based on valid strategies that are proven over time. You might use hard statistics, such as how markets react to economic events or investor psychology and enthusiasm. Some people call this "knowing the ropes" or the "tricks of the trade." No professional can survive without knowing such things deeply and instinctively.

Trading theories fall into one of two camps: "technical" or "fundamental." Technicians try to predict the market's future based on past price activity, investor sentiment, and other market indicators. Discovering patterns of behavior that predispose investors to act a certain way is technical trading at its best. For example, using statistical analysis you may discover situations where people are so emotional that they just can't help themselves. Remember, all you're looking for is a small edge. People are not robots; their emotions guide them. Is it any surprise that people file more tax returns on April 15 than any other day of the year? Human nature is not completely predictable, but it is not completely random either; it takes shape and form in the research done by smart technical traders.

Fundamentalists are the other camp. They believe that everything is based on the economics of supply and demand. Applying this concept to the value of shares of stock, they have developed a very useful theory called "value investing." Focusing on earnings and interest rates, they try to strip all emotion and opinion from the market and discover what "fair value" is for a stock. Then they buy only when it trades below this fair price. In options trading the analogous fundamental for establishing a "fair price" is future volatility. We talk about volatility next.

Volatility Is *the Key* to Beating Options

There is one piece of option information that stands head and shoulders over all others as a prognosticator's tool: *future* volatility. If granted a wish by a genie, this is the one piece of market information that tried and true option traders would ask for; it's what they dream about, their Holy Grail. The trader who can most accurately assess future volatility will win the prize.

Most traders adopt a statistician's view when trying to map out the future. The statisticians expect that given past volatility, today's activity will look very similar. Now, you cannot prosper more than the average by taking such a view. It is up to you to find possible holes in the theory and ways to predict change. If you are trying to predict *future* volatility by using historic volatility, you had better plan on having more than elementary statistics to help you or you'll end up doing *poorer* than average. Even the rankest beginner recognizes that using plain historic volatility will get you clobbered. You cannot expect the past to reveal the future without understanding the many twists and turns that the road normally takes. Only long experience and knowing the "tricks of the trade" can give you a handle on this.

One of the best books on this topic is *Option Volatility and Pricing* by Natenberg. Despite the title and the fact that it is a very good book, you still won't find half the information you need to become truly knowledgeable about volatility. This is actually good news. It shows you how broad the subject is and how wide open the field is. It is by no means a fully explored topic, so there is room for all of us to find our own niche. But understanding volatility requires working with statistics; it isn't a walk in the park. First you must learn what statistics can tell us about using prices to calculate volatility. Then you must learn what the limitations are of these methods. At that point you begin to see how other traders are also handcuffed by these methods' limitations. You may slowly begin to see that certain market situations are poorly understood; focusing on these can give you an advantage.

Once you discover how the market arrives at its implied volatilities (its expectation of future volatility), you might then try to develop a method that does it a little bit better. The market's decision-making process is a complicated blend of technical market patterns, gut feel, and historical vols. If you find a better way, then you are in business.

Market Prices Are Not Stationary Statistics; They Do Not Repeat Themselves

One reason statistical analysis comes up short when predicting markets is that the markets are not stationary; they are not a repeat of the same thing over and over again. Surprises happen all the time, some of them quite severe. The road behind us is not even remotely close to the one in front of us.

Classical statistics works something like this: we have an unknown population in an urn. There are 100 balls in this population, but we do not know how many are black and how many are white. If we are allowed to pull samples from the urn, can we deduce the actual mix of this population? The answer is a qualified "yes." If we take a few small samples we might venture a prediction, but confidence in our accuracy is low. Our knowledge of the population increases as we make more tests and take more samples. And large samples are better than small samples.

Given enough sampling, our confidence is very high that we can predict very closely what the true population looks like even though we never get to crack open the urn. One key point, however, is that we must keep sampling *from the same population*, that is, it must remain stationary.

But markets are not urns. When we try to analyze markets it seems as if a new urn is being switched in after every sampling. The population from which we are drawing samples does not remain constant. *Markets change dramatically over time; they are never constant.*

The bear markets at the height of the Great Depression in 1932 are similar in many ways to the bear markets we have seen in 2001 to 2003, but there are also many differences. No period ever mimics another period perfectly. So our statistical methods are handicapped by the inconstant nature of the data being supplied. It's one of the more daunting issues to deal with when we analyze markets. One day we may discover more accurate statistical methods for predicting future price moves. Until then the field is wide open to every trader's interpretation. Some interpreters are better at this than others. And some traders are shrewder and more disciplined than others. That's what makes markets so complex. As Mark Twain said: "It weren't meant that we should all think alike. Difference of opinion is what makes horse races!"

People Make the Prices and People Are Often Emotional

While the formulas and models may be computer driven and as coolly unemotional as robots, the markets are not comprised of robots; they are made up of people. And people can be plenty emotional. Having sat through many thousands of trading days and many hundreds of mini-panics, we can say without equivocation that people can get nuts when their money is on the line.

And it doesn't happen only in doomsday crashes like 1929 and 1987. It happens every day in mini-fashion, in some market, somewhere in the world for a short burst of time. New highs are made and new lows are made, and while the market is probing those extremes there are traders yelling and screaming and investors turning white and panicking. They just don't do it all at once. They do it a few individuals at a time and are easily offset by the more rational elements of the investment world. Those more rational elements are the other investors who are getting it right at the time and smiling beatifically at the morons being stampeded into their nets. When you're winning it's such an easy game!

It's when everyone is aligned just the same way and they all start to turn various shades of pale that the real panic begins. When a market move that was unthinkable starts to unfold in front of you and you've miscalculated badly about the possible magnitude. When you're helpless to act because you've already reached your position limits and lost more money than you can stomach, that's when the really sharp moves begin. And every single trader and investor has a different position limit and a different ability to stomach losses. If you want to see the raw emotions of fear and anger, just watch a trader trying to dump his position into a free-falling market. It's fight and flight competing with each other and then augmenting each other at the very same moment. It's a bloody mess is what it is.

Yes, people are emotional and money brings out the emotional sides of us. Given this fact, what use can we make of this insight?

Well, we said earlier that the option formulas and models had a robot's view of the world when it came to the markets. That is, they are totally unemotional and couldn't care less what the future might bring. People are exactly the opposite. They *are* emotional and they care a *great deal* about what the future might bring. In fact, they care so much that their opinions are often clouded by their need to have their positions work out well. They suffer from the thousand biases that beset all humans and plague emotional humans even more so. There are few more emotional humans then those who are winning or losing lots of money.

All you need to know is that emotions are anathema to rational thought and that the markets are filled with emotions every day, but never more so than in the midst of a large and roaring parabolic blow-off (up or down). Such moves parallel high volatility. Thus option traders must learn firsthand how emotions translate into volatility. If you ever wanted a direction to follow on market research, this is it.

The great economic thinkers of our time have concluded that the markets are efficient and rational. But we think they would change their opinions quickly if they were forced to stand in a trading pit executing orders when a hundred screamingly crazy brokers were trying to grab hold of them to consummate a trade and, in the ensuing melee, had their shirts pulled, twisted, and ripped off. The fact of the matter is, theorizing about how it must feel to be in a foxhole is about a thousand human emotions short of being in the foxhole when the cold and the mud and the dark and the fear overtake you. That's the part of trading and investing that the economists missed, the emotions. Don't you make the mistake of missing it too.

KEY CONCEPTS REVIEW

♦ Good trading requires managing risk/reward scenarios. Before Black-Scholes no one knew what the risks really were or how to weigh them.

* Black-Scholes was the first formula to give traders the ability to make sense of the immensely complex world of options.
* Most option traders have only superficial knowledge of the option formulas. To many, the models are merely "black boxes" used for computations.
* Understanding the option formulas in detail gives us some insights that go far beyond the average option trader's and can help us become far better-than-average traders.
* No set of rules or insights can guarantee success, however. Only hard work, hands-on experience, superior knowledge, flexibility, and discipline can do that.
* There are no automatic winning option strategies that blindly generate profits. Every apparent winning strategy succeeds due to the type of market prevailing at the time.
* Option models cannot predict the future and they have no interest whatever in the market's future. Instead, they use the data we input and the normal curve embedded in their formula to define the necessary probabilities and payoffs, *based on the inputs.*
* Maintaining a delta neutral position is rarely profitable. On average it should break even *if there are no expenses.* In the real world the expenses will eat you alive.
* Option mispricings are often discussed, but never quite found. Since no one knows the correct future volatility to plug into the formula, our ability to identify mispriced options is severely diminished.
* To make money in options you must be able to assess the future better than the market does. If the market does it more accurately, you will lose money.
* If there is a *single key* to beating options, it is understanding volatility. Just as the secret to real estate is location, location, location . . . the secret to option trading is volatility, volatility, volatility.
* Market price movements are not stationary statistics; they do not repeat themselves. As such, any model based on the past will be inaccurate when foretelling the future.

• People make the prices and people are often emotional. The key to finding patterns in markets rests on the biases brought to the table by the participants—emotional people.

THINGS TO THINK ABOUT

Poker and Trading   Imagine you are in a poker game with nine other players. You each buy $1000 in chips and the smallest chip is $10 (this is serious poker here). The game goes on until one player wins it all and you can't leave the hotel room until you are busted or the game is over. At the end of many hours or a few days, one player will have won all the money. If you replayed this event 100 times you would find the same two or three players would win the lion's share of the sessions. Over time and many thousands of hands the luck will even out, but the players with superior strategies, instincts, and disciplines will win all the money.

There are many hard-to-define qualities that are essential to being a great poker player and just as many hard-to-define weaknesses that mitigate against a person being successful at poker. But in the end, because we are inherently different from one another, there will always be a best player and a worst player. The very same thing is true of trading, which is really just poker played in a different forum. There are a thousand nuances and tricks of the trade to learn, but not everyone can learn the lessons. And even those gifted enough to learn them all aren't necessarily gifted enough to execute what they've learned *and adjust to what they haven't yet learned*. Many are called, but few are chosen.

Answer Key

Chapter 1

1. What are the three basic derivatives? Options, forwards, and futures.

2. What are the three primary markets or assets that underlie all financial derivatives? Stocks, bonds, and commodities (which includes currencies).

3. What are delayed or deferred deliveries? When you are allowed to deliver beyond the typical 2 to 3 days of the cash and spot markets, this is called delayed delivery or deferred delivery. Forward and futures markets specialize in such deferred deliveries. In fact, without deferred delivery the forward and futures markets would cease to exist.

4. Why are cash, spot, and forward markets often called *physicals* **or** *actuals* **markets?** The actual physical object, be it a barrel of oil, a bar of gold, or a stock certificate, are usually delivered in these markets. Those who need the physical items trade heavily in these markets. While such trades can often be offset by liquidating or rolling forward before actual delivery takes place, it is normal and expected to go through with the physical delivery in these markets. Notice how this differs from "paper" markets.

5. Why are futures and options markets considered "paper" markets? Less than 2 percent of all the contracts traded ever go through with actual delivery in these markets. It is normal and expected in these markets that traders will offset their trades before delivery day by liquidating them or rolling them forward. While physical delivery is possible for those who want it, most traders prefer to use the cash, spot, or forward markets to make or take such actual deliveries because the range of asset choices is very narrow in futures and options markets. For example, a trader might need 0.9999 pure gold kilobars (32.15 ounces each), but the futures exchange only delivers the bigger 100-ounce bars and the purity is only 0.995.

6. Where are forwards traded? Where are futures traded? Forwards are traded over-the-counter by telephone through the network of investment bankers choosing to make markets in that asset. No formal central location exists (although certain metropolitan areas naturally attract financial market makers: New York, London, Zurich, etc.). Futures markets require a physical exchange floor "downstairs" where traders congregate and transact with each other. In commodities markets there might be a dozen "pits" arranged on the exchange floor, each pit being associated with a single commodity. [This is similar to the NYSE where the crowd interested in a certain stock congregates around a "post" specializing in that stock. The NYSE is a cash market, however.] Electronic Internet trading is gradually changing the face of exchange-traded assets, and clearly a trading floor is not needed for this. While futures are slowly going this electronic route, it will be years before the pits are completely outmoded. At least for now, however, we can still note that an exchange floor helps differentiate futures from forwards. It's not a critically important aspect of the market, but it makes a nice visual aid to separate the two.

7. Why are futures like eating at McDonalds and forwards like eating at "Alice's Restaurant"? In the futures market the prices are cheap and the products are prepackaged and very limited. If you don't like hamburgers, you'd better not go to McDonalds. In the forward market, however, an investment banker will hand-tailor an asset that fits you to a tee. This is akin to Arlo Guthrie's song where we learned: "You can get anything you want, at Alice's Restaurant." But we all know that if you get pampered and waited on in a sit-down restaurant, it's usually going to cost a lot more than McDonalds.

8. Which are more competitive prices, futures or forwards? The insiders' price is essentially the same in both markets. The problem is that futures markets are mass-production conveyor belts that can afford to give everyone the same price, insider or outsider. The exchange does not make a profit on each trade aside from a tiny fee. The only other costs to you are brokerage charges. The forward market-makers, however, only make money to the extent that they get their customers to pay up a little (or a lot). The customers are essentially outsiders and thus get the retail price not the insiders' wholesale price. Futures exchanges do not mark up the insiders' price and thus are incredibly good deals for those that can use them.

9. What is fungibility? Why is it important to markets? When all items of a kind are considered identical with one another for purposes of transfer, then they are fungible. Coins that we use (pennies, nickels, dimes, quarters) and dollar bills (singles, fives, tens, twenties) are an example. Each one dollar bill is considered exactly equal to every other one dollar bill for purposes of money transfer. If not, it would take forever to go shopping or buy gas for your car. On the NYSE each share of IBM stock is considered identical to every other share of IBM. And each warehouse receipt for a commodity is identical to every other warehouse receipt for the same type of commodity (as far as the exchange's delivery rules are concerned). This allows easy transfer of ownership and an easy ability to offset one for another. Without this ability there would be zero liquidity in a market.

10. What is liquidity? Why is it important? Liquidity means easy exchangeability. If you can easily buy, sell, and transfer an asset, it is very liquid. The amount of liquidity is measured by its volume (the number of units traded in a day). When one trade takes place a day, it is a very *illiquid* market. When, like shares of Intel Corp., 50 million shares trade each day in the course of 50,000 trades, that is very, very liquid. It doesn't get any more liquid than that. There are many other uses of the term *liquidity*, but in the end, financial liquidity comes down to the ability to "flow" in and out of an asset. A person holding real estate is not in a liquid investment because it might take weeks or months to sell and transfer, whereas someone sitting on cash or T-bills is very, very liquid. He or she can easily flow out of cash or T-bills in minutes.

It is very important to traders not to trade in illiquid markets unless they plan to maintain their position for a long time. The price difference between bid and offer can be enormous in illiquid markets. This is a bad scenario for traders.

11. How do futures exchanges magnify liquidity? By identifying the most popular and widely traded asset and sticking to only that single asset the exchange can funnel all the available business into a single contract. For example, the S&P500 index is one of the most popular stock indexes in the world. But there are dozens of other indexes. And the Chicago Merc chose to allow trading only in the S&P500, not the S&P499 or S&P498. No variation on the theme at all. Also, the delivery date is the third Friday of only 4 months a year: March, June, September, and December. If it is January or February right now, then 95 percent of the traders are trading the March S&P future, not that of June or September. This takes all the interested traders and forces them to trade against one another in a single asset instead of spreading the business all over the map. This increased liquidity attracts other traders who might not have considered trading an illiquid asset. Success attracts other participants.

12. How are options a separate class from any other financial contract? Only options offer you a choice when delivery rolls around. Every other financial arrangement demands that you make delivery or take delivery on the appointed date; there is no choice, you are obligated by law. But if you buy an option you can choose to make or take delivery as it suits you. For this you pay a fee up front called a *premium*, just like in insurance policies.

13. How are insurance and options linked? Options are really price insurance. You can protect against upside or downside moves in the price of an asset such as shares of IBM. Or, as many traders do, you can speculate with options if you have nothing that must be protected. The law doesn't normally let you speculate with insurance; for instance, you cannot buy insurance on your neighbor's car unless you have an "insurable interest" (maybe you loaned your neighbor the money to buy it). But you can use options on stocks to speculate if you wish and you may also write options against your portfolio, if appropriate. In any event, options are priced and analyzed in the same ways that actuaries analyze and price every other type of insurance. Also, the price you pay up front for insurance and options is called the premium.

14. Suppose you decide shares of Amazon.com are going to run up in price shortly. Which market can help you more clearly define and limit your risk: spot, cash, forward, futures, or options? The answer is options. Let's go through some details to explain why. First of all, spot and cash are the same as far as we are concerned and refer to buying Amazon on the NASDAQ for 3-day delivery. You must pay full price, let's call it $30 a share. That's your risk, $30 a share. You are unlikely to lose it all, of course, but there is no protection against doing so. The forward and futures markets would price 3-month delivery Amazon at, say, $30.25. That then would be your risk. Just because you might only have to put down $6 a share as a margin deposit doesn't exempt you from the exposure if Amazon falls to $22 or $18. You are liable for the whole difference between your purchase price, say $30.25, and the price at which you finally liquidate (sell) it. Finally, let's look at options. The 3-month $30 call option might be trading at $4.50, for example. This $4.50 per share is your total risk. But you will lose all $4.50 in 3 months if Amazon just sits at $30, whereas you would have broken even in the other markets. There is no free lunch. Your risk is limited and well defined, but there is a cost. It's called the *premium*.

15. What is a swap? A swap is a complex two-sided financial deal wherein something is taken and something is given. The most popular swaps these days are interest rate swaps. A simple swap might have you paying the T-bill rate for the next 2 years and receiving the U.S. T-bond rate for the same period. Since T-bonds may be running at 5 percent and T-bills only at 2 percent, part of the deal might specify that you pay 3 percent extra as the fair offset. The variations on this theme are endless. Many swaps heavily use forwards and futures as part of the agreement. If options are involved, it is called a *swaption*. In the end, the basics we learn here about our three basic derivatives (options, forwards, and futures) set you up nicely to advance to more complex derivatives such as swaps should you decide to do so.

Chapter 2

1. What is a binomial? *Binomial* means "two names" or "two terms" as in the heads and tails of a coin toss.

2. How can coin tosses be linked to binomials? A coin toss is a perfect random generator with only two possible outcomes.

We might, therefore, consider the coin to be a physical representation of a binomial in motion. Binomial math laws allow us to analyze the many possible outcomes in a neat and orderly way.

3. If we toss a coin one time, how many different head-count outcomes are possible? What are they? There are only two headcount outcomes possible, 0H and 1H.

4. Answer the same question for tossing a coin two, three, and four times. For a coin tossed two times there are three possible outcomes: 0H, 1H, 2H. For a coin tossed three times there are four possible outcomes: 0H, 1H, 2H, 3H. For a coin tossed four times there are five possible outcomes: 0H, 1H, 2H, 3H, 4H. Notice a pattern here?

5. What is a binomial tree? A diagram that looks much like a tree. Each path branches into two new paths at a junction called a *node*. It displays each and every possible path that can be taken by a tossed coin (or any other two-choice mechanism). The diagram allows us to visualize all the possible outcomes that might occur when we toss a coin N times.

6. Figure 2-1 depicts a binomial tree diagram for a coin tossed four times. Use this diagram and table that accompanies it to answer the following questions: How many 3H outcomes were there? How many 2H outcomes? There were four distinct paths that led to the 3H outcome, thus there were four cases of a 3H outcome. There were six paths that led to the 2H outcome.

7. How do we mathematically express the number of possible paths and number of possible outcomes for a coin tossed N times? If we let N equal 3, what are the number of paths and outcomes? The number of possible paths are calculated by 2^N, and the number of possible outcomes are calculated by $N + 1$. For the case where $N = 3$, then 2^N means 2^3 which translates to $2 \times 2 \times 2$ (which is, of course, 8) and $N + 1$ means $3 + 1$, which is 4. So the number of possible paths are eight and the possible outcomes are four. See previous question 4 for details on what the outcomes are for tossing a coin three times.

8. Is there a difference if we say "a coin tossed three times" or "three coins tossed once"? Not in terms that matter to us such as the number of possible paths or possible outcomes. We can, for our purposes, consider them to be *mathematically indistinguishable* (as we said in the chapter). One tiny difference occurs when we describe the tossing process and try to help students visualize how it works. Since tossing one coin, recording the result, and then tossing again gives us an extremely clear and well-defined series of outcomes, that is the picture we sought to emphasize. The problem with tossing three coins at once is that they do not take place as a series of outcomes, but occur simultaneously in one split second of chaos. While it gives us the identically same outcomes as tossing one coin three times, when we toss a bunch in the air, how can we say exactly which coin should be listed as the first result? It's difficult to track the coins as they never stay in order and tend to spin and dance all over the table. Should we paint each coin a different color or mark each with a different letter? What a mess! What we end up with is a confused reading audience trying to figure out if it makes a difference and how important the difference might be. We avoided that confusing imagery by methodically tossing one coin at a time. As far as mathematicians are concerned, however, tossing one coin N times generates the same identical results as putting N coins on a trampoline and causing them to bounce into the air once.

9. Compute $N + 1$ and 2^N when we let $N = 1, 2, 3, 4,$ and 5. The results are given in the following table:

N	$N + 1$	2^N
1	2	2
2	3	4
3	4	8
4	5	16
5	6	32

10. Are the number of possible paths typically more or less than the number of possible outcomes? Why? There are typically far more possible paths than possible outcomes. Using their mathematical expressions 2^N and $N + 1$, we can see that as long as N is more than 1, then 2^N will always be larger than $N + 1$. As an obvious example, when we toss a coin 10 times ($N = 10$), then the number of possible paths is 1024, but the number of possible outcomes is only 11.

11. What is meant by possible outcomes and possible paths? When we get done tossing a single coin, say five times, we will count the number of heads that have arrived in the five tosses (regardless of order). This count is the outcome we are looking for. We also called it the final outcome or the head count outcome.

The exact order is not important to the head-count outcome. It is, however, very, very important in defining the path. The exact order in which the heads and tails arrived is what creates the path. For example, if the coin tosses result in HTHTH, then the outcome is 3H, but the path is HTHTH. Other paths, TTHHH and HHHTT and THHHT, for example, can and do result in exactly the same 3H outcome. This means there are often multiple paths for each outcome. Clearly, when we toss a coin 10 times, you can see this: there are 1024 possible paths but only 11 possible head-count outcomes!

12. If it doesn't matter which path was followed to get to the head-count outcome, why are we so interested in tracking and counting the number of paths? Hopefully you remember that in this chapter we said, "Now pay attention here: It does not matter which path was followed, but it is immensely important that there were four paths (for the 3H outcome), since it is the way to *measure the probability of winning*. The *number of paths* to any final outcome is critical to our later analysis." For a coin tossed four times, we can figure the probability of each head-count outcome *only if we know how many paths lead to each outcome.*

13. Tossing a coin three times yields how many different possible paths? List each path. For a coin tossed three times, there are eight different possible paths: HHH, HHT, HTH, HTT, THH, THT, TTH, TTT.

14. If tossing a coin 9 times yields 512 different possible paths, how many different possible paths are expected when we toss a coin 10 times? Twice as many, 1024. Each new toss doubles the possible paths.

15. For tossing N coins the number of different payable head-count outcomes is $N + 1$ and the number of different possible paths is 2^N. If we toss five coins calculate these two values. Do the same for 10 coins. Tossing five coins once or tossing a coin five times (which give identical results) can result in six possible different head-count outcomes and 32 different possible paths. For 10 coins the results can have 11 head-count outcomes via 1024 paths.

16. When we toss a coin four times, how many different paths lead to an outcome of exactly 3H ? List all the paths. Is this more or less likely than an outcome of exactly 1H? (*Hint*:

Use the binomial tree diagram in Fig. 2-1 to compare 1H paths versus 3H paths). There are four paths that lead to outcomes of exactly 3H: HHHT, HHTH, HTHH, THHH. Similarly there are four paths that lead to outcomes of exactly 1H: TTTH, TTHT, THTT, HTTT. Obviously, then, they are equally likely.

Chapter 3

1. **What is Pascal's triangle?** It's a triangle formed completely by numbers that are the coefficients for the binomial theorem. Each row is tied to a different power of binomial expansion. That is, the first row represents the zero power, the second row represents the first power, the third row represents the second power, and so on. As an example, the fourth row represents an expansion to the third power and the numbers in the row are 1, 3, 3, 1. While we explained an easy method for constructing the triangle by simply adding the two numbers above, there is a more complex formula related to probability theory that also dictates each value in the triangle. You'll run into this if you study the binomial option pricing method by Cox-Ross-Rubinstein, but we really didn't need it for our lessons, so we spared you that!

2. **What does *binomial expansion* mean?** It means you should perform all the multiplications rather than use the exponents (powers) that simplify the expression. For example, the binomial $(H + T)^2$ is not expanded. The exponent 2 implies that we must multiply $(H + T) \times (H + T)$, but it has not been done because the expanded form can get quite long and messy. Expanded it is $H^2 + 2HT + T^2$. When we get higher powers like 3, 5, or 10, the expanded version is an absolute nightmare. But it has some wonderful help for coin toss analysts, which is why we study it.

3. **How does the binomial theorem help us?** The binomial theorem tells us simple rules to easily perform an expansion on any binomial regardless of the number of multiplications required—even millions. No matter how messy it could become without this theorem, the results are kept neat and orderly; the quickness with which you can find an answer is astonishing.

4. **What is a coefficient? What is an exponent?** In algebra each algebraic variable term has three parts to it even though some are unstated:

1. The leading number (with its plus or minus sign) called the *coefficient*
2. The letters comprising the variable's name (like X or Y or H, etc.)
3. The power (*exponent*) to which it is raised.

5. What are the coefficients for the following algebraic terms: A, $-H$, $3X$, $-2Y$, $256Z$? Typically, to make things easier, mathematicians don't state when a coefficient or exponent is 1. It's just understood. Also, minus signs (negatives) are required, but plus signs (positives) are not stated. A number is assumed positive unless a minus sign appears. So, A has an unstated leading number of $+1$ which is its coefficient. For $-H$ the coefficient is -1. The $3X$ coefficient is $+3$. The $-2Y$ coefficient is -2. And the $256Z$ coefficient is $+256$.

6. What are the exponents (powers) for H^2, X, $(A + 1)^2$, $(H + T)^4$? H^2 has an exponent of 2. X shows no exponent and thus has an unstated exponent of 1. For $(A + 1)^2$ the whole binomial $(A + 1)$ has an exponent of 2, but the A inside the parentheses has an exponent of 1 (unstated). Similarly, $(H + T)^4$ has an exponent of 4 for the entire binomial $(H + T)$, but both the H and T inside the parentheses have exponents of 1 (unstated).

7. How do coefficients and exponents help us in our coin toss analyses? The coefficients tell us the total number of paths to an outcome. The outcomes are designated by a sort of shorthand using the letters $H + T$ and their exponents. For example, $252H^5T^5$ translates as 252 paths to the five heads and five tails outcome. Since we only measure outcomes by head counts (not tail counts) we might say "252 paths to the outcome of exactly five heads." The five tails help us note that this expected result must be linked to tossing 10 coins.

8. The expanded binomial representation of $(H + T)^3$, which means $H + T$ to the third power, multiplies out to be equal to $H^3 + 3H^2T + 3HT^2 + T^3$. Translate what this means in terms of paths and outcomes for a coin tossed three times? First we translate into heads and tails using the power (exponent) as an aid in counting : H^3 means HHH, $3H^2T$ means 3HHT, $3HT^2$ means 3HTT, T^3 means TTT. Next we look at the associated co-efficients (the numbers in front of each series of letters). This is the number of occurrences or paths to that outcome (1s are unstated). Continuing our translation: three heads (HHH) occur once, two heads (HHT) occur three times, one head (HTT) occurs three times, and zero heads (TTT) occurs just once. This is a total of eight possible paths, which is what we would expect for a coin tossed three times.

9. The eleventh row (or tier) of Pascal's triangle is 1 10 45 120 210 252 210 120 45 10 1. This row represents the coefficients for a 10 coin toss (the row's number is always one higher than the coin toss number). Since the coefficients tell us the number of paths to each of the 11 possible head-count outcomes, what are the total number of possible paths and can you associate these 11 coefficients with their 11 head-count outcomes? Total paths = 1024, 1 case of 10 heads, 10 cases of 9H, 45 of 8H, 120 of 7H, 210 of 6H, 252 of 5H, 210 of 4H, 120 of 3H, 45 of 2H, 10 of 1H, 1 of 0H.

10. In Chap. 4 we will begin discussing *frequency of occurrence* **and show how it helps us analyze the probability of an event. We already discussed frequency a bit when we showed the number of paths to each outcome via Pascal's triangle. Based on the eleventh row of Pascal's triangle (see question 9) which event do you expect to happen more frequently: 10 heads or 9 heads? 7 heads or 5 heads? 6 heads or 4 heads? Write down the frequency of each event.** Ten heads occur just once out of every 1024 tosses while nine heads occur 10 times. Seven heads occur 120 times per 1024, while five heads happen much more frequently, 252 times. And finally, both six heads and four heads are expected to occur 210 times each per 1024 tosses. Note these analyses are average expectations. On any given series of 1024 results of a coin tossed 10 times (or 10 coins tossed at once, which is identically the same) there can be wide swings away from these averages. But these are the results that would shake out after millions and millions of 1024 groupings of 10 coin tosses.

Chapter 4

1. What is a distribution? A table or graph with many answers. Not just one answer, but a whole army of answers. If we ask, How much is a house in California worth?, there just isn't one answer, is there? But there are many, many possible answers that vary according to the neighborhoods you look at. The full and correct answer is therefore a distribution that shows about a million possibilities.

2. What is frequency? A measure or count of how often an event occurs.

3. What is relative frequency? A comparison as a fraction of all events; how frequently one event occurs compared to the number of total possible events.

4. What is probability? The same as relative frequency. If an event *always* takes place it has proven to have 100 percent probability. If an event *never* occurs, it has proven to have zero percent probability. Of course, we are talking about looking at past events here. We already know the results and can count them. The future never follows the past exactly or we'd all be rich.

5. What is a frequency distribution? A listing in a table or on a bar graph of all the frequencies of occurrences of certain events, like coin tosses, for example.

6. What is a relative frequency distribution? The same as a frequency distribution except we must divide all the data by one special number. If we take a frequency distribution and divide each data point by one number (the total number of possible events), the data become relative frequencies and the table or graph automatically becomes a relative frequency distribution.

7. How do relative frequency distributions differ from probability distributions? They don't. Probability is just another name for a relative frequency. They are identical and interchangeable. A distribution of one type is identical to a distribution of the other type.

8. Can you define probability by a formula? The number of favorable events divided by the number of possible events. Probability = favorable events/possible events. Say we want the probability of an outcome of exactly two heads in a four coin toss game. There are 6 paths to get exactly 2H and 16 paths overall. The probability = 6 favorable/ 16 total = 3/8 = .375 or 37.5 percent (whichever number style you prefer).

9. What is a histogram? A bar chart that shows frequencies or relative frequencies or probabilities.

10. Is a histogram a distribution? It's a visual representation of a distribution, anyway. Technically speaking, the distribution is the data and the histogram is a type of graph that statisticians use to show the data. It's easy on the eyes and the brain and much more appealing than a boring table of data.

11. When we toss a coin four times, is there one single outcome that must occur? No, there are five possible head-count outcomes: 0H, 1H, 2H, 3H, 4H. Some are more likely to occur than others because there are more paths to them. Certainly, without a doubt, there is no single outcome that *must* occur; the outcomes are spread over a range of possibilities called a distribution. That's why we study distributions, to be able to see all the possibilities and make judgment calls on them. That's what the best traders do and what good trading is all about—understanding the many possible outcomes and their likelihoods.

Chapter 5

1. What are odds? The ratio of cases against you divided by cases for you.

2. In the newspaper sports section last Sunday we saw an "odds line" for a football game quoted as +7 and in a baseball game as −125/+115. These don't look anything at all like the odds described here in the book. Why not? As we said early on, there are dozens of ways to express odds and not all of them make sense within the context of our discussions on coin tosses and markets. Our discussions of odds have been limited to the most generic, basic usages to help describe coin tossing and familiarize you with the interrelationship of probabilities, odds, and payoffs. We avoided discussing the frills and special conventions that are used in the real wide world of gambling. In many sports the odds lines have grown up and out in different directions over the last 50 years. Each sport attracts a different betting clientele, and the casinos and sports books try to keep the customers happy by adjusting to their preferences. The odds line for each sport has come to have different terms, conditions, and meanings which vary according to the practices that are well known only to the inveterate players who follow them.

As to the odds lines we mentioned from the newspaper: football bets typically involve a point spread, which is what +7 means. If you bet on the underdog team, you get to add seven points extra to your final score. The odds are essentially "even money" (1 to 1) *less a takeout*. But that's all implied, not written.

If you're not a seasoned bettor, you wouldn't have a clue. The baseball odds line above reflects that you can bet $1.25 to win $1.00 on the favorite or bet $1.00 on the underdog to win only $1.15. The takeout is the difference in payoffs, and the house can't lose if its book has appropriately balanced bets on both sides. These are not fair odds or fair payoffs since there is a takeout involved.

3. What is a fair game? A game where no player has special knowledge or an advantage going in and all players are expected to break even over the course of many games. Tossing a coin and winning or losing $1 per toss is an example. No one knows the outcome ahead of time, and the payoff is properly calibrated to the likelihood of occurrences.

4. Option formulas are built on the central concept of breaking even. What is the simple formula that defines breaking even for a zero-sum game? There are two versions of the very same break-even formula. The first is total winnings = total losses and the other is total winnings − total losses = 0.

5. What is break-even analysis, and how does it help us set up fair payoffs? The concept that all players will break even on average and, therefore, that the sum of expected winnings will be exactly equal to the sum of expected losses. Said another way, all expected winnings minus all expected losses equals zero. Since expected winnings or losses are calculated by probability times payoff, we can set up simple formulas to help us deduce fair payoffs if we know the probability of an event.

6. Tossing a coin three times leads to four outcomes (0H, 1H, 2H, 3H) with eight different paths. List all eight paths. How many result in an outcome of 0H, 1H, 2H, and 3H? What are the probability, fair odds, and fair payoff for 2H assuming a $1 bet? The eight possible paths are HHH, HHT, HTH, HTT, THH, THT, TTH, TTT. The outcomes of 0H, 1H, 2H, 3H occur 1, 3, 3, 1 times in that order. For the case of 2H the probability is 3 out of 8 which can also be stated 3/8, .375, and 37.5 percent. The fair odds are five paths against with three paths for which computes as 1.66 to 1 against. Done another way, the probability is .375 for versus .625 against; dividing .625/.375 yields 1.66 to 1 against also. For betting $1 your payoff should be $1.66 (actually $1.66666666 . . .) plus your $1 returned.

7. Odds, payoffs, and returns are inextricably linked together. How are they linked? All three terms refer to the amount collected on winning bets (or investments). They are alternative ways of describing the same end result. We need to describe how much is won and how much is lost on each investment, and these three terms describe this in varying ways.

8. We are playing a game where it is determined that our fair chance of winning is .20 (same as 20 percent). What fair odds and payoff should we receive? We need to determine what the percentages for and against us are. The problem stated the percentages for us were .20 or 20 percent, and, therefore, the percentages against us must be the complement: .80 or 80 percent. We compute the ratio of against and for by dividing .80/.20. This shows the fair odds to be exactly 4 to 1 against. For a $1 bet we should receive a $4 payoff plus our $1 bet back (if we win, of course).

9. What do we mean by the phrase *mathematical expectation*? This phrase is sometimes called the average expected value as it is a type of average result which has been properly weighted by probability. The mathematical expectation is the amount you could expect to receive, on average, if you repeated the experiment or study many, many times. You won't necessarily get that result next time or the time after or even the 10 times after, but if you did the experiment or study again and again for say, a thousand or a hundred thousand tries, then you would get very close to that result, as an average. As an example, the mathematical expectation of the number of heads received from tossing a coin 10 times is five heads. You might get three heads this try and eight heads on the next try, but if you make a thousand tries, the average result will likely be between 4.8 and 5.2 heads.

10. Explain the formula: Individual expected return = $prob_{win} \times payoff_{win} - prob_{lose} \times payoff_{lose}$. This formula simply shows us how to calculate the amount we can expect to win (or lose) for an individual event within a game. For example, if we elect to bet on zero heads arriving when we toss a coin twice, we must calculate the probability of winning times the payoff for doing so. From this we must subtract the probability of losing times the amount we must payoff for that! Analysis will show that the probability of zero heads arriving is 1/4, and, therefore, the probability of zero heads *not* arriving must be 3/4. The payoffs, to be fair, must also be different for the two since the chances are different. The fair payoff for zero heads arriving is $3, while the fair payoff for zero heads *not* arriving is $1. Thus we can compute the individual expected return on zero heads as: $1/4 \times \$3 - 3/4 \times \$1$ which is $\$3/4 - \$3/4 = 0$. In a fair game each individual expected return will equal 0 as will the total sum of all the individual expected returns. The whole game has an expected return of 0. This is guaranteed because we created the fair payoffs in such a way as to make each and every event a break-even result for either side of the bet. To run a casino all we need do is trim the payoffs slightly below these fair values and we would have a positive expectation if everyone had to bet with us (because we became the house).

11. The symbol Σ is sigma, a Greek letter often used in math. In what context is it usually used? The symbol Σ is merely used to sum up a bunch of numbers. It's the capital of the Greek letter sigma, much like our capital S (as in sum). If placed before a group of numbers, it simply means sum these numbers up and write down the result.

Chapter 6

1. What was the first option we created, and how much did it cost? In a game where we tossed a coin four times we granted your friend the right to be paid $1 if exactly four heads came in. Regardless of outcomes (win or lose) your friend wasn't required to pay a cent when the game was over—a no-lose situation. To allow you to break even we charged him $1/16 (one sixteenth of a dollar) before each game started. Over the long haul this charge will wipe out his winnings and cause him, and you, to break even.

2. What do we mean by probability complements? We spent a lot of time describing probabilities *for* you and *against* you. These two complete the whole and complement one another, not unlike yin and yang, and they always add up to 1.00 or 100 percent, which is the total probability for all possible outcomes.

3. How does a probability distribution help us with coin toss analysis? A probability distribution is a precomputed answer to our questions on outcomes and probabilities. The bar graphs (histograms) in Fig. 4-3 showed six different probability distributions for coin tosses (1, 2, 3, 4, 5, and 10 tosses). The information available on each graph gives us quick and easy answers to our questions and eliminates the nasty, tedious work of figuring out each scenario step by step. In other words, the results of tossing a coin 10 times hasn't changed in the last thousand years and mathematicians decided to write down the results on a graph for their own reference. By learning this trick we get to use their short-cut. This also sets us up to learn the ropes for using their more advanced tools that can help predict stock price moves via the normal distribution which is merely a more powerful type of probability distribution. We're learning how to properly cut wood with a handsaw before we are thrown into the world of power saws.

4. Which is a better way to calculate odds and payoffs: using paths or probabilities? They are both the same and give the exact same answers. But as we use probability distributions to analyze more complex situations it will become increasingly difficult to count the paths and increasingly more advantageous to rely on probabilities.

5. What does *expected gain* mean? The amount that you can expect to win, on average, if you play over and over.

6. What does *expected loss* mean? The amount that you can expect to lose, on average, if you play over and over.

7. How are expected gain and expected loss linked? They exactly equal each other in a fair game. To perfectly offset each other they have to be equal; the sum total of all gains and losses is zero. In a two-player game, one player's expected gain equals the other player's expected loss.

8. What is a prepayment? A payment that must be made before an event occurs.

9. What is a premium? The amount you must pay up front to buy an option. The cost to buy an option.

10. How are insurance and option analysis linked? They are both actuarially sound businesses that sell products to limit risk. That is to say that statisticians, called actuaries, analyze historic data and use the math of statistics and probability to find out the proper break-even value for writing an insurance policy on a given event. Insurance companies might sell health insurance or life insurance. Options are price insurance. The same thought processes and concepts apply to both.

11. Why must you prepay for an option? At the expiration date, an option owner chooses to exercise the option or not. If the option is a loser, the owner will walk away, but if it is a winner, the owner will cash it in. Therefore, option owners never pay a penalty at the end of the deal. If they aren't forced to pay up front, the option *seller* will never see a cent.

12. What does it mean to say that options premiums are "prepayment for your expected gain"? The cost to buy an option is called its *premium*, the same name given to the cost of buying other types of insurance. You must pay for an option before the event takes place, just like you must buy any other type of insurance before the event. Flood insurance is not for sale when the water is rising up through your floorboards. Paying before the event is called making a *prepayment*. The buyer of an option has the choice at expiration to cash in the profits or walk away without paying a cent (if there are losses). As such the buyer can never lose, but can often win. Therefore, the buyer automatically has an expected gain. When the seller charges the amount of this expected gain up front, through a prepayment, the two offset and the buyer will be expected to break even over the long haul. The fair price is the one that gives no advantage to any player.

13. We said in the chapter, "If you learn only one thing from our studies, learn this lesson." What was that lesson? We quote from the chapter: "If you learn only one thing from our studies, learn this lesson: Every option formula you will ever run into is merely trying to compute the prepayment required to break even. Put another way, the option formulas are trying to calculate what the expected gain is and charge that amount up front."

14. In a four coin toss game we might use the following phrases for outcomes: four heads in a row, exactly four heads, more than three heads, and no tails at all. How do these outcomes differ? They don't. They all refer to the very same outcome, HHHH, which occurs 1 out of 16 times.

15. In a four coin toss game if you select all tails, what are the odds and fair payoff? (*Hint*: It's the same as all heads.) There is just 1 chance out of 16 to get TTTT. That is 15 to 1 odds against and a payoff of $15 for a bet of $1. In other words it's identical to the odds and payoff for HHHH, all heads.

16. In a game where you will win .20 (20 percent) of the time and the payoff is $1, what is the price for an option to play

the game? If you play the game five times you will, on average, win once and be paid $1. This averages $0.20 per game profit since you don't pay for losers because you are buying an option. That is the appropriate premium you should pay up front for the option, $0.20. An alternative analysis: Probability × payoff = .20 × $1 = $0.20 which is your expected gain (again assuming you needn't worry about any expected losses). The option premium equals the prepayment of your expected gain.

17. **In the same game where your winning chances are larger, say .50 (50 percent), and the payoff is $1, what should you pay for that option to play the game?** Probability × payoff = .50 × $1 = $0.50 expected gain per game. That's how much you should pay for the option.

18. **What does** *plain vanilla* **mean?** When an option is standard or run-of-the-mill it is sometimes called plain vanilla likening it to the most basic, unimaginative, and ordinary type of ice cream.

19. **We described path-dependent options and mentioned that they are sometimes called exotic options. What was meant by that?** The term *exotic* implies a more complicated product with all sorts of extra bells and whistles. In terms of complexity it is at least a step or two above the plain vanilla types.

Chapter 7

1. **The title for this chapter is Sectors, Strike Prices, and Summation Signs. What sectors are we referring to?** The term *sectors* refers to "coin toss sectors" or more precisely "cumulative coin toss sectors." In a four coin toss game you can choose from five outcomes or simple sectors (0H, 1H, 2H, 3H, 4H) or you can choose multiple continuous sectors like "more than 1H" or "less than 3H." We called these *cumulative sectors*.

2. **What is a cumulative sector when referring to coin tosses?** When you toss a coin four times, there are five possible outcomes (0H, 1H, 2H, 3H, 4H). Whereas we had been discussing individual outcomes earlier in the book (such as 2H or 4H), we are now interested in discussing multiple outcomes, but they should be consecutive. A sector is defined as including multiple consecutive outcomes. For example, the "2H or higher" sector means that 2H, 3H, and 4H would all be deemed winners. Cu-

mulative sectors closely parallel the strike prices used in options; that's why we've followed this route.

3. What is a strike price? Options have a kick-in level associated with them known as the strike price. A $100 call option on IBM, for example, will not be worth anything at expiration unless the $100 strike price is exceeded at that time. In effect, the option doesn't kick in until IBM hits $100, but once $100 is reached you will get paid more and more for all the prices above and beyond it. In this sense the strike price is the starting point of the option's cumulative sector and implies you are betting on all the prices greater than that (for a call option).

4. Why did we compare cumulative coin toss sectors to strike prices? Whereas coin toss games typically pay off for individually selected outcomes such as 1H or 3H, stock options pay off across multiple price areas beginning at the strike price. We were trying to show a closer link between coin toss payoffs and option payoffs.

5. What is Σ, and what does it represent in math? The symbol Σ is the Greek letter sigma and is equivalent to our letter S. Mathematicians use it as a formal method for summing up numbers. It's known as the summation sign. It is typically accompanied by tiny subscripts below it and above it, and there are rules that tell us how to interpret the subscripts. It is also the precursor to the more advanced math called integral calculus which is used to add up the many, many tiny pieces of a curve and give us the value of the whole. We are going to work around the need to involve calculus in our explanations, but hopefully you will begin to see that it can be a very powerful and useful tool that eliminates an enormous amount of work. That's why it's associated so often with options and other derivatives—the mathematicians don't know how to do the work any other way. Unless they want to slog through all the step-by-step details like we are!

6. Why do we need Σ for our purposes? When computing the value of an option, we will have to add many, many tiny values. The value of an option is directly related to the sum of an infinite number of payoffs × probabilities. We cannot sum these all without help from mathematics.

7. Betting on a high probability event is not always the best idea. Why not? There are many sure things in the world, but their payoffs are meager. People tend to overbet the sure things, making the returns pitiful when they win and devastating when they lose. What matters most is the net expected return, not the certainty of getting paid on the next roll. Also, it's very important for traders to choose wagers with likelihoods that fit their psychological profiles. Traders will not be able to weather the ups and downs, which are sure to occur, unless they believe in the investment and their heads and stomachs are not aching from the stress of the wager's return patterns.

8. What does the following formula tell us: cost = probability × payoff? The appropriate price to charge (the cost to the buyer) for any asset is equal to its expected gain, which is calculated by its payoff weighted by its probability.

9. What do we mean by option fair value = expected gain (discounted)? The fair price to charge for an option is its expected gain, which is the amount that the buyer can expect to win on average. But let's say this average gain will take place a year from now. Then the amount you should pay for it today must be lowered by the cost of borrowing money (since you won't get paid for a year). This is called discounting.

10. We've mentioned on occasion that expected gain = expected loss. Why does this make sense? We are dealing with break-even scenarios throughout our studies. This means that neither side should win, on average. It also means that winnings must equal losses. If a situation develops that allows someone to expect to be a winner, then the flip side is that the person playing against him or her must expect to be a loser. Thus all expected gains for the buyer of an option are at the very same time expected losses for the seller of the option. We can discuss either side and still be speaking of the same option.

11. From the optional math tutorial: Here is a summation sign with several subscripts. What do they all mean?

$$\sum_{i=1}^{8} G_i$$

Quickly translated this means we want to sum up all the G values starting at G_1 and ending at G_8. The G is the variable we are trying to sum up and the i just below it means we should expect it has more than one associated value. How many associated values is described by $i = 1$ at the bottom of Σ through 8 on top of Σ. This means that we must allow *i* to be worth 1, 2, 3, 4, 5, 6, 7, 8 one at a time and sum up all the values they imply. That is, sum up all eight of the G_i.

Chapter 8

1. We said the following in the chapter: "We can't tell the payoff until the result comes in, but we now have a payoff schedule for each possible outcome." What was meant by this? In a game where there are many possible outcomes and each outcome has a different payoff, we can build a table that explains all the payoffs, but we don't know which will occur until it happens. Each outcome has a probability and some are more likely than others, but none is a certainty. So, if outcome 1 occurs, then its associated payoff 1 will be made, but if outcome 2 arrives instead, then payoff 2 will be paid out, and so on.

2. We created a simple four-step list to calculate expected gains at the beginning of the chapter. We added, however, that the list was difficult to execute. Why is that so? The first difficulty arises because finding the probability associated with each payoff gets tougher as the complexity of the game increases. Coin tosses are easy compared to stocks. The second difficulty is in the multiplying and summing of an enormous number of payoffs and probabilities. As we approach reality we need more and more payoffs to represent the way stock prices can move. This causes us to have zillions of payoffs and thus zillions of probabilities too. This is far too much calculating to do by longhand.

3. We repeated a statement from Chap. 7 that "the fair value of each option was equal to the expected gain (before discounting)." What has discounting got to do with it? Your expected gain will not come until some time in the future when and if events turn favorable for your bet. A future gain is worth less than a gain today due to the time cost of money (interest rates). The financial process of translating a future gain into a gain today is called *discounting* or *present valuing*. We haven't shown the discounting process as yet, but we will need to do so later on.

4. We showed the math shorthand: Σ payoff$_i$ × probability$_i$. This is the same formula covered in the optional math tutorial in Chap. 7. How would you translate it for a beginner? This expression says we must sum up all the multiplicative products that result when we multiply each associated pair of payoffs and probabilities. Suppose an event has three pairs of linked payoffs and probabilities. We number them payoffs 1, 2, and 3 and probabilities 1, 2, and 3. The formula tells us we must pair payoff 1 to probability 1 and multiply them. Do the same for payoffs and probabilities 2 and 3. Each of these multiplications creates a separate product. We then sum up all the products to reach the final answer.

5. Why is the following formula called the sum of the products: Σ probability$_i$ $\times$ payoff$_i$? As per earlier instructions, the formula is simply asking us to first create a product for each pair of equally numbered payoffs and probabilities. The Greek letter sigma (Σ) tells us to sum up all the values next to it which just happen to be the products.

6. We switched the order of probability$_i$ and payoff$_i$ in a few of the formulas. How does this switching of order impact the results? Not at all. Suppose we use any of the five following expressions: Σ probability$_i$ $\times$ payoff$_i$, Σ prob$_i$ $\times$ payoff$_i$, Σ payoff$_i$ $\times$ probability$_i$, Σ payoff$_i$ $\times$ prob$_i$, Σ pay$_i$ $\times$ prob$_i$. They all mean precisely the same thing and give the very same answers. As long as we are dealing with the same two variables, payoff$_i$ and probability$_i$, what we call them is irrelevant. And it is also irrelevant which comes first when we multiply them. The answer will come out the same.

7. We mentioned in the chapter that "The payoff schedule is crucial." Suppose we doubled the payoffs in our example in this chapter. What would that do to the fair option value? Suppose we tripled the payoffs? The payoff schedule is indeed important to calculating the fair option value. Since the fair option value equals the expected gain, we are very interested in what the expected gain will be, and it varies directly with the payoff schedule. Suppose the payoffs are in pennies instead of dollars. Suddenly every option worth $2.00 originally would fall to $0.02 (two pennies). Likewise, if we double or triple the payoff schedule across the board, then the fair option values will double or triple, respectively.

Chapter 9

Use the expression max $[S - K, 0]$ to help with questions 1 to 4.

1. IBM closes at $109. The strike price is $90 for a call option expiring at the close. What is the option worth at expiry? $19 because $S = \$109$, $K = \$90$, $S - K = \$19$.

2. **IBM closes at $96.50. The strike price for a call option expiring at the close is $100. What is the option worth at expiry?** Zero because S = $96.50, K = $100, $S - K$ = − $3.50. Options are not allowed to ever have a negative payoff at expiration.

3. **IBM closes at $89. The strike price for a call option expiring at the close is $85. You had to pay $4 to buy the option. What is the option worth at expiry and how much profit did you make?** The option is worth $4 because S = $89, K = $85, $S - K$ = $4. You made no profit because your initial cost was also $4.

4. **IBM closes at $115. You own two call options expiring at the close. Their strikes are $105 and $125. You paid $5 and $2 for them in the morning. What are the options worth, and what is your profit for the day?** The first option is worth $10 because S = $115, K = $105, $S - K$ = $10. The second option is worth zero because S = $115, K = $125, $S - K$ = − $10. Thus you *net* (made) $3 for the day: $10 − $5 − $2 = $3.

Use the histogram in Fig. Q–1 to answer questions 5 to 7.

FIGURE   Q–1

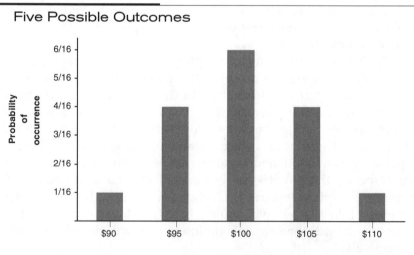

Five Possible Outcomes

Today's Closing IBM Price

5. **If you buy IBM at $100 in the morning, what is your expected gain at the close? (*Hint*: You should sum all the probabilities × payoffs.)** We must sum (1/16 × −$10) + (4/16 × −$5) + (6/16 × $0) + (4/16 × $5) + (1/16 × $10) = − 10/16 − 20/16

+ 0/16 + 20/16 + 10/16 = 0. There are equal wins and losses, and they zero out. Therefore, there is no expected gain.

6. Assume you have a call option struck at $100 that expires at the close. What is its expected value at the close? How much should you be willing to pay for it before the close? If IBM closes at $90, $95, or $100, the option is worth zero. Thus the only two bars that need calculating are the $105 and $110 closes. The $105 close will create an option value of $5 and will occur 4/16 of the time. For the $110 close the option will be worth $10, but it only occurs 1/16 of the time. Multiplied out and summed these are $5 × 4/16 + $10 × 1/16 = $20/16 + $10/16 = $30/16 = $1.875. This is the expected value at the close. It's also the limit of what you should be willing to pay. Buying it for less would be preferred, of course.

7. In questions 5 and 6 we found there was no expected gain for IBM stock at the close but that the call option had an expected value at the close of $1.875. Why does the option have value if we don't expect the stock to gain (on average)? The stock can lose $5 or $10 by the close according to the histogram in Fig. Q–1, but the option can never fall below zero. So the expected gains on the stock are offset by the expected losses. This does not happen with options. Options give you a chance to share in the winning pile but no chance to share in the losing pile.

For questions 8 to 12 we will ask you to evaluate a call option (strike price of $100) that expires at the close. For these examples we create overly simple probability distributions (there are only two possible closing prices, and each has 50 percent likelihood).

8. If the stock can only close at $90 or $110, what is the option worth? Half the time the option is worth zero, the other half it's worth $10. We compute the option's value as (0.50 × $0) + (0.50 × $10) = $0 + $5 = $5.

9. If the stock can only close at $85 or $115, what is the option worth? Half the time the option is worth zero the other half it's worth $15. We compute the option's value as (0.50 × $0) + (0.50 × $15) = $0 + $7.50 = $7.50.

10. If the stock can only close at $70 or $130, what is the option worth? Half the time the option is worth zero, the other half it's worth $30. We compute the option's value as (0.50 × $0) + (0.50 × $30) = $0 + $15 = $15.

11. If the stock can only close at $0 or $200, what is the option worth? Half the time the option is worth zero, the other half it's worth $100. We compute the option's value as (0.50 × $0) + (0.50 × $100) = $0 + $50 = $50.

12. Now notice that in questions 8 to 11 we suggested a closing price range that kept getting wider (which is a measure of increased volatility). But the expected gain for the stock stayed steady at zero, since the downside offset the upside exactly. Despite this the worth of the options kept increasing more and more. What was happening? How did increasing volatility affect the option values? The fact that the expected gain on the stock was zero has no impact whatsoever on the value of an option. What matters is the size of the potential winning pile, the upside. As the volatility increases, there is more upside and more downside, which will tend to offset each other and not impact the expected gain for the stock. But options benefit from an increased upside potential and totally ignore the increased downside. The worst case never gets worse because the option is never worth less than zero, but the best case keeps getting better as the upside potential expands. This is why increased volatility is good for option holders and why the cost of options goes up.

Chapter 10

1. Why do we call the average a sort of middle-of-the-road measurement? The purpose of the average is to find a quick and easy measurement that represents the center point of the data you are working with. Being at the middle of your data it does not, by any stretch of the imagination, represent all the data, but it is the best single number we can come up with. Looked at another way, if you randomly picked your data numbers from a hat, it is the weighted result you could expect over the course of many pickings.

2. What is the average of these five data points: 23, 16, 19, 27, 15 ? The sum of the five points is 100 which we divide by the number of points (5) to give us exactly 20 as the average. Notice that 20 is near the center of the data, in keeping with the purpose of an average which is to find a reasonable center point.

3. What is the mean for the five data points in question 2? The mean is simply another name for the average. So the mean of the data is also 20.

4. What is the meaning of the term *central tendency* **as related to clusters of data points?** When we plot many data points on a graph, they tend to cluster together in an area which is neither near the high nor the low end of the data point values. Most typically the cluster tends to be near the center. Many statistical distributions display this tendency, and much of statistical theory depends on the concept of central tendency.

5. Does the average or mean tell the whole tale? What do they leave out? The average and mean (which are the same thing) simply tell us where the center of the data is located. Very often the center is interesting, but less important than the extremes. The average and mean tell us nothing about how far the other data points stray from the center and how extreme they can get. This tendency to *vary* from the average or mean is called variance, a very important statistical measurement.

6. In our lab experiment the paid volunteer was kept on average at a very comfortable 70°F. Do you think the extreme temperatures averaged out in his opinion? What was the likely physical result of the extreme temperatures? The volunteer will not be volunteering again, unless he was brain damaged by the experiment and got amnesia. His bad experience taught him a very important lesson: he definitely did not want to do this for his livelihood! Sometimes such life lessons are worth the pain. Physically, he no doubt suffered blisters on his toes and frostbite on his scalp. There is no way he could believe that he wasn't exposed to bizarre and extreme temperatures. Extremes often matter most to the people who must suffer through them. Too many traders think it can't happen to them—but it does.

7. Can we make accurate predictions without noting similar experiences from the past? No. Our ability to predict the future is based on our experiences or the experiences of others. Without any sort of comparable experience we might make educated guesses, but even educated guesses are based on paralleling the past: "If it happened this way under those circumstances, then maybe it will happen this way now." All knowledge is based on experience. Otherwise it is unproved theory.

8. What is the variance of the five data points we averaged in question 2? Use the results to compute the standard deviation also. We know the average or mean is 20, so the respective deviations from the mean are $+3$, -4, -1, $+7$, -5. We must square each (9, 16, 1, 49, 25) and then take their average. They sum up to 100 (which is pure coincidence), we divide by 5 and get 20 (another coincidence). Thus the variance is 20. (We divided by N here, not $N - 1$, to keep the explanation simple.) Now, it seems to us that 20 *feels* very high as a variance, but if we use the more helpful measure, the standard deviation, which is the square root of the variance, we get 4.472. Now, that feels more accurate, don't you think? We said the deviations from the mean were $+3$, -4, -1, $+7$, -5 which makes 4.472 right in the ballpark. Thus the standard deviation tends to be more reflective of our gut feel than the variance does.

9. What is the variance of these five data points: 22, 17, 20, 25, 16? Use the results to compute the standard deviation also. The average or mean is 20. The deviations from the mean are $+2$, -3, 0, $+5$, -4 which squared are 4, 9, 0, 25, 16. This sums to 54, and dividing by 5 (N instead of $N - 1$) gives a variance of 10.8. The standard deviation is the square root of this which is 3.286. Notice that these data are similar to the five data points in question 8 except more tightly wrapped around the bulls-eye (the mean). Therefore, the variance and the standard deviation are smaller.

10. What is the variance of these five data points: 18, 19, 20, 21, 22? Use the results to compute the standard deviation also. The average or mean is 20. The deviations from the mean are -2, -1, 0, $+1$, $+2$ which squared are 4, 1, 0, 1, 4. This sums to 10, and dividing by 5 (N instead of $N - 1$) gives a variance of 2.0. The standard deviation is the square root of this which is 1.414. Notice that these data are even more tightly focused near the bulls-eye (the mean) than those of question 9. The variance and the standard deviation are quickly approaching zero. If the five data points were 20, 20, 20, 20, 20 (all identical), then there would be zero deviation from the mean of 20 and both the variance and standard deviation would be zero.

11. Can we predict an event exactly if historically it often varies? No. The more variation that is possible, the less precise our prediction can be. When variations exist, we may be able to assess probabilities, but never certainty.

12. How does the variance and standard deviation relate to our study of the Black-Scholes option formula? We already know that standard deviation is simply the square root of the variance.

It turns out that the annual standard deviation of a stock's return is what the Black-Scholes option formula requires as a stock's volatility. And volatility is by far the most difficult input we'll need to compute the Black-Scholes option formula.

Chapter 11

Questions 1 to 3 refer to Figs. 11–1 and 11–2.

1. Are there any noticeable differences in the bar heights of the two charts, and, if so, how would you describe the differences? Yes, the graph in Fig. 11–1 shows higher bars in the center and higher bars at the extremes (the tails). Two bars are much taller than any of the bars in Fig. 11–2. The bars in the tails in Fig. 11–1 are barely visible, but they are, nonetheless, more visible than for those in Fig. 11–2.

2. Assuming the typical trading market has a higher center and thicker tails than a perfectly symmetrical model, where does the difference get made up? The Dow Jones graph in Fig. 11–1 and other trading market graphs like it have shorter bars in the areas that are just off the few center bars, but not quite far out on the tails. Since the center tends to represent zero price change, we can translate this to mean that the market has many extra days where things are quiet and sleepy, closing unchanged for the day. Every once in a while the extreme moves occur, however, and these also happen more frequently than expected by theory. This implies that the moderate moves, which make up the rest of the distribution, occur less frequently than theory would dictate.

3. The far-out fringe data points (called *outliers*) are what the tails of the distributions are made of. Why are these data points much more important to a trader than the ones at the center? The center is comprised of price moves that are close to unchanged. As such they don't impact a trader's profits and losses too much. The most explosive market moves are the few that occur on the tails of the distribution. They represent huge down days and huge up days. Sometimes a trader's whole month or quarter can be unduly affected by just one of these days.

4. Briefly describe the concepts of discrete math and continuous math. Discrete math is the math we learn in elementary school to count things. It typically involves the use of whole numbers (integers). As we get older we later learn about fractions and decimals and come to realize that there are a zillion possible numbers in between every two integers. Paying attention to all these zillions of possible numbers is what continuous math does.

5. Which uses discrete math: the binomial distribution or normal distribution? Why? The binomial distribution measures events that have only two possible outcomes. We can, as we have shown with the binomial theory, get a good count on these if we wish to do all the work necessary. Therefore, discrete math, where each event can be counted, is highly suited to the binomial distribution.

6. Which uses continuous math: the binomial distribution or normal distribution? Why? The normal distribution measures events that have an infinite number of possible outcomes. We cannot get a good count on these no matter how much work we wish to do. We have to find other ways to measure these many, many outcomes. Continuous math gives us the ability to get a handle on this. The normal distribution can only be evaluated with the use of continuous math.

7. What does CDF stand for? What does it mean? How does it help us? Is there a separate CDF for the binomial distribution and the normal distribution? CDF stands for cumulative distribution function. It simply means it is a formula for accumulating (adding up) all the probabilities under a distribution's curve. It helps us because we are studying options that require us to sum up a great many probabilities and payoffs. The CDFs do our work for us. There are separate CDFs for every type of distribution, and the binomial and normal are simply two examples.

8. After spending a great deal of time learning about the binomial distribution, we are suddenly shifting to the normal distribution. Why? Stock price moves cannot be precisely measured with only a few price groupings. We ran into a problem of bracketing. When we used 21 outcomes and tried to measure a $40 closing range for IBM of $80 to $120, we had to make each bar represent a $2 bracket. Thus $100 was stuck in the bracket of all prices from $99 to $101. This is far too imprecise and led to errors in assigning probability. We needed a more precise, *continuous* set of prices.

9. How many standard deviations wide is the normal distribution? The typical normal curve is six standard deviations wide, three on either side of the center.

10. Does each standard deviation measure the same percentage of the curve? No. While the standard deviations are set up to be equal in width, it is clear that the curve is not equally high in all places. The 2 SD width that we call $+/-$ 1 SD (one right of center and one left of center) monopolizes the central zone and represents 68 percent of all the area and, therefore, 68 percent of the probabilities. Less area and therefore less probability must be divided among the four remaining SDs.

11. What is significant about three standard deviations? When we speak of $+/-$ 3 SDs, we are essentially talking about the entire width and area of the normal curve. Thus 99.74 percent of the area under the curve, 99.74 percent of the data points, and 99.74 percent of the probabilities are expected to fall within that 6 SD range known as $+/-$ 3 standard deviations.

12. When traders describe a move that has just occurred as a "three standard deviation move," what are they referring to? They mean that a huge move has just occurred and that it had only a tiny probability of happening. Since 99.74 percent of all moves take place inside the $+/-$ 3 SDs zone, that leaves only the very rare and extreme moves. They are the remaining 0.26 percent of the cases which occur every $1\frac{1}{2}$ years (in theory) or about 1 out of every 400 trading days. In reality they happen a bit more often.

13. Is there a link between standard deviations and the volatility used by the Black-Scholes formula? Yes, there is a direct link. The Black-Scholes formula needed a probability measuring tool, and the normal curve CDF provides it. The more a stock price strays from unchanged (the typical center of our normal curve), the more volatile it is. In keeping with the rules set up for using the normal curve we needed to turn these "distances strayed" into a more standard measure: the standard deviation. The Black-Scholes formula decided that a good measure of a stock's volatility would be one standard deviation, but it had to be the annual standard deviation, not the daily ones we looked at in this chapter. We can adjust daily to annual with a simple scaling factor. Knowing a stock's volatility in terms of standard deviations allows the Black-Scholes formula to search through the normal curve CDF and obtain quick and easy probability readings.

Chapter 12

Use the graph in Fig. 12–1 for questions 1–9.

F I G U R E   12–1

(Reprinted)

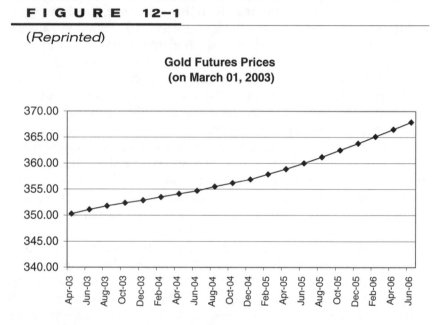

**Gold Futures Prices
(on March 01, 2003)**

1. What market type is represented by the graph in Fig. 12–1? This is called a normal, or contango, market. Notice that prices are higher for the later delivery dates. This is typical of a market where the supply is sufficiently adequate to meet nearby inventory needs. Sometimes there is a glut of material on the market and the contango widens dramatically because there is more spot material available than the market cares to hold. Which brings up the very colorful riddle that, as a rite of passage, is posed to all new traders: What market has the steepest contango in the world? Answer: Camel dung. . .because nobody wants to hold the spot!

2. You have bought an April 03 gold future, and it is now March 27. You will get delivery if you don't get out in the next few days. You feel it is important to own gold, but you are afraid (or unable) to take delivery. What can you do? You can do what most traders do: a rollover spread. You put in a spread order to sell in April and buy in June simultaneously. This liquidates (offsets) your April position so that you are "flat" (i.e., no position) and makes you the owner of a June future contract. Come May 25 you have to do it again to avoid June 1 delivery, and so on.

3. **April 2003 gold closed today at \$350.30 and June 2003 gold closed at \$351.10. How much will it cost to roll over?** Well, closing prices are not the same as trading prices, but the spread (which closed at \$0.80) is probably buyable at \$0.90, and then there are commissions, of course. The prices mentioned are per ounce and one gold futures contract is 100 ounces.

4. **The April gold contract trades until almost the last day in April. What will happen to the spread in price between April and June as time moves on?** While there are no certainties, it would be most usual in a contango market that the contango (another name for the spread) will get smaller to reflect the smaller amount of time remaining. If the overall spread structure of the gold market remains steady, then by the end of April the spread should fall to about \$0.40 because what started as a 2-month spread has now, through the passage of time, become a 1-month spread.

5. **What are the factors affecting how wide or narrow the April/June spread is?** As we discussed in the chapter there are carrying costs and carrying benefits which vary widely from one asset group to another and can also change as market perceptions shift. Our prime discussion in the chapter was about stocks. Stocks have a very simple cost structure that only incorporates an interest cost (at least in the hypothetically constrained world of the Black-Scholes formula). Just like stocks the main cost to carry gold is the cost of financing the purchase, meaning interest costs. But owning gold also means holding it in a vault and incurring monthly storage and insurance charges. Furthermore, there is a liquidity premium for gold (a cost to borrow) which at times can be pretty steep, at least for a financial asset anyway. This liquidity premium (the cost to borrow) narrows the spreads, while the cost of interest and storage widen the spreads.

6. **At this point in time short-term interest rates are at very low levels (1.45 percent). If gold storage costs 0.3 percent a year and the liquidity premium is a low 0.4 percent, how would you calculate the annualized return for carrying Gold?** These estimates give us a projected contango (spread) of $1.45\% + 0.3\% - 0.4\% = 1.35\%$ annual rate. This is in line with the April/June spread which is \$0.80 for 2 months (\$4.80 year/ \$350 spot = 1.37\%). Don't forget, however, that these are rounded numbers, and every extra \$0.10 you pay on the spread plus every commission can have a big impact on the final percent return.

7. What does it mean when we say "a 1.37 percent annual return for carrying gold"? It means you have entered into a two-sided position wherein you have bought spot gold and sold it forward at the same moment, locking in a price differential of 1.37 percent per annum. You are carrying gold inventory but have already arranged to redeliver it at some forward date and have set the price. You do not own gold in the usual sense, but have it on a spread position called a *carry* which earns 1.37 percent on the dollars you have invested in gold inventory. If gold goes up and down in price, it has little impact on you (aside from margin calls) because you have already bought and sold (just for different dates is all). You can use the gold in your inventory as you wish as long as you get it back in shape to redeliver on the forward date. In effect, you are renting or borrowing metal like many people rent or borrow apartments. Metal traders constantly speak of such spread positions in terms of being a borrower or lender. If you lend out the gold you can earn the 0.40 percent we spoke of in question 6 and also avoid the storage fees of 0.3 percent. If you leave it in the vault you'll have to pay the 0.3 percent.

8. What is your guess as to the typical price curve for individual stocks like IBM or AT&T? Does it look similar to the forward price curve for gold in Fig. 12–1? In general, the forward price curve for stocks is a contango and looks very similar to the gold price curve. However, stocks do have dividends (despite what the Black-Scholes formula prefers), and this is a carrying benefit called a cash flow, and it narrows the spread. Since interest rates right now are 1.45 percent and stock dividends tend to run in the 2 or 3 percent area, these stocks will *not* have a contango as their forward price curve, but instead will display a slightly inverted curve (also known as a backwardation). Stocks with no dividends will, however, continue to trade in contango mode. When interest rates rise, which they will do when the economy picks up, it will force all stocks into the contango mode as the spreads widen. This is one of the many types of specialized plays that spread traders will occasionally make. Some consider it a form of risk arbitrage.

9. What is your guess as to the typical price curve for U.S. government long bonds? Does it look similar or different than the forward price curve for gold in Fig. 12–1. Typically, the coupon rate on bonds is higher than the cost of short-term interest rates. This leads to all sorts of interesting carry trades and colorful descriptors like "riding the yield curve." For our purposes here the bonds are very similar to stocks with large dividends. Since the carrying benefit (the coupon rate) is higher than the carrying cost (short-term interest rates), this causes a negative spread which we call an inverted or backwardation market. This is different than gold which is a contango market.

[*Note*: You might notice that a paradox exists between financial assets and commodities. The bond market is typically inverted even though there is a plentiful supply of bonds. This is because the forward price market structure of financial assets like stocks, bonds, and currencies is typically driven more by their cash-flow benefits than by any liquidity premium (a desire to hold inventory). Most financial assets are created by governments and corporations out of thin air with an almost unlimited supply, so real shortages are rare. And aside from being agreements on paper they have no physical existence either. This is an advanced concept and points out some of the loopholes we run into when we try to explain complex entities, like markets, with a few simple rules. This is why it takes traders years to understand the ins and outs of forward price curves. But don't despair, since our formulas still work fine. Following is a rule of thumb to help you get a grip on this. You should remember that for the financial asset groups the biggest drivers of forward pricing are cash flows and short-term interest costs and that liquidity premiums are often near zero. The opposite is true for touchable commodities like oil, gold, and cattle: cash flows are usually near zero and liquidity premiums can often soar. And there are always exceptions to these rules of thumb. We live in a complex world.]

Use the graph in Fig. 12–2 (*Reprinted*) for questions 10 and 11.

10. What type of market is displayed by the crude oil market in Fig. 12–2? This is an inverted, or backwardation, market. The liquidity premiums in a "back" such as the crude oil market dwarf every other cost or benefit.

11. What rational explanation could there be for such a steep price curve in oil? This chart shows there is a mini-crisis in supply versus demand. This mini-panic was prompted by an historic occasion: the 2003 war in Iraq. In the months leading up to this price chart it was increasingly clear that a March/April mil-

F I G U R E   12–2

(Reprinted)

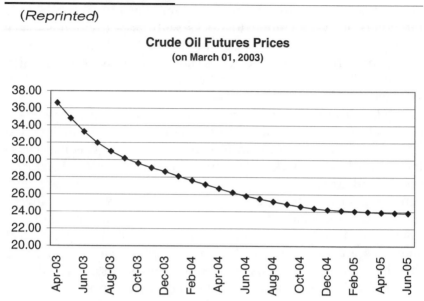

Crude Oil Futures Prices
(on March 01, 2003)

itary showdown was coming between the government of Iraq and the United States led "coalition forces." Iraqi President Saddam Hussein said he would "light up the skies and burn his oil fields to the ground" before giving in to the coalition demands. The largest oil companies in the world were terrified that supplies would be cut off and they'd lose market share if they didn't get hold of enough inventory—just in case. So you can see what happened to the nearest delivery prices; they went through the roof. Meanwhile most rational people figured that within a year everything would be back to somewhat more normal conditions and they wouldn't pay such steep prices for oil in 2004. This is what markets do, analyze the probabilities of supply and demand over different time frames. It's not usually so clear what their fears and thoughts are, however.

Chapter 13

1. **The key to all option pricing is the ability to sum up all the payoffs × probabilities, which can be shown as Σ pay$_i$ × prob$_i$. Why is this easy to say, but hard to do?** When we were dealing with a few coin tosses, it didn't take more than a few minutes to analyze all the possible outcomes, the paths for each, the probabilities, and the payoffs. When we talked about the 20

coin toss game, we showed the paths had increased to over a million! The calculations were still doable if we used the binomial theorem, but we learned that the accuracy of the probabilities failed when we tried to place stock prices into only 21 individual brackets. Whereas a 20 coin toss has 21 possible outcomes, we were more interested in the thousands of possible closing prices we could determine for IBM by separately bracketing every penny. The number of possible paths was quickly rising above the trillions! No one could figure out all the individual probabilities let alone pair them with their payoffs, multiply them, and add them all up.

2. **In Σ pay$_i$ × prob$_i$ what does the subcript i mean?** The subscripted, lowercase letter i represents all the possible payoffs with all their possible probabilities (there is an equal number of each since they are pairs). In the optional math tutorial in Chap. 7, which used George Foreman and his eight sons as an example, we set i equal to 8, for the 8 sons. We could set i equal to any number that suits us, but in the continuous math world we must operate in, there are basically an infinite number of possibilities, so we keep the value of i open to be as large as necessary. For purposes of an example that we can be comfortable with we might say that i can be all the numbers from 1 to 1,000,000. That is, i equals 1, 2, 3, 4, 5, . . . , 1,000,000. How do we then use these i's? First we compute pay$_1$ × prob$_1$ simply by multiplying payoff 1 by probability 1. We put that aside. Then we compute pay$_2$ × prob$_2$ by multiplying payoff 2 by probability 2. We put that aside. Then we compute payoff$_3$ × prob$_3$ and so on until we have computed all 1 million through payoff$_{1,000,000}$ × prob$_{1,000,000}$. Then, and only then, we add them all up to arrive at the final value of Σ pay$_i$ × prob$_i$ (where i = 1,000,000). So, i can be any number and every number if we choose to define it as such. In our option analysis it is essentially equal to an infinite number we like to call a *zillion*. How is anyone able to add a zillion numbers? Thank goodness for geniuses like Gauss, Newton, and Leibnitz—the last two created calculus which is considered the mathematics of the infinite.

3. **We replaced payoff$_i$ with the expression $S_i - K$. What does $S_i - K$ mean, and why are we allowed to substitute this expression?** From Chap. 9 you will remember we defined an option's final payoff value as max $[S_i - K, 0]$. That expression means you get the pleasant choice (because it's an option) of receiving

the maximum of $S_i - K$ or zero. So, if $S_i - K$ has a positive value, you'll get that. The term S_i stands for the final spot price of the stock on expiration day. The other term K stands for the strike price of the call option. In algebra, whenever two expressions are identically equal, we are allowed to substitute one for the other at our convenience.

4. **Using $S_i - K$ calculate the payoff at expiration for an IBM $90 call option if IBM's spot price S_i closes at $80, $90, $100, and $104.** Using the max $[S_i - K, 0]$ explanation from the answer to question 3, the four option payoffs are zero because $S_i - K$ is negative, zero because $S_i - K$ is also zero, $10 because $S_i - K$ is 10, and $14 because $S_i - K$ is 14.

5. **Assume the interest rate is 10 percent, IBM spot is $100, and you need to compute a 6-month forward IBM price. How would you do it? (*Hint*: Use e^{RT}.)** The forward price is defined as $S \cdot e^{RT}$. We know that spot IBM (S) = $100, R = 0.10 (same as 10 percent), T = 0.5 (same as a half year), and e always equals 2.71828. First calculate the tough part e^{RT}, which we know from Chap. 12 as the interest rate multiplier. We need to raise e to the RT power. First, RT means multiply $R \times T$, which is 0.10 $\times$ 0.5 which equals 0.05. We can either raise 2.71828 to the 0.05 power or in Microsoft Excel calculate the value "=Exp(0.05)" which does the same thing. In any event, e^{RT} equals 1.051271 which is our interest rate multiplier. We multiply that times S, which is $100, and come up with $105.1271 for the 6-month IBM forward value. This explanation took about 100 times longer than it will take you to compute e^{RT} with a little practice. Notice we were using an annual rate of 10 percent for half a year, which is obviously close to a 5 percent return. Our computation showed a 5.1271 percent return because e^{RT} is based on continuous compounding. Regardless, it doesn't hurt to recognize you were looking for about 5 percent, as this helps prove that your answer is reasonable, especially when dealing with abstruse concepts like e^{RT} where even wizards can make errors and get lost in the sauce.

6. **We talked about discounting and present valuing in the chapter. Take the 6-month forward IBM price (the answer to question 5) and reverse the process to show how this discounting process works. (*Hint*: Use the inverse of e^{RT} which is e^{-RT}.)** We found the 6-month forward IBM price to be $105.1271 in ques-

tion 5. We want to find the present value or discounted value of this forward price. In other words, if the 6-month forward price is \$105.1271, what is spot worth now? The formula for reversing the process is forward price • e^{-RT}. So, again, let's compute the tough part first, e^{-RT} equals 2.71828 to the -0.05 power which is 0.951229 (it's an inverse process that shrinks the forward value). Multiply \$105.1271 × 0.951229, and we get \$99.99999 or, as we noncomputers know it, \$100.00. So, the inverse function (e^{-RT}) did its job and reversed the original e^{RT} growth rate. That's because when you multiply: $e^{RT} \times e^{-RT}$, they cancel each other and equal 1.

7. **We split apart our payoff × probability expression, $(S_i - K) \times \text{prob}_i$, into two parts: $S_i \times \text{prob}_i$ and $-K \times \text{prob}_i$. Why is this okay?** In algebra, any math procedure which equals any other math procedure is allowed to be substituted at our convenience. Suppose we were trying to find $(2 + 7) \times 4$. We can say this equals 9×4 which is 36, or we can say it equals $2 \times 4 + 7 \times 4$ which is $8 + 28$ which, of course, also equals 36. Both procedures are equal and, therefore, substitutable for each other.

8. **We said in the chapter that our final formula and the Black-Scholes formula were identical if we could show that Black and Scholes' $N(D_2)$ = our prob_i and if Black and Scholes' $N(D_1)$ = our $\text{prob}_i \cdot S_i/S$. Can you do the algebraic substitution to show that what we said makes sense?** Here are the two formulas together:

Black-Scholes formula: $\qquad S \cdot N(D_1) - e^{-RT} \cdot K \cdot N(D_2)$

Our final formula: $\qquad S_i \cdot \text{prob}_i - e^{-RT} \cdot K \cdot \text{prob}_i$

First, look at just the right-side pieces of the two formulas. Clearly, if $N(D_2) = \text{prob}_i$, then our right-side piece is identical to the Black-Scholes formula's right-side piece. Second, if we adjust our left-side piece by multiplying by S/S (which is equal to 1) and rearrange the order slightly, we end up with $S \cdot S_i/S \cdot \text{prob}_i$ which we separate by parentheses to show the effect more clearly: $S \cdot (S_i/S \cdot \text{prob}_i)$ is our new left piece, identically equal to the original, just changed a little by algebraic manipulation. So, we are trying to show that the Black-Scholes formula's left piece $S \cdot N(D_1)$ equals our left piece $S \cdot (S_i/S \cdot \text{prob}_i)$. And it is true if what is inside the parentheses $(S_i/S \bullet prob_i)$ equals $N(D_1)$, which was our original claim. This is not a rigorous proof, but it does make the prima facie case for now.

9. To show how our formula is equivalent to the Black-Scholes formula we found it was convenient to use the expression S_i/S, which, it turns out, has a meaning of special importance to stock traders. What does S_i/S mean? S_i/S represents all the possible *returns* of the stock at expiration. For example, if IBM is $100 now (which is S) and closes at $113 at expiration (which is only one possible S_i), then S_i/S would be 1.13 (its gross return), the same as 113 percent. The net return would, of course, be simply 0.13, the same as 13 percent.

10. Why does the Black-Scholes formula have two probabilities $N(D_1)$, and $N(D_2)$, while we only have one, which we call $prob_i$? There is only one true probability for an option. We can call it $N(D_2)$ like Black and Scholes did or $prob_i$ like we did. We discussed before that Black and Scholes' other probability $N(D_1)$ is equal to our probability with an adjustment factor: $S_i/S \bullet prob_i$. This says that the Black-Scholes formula is multiplying the possible payoffs (returns) times their true probabilities: $S_i/S \bullet prob_i$. They found a way to adjust the true probability to compute the most difficult piece of the option puzzle, the sum of all the payoffs × probabilities. Thus, they only really use one true probability and the other is an adjusted summing of payoffs × probabilities.

Chapter 14

Questions 1 to 5 relate to the Black-Scholes formula:

$$C = S \bullet N(D_1) - K \bullet N(D_2) \bullet e^{-RT}.$$

1. We must figure out the value of the five components on the right side of the equation and insert them to compute a call option premium. Name the five components. S, $N(D_1)$, K, $N(D_2)$, e^{-RT}

2. Briefly describe each of the five components from question 1. Also describe C.

C = call premium, also known as the fair value of the option.

S = spot price of the stock.

$N(D_1)$ = probability 1 from the normal curve CDF (evaluated at point D_1).

K = strike price of the option, also known as the kick-in exercise level.

$N(D_2)$ = probability 2 from the normal curve CDF (evaluated at point D_2).

e^{-RT} = discounting factor (the value e to the power "minus $R \times T$," where R is the interest rate and T is time in years).

3. In the chapter we said finding the values of S and K is a snap. Why is that so? The spot price S of the stock you are trading, like IBM, is simple enough to locate and the strike price K of the option you want to analyze is *chosen by you.*

4. We mentioned that the value of e^{-RT} (the discounting factor) is simple enough after a little practice. Let's get a little practice now. Compute e^{-RT} for two time periods (6 months and 1 year) and three interest rates (0, 5, and 10 percent). For 6 months input $T = 0.5$, and for 1 year $T = 1.0$. The three interest rates should be input as $R = 0.00, 0.05,$ and 0.10. We must calculate $-R \times T$ for each of the six combinations and then evaluate e^{-RT}.

$$0\% \text{ for 6 months} = e^{-0 \times 0.5} = e^0 = 1.0000$$

$$5\% \text{ for 6 months} = e^{-.05 \times 0.5} = e^{-.025} = 0.97531$$

$$10\% \text{ for 6 months} = e^{-.10 \times 0.5} = e^{-.050} = 0.95123$$

$$0\% \text{ for 1 year} = e^{-0 \times 1.0} = e^0 = 1.0000$$

$$5\% \text{ for 1 year} = e^{-.05 \times 1.0} = e^{-.050} = 0.95123$$

$$10\% \text{ for 1 year} = e^{-.10 \times 1.0} = e^{-.100} = 0.90484$$

5. As we said, finding $N(D_1)$ and $N(D_2)$ is much more complicated so we'll provide values to use. We want you to calculate the fair value of the following five IBM call options using the information provided. Assume IBM is trading at $100 now and that interest = 10 percent.

$80 call, 3-month expiry: $N(D_1)$ = .9581, $N(D_2)$ = .9429
$90 call, 4-month expiry: $N(D_1)$ = .8126, $N(D_2)$ = .7625
$100 call, 6-month expiry: $N(D_1)$ = .6337, $N(D_2)$ = .5516
$110 call, 6-month expiry: $N(D_1)$ = .4572, $N(D_2)$ = .3746
$120 call, 6-month expiry: $N(D_1)$ = .3023, $N(D_2)$ = .2327

Let's use the formula: $C = S \cdot N(D_1) - K \cdot N(D_2) \cdot e^{-RT}$

$80 call = 100 × .9581 − 80 × .9429 × .9753 = 95.81 − 73.57 = 22.24

$90 call = 100 × .8126 − 90 × .7625 × .9672 = 81.26 − 66.38 = 14.88

$100 call = 100 × .6337 − 100 × .5516 × .9512 = 63.37 − 52.47 = 10.90

$110 call = 100 × .4572 − 110 × .3746 × .9512 = 45.72 − 39.20 = 6.52

$120 call = 100 × .3023 − 120 × .2327 × .9512 = 30.23 − 26.56 = 3.67

Chapter 15

1. What does SKIT-V stand for? It's an acronym we created to help remember the five basic inputs for the Black-Scholes option formula.

2. Name the five inputs that comprise SKIT-V. Spot stock price, strike price, interest rate, time to expiry, volatility.

3. Which inputs are easy to find, which are hard? The first four are simple to find; the last one, volatility, is a lot more difficult to find.

4. What are the three types of volatilities that traders use? Historical, implied, and future volatility. We sometimes think of them as past, present, and future.

5. How can we compute historical volatility? All you need is some closing stock prices going back a reasonable distance, say the past 30 trading days. You then compute the statistical measure known as the standard deviation and annualize it. The Black-Scholes formula requires the *annual* volatility.

6. How can we compute implied volatility? If you know where a call option is trading right now (its premium C) and you can also get the four inputs we call SKIT, then you can solve for volatility using the Black-Scholes formula in reverse. The answer is the present volatility, that is, the volatility implied by the option's premium.

7. How can we compute future volatility? You can't. Nobody knows how to predict future volatility.

8. Why would you be able to make big money if you knew the future volatility? Let's suppose that you know that future volatility will be 33 percent, but the market is trading at 25 percent now. You could buy call options now and hedge them by selling shares of stock against them. You would have to rebalance your hedge all the time to protect yourself by selling rallies and buying dips. The future will bring higher volatility in the stock than the market is guessing now. This allows you to make more money on your selling and buying than you pay out for your call options. This is one of many possible scenarios and is oversimplified, but that is how the concept works.

Chapter 16

1. Name three things that are positive about the Black-Scholes formula. Here are six positive attributes, choose any three: It was the first accurate option formula, it is now universally accepted by traders, it is very fast and easy to implement, it uses elegant mathematics, the formula is easily modified for adjustments, the math allows quick and clean derivatives such as the delta, $N(D_1)$.

2. Name three things that make the Black-Scholes formula less than ideally perfect. Here are six problems that make Black-Scholes less than perfect: It was based only on spot stocks that have no dividends, it generates only call premiums—it's not for puts, no early exercise is allowed, it requires modified versions to more closely approach the real world, there are many unreal assumptions and conditions that can never be satisfied, it uses a log-normal model which is the best available but is still inaccurate.

3. What modifications, also called "relaxing of restrictions," would you think might be required for someone to create the perfect formula? We've mentioned about a dozen problems in the chapter, all of which would be good answers. Here are a few of the more important ones. First is the "no dividend" restriction. Too many assets have dividends or their equivalents. Second is the "no early exercise" restriction. Next is the asset types: we need to be able to trade more than spot stocks. That means extension into futures and forward markets as well as bonds and commodities (including currencies). Then there is the ability to price put options as well as calls. After this there is a whole slew of other non-real-world assumptions like the expectation of constant volatility and interest rates, and the requirement to hedge continuously and be able to do so at any time, in any amount, at no cost.

4. Some studies say that the Black-Scholes formula slightly misprices the at-the-money and deep out-of-the-money options. Does this sound right, and if so, why? There have been many studies that try to test the effectiveness of the Black-Scholes formula in accurately predicting how the marketplace will price options. There are many arguments as to the results of the studies and to the validity of the studies. One of the least contested findings is that the Black-Scholes formula has shown a tendency to overprice the at-the-money options and underprice the deep out-of-the-money options. One reason it isn't as strongly contested is because of the phenomenon we've mentioned before: in the real world of trading there are more sleepy, quiet days than a normal distribution suggests. There are also more wild and crazy days than the normal distribution would suggest. Since the Black-Scholes formula depends on the normal distribution to make these probability assessments, that would naturally cause a problem. There is no probability model that accurately portrays how markets move, and this automatically makes it unlikely that any model will work without flaws.

5. Some traders worry a lot about the Black-Scholes formula's assumption of constant volatility. What does the assumption mean, and why is it flawed? To make their formula workable Black and Scholes hypothesized a world where stocks had a consistent normal curve that described their movements. The width of a normal curve, you will recall, is six standard deviations wide (three on either side of the center). Volatility is defined as one standard deviation. If volatility keeps changing, then the normal curve keeps widening and narrowing. This would naturally change the probability and payoff estimates from day to day and therefore change the delta hedge requirements abruptly and sharply without any warning. Changing volatility does not work well in the Black-Scholes world, but unfortunately it is what we deal with in the real world. There are very advanced formulas being worked on that modify the Black-Scholes formula and allow for the real world of volatility. Just remember, the Black-Scholes formula isn't perfect, but neither is any other model. It's a terrific starting point and guideline for analyzing options, but just like for any other rigid guideline, if you don't make adjustments for the real world you will soon find yourself hopelessly outplayed and outdistanced.

Chapter 17

1. Oftentimes traders find an attractive, predictable, and profitable short-term correlation between two assets. Is this a

good start for a hedging operation? Every idea that shows a profit is an interesting start, but a great deal more research is needed before it can be considered worthwhile. There are a zillion short-term relationships that pop up in markets and disappear just as quickly. These are rotten hedges. If you can't depend on the relationship to be maintained during times of market stress, then the hedge is useless. The proper basis for any hedge is a reliable cause and effect. For instance, the spot prices for IBM shares and the future prices for IBM shares, while not a perfect match, have a strong cause-and-effect relationship. The spot shares can one day be delivered against the futures contract, and thus traders know that the two are inextricably linked together. There can be slight differences, which is why it isn't a perfect match, but for the most part one should move in line with the other minute by minute, day by day. If, however, a wheat trader finds that corn has made a wonderful hedge over the past 2 years, he or she will be in for a rude awakening when the spread diverges and there is no way to deliver one against the other come delivery day. Disaster awaits those who depend on such relationships to protect them.

2. A trader has a "fully hedged" portfolio. Soon the daily profit and losses start to become larger than that of a similar portfolio that is unhedged. What does this tell us? The hedge stinks. For some reason there is more risk with the hedge than without it. This means that the hedge is failing miserably. The hedge not only fails to lower the risk, it is actually increasing it. Since this is the opposite of what a hedge should do, you must immediately replace the hedge with something more suitable.

3. A trader owns spot shares of IBM and decides to hedge in the futures market. He now has a two-legged spread position known as a *carry*. On our subjective hedging scale, how well hedged is the position and what types of things can go wrong with a carry position hedged with futures? On our subjective hedging scale we suggested this position is 95 percent hedged. If the trader is borrowing money to hold the spot shares of IBM on a day-by-day basis, then interest rates might go up. This would be an extra expense for the period of time before delivery. If the shares owned cannot be readily delivered on the day the futures contract comes due, there could be extra expense with that. And, like our poor silver producer who had sold the futures, if IBM prices double (say a takeover bid happens), the trader will get variation margin calls from the brokerage house. If he or she can't come up with the cash to pay the margin call, the position will be liquidated the next day voiding the hedge entirely. Even if the extreme case scenario doesn't occur, there are still plenty of small IBM price moves that require nominal variation margin payments day to day. Professional traders adjust for this with a variation margin hedge.

4. A trader owns spot shares of IBM and decides that she can write call options against the shares to earn a little money and also protect against the price of IBM going lower. How much is she hedged, is this a good idea, what's wrong with it? If she sells the at-the-money call options, she will be roughly 50 percent hedged against the price of IBM falling. Out-of-the-money options will give less hedging protection. And the trader is not earning extra money although many people seem to think so. She is being paid a fair amount to give away her IBM upside potential, while she keeps her downside risk. It's not necessarily a good idea or a bad idea. It's more a question of what suits her market views at the time. As long as the trader understands she only has partial protection and is also giving away upside for the premium received, then it's a reasonable trade.

5. Assume the trader in question 4 sold at-the-money call options and was thus hedged 50 percent. Will the percent protection be the same tomorrow and next week? No. Option hedges are always in a state of flux. Given the number of possible changing conditions the protection can vary widely over time. It is never a constant, unchanging thing. Tomorrow the protection might be 40 or 60 percent. It depends on all the variables that go into the Black-Scholes formula, many of which can change minute to minute.

6. In the chapter we proposed a crazy takeover attempt: Intel offered to buy all IBM shares by paying three Intel shares for one share of IBM. Before the announcement Intel was trading at $25 and IBM was trading at $60. After the announcement, Intel went down to $23 and IBM went up to $67. Explain the buy/sell dynamics that made Intel go down and IBM up. What might some reasons be? Clearly, traders were selling Intel while buying IBM. The most obvious reasons for this are related to how the takeover bid will affect each company. First, many traders might believe that the burden placed on Intel will affect its ability to earn future profits and also impact its credit ratings with new debt it will likely incur. Second, traders see a corporation willing to pay $75 (three times the original Intel price of $25) for IBM and thus it looks cheap at $60. Third, risk arbitrage traders go into action and buy 1000 IBM/sell 3000 Intel every chance they see. If they believe that there is a good chance the deal will go through, then the starting ratio of 2.40 (IBM $60/ Intel $25) was cheap with a company saying they would pay a ratio of 3.00. The risk arbitrage traders are simply arbitraging the ratio, but this sells Intel and buys IBM. Fourth, traders might also believe this could start a bidding war and cause IBM to go up even further. There are a dozen different ideas and beliefs that spring up for each trade, including takeovers. We discussed the most evident ones here, but be assured that there are shrewd traders making more sophisticated analyses and betting accordingly. In the end, all you know is the final outcome of the prices on any given day. This day Intel went down $2 and IBM went up $7. On that fact alone we know there had to be aggressive selling in Intel and aggressive buying in IBM, no matter what the rationales.

7. **Referring to question 6, why does there still seem to be a guaranteed profit in the present prices ($23 and $67)? What would you do to arbitrage these guaranteed profits? What problems would you run into?** As we have said time and again, there are no guaranteed profits. What's happened is the arbitrageurs started to get nervous just short of the 3.00 ratio. The price paid for IBM is strictly related to Intel's price. At $23 that means the takeover is worth $69 a share for IBM. But everything has to go smoothly for that to occur. So the apparent last $2 that is being left on the table is due to uncertainty. Many deals are scuttled leaving the arbitrageurs out to hang. There are many ways the deal can fail to go through. If we want to step up to the plate to make that last $2 (left by the smartest traders in the business), we would buy 1000 IBM and sell 3000 Intel (if we can borrow the Intel shares). Just remember, if the deal falls apart and prices revert to where they were earlier ($25 and $60), we'll lose $2 times 3000 on Intel and also $7 times 1000 on IBM for a total loss of $13,000. This compares unfavorably to the $2000 we are trying to make. And when deals fall apart they can overshoot the original prices as arbitrageurs get killed and run for the hills. It's not a pretty picture. Remember: There are no guaranteed profits.

8. **When a management begins to investigate trader activity, it seems that the traders are often over their limits and are losing money. The discovery of over-the-limit positions usually**

goes hand in hand with losing positions, not winning ones. Why is this? This is because managers never investigate or argue with excess profits. No one wants to "look the gift horse in the mouth." Investigations only occur when losses start to show up, not when the traders are piling up the winnings.

9. Everyone knows that you can't get out of a hole by digging deeper. Why does it seem, then, that traders keep digging deeper? That is, why do they hold onto the same losing positions and often add more? The traders in question are merely following their hard-wired instincts to hope for the best. Tomorrow is another day. The sun will come out tomorrow. When you're at the end of your rope, tie a knot and hang on. Winners never quit and quitters never win. There are thousands of sayings and proverbs that go into making up the way we think and feel. It is human nature to be optimistic or we would never strike out on adventures. Within every successful person is grit and determination not to let adversity get them down, to stand their ground and fight back. Perversely, all these things can be turned to your disadvantage in the markets. To succeed, traders have to learn how to lose and give up—but at the right times, particularly when they are losing. This is very, very hard to do for successful, hardnosed people. So, we could say that the traders who destroyed their trading firms with billions of dollars in losses were merely holding fast to the ideals embraced by millions of successful people. It's just that the trading markets turn emotions and postures against you at every turn. If you can't learn to play the game, and it is a complex and intricate game, you can't become a successful trader. Holding fast in the face of adversity will plain destroy you in the markets. One top trader said it: "You've got to swim upstream against human nature to be a good trader." Easy to say, hard to do.

10. Many people don't realize that most of the trading firms that were wiped out by huge losses were very profitable traders for years. They showed large profits at first, but they were unreasonably large profits. And this was their downfall. Why does this make sense and to what degree is this a simple example of human nature in action (greed and fear)? Most corporate managers come from different backgrounds than traders do. They don't understand trading, and they don't understand traders. They believe that a successful trader should make money automatically, much like a rodeo star can ride a bucking bronco and a good architect can design a building. The philosophy often is: When the traders are on a roll, let them go for it.

Unreasonably large profits can be the result of taking unreasonably large risks. They can also be due to thinly traded markets that tend to overstate the results. Everybody hopes and expects the traders will make the firm good money, and so after a string of great results the traders are given more autonomy and told to go get 'em.

But markets reverse all the time and when the risks are too large, the resulting backlash can be devastating. As the losses start to pile up, the traders are apt to dig in, saying that they know what is going on. If they truly did, they wouldn't have chosen the losing side, would they? At some point the huge risk leads to losses that are too painful to accept, so everybody involved votes to tie a knot when they get to the ends of their ropes and hang on. Or they choose to double up. If it was a buy at 60, its a steal at 45! Then the market bails them out (and you never hear about it) or the market plummets lower and they end up on the front page of the *Wall Street Journal* as an abject lesson in the "Disasters of Dabbling in Derivatives." In the end it was an overabundance of greed that encouraged overtrading and then fear that enabled them to keep digging faster as the hole got much, much deeper.

Chapter 18

1. What are the three phases of risk management? (1) Identify and measure every knowable risk. (2) Create hedges that offset all hedgeable risks. (3) Continuously monitor to catch surprises early and readjust.

2. How do we eliminate the risk after we've identified and measured it? We must offset the risk with an appropriate hedging vehicle. Hedges must be selected for their ability to offset S (spot price), T (time), and V (volatility) as well as the lesser risks we call rhos. If we fail to hedge all the multidimensional risks, there is some market movement that will ambush us in the end.

3. What are the names of the most important of the Greek risk tools? Delta, gamma, vega (kappa), theta, and rho are by far the most important names, but there are other, less well known measures also.

4. What risk tool monitors spot price movements? How is it expressed mathematically? Delta monitors the call premium change versus the IBM spot price change. Mathematically it is shown as $\partial C/\partial S$.

5. What risk tool monitors strike price movements? How is it expressed mathematically? There is no strike price movement, and so there is no need to monitor it. When you take a position, you have already selected your option's strike price and it always stays the same. You can liquidate the position, but you cannot alter the strike price of a plain vanilla (ordinary) option. There are very advanced exotic options that allow this, but needless to say, we aren't going there.

6. What risk tool monitors interest rate movements? How is it expressed mathematically? Rho monitors the call premium change versus the interest rate change. We expressed it as $\partial C/\partial I$.

7. What risk tool monitors time decay? How is it expressed mathematically? Theta monitors the call premium change versus the time change. Mathematically it is shown as $\partial C/\partial T$.

8. What risk tool monitors volatility movements? How is it expressed mathematically? Vega monitors the call premium change versus the volatility change. Mathematically it is shown as $\partial C/\partial V$.

9. What is gamma, and how is it different from other risk tools? How is it expressed mathematically? Gamma does not analyze any of the SKIT-V inputs directly like the other risk tools we described. The others are known as first derivatives, whereas gamma is a second derivative mathematically expressed as $\partial^2 C/\partial S^2$. Notice the 2 in the math expression. That means it is a second derivative derived directly from the first derivative. Notice also that the same symbol $\partial C/\partial S$ (without the 2) is the delta. Thus gamma is derived directly from the delta and measures the rate of change of the delta.

10. How many option premiums do you need to calculate the delta? Each pair of premium values will generate a single delta value. For example, if the premium for an IBM call option is $2.95 when IBM is $100 and $3.10 when IBM rises to $101, then the change in premium is $0.15 for a $1 IBM move and the delta is thus 0.15. We need two premiums because we are measuring the change in premium. That's how we define the delta.

11. How many deltas do you need to calculate the gamma? Each pair of deltas generates only one gamma value. This means you need three premiums to generate a single gamma. Using the same premium structure from question 10, for IBM at $100 the premium is $2.95, for IBM at $101 the premium is $3.10, and for IBM at $102 the premium is $3.30. This allows us to compute the pair of deltas we need. The $100/$101 delta is 0.15 and the $101/$102 delta is 0.20. Thus the delta has moved from 0.15 to 0.20 in the span of a $1 IBM move. This is a change of 0.05, and we call this the gamma. We need two deltas because we are measuring the change in delta. That's how we define the gamma.

12. Theta is the risk tool that measures time loss. Why do traders only measure theta one day at a time? Why not each hour? In theory we could measure any amount of time loss that we wanted. The reality is, however, that the most convenient and practical unit is a daily measurement. What would be the point of knowing your time loss every minute, anyway? You couldn't trade in and out of the option every 5 minutes even if you came up with the most ingenious trading strategy in the world. Say you knew that the market was hectic for the first hour, deadly quiet around lunchtime, and hectic again at the close, like many markets are. If you tried to buy at the open, sell an hour later, buy an hour before the closing, and sell out right at the closing bell, the other floor traders would absolutely kill you in execution slippages. Try it sometime. It's a real eye opener. Welcome to the wonderful world of trading.

13. Vega measures volatility. If your position has positive vega, it means that rising volatility will be profitable for you. Volatility tends to move in the same direction as option premiums (higher volatility means higher option premiums). If you have positive vega, are you more likely a net owner of options or a net seller of options? Why? Being an owner of options gives you a positive vega exposure. Say you own several different call options. When volatility goes up, the premiums on all the calls will tend to get pumped up to give you a profit. That is what is meant by positive vega, that you participate as if you had bet on volatility to go up. If volatility goes down, you'll lose.

14. Perfectly hedged positions do not experience P&L shifts. Therefore, what do you know about a position that shows

varying profits and losses every day? Clearly the position is not perfectly hedged. If a position is hedged perfectly, then every day is a big zero, i.e., a whole lot of nothing happening. There is hardly a trader alive who is comfortable with a zero P&L day after day. They tend to crave action and exposure. If a trader tells you he or she is hedged, but is making or losing a chunk of money every day, then it's time to review what the hedges are, because something is not quite kosher.

15. You are a trader and you receive your daily P&L breakdown. You essentially broke even for the day, but it turns out you made $10,000 in vega profits and had $10,000 in delta losses. What does this mean in terms of risk, and where are the risks coming from? Even though you broke even for the day, your exposures were not properly hedged. Tomorrow you could see a $20,000 net gain or loss if the two fail to offset—and vega does not normally offset delta exposure, so you ought to be ready for some big swings. You have both volatility exposure and spot price exposure. As one possible explanation (and there are others) if you owned IBM call options and the price of IBM went down, you lost because IBM fell in price, but you made because the volatility got pumped up—for the moment. The two offset, but probably won't tomorrow. Unhedged exposures give you the rope you need to lasso some profits, or to hang yourself with losses.

16. What does delta neutral mean? Delta neutral means maintaining your delta at zero. That's how traders hedge their delta risk.

17. What is delta neutral hedging? What other names is it called? When traders readjust their delta position to try to keep it always at zero, they are hedging to become delta neutral. To stay delta neutral the traders must sell excess long positions or buy back excess short positions. This is typically done once a day, but in Black-Scholes theory it must be done the instant the delta moves from zero, which could be 84 zillion times a day. This process is known as dynamic hedging (also called rebalancing or rehedging).

18. What is a gamma positive position? A trader that is a net owner of options typically has a positive gamma position. Because it does matter which options you own and which you are short, let's simplify this to say that if you only buy options you are gamma positive. Being gamma positive means that your delta will change in the direction of the price move. If prices go up, you will become longer (your delta will become more positive). If prices go down, you will become less long (your delta will become less positive). With the proper mixture of hedges and put options you can actually get shorter as the spot price falls. Thus you are following the trend (in a sense) by effectively buying into rallies and selling into dips.

19. What is meant when we say that the hedging vehicle must offset the driving force of the risk you have? Clearly, option risks have many dimensions to them and all are not driven solely by the spot price, so we cannot merely hedge with shares of IBM to neutralize all the possible exposures. IBM shares will help us hedge delta only (and gamma a little bit). Time decay (theta) and volatility (vega) are totally unrelated to the closing price of IBM shares. So, try as we might, we cannot hedge away theta or vega by trading shares of IBM as our hedging vehicle. Only other options that have offsetting theta and vega characteristics are worthy of consideration as the proper hedging vehicles.

20. We have said that traders worry not just about S, but about the big three, STV. What does the expression STV mean, and how can traders hedge against it? The big three option risks are the underlying spot stock price (S), time decay (T), and volatility (V). The three Greek risk monitors for these are, in order, delta, theta, and vega. We've explained where to find offsetting hedges many times before.

Questions 21 and 22 refer to this: Thetas between two options are related by an inverse "square root of time" rule.

21. Assume a 90-day IBM option is worth \$3.60 and the same option for 360 days is worth \$7.20. At first glance it seems that the first option's time value is priced at 4 cents a day and the second option's time value is priced at only 2 cents a day. Assuming for the moment that they will lose 4 cents a day and 2 cents a day, respectively, how does this relate to the inverse "square root of time" rule? The 360-day option has four times as long to maturity as the 90-day option. The square root of 4 is 2. This square root has two uses: all other things equal, the premiums will vary very roughly by a ratio of 2 and the daily theta will vary very roughly by the inverse of the ratio (that is, $\frac{1}{2}$). Notice that the 360-day option premium is, in fact, two times as expensive as the 90-day option ($7.20 vs $3.60). Also, we are suggesting that the longer option only loses time value at $\frac{1}{2}$ the rate of the shorter option (2 cents a day versus 4 cents). See question 22 for further information.

22. Options do not, in fact, lose time value at the same flat amount every day. Option time decay accelerates rapidly as the last days of an option's life are approached. We assumed that the two options might lose time value at the flat rate of 2 and 4 cents a day. Calculation shows, however, that the 360-day option would lose 1.1 cents the next day and the 90-day option would lose 2.1 cents the same day. How does this fit with the inverse "square root of time" rule? Even though the actual rate of time decay is different than our assumption of a flat rate, the ratio is still just as predicted. The option which has four times the length of time to maturity should lose time value at one-half the rate of the shorter option. Restated in terms of theta (time decay), the theta of the shorter option is much larger than the longer option. As a rule of thumb, the square root accuracy works very nicely.

23. Why is staying delta neutral much more expensive than the Black-Scholes formula suggests? Black and Scholes created a world where there were no fees, commissions, slippages, or bid/asks. This is far different than the world that traders find themselves in. Therefore, traders who try to maintain a perfectly neutral portfolio are constantly getting hit with expenses every time they hedge. Since the average expected result of all the hedging is a zero gain or loss, the real result ends up a net loss after including expenses.

24. How can a delta neutral trader manage to become profitable given the costs of hedging? If the trader only trades on fairly valued options, he or she cannot expect to be profitable. Clearly, then the trader must find a way to buy below and sell above fair value. In other chapters we've called these mispriced options. We discuss this concept in more detail in Chap. 19.

Chapter 19

1. We suggested there are only two ways to make money in business. What are they? Either you make money from the other professionals in your market (could be the pharmaceutical market, it need not be a trading market) or you make money from your customer base by marking up the products they want.

Sometimes professionals can be your customers, but if you find you aren't making a consistent profit from them, you should consider the fact that they may be wolves in customers' clothing. Very few companies can make money from professionals who aren't happy to fully play the role of customers. Customers know you need to make a little to stay alive; professionals couldn't care less.

2. How important is a client base to the profitability of a company? The success and profitability of most companies relies almost entirely on their ability to find clients for their products. Without someone to sell products to you'll end up with a warehouse full of useless merchandise. Many first-time entrepreneurs think all they need do is make a decent product at a reasonable price and they'll prosper. Nothing could be further from the truth. Plenty of decent new companies go out of business because they fail to properly recognize the importance of moving products into customers' hands at a profit. Meanwhile, many substandard companies have existed for years and years even though their products and extra value are lacking. They know how to hold onto their customers and continue to overcharge them. If life is not fair, then by comparison the corporate world of products and distribution systems is downright tragic. But it's a twisted, complicated game and "if you're gonna play the game, boy, you better learn to play it right!"

The old proverb about the world beating a path to your door for designing a better mousetrap is pure nonsense. The world has become full of jaded consumers due to all the promises made and broken time and again. Nowadays, consumers have a very limited attention span and totally ignore anything that isn't sold, pushed, and hyped over and over. If you build a better mousetrap and the world has never heard about you, you'll see no new business at all. Getting customers is everything.

3. What's the difference between a dealer and a trader? Both are heavily involved in buying and selling and trying to make money out of the markets, but a dealer quotes a two-way market to customers all day long whereas a trader only trades whenever it suits. Dealers can get "hit" or "lifted" according to the flow of clients' business, which may jam them with unwanted positions, but traders need only trade when the time seems right and a choice is made.

4. How does a dealer make money from the bid/ask spread? How important is the width of the spread and the active, two-way order flow? The benefit of being a dealer is getting hit on your bid and being taken or lifted on your offer. It is an automatic profit when it happens quickly. That's the key. If it takes 2 days to complete a buy/sell cycle, you are, for all intents and purposes, a dead duck. There is nothing more fun than making the cash register ring every few minutes with winning trades. Unfortunately the real world doesn't work that way most of the time. What happens far more often is that the dealer gets stuck with an imbalance (too much position on one side of the market) and the market moves the wrong way just long enough to wipe out the day's proceeds from the easy trades. The width of the bid/ask spread has an interesting impact on the dealer's business. A wider spread is more profitable, but it drives away customers and slows two-way order flow. A narrower spread is less profitable, but it attracts customers and speeds up two-way order flow. The key is to optimize the two for the best results. That is one of the secrets to being a good dealer. Keeping your clients happy helps, too.

5. What are the dangers of being a dealer? Dealers who take on all comers, meaning they're always ready to trade regardless of circumstances, will get the lion's share of the business, but they will also get smacked hard when news is released or a market breaks out big-time. A dealer who is too slow to react (by fractions of a second sometimes) can get stuck with bad positions just as a market is about to swoon and find an awesome gap in prices about to occur. Sometimes a dealer gets a bad position and rides it far too long. Taking home losers can lead to big, big downdrafts in P&Ls the following days as the market fails to recover. There are about a thousand tricks of the trade to surviving as a dealer, but the biggest of all is, don't lose more than you made last month! People naturally hold on to losers in hope that they'll come back, but a dealer can't do that too long and survive.

6. What does it mean to take a pip or a tick as a markup on a trade? Why do some traders take a single tick while others seem to take far more than that? A *tick* and a *pip* are names that refer to the tiniest of price moves. When stocks traded in one-eighth point increments (before decimalization), each tick on the ticker tape would be one-eighth. The size of a tick or a pip varies from market to market. When traders take a markup of a tick or a pip, it means they are giving the customer a tiny fraction worse than they were able to execute in the market. Some traders are happy to make such a tiny profit and keep the customer satisfied. Others are less generous and might be trying to make up for poor trades done elsewhere. If the trader takes too much, too often, the customer gets aggravated and goes elsewhere.

7. Some quick traders scalp the markets. What is meant by this? A *scalp* is a very short-term trade where the trader is trying to make a couple of ticks, usually. As with all things in trading there is a wide range of what short term means and how much profit is sought out. The typical scalper tries to buy on the bid and sell on the offer within a few minutes of each other, trying to make the bid/ask spread without being a true dealer.

8. We've described many different categories of trade types and styles. Must they always be separate, or do they sometimes overlap between the types? There are frequent overlaps between the categories and sometimes it's hard to say which category a trading style falls into. The scalp we described in the answer to question 7 was also a bid/ask dealer play. A scalp can also be an arbitrage. A spread player can act as a dealer, an arbitrageur, a scalper, or an overnight proprietary position player. The descriptions of who a trader is and what types of trades he or she specializes in must be kept fluid because very little stays constant in a trading environment. Traders are, by definition, opportunists. And opportunists move to wherever the opportunities flow.

9. What are rollovers, and how can they be profitable for traders? Rollovers refer to positions that are coming due and must either be delivered or rolled over, that is, moved forward in time. By becoming expert in the tendencies of people who wait until the last minute to get out of their positions, a trader can see patterns develop. Making money trading is all about pattern recognition and deciphering the probability that the patterns will repeat this time.

10. What are back-month differentials, and how can they lead to profits for traders? The back months in futures or options contracts are the months which are farther out in time, least traded, and most ignored. Whenever you have a familiarity that others do not, you have an edge. By becoming very knowledgeable about these back months you will be able to make accurate markets in them and you'll encounter less competition. You may not see frequent trading activity, but opportunities for profit will come if you are patient.

11. Why are some traders able to be successful at spreading, more so than others? They become successful spreaders by developing skills far more specialized than their rivals. Patience is a virtue here. Spreaders are better off for having had longtime experience and background in rollovers and deliveries. After you've seen a few hundred delivery months go by, you'll get the picture pretty well if you keep your eyes and ears open. Most traders want nothing to do with spreading and deliveries. One of the biggest traders in the business went on record as saying, "I'm someone who knows absolutely nothing about deliveries." So he gets out before delivery takes place and lets the specialists earn their money. Being a specialist gives you a niche and an edge.

In the good old days there was a Fresh Egg futures contract in Chicago (22,500 dozen eggs per contract). Aside from the glee of order desk clerks screaming "buy 10 Easter Eggs" or "sell a hundred Christmas Eggs," there were also smiles on the faces of the guys who specialized in distressed deliveries. Anyone outside the business who got delivery by accident had distressed merchandise, because you couldn't redeliver the eggs. These merchants of gloom would make Scrooge look like a generous man as they offered to pay you half price for your distressed delivery. The alternative was to hang on and watch the eggs rot as they sat in an unrefrigerated warehouse. These days there are very few commodity contracts that can give you anything close to the same pain for the buck. Almost all deliveries give you a warehouse receipt, and almost all of these are transferable or redeliverable. But there are exceptions, and you must give the spreaders and rollover experts their due: pay them their bid/asks and stay away from deliveries.

12. Suppose you have important clients come to you and request that your trading desk price a special product for them. They describe the product and the large quantity needed and tell you this is all very hush-hush and yours is the only desk that they are interested in dealing with. Do you think that you could find a way to make a profit on this? Do you think your margin of profit would end up better or worse than most of the

competitive deals you've worked on all year? If you can't find a way to make a profit on this private pricing deal, then you had better consider going into government work where profits don't count. The margin of profit will no doubt be one of your best all year, as long as the client isn't bent out of shape by it. There is no competition here, and so it's all strictly between you and the customer. Somehow the big spielers are always brought in on a deal like this to stroke the client and puff up the rationales as to why such hefty profits are not only necessary, but good.

13. Lately in the news there have been some trading scandals involving the possibility of *front-running.* **This is a form of going with order flow where the client never gets a chance for an execution. The trader involved in front-running a buy order, for example, tries to buy the market ahead of the customer's order and doesn't fill the customer's order unless the market breaks down. If the market keeps going up, the customer gets nothing and the trader reaps the benefits. How is this advantage different from the edge of going with order flow that we've described?** Our description of going with order flow was specifically referring to cases where the clients got their orders filled. The trader would use the information that such orders create to firm up his or her judgment on the future direction of the market. This future might only be minutes away, but it would still be *after* the client's order got filled, not *before.* Front-running is less a problem when there are alternative traders and trading firms to give orders to and they know they can lose the business if they try this nonsense. The scandal in question is under ongoing investigation, as the phrase goes, and no results are yet in.

Chapter 20

1. What is the basic relationship between owning shares of stock versus puts and calls? Owning shares of stock has an upside and a downside. This can be shown to be equal to buying a call and selling a put on the same shares.

2. What does Corporal Paces mean to us? It means CPL.PCS which is our acronym for remembering put and call conversion formulas.

3. What does CPL.PCS stand for? It means a call = put + long and a put = call + short.

4. How did we derive the two formulas in CPL.PCS ? They are just a reworking of the most basic equality: Long IBM = + IBM call − IBM put.

5. What are the two main conditions that are required before puts and calls can be converted into each other? They must have the very same strike price and expiration date.

6. How are puts and calls kept in line on the floor of the exchange? Some floor traders specialize in arbitraging the conversions for a tiny profit whenever they get out of whack. This brings them back in line.

7. What is meant by a synthetic position? How does this differ from a natural position? When you buy shares of IBM in the open market, that is considered a natural position. Alternatively, you can create an equivalent to this by buying calls and selling puts. This will create a synthetic long position in shares of IBM. You will have identically the same cost to purchase the shares and the very same upside and downside; so on the basis of cost or risk exposure they are indistinguishable. When you buy or sell the asset in the marketplace, we call that position a natural position. When you create the position using other assets, it is called a synthetic position.

8. How would you create a synthetic AT&T $20 call if you could only trade the AT&T $20 puts and the AT&T shares? Use CPL.PCS for help. The first piece, $C = P + L$ tells us we can create a call by buying a put and going long shares. So, if we buy an AT&T $20 put and buy 100 shares of AT&T also, we will own a synthetic call.

9. Suppose the AT&T $20 calls are trading at $9.00, the AT&T $20 puts are trading at $5.50, and the AT&T shares are trading at $24.00. Is there a profitable arbitrage to be done, and, if so, how would you do it? Do the conversion: buy the calls at $9.00, sell the puts at $5.50, and sell the shares at $24.00. This will give you a 50 cent profit before commissions. Since you pay $9.00, get $5.50, and get $24.00, you'll receive $20.50 net. On expiration day the three positions will net out and cost you only $20.00 to repurchase the shares. You'll pay only $20.00 because you exercise your call if the price is up or someone puts the shares to you at $20.00 if the price is down. Sounds complex, but it's pretty simple once you get used to it.

10. How does a synthetic position vary in risk from a natural position? Synthetic and natural positions are identical in risk and cost. There is no difference in the two.

11. How does understanding synthetics allow us to better understand a complex portfolio? Many large portfolios have positions all over the map: puts and calls, longs and shorts. If you can match off the ones with the same strike and same expiration date, you can often find a way to pair them into synthetic equivalents and even conversions where they fully neutralize each other. This can help convert a rather complex and unwieldy position into a much simpler one.

Chapter 21

Use this table to help answer questions 1 to 15:

IBM Call Options

	Jan	Apr	Jul
$90	10.60	13.25	15.40
$95	6.60	10.00	12.40
$100	3.50	7.30	9.80
$105	1.70	5.10	7.60
$110	0.70	3.60	5.80
$115	0.30	2.30	4.40

1. Assume IBM shares are trading at $100. If you wanted to write a naked $10 out-of-the-money call expiring as soon as possible, how would you do it? All you need do is sell one January $110 call. *Writing an option* means selling it, and naked means that it is uncovered, that is, there is no hedge against the sale. The $10 out-of-the-money call is the $110 strike and the soonest to expire is the January call.

2. Assume IBM shares are trading at $100. How would you create a covered write using the nearby at-the-money call? What type of market scenario would benefit this position the most? You would buy 100 shares of IBM at $100 and sell one January $100 call for $3.50 (per share). If IBM closes below $96.50 at January expiry, you will have a net loss for the transaction, so you want the price to close higher than that. From $96.50 to $100 you will have a profit that increases penny for penny to a maximum of $3.50 per share. Above $100 you will have the shares called from you for $100, so you won't participate any further. You have given away your upside for $3.50. This is why a covered write strategy best suits a neutral-to-slightly-bullish market view. Typically, people sell a higher strike instead of the at-the-money because they are more bullish.

3. What's the difference between a covered write and a buy-write? There is no difference at all. They are different names for the very same position.

4. What is a vertical spread? A buy and a sell in the same expiry month, but using two different strikes, for example, a spread containing the July $90 call versus the July $110 call.

5. What is a bull spread? A vertical spread where you are long the low strike, for example, where you buy the January $95 call and sell the January $115 call against it.

6. What is a bear spread? It's the reverse of a bull spread: a vertical spread where you are *not* long the low strike, for example, where you sell the July $100 call and buy the July $110 call.

7. How much would it cost to put on the April $90/$100 bull spread, and how would you do it? You must pay out $5.95, the difference between a credit of $7.30 and a debit of $13.25. In a bull spread you go long the low strike, so you would buy the April $90 at $13.25 and sell the April $100 at $7.30.

8. What would be the optimum IBM closing price at April expiry for the $90/$100 bull spread? If IBM closes at $100 or above, you will max out on profitability. The spread will be worth its maximum possible: $10.00 because the $90 call will be worth $10 more than the $100 call at expiry.

9. What is the maximum profit for the scenario in question 7? You paid $5.95 and the maximum spread is $10.00, so the maximum profit is $4.05.

10. What is the worst case scenario at expiry for the scenario in question 7? If IBM closes below $90, then both calls are worth zero and the spread closes at its minimum, which is zero.

11. What is the loss for the worst-case scenario in question 10? With the spread closing at zero you have lost your whole $5.95 investment.

12. What is a horizontal spread, and what are two other names for it? In a horizontal spread the expiry months are different but the strikes are the same, for example, a January $90 call versus a July $90 call. Horizontal spreads are also known as time spreads and calendar spreads.

13. How does defining a horizontal spread as a debit or credit tell you which option was bought and which was sold? Since calendar spreads use two different expiry months, but the same strike, the nearby expiry month is almost always cheaper than the far out month because it expires sooner (the exceptions are too few and too complex to mention). This means that if you buy the nearby month and sell the far out month, you will have money credited to your account. Thus we can tell which leg is bought and which is sold by the credit or debit.

14. What is a diagonal spread? A hybrid combination of both a vertical spread and a horizontal spread, for example, spreading the January $90 call versus the April $105 call. Expiries *and* strikes are different.

15. Suppose you believe IBM shares are not going to budge over the next few months and wish to do a 3-to-1 ratio write with the Jan $105 call. If IBM is $100 now, how would you do it, and what are the possible outcomes at expiry? This is not quite a covered write since it is not 1 to 1, but the mechanics are the same. You would buy 100 shares of IBM at $100 and sell 3 January $105 calls at $1.70 each. Therefore, you will immediately receive $5.10 in premiums. If IBM closes below $94.90, you will have a loss. Above that you will have a profit penny for penny until $105 where it maxes out at $10.10 (the $105 paid to call your 100 shares, less their $100 cost, plus the $5.10 in premiums). But from $105 upward you will lose three pennies from this $10.10 profit for every penny up since you will owe 300 shares at $105 and the market is higher. At $108.40 you will have exhausted all your $10.10 in profits and be in the hole a thin dime (−$0.10). From that point upward you will lose more and more money since you have no protection whatever. Ratios can get very nasty when they go wrong.

Use the puts and calls in the following table to help answer questions 16 to 21.

IBM Puts and Calls
(IBM Spot Price = $100)

	Jan Calls	Jan Puts	Straddle
$90	10.60	0.70	11.30
$95	6.60	1.70	8.30
$100	3.50	3.50	7.00
$105	1.70	6.60	8.30
$110	0.70	10.60	11.30
$115	0.30	16.00	16.30

16. We want to create a synthetic long IBM position using the January $100 put and call. What should we do, and what price would we be long the shares of IBM at? A long position is equivalent to buying the call and selling the put. If we buy the January $100 call at $3.50 and sell the January put at $3.50, we would have no debit or credit assigned to our account as the two premiums exactly offset each other. This means that we would be long shares of IBM at $100 plus the debit/credit which was zero. Our effective price for our IBM long position is therefore $100.00.

17. What is the difference in risk and cost for this synthetic long position versus a natural long position in IBM shares? There is essentially no difference in risk exposure or cost for buying IBM synthetically rather than naturally. For all intents and purposes they are the same.

18. We decide the market is going to be very volatile for the near future, and we want to buy the $95 IBM straddle. How would we do it, what would it cost, and what are the possible outcomes at expiration in January? Buying a straddle means buying the same strike put and call. We would buy the $95 call for $6.60 and buy the $95 put for $1.70, for a total cost of $8.30. At January expiration if IBM is below $86.70 ($95.00 − $8.30) or above $103.30 ($95.00 + $8.30), we will have a profit, otherwise we can lose as much as the full $8.30 straddle cost as IBM closes nearer and nearer to $95.00.

19. What is the difference between a straddle and a strangle? Straddles require that the put and call be the same strike.

Strangles use different strikes for the put and call, typically both are out-of-the-money.

20. How would you buy the $95/$105 January strangle? What are the possible expiry outcomes? We would buy the January $95 put (which is out-of-the-money) and buy the January $105 call (also out-of-the-money) for a total cost of $3.40 for the strangle. If IBM closes below $91.60 or above $108.40, we will have a profit. Inside that we will gradually lose our original investment of $3.40. If IBM closes between $95 and $105, our full $3.40 outlay will be lost.

21. What is a conversion, and why would traders do them? A conversion is a three-legged trade wherein the trader buys a put, converts it into a synthetic call by buying shares of stock, and then sells the natural call against it to essentially zero out the position. Traders tend to do conversions to neutralize open put positions or open synthetic calls in their portfolios.

INDEX

A

Algebra, 38
American-style options, 213
Answer tables, distributions as, 69–70
Arbitrage, 224, 228–229, 280
Arbitrageurs, 26
Assets:
    financial, growth in variety of, 5
    qualifying as derivatives, 8, 11
    underlying, 12, 13, 15
At-the-money (ATM) options, 18, 19, 131
Average expected value, 79
Average (mean), 12, 13, 103, 138–141
Averages, law of, 43, 113

B

Backwardation, 164
Bar graphs, 64–66
Barings Bank, vii
Barry, Dave, 258
"Basket of stocks" concept, 12
Bell-shaped distribution, 147
Bias, 74
Bid/ask spread, 275–277
Binomial distributions, 34, 67–68, 147–148
Binomial expansions, 51, 53
Binomial theorem, 47, 50–54
Binomial tree, 36, 37, 39
Binomials, 33–34
Black-Scholes formula, 100, 195–201, 322–337
    assumptions underlying, 169, 214, 263–264
    and author's final options formula, 186–189
    components/inputs of, 196, 203–206
    converting spot prices into forward prices, 160
    Cox-Ross-Rubinstein model vs., 193
    cumulative normal distribution function in, 149
    development of, 181–182
    e^{RT} variable in, 170
    modified versions of, 211–212, 214

Black-Scholes formula (*Cont.*):
    and normal distributions, 87
    payoff weights in, 189
    positive attributes of, 210–212
    problems with, 212–216
    pros and cons of, 209–217
    restrictions of, 170–171
    theory behind, 298
    two probabilities in, 186
    universal acceptance of, 219
    for valuing IBM options, 196–199
Bonds, 9–12
Borrowing money, 280–281
Break-even analysis, 74, 100
Brief History of Time, A (Stephen Hawking), 274
Bull spreads, 304–305
Buy-writes, 226, 300–303

C

Calculus, 212, 250–251
Calendar spreads, 305–307
Call premium, 196, 205, 213 (*See also* Black-Scholes formula)
Calls, 18, 317
    converting puts and, 289–293, 295–296
    moneyness of, 18–19
    in trading strategies, 299–300
Carry position, 226
Carrying costs, 167–169
Cash flows, 168
Cash markets, 14, 19, 20, 160–162
Cash prices, futures prices vs., 26
CBT (Chicago Board of Trade), 15
CDF (*see* Cumulative distribution function)
Central tendency, 139–140
Certainty, 120
CFTC (*see* Commodity Futures Trading Commission)
Chicago Board of Trade (CBT), 15
Chicago grain market, 14–15
Chicago Mercantile Exchange (CME), 15
Client's price, 74

Futures (*Cont.*):
forwards vs., 20–22
origin of, 14–15
single stock (*see* Single stock futures)
of stocks, 15
Futures exchanges, 20
Futures markets, 19, 20, 160–162
Futures pits, 21–22
Futures prices, 26, 160

G

Gain, expected (*see* Expected gain)
Gambler's fallacy, 113
Games of chance, 7, 74
Gamma, 252, 253, 258–260
Gauss, Karl Friedrich, 147, 156
Gaussian distribution, 147
The General Theory of Employment, Interest and Money (John Maynard Keynes), 171
Gooding, Cuba, Jr., 80
Grain market, 14–15
Graphs (*see* Histograms)
Greek symbols/names, 249–252 (*See also* specific symbols/names)
Gross return, 77

H

Hawking, Stephen, 274
Head count, 37, 39, 50, 53
Hedge ratio, 190, 200
Hedges and hedging, 224–225, 256–264
and arbitrage, 227–229
and correlation, 229, 230
cross hedges, 233–235, 237
crude oil example, 235–237
delta, 257–258
dynamic hedging, 258
gamma, 258–260
IBM example, 225–227
with large portfolios, 248
with low correlation vehicles, 237
of option risk, 256–264
perfect, 229–233, 236, 244–245
replication in, 229
rho, 260
theta, 261–262
and use of Black-Scholes formula, 263–264
vega, 262–263

Hedging vehicles, 257
Histograms, 64–66, 123, 126, 127, 131
Historical volatility, 205
Hoarding, 168
Horizontal spreads, 303, 305–307
"House take," 73–74

I

IBM options examples, 17, 289–290
applying CPL.PCS to, 292–293
Black-Scholes formula for, 196–199
covered write (buy-write), 301–303
hedging, 225–227, 257–260
long straddles, 309–310
long strangles, 310–311
synthetic long position, 308–309
valuation of, 119–131
and vertical spreads, 304–305
Implied volatility, 205–206, 262, 328
Indifference, delivery date, 166
Indifference spread, 167–169, 175
Individual expected return, 80–81
Inside information, 281
Integral calculus, 250–251
Interest rate discounting, 119
Interest rate markets, 24
Interest rate multiplier (e^{RT}), 170–171, 173, 184–185 (*See also* Black-Scholes formula)
Interest rate risk (rho), 253, 257, 260
Interest rates, 24, 196, 204 (*See also* Black-Scholes formula)
Internet trading, 22
In-the-money (ITM) options, 18, 19, 131
Inverse functions, 184
Inverted market, 164
Investors:
inexperienced, 4–5
markets traded by, 19, 20
recent technical trading by, 4
Irresponsible trading, viii
ITM options (*see* In-the-money options)

J

Jordan, Michael, 277

K

Kappa (*see* Volatility)
Keynes, John Maynard, 171

ABOUT THE AUTHOR

Robert Ward is an independent consultant to Prudential Securities, JPMorgan-Chase, Dresdner Bank, and other global financial institutions. Ward gained extensive experience in the realities of trading by working as a head trader and manager of Merrill Lynch's gold department. He has also taught courses on trading and options at New York University.